广东省在线开放课程"现代生活的文化解读"（慕课）教材
首届"智慧树杯"课程思政示范案例教学大赛优秀课程教材
华 南 农 业 大 学 首 批 慕 课 建 设 项 目

现代生活的文化解读

Cultural Interpretation of Modern Life

廖杨 蒙丽 编著

科学出版社

北 京

内 容 简 介

本书是广东省在线开放课程"现代生活的文化解读"的配套（慕课）教材，主要从文化的角度，对现代社会日常生活中的衣、食、住、行、游、购、娱、婚、丧、生、老、病、死、葬、祭等基本生活领域（方面）进行解读，以帮助人们运用文化人类学的相关知识来正确看待社会生活、认识社会生活和过好社会生活。为适应优质慕课国际化的发展需要，本书采用了中英文合版的方式进行编写。

本书可供国内外高校学生和社会文化爱好者阅读参考。

图书在版编目（CIP）数据

现代生活的文化解读 = Cultural Interpretation of Modern Life：汉、英 / 廖杨，蒙丽编著. —北京：科学出版社，2022.2
广东省在线开放课程"现代生活的文化解读"（慕课）教材
ISBN 978-7-03-068450-9

Ⅰ.①现… Ⅱ.①廖… ②蒙… Ⅲ.①文化人类学－教材－汉、英 Ⅳ.①C958

中国版本图书馆 CIP 数据核字（2021）第 049087 号

责任编辑：郭勇斌 彭婧煜 杨路诗 / 责任校对：杜子昂
责任印制：张 伟 / 封面设计：玖思文化

科学出版社 出版
北京东黄城根北街 16 号
邮政编码：100717
http://www.sciencep.com

北京科印技术咨询服务有限公司数码印刷分部印刷
科学出版社发行 各地新华书店经销

*

2022 年 2 月第 一 版 开本：720×1000 1/16
2024 年 8 月第二次印刷 印张：19 3/4
字数：464 000
定价：128.00 元
（如有印装质量问题，我社负责调换）

前　言

　　随着互联网和信息技术的发展，人们获取知识的方式越来越多元，也越来越碎片化。按照我国中小学正常的学制计算，1995 年生人跨入大学校门，应该是在2013 年。这一年，我国的慕课（massive open online course，MOOC）建设才刚刚起步。在千禧之年出生的人，一般在 2018 年升入大学。从 2013 年到 2018 年，我国慕课发展迅速。2019 年底至 2020 年初暴发的新型冠状病毒肺炎疫情（以下简称"新冠肺炎疫情"）不仅危害人们的身体健康，也打乱了 2020 年春季学期传统的面授教学秩序。新冠肺炎疫情防控期间，全国乃至全球大中小学大规模的网络授课，进一步凸显了慕课依托在线教育教学平台的天然优势和重要价值。慕课以视频教学为主，课程视频、练习、测试、题库等相关资源丰富，但配套的慕课教材建设却相对滞后，特别是同时面向国内和国际留学生开发开放的慕课及其配套教材较为少见，难以满足"微时代"和全球化时代的教育教学要求。

　　随着微信等互联网通信应用的发展和抖音、快手等直播平台的出现，人们越来越倾向于从碎片化的资讯中获取自己所需要的信息，适应年轻人特点和社会需要的慕课建设及配套的教材编写出版势在必行。

　　本课程从文化特别是文化人类学的角度引导青年人（包括在校大学生和社会青年）关注社会，融入社会，解读生活，思考人生，助力人类命运共同体建构和世界和谐发展。

　　本课程主要依托广东省精品视频公开课"人类学与现代生活"和广东省在线开放课程"现代生活的文化解读"，兼顾社会公众学习的人文素质教育要求，主讲教师广泛涉猎文学、历史学、哲学、民族学、宗教学、民俗学、社会学、人类学、公共管理等相关学科，而且曾游学海外，具有良好的学术背景和教学资源。

　　现代社会纷繁复杂，现代生活丰富多彩，现代文化魅力无穷。可以说，我们生活在文化的轨道上，或者说，我们居住在文化的空间里。可是，我们真的了解社会，认识生活，读懂文化吗？本课程将带领您从文化的角度观察多彩社会，从生活的角度品味多元文化。希望您更加积极主动地关注社会，解读生活，了解他者，反思自我，品鉴文化，思考人生，大家一同携手共建和谐美丽的世界。基于这一定位，本教材的编写着眼于如下目标：一是介绍人类学的基本知识，从文化的角度理解文化与现代社会、现代生活的关系。二是分析具体的日常生活现象，培养人们对现代生活的观察能力、分析能力和通识能力，提高人们对现代社会生活的整体认知和科学认识。三是融入思政元素，帮助人们从文化的角度来看待社会生活和更好地适应生活，促进社会和世界和谐。

本教材的课程设计体现如下原则：一是根据慕课特点，以现代生活领域的基本问题为导向，通过问题串联知识点，重整教学资源。二是细化单元内容和阶梯式测试，通过学生自主学习、生生互动和师生联动等方式，促进教学质量的提高和学生学习能力的提升。三是以生活美育和美化生活为目标，通过课程学习，促进青年学生人文素质和品质的提升。

本教材的课程 APP 二维码见封底，微信扫码下载学生端 APP 后打开，搜索"现代生活的文化解读"即可。

如果您想进一步了解本教材的在线课程，敬请打开网址：https://www.zhihuishu.com，搜索"现代生活的文化解读"，它将带您走进"和而不同"的人文世界。

Preface

As both the Internet and information technology have developed, the methods by which people obtain knowledge have grown more diverse and fragmented. Young people born in 1995 who went through China's regular primary and secondary school system started attending university in 2013. China's MOOC(massive open online course)construction has just started from this year. Similarly, people born in 2000 were generally admitted to university in 2018. From 2013 to 2018, MOOC in China developed rapidly. The outbreak of the novel coronavirus (COVID-19) from the end of 2019 to early 2020 not only threatened public health but also disrupted traditional face-to-face teaching throughout the spring semester of 2020. During the prevention and control of the pandemic, the large-scale online teaching at universities, middle schools and primary schools in China, and even around the world, further highlighted the advantages and value of MOOC, which rely on online education and teaching platforms. MOOC is mainly taught via video. MOOC videos, exercises, tests, question banks and other related resources abound, but the compilation of MOOC textbooks has lagged, especially for MOOC that is open to both domestic and international students. These teaching materials cannot meet the educational and teaching requirements of this era of short attention spans and globalization.

With the development of Internet communication applications such as WeChat and the emergence of live streaming platforms such as Tiktok and Kuaishou, people are increasingly inclined to obtain the information they need from fragmented sources. Thus, course books and teaching materials must be updated to cater to younger generations.

This course provides guidance for young people (including college students and young employees) from the perspective of culture and, in particular, cultural anthropology, thus helping them pay closer attention to society, integrate into society and understand the meaning of life—all while building a community with a shared future for mankind and promoting harmonious world development.

This course mainly relies on Guangdong province's excellent open video course "Anthropology and Modern Life", as well as Guangdong province's open online course "Cultural Interpretation of Modern Life". It takes into account the need for cultured education in public learning, and its lecturers are proficient in a wide range of disciplines, including literature, history, philosophy, ethnology, religion, folklore, sociology, anthropology and public administration. Along with experiences of studying abroad, they also have excellent academic backgrounds and teaching resources.

Modern society is complicated, modern life is abundant and colorful, and modern culture is full of charm. It can be said that we live on a cultural trajectory or in a cultural space. However, do you really understand society, life and culture? This course will guide you as you observe a colorful society from a cultural perspective, experiencing multiculturalism from a life-oriented perspective. The authors sincerely hope that by taking this course, you will pay more attention to society, better interpret life, better understand others, reflect on yourself, appreciate culture, think about life and work together to build a harmonious and beautiful world. This textbook focuses on the following teaching objectives. Firstly, understand the basic knowledge of anthropology, and understand the relationships between culture, modern society and modern life from a cultural perspective. Secondly, beginning with an analysis of concrete phenomena in daily life, develop students' abilities for observation and analysis, as well as their general knowledge, so that they may better comprehend modern life; in addition, improve learners' overall awareness and scientific understanding of life in modern society. Thirdly, incorporate philosophical and political elements into the curriculum to help students view life in society and better adapt to real life from a cultural perspective, thus promoting harmony in society and the world.

The curriculum design of this textbook reflects the following principles. Firstly, working within MOOC characteristics, this textbook is oriented towards discussing the basic problems in modern life, thus connecting knowledge points through problem solving while also reorganizing teaching resources. Secondly, by refining the content of each unit and quizzes, this textbook aims to improve teaching quality and learning ability through independent student learning, student–student interaction and teacher–student communication. Thirdly, seeking to offer an aesthetic education and the beautification of life, this textbook is committed to building the character of young students and making them more cultured through coursework.

If you would like to learn more about the online courses of this textbook, please visit https://www.zhihuishu.com, search "Cultural Interpretation of Modern Life", where you will be led into a cultured world of "harmony through diversity".

目 录

Contents

1 现代、现代生活及文化解读

1.1 现代与现代生活

1.1.1 何谓现代？

现代是相对于传统而言的。"现代"有别于"传统"什么呢？不同的人当然可能会有不同的答案。

如果从生产和生活的角度去观察，"现代"的特征是十分明显的，那就是：以机器大生产取代传统的手工生产方式；个人生活时间让渡和服务于工业化的"流水作业"时间；机器大生产和工业化、标准化、市场化、效益化，构成现代社会的标准配置，时间、金钱和效率则构成了现代生活的主要变量。

1.1.2 何谓现代生活？

顾名思义，现代生活是和现代及现代社会相联系的。相对于传统的、自给自足的自然经济时代的农耕生活、手工业社会生活来说，现代生活是与工业社会的机器大生产方式相适应的。简单地说，与工业社会相联系的生活就叫现代生活。那么，现代生活究竟有什么特征呢？

首先，现代生活时间受工业社会"流水作业"的生产或工作时间支配。

其次，现代生活空间受工业社会的空间制约。

再次，现代生活内容受工业产品种类影响。

最后，现代生活质量受工业产品质量、市场价格和社会环境等因素影响。

1.1.3 现代生活的初步认识

现代生活包罗万象，也非常复杂。不同的人，对现代生活可能会有不同的了解和认识，当然也会有不同的生活方式。

我们知道，现代是和工业社会相联系的。机器大生产和流水作业是工业社会生产方式的主要特征。这种流水线上的机器大生产，客观上要求标准化和模型化。比如说，标准化的技术、标准化的生产线、标准化的价格机制、标准化的销售渠道、标准化的时间、标准化的空间（厂房、库房、商场、直营店、体验店等）。和这种标准化、模型化、工业化相适应的生活，是现代生活，它和传统的、基于自给自足自然经济的传统生活是完全不同的。因此，大家不难发现，日常生活中的衣、食、住、行、游、购、娱、婚、丧、生、老、病、死、葬、祭等，无一例外都带有太多工业化的烙印和痕迹。

在现代生活当中，人们看似有很多选择，其实也没有太多选择。尽管不少人喜欢 DIY，但这种 DIY 其实也只是在有限的时间、有限的空间和标准化的工业材质当中进行有限的自我设计和制作而已。它本质上是对现代生活方式的背离，也可以在一定程度上看作是对传统生活的自我回归。传统与现代是相对的，不是绝对的。从传统生活向现代生活的转变过程中，文化发挥了十分重要的作用。

1.1.4　本节小结

本节我们讨论了现代和现代生活的含义，阐述了现代生活的主要特征和基本维度。希望通过本节内容的讨论，能够加深大家对现代、现代生活的初步理解，为后面章节内容的学习和讨论奠定良好的基础。

知识拓展与链接：

文化价值观和态度可以阻碍进步，也可以促进进步，可是它们的作用一直大体上受到政府和发展机构的忽视。我相信，将改变价值观和态度的因素纳入发展政策、安排和规划，是一种很有意义的办法，会确保在今后 50 年中世界不再经历多数穷国和不幸民族群体过去 50 年来所陷于其中的贫困和非正义。

——［美］塞缪尔·亨廷顿、劳伦斯·哈里森：《文化的重要作用：价值观如何影响人类进步》，程克雄译，北京：新华出版社，2002 年版，第 24 页。

推荐阅读：

《文化的重要作用：价值观如何影响人类进步》是当代著名政治理论家、思想家亨廷顿参与主编的一部书。该书从文化与经济发展、文化与政治发展、文化与性别、文化与美国少数民族、亚洲危机和处境变革等几个方面论证并阐述了文化广泛而深刻的影响，回答了文化价值观是如何影响人类进步的。埃通加·曼格尔在该书中提出的"文化是制度之母"的学术命题，可以视为该书的点睛之笔。

——常青藤译丛编者序言

1.2　文化与现代生活的关系及其解读

1.2.1　文化与现代生活的关系

什么是文化？据不完全统计，文化的概念有两三百种之多。不同的人对"文化"的理解可能都不一样。从人类学的角度看，凡是带有人类活动烙印的一切事物都属于文化。因此，可以这么认为，文化是人类活动的产物。或者说，文化是人类一切活动的总和。我们吃的是文化，穿的是文化，住的是文化，行的也是文化，我们生活在文化的世界里。不同的国家、不同的地区、不同的民族或族群，在与自然界、与他人、与自我长期的交往实践中形成了不同的文化，构筑了不同的人文世界和多元的"文化星球"。和而不同的文化景观，构成了当代世界基本的文化图像。

文化是社会的基因，它本质上是历史性的。文化反映历史多于反映现实社会，或者说，文化反映现实社会少于反映历史。为什么这么说呢？因为文化是社会的"黏合剂"。离开了文化的黏合，社会将无法形成共同体或组织单元。因此，从文化的角度去看待现代生活，便具有特殊的意义。

文化与生活关系密切。生活乃文化，文化即生活。生活与文化，互为表里，构成了具象与抽象的关系。文化是社会的"黏合剂"和生活的"调味品"。离开文化的社会，将无法成为社会，而是一盘散沙，无法正常和有效运转。

1.2.2　如何从文化的角度解释现代生活？

文化有哪些分析视角？不同的学科对文化有不同的分析视角。大多数的社会科学和人文科学是从狭义的角度去理解文化的，它们把文化仅仅看作精神层面的东西，如精神文化等。即便包括了从精神文化延伸出来的制度文化等，实际上也是不全面的。为什么呢？

从人类学的角度看，文化其实是一个有机联系的整体。我们认为，无论是文化的"二分法"（物质文化和精神文化）、"三分法"（物质文化、精神文化、行为文化），还是"四分法"（物质文化、行为文化、制度文化、精神文化），文化实际上都是一个有机的整体，如果对文化做一个横截面的解剖，可以发现：文化由外到内的圈层结构依次是物质文化→行为文化→制度文化→精神文化。[①]

现代生活的衣、食、住、行、游、购、娱、婚、丧、生、老、病、死、葬、祭，构成现代社会的基本生活领域或维度，覆盖了文化的物质、行为、制度和精神层面。在现代社会中，生活的世俗空间与"神圣"空间并非截然对立，而是相

---

① Yang L, Li M. Cultural understanding of global governance: a perspective of religious culture[J]. Advances in Applied Sociology, 2018, 8(5): 359-365.

对的，空间隔离的时限取决于当地社会（群体）的文化需要。因此，我们需要从整体上去分析现代生活。"人类学家与其他围观访客之间的真正区别在于，他们会从研究对象的文化的角度去思考人们的所作所思。"①文化的整体观、相对观和比较观，构成了现代生活文化解读的有效视角。

1.2.3　本节小结

本节分析了文化与现代生活的关系，讨论了现代生活文化解读的基本领域和分析视角，以及现代生活与文化解释之间的逻辑关联，希望能够帮助大家运用文化人类学的相关知识来看待社会生活和更好地生活。

知识拓展与链接：

少数民族服饰的蜡染工艺，在宋代已有详细记载。宋代桂林通判周去非在《岭外代答》中写道：

"瑶人以蓝染布为斑，其纹极细。其法以木板二片，镂成细花，用以夹布，而熔蜡灌于镂中，而后乃释板取布，投诸蓝中。布既受蓝，则煮布以去其蜡，故能受成极细斑花，炳然可观。"

——周去非：《岭外代答校注》，北京：中华书局，1999 年版，第 224 页。

推荐阅读：

美国纽约州立大学波茨坦分校人类学系杰出教授约翰·奥莫亨德罗（John Omohundro）编写出版的《像人类学家一样思考》，每章都围绕一个关键问题精心组织，用相关田野故事揭示身处田野的人类学家将会遇到的潜在问题、挑战和后果。通过亲身田野经历，作者生动地展现了人类学家所面对的核心概念与问题，有助于学生深入掌握人类学研究人类行为和观念的方法，并有机会在读过本书后，在本文化和异文化的生活中，像人类学家一样思考。

---

① 约翰·奥莫亨德罗. 像人类学家一样思考 [M]. 张经纬, 等, 译. 北京: 北京大学出版社, 2017: 16.

2 衣和食：人类社会的文化偏好

人以衣遮体，民以食为天。裹衣腹食是人维持生命的基本需求。但是，在工业化的现代生活当中，衣食问题不仅仅是一个基本的维生问题，它在很大程度上也反映着人类社会的文化偏好。

2.1 衣服的含义与起源

2.1.1 衣服的含义

现代汉语中的"衣服"是一个名词，一般是指人们穿在身上遮挡身体或御寒、防风、防潮、防晒、防尘护肤的东西。但是，在古代汉语中，"衣"和"服"具有不同的含义。汉代许慎《说文解字》中说："衣，依也。上曰衣，下曰裳。象覆二人之形。凡衣之属皆从衣。"①对于"服"的解释，《说文解字》说："服，用也。一曰车右騑，所以舟旋，从舟。古文从人。"②《辞海》说"衣"有"衣服"的含义："古时上曰衣，下曰裳。"③古代"衣裳"，《诗经》已有记载。《诗·齐风·东方未明》谓："东方未明，颠倒衣裳。"这说明，最迟到战国时期，古人对上衣下裳已有了明确区分。

由此可见，在中国古代汉语的语境当中，"衣"和"服"的含义是不同的。至于"衣"和"服"连用成为"衣服"，则是近现代以后的事情。

2.1.2 衣服的起源

关于衣服或服饰的起源问题，学者们有不同的看法。概括起来，大概有"气候适应说"、"人体保护说"、"护符说"、"象征说"、"审美说"和"遮羞说"等不同的说法。从本源上讲，衣服应该是人类适应自然环境的结果。

现代科学的研究发现，人类在起源和发展过程中经历了气候的变化，特别是第四纪冰期，人类为了保温防寒开始使用动物毛皮裹体御寒，气候环境的变化促进了树叶兽皮等服饰的出现。中国古代服饰，"是在人类不断面对、克服和改造自然的动态发展过程中逐步创造和积累出来的。这是一个由简单到复杂、由生理到

---

① 许慎. 说文解字: 附检字（卷八上）[M]. 北京: 中华书局, 1963: 170.
② 许慎. 说文解字: 附检字（卷八上）[M]. 北京: 中华书局, 1963: 176.
③ 辞海编辑委员会. 辞海 [Z]. 1999 年版缩印本. 上海: 上海辞书出版社, 2000: 2306.

精神、由物质到文化不断升华、演进和丰富的过程"①。在初民社会中，自然的生理适应应该比社会适应更符合人类的进化。"服饰的起源，其根本是出于实用。但是人类分布极其广泛。各地气候、自然地理环境、条件各异，因此，不同地区的原始部落在发明衣服方面，都有其特殊的形式。在寒温带地区，人类为了防御寒冷、保护身体，很早就披上了兽皮或树叶。在热带，御寒的问题虽不存在，却另有危害人类生存的因素。"②"服饰的产生是人类在从猿到人的转变过程中，由于身体结构和生理器官发生变化，为了适应自然界的需要而产生的。"③"气候适应说""人体保护说"可能更接近远古人类服饰起源的真实状况，"护符说"、"象征说"、"审美说"和"遮羞说"等学说，则是人类步入文明社会之后产生的结果。

　　文化是人类区别于动物的重要标志。但是，文化是有圈层结构的。从广义上的文化结构来看，"二元"文化结构的最外围应该是物质文化，最里面是精神文化；"三元"文化结构的最外围仍然是物质文化，最里面是精神文化，处于物质文化和精神文化之间的是行为文化；"四元"文化结构由外到内依次是物质文化、行为文化、制度文化、精神文化。人具有生物属性和社会属性，生物属性是本源性的，社会属性则是派生或演化出来的。从这个意义上说，衣服的起源，应该是满足人类适应自然环境特别是气候变化的结果。毕竟，适应自然环境变化的生理需要远比心理需要重要得多，也更符合初民社会的特点。

2.1.3　本节小结

　　现代汉语中的"衣服"是一个名词性词语，但古代汉语中的"衣"和"服"具有不同的含义。"衣"和"服"连用成为"衣服"是近现代以后的事情。衣服的起源，应该是人类适应自然环境特别是气候变化的结果。

知识拓展与链接：

　　少数民族服饰尽管有地域上的差别，但它往往保持着中华民族古代服饰的传统款式特征，残留着诸多的原始文化遗迹，展示出人类古代服饰的发展轨迹，是我们了解和佐证人类早期服饰状况的"活化石"。在这里，我们发现了服饰的缘起演变规律：它起源于障风避雨、防御自然，得助于性的夸示或躲避两性间的性吸引，繁荣于大自然的启迪，兴盛于夸富心理的支配……
　　——杨鵾国：《符号与象征：中国少数民族服饰文化》，北京：北京出版社，2000 年版，第 6 页。

---

① 贾玺增. 中国服饰艺术史 [M]. 天津: 天津人民美术出版社, 2009: 1.
② 戴争. 中国古代服饰简史 [M]. 北京: 中国轻工业出版社, 1988: 2.
③ 朱和平. 中国服饰史稿 [M]. 郑州: 中州古籍出版社, 2001: 52.

2.2 现代服饰的主要特征

我们刚才谈到，现代社会是和工业社会的机器大生产及流水作业的生产方式相联系的，现代社会中的服饰嬗变实际上是工业化影响的结果。这种变化主要表现在以下几个方面。

2.2.1 服饰的面料材质多元化

传统服饰的面料材质大多就地取材，取自当地的纯天然植物，经过手工加工而成。例如，中国传统农耕社会中的种桑养蚕、纺纱织布等，基本上都是纯天然的，即便有些蜡染加工，其原材料也主要是天然的矿物或植物。①

在现代社会中，由于工业技术的进步和审美能力的普遍提高，现代服饰的面料材质已经不再局限于天然的动物、植物或矿物，而是出现了一些经过化学合成工艺制作的材质或面料，如人造纤维、玻璃纤维、铜氨纤维、金属纤维、涤纶、人造皮革等，它们和棉、麻、丝、毛、皮等传统材质，共同构成了现代社会服饰的多元化面料材质。②③

2.2.2 服饰的制作工艺精细化

传统服饰的制作工艺相对简单，主要靠人工量体、手工裁剪布料，使用手缝针和顶针箍进行手工缝制，不同的面料使用不同型号的针头，如丝绸等纤维较细的织物用 7~9 号针，锁眼钉纽用 4~5 号针，一般毛料则使用粗细适中的 6~8 号针。另外，传统的镶、嵌、滚（也称绲）、荡、盘等装饰工艺耗费的时间较长，难以量化生产。④

现代服饰使用批量裁剪（又称工业裁剪）、机器缝纫、特殊工艺缝纫和电熨等方式加工，制作工艺更加标准化和精细化，即便是单件量身定做，制作工艺也更为精细。20 世纪 50 年代除手工铺料外，开始采用手推车或往返式电动铺料机操作。20 世纪 80 年代应用微电脑控制自动铺料机，能自动进行正、反面交叉或单面铺料，自动理边、记数等。⑤

从裁剪方式上看，20世纪60年代末已经出现使用电脑控制的自动裁剪机。从缝纫工艺上看，现代服装加工的主要机缝设备，除高速平缝缝纫机外，还有多针多线包缝缝纫机以及取代手工的开袋、锁眼、钉扣、扎驳、复衬（衣面与衣衬组

① 戴争. 中国古代服饰简史 [M]. 北京: 中国轻工业出版社, 1988: 8-21.
② 马新敏. 服装面料艺术再造的多元化 [J]. 纺织导报, 2012, (4): 92-93;
③ 佚名. 传统面料如何多元化 [EB/OL]. (2002-02-06) [2019-09-01]. https://www.tnc.com.cn/info/c-001001-d-61906.html.
④ 李华麒. 从服装缝制工具的演变看手工制作的意义和作用 [J]. 武汉纺织大学学报, 2019, 32(1): 3-6.
⑤ 程启, 荀秉志. 现代服装流行趋势 [J]. 天津纺织工学院学报, 1987, (4): 116-122.

合)、装袖、装裤腰、打褶等各种专用单机，并有多功能自动调速固体电路电子缝纫机问世。[①]

20 世纪 80 年代，采用工业摄像机和电子计算机监控，能自动识别裁片的样式，传送并进行自动分类控制的比较先进的自动缝纫系统问世。与此同时，先进的电脑绣花机也开始出现，它采用九色彩绣，24 个机头同步工作，并配有 2 针到 25 针机的 10 多种装饰机，可在织物上创造出复杂的美术图案，进一步改良了现代服饰的制作工艺。[②]

此外，20 世纪 50 年代起使用电熨斗较普遍。50 年代后期，中国第一代"三领机"研制成功，开始用于衬衫领的黏合和弧定型；英国则发明了以热压方式黏合可熔性衬布的专用黏合机。这种黏合机包括能控时、控压、控温的滚压和平压式两种，成为与缝制新工艺配套的新型熨烫工具。[③]对半成品和成品的熨烫，已应用模压、充气、多工位回转等蒸汽熨烫机和衣片归拔机。一套西服蒸汽熨烫设备可完成熨烫衣袖、衣身、立体整形等 12 种最终熨烫和分缝、归拔等 18 种中间熨烫，使产品干燥、烫迹定型、无亮光。这些现代熨烫新设备、新工艺的出现，极大地提高了产品的熨烫质量。[④]

2.2.3　服饰的款式风格时尚化

服饰的风格和款式往往带有明显的时代特征。有人概括了八种女性服装风格类型，它们包括经典型、运动型、休闲型、民族型、优雅型、中性型、前卫型和轻快型。[⑤⑥]

经典型风格具有传统服装的特点，相对成熟，适合大多数中年女性和相对保守的青年女性穿着，能被大多数女性所接受。这种风格平实、朴素，个性化特征不强烈，时尚感稍弱，但适应面广。

运动型风格借鉴运动装设计元素，充满活力，较多运用块面分割与条状分割及拉链、商标等装饰，穿着面较广。

休闲型风格以穿着轻松、随意、舒适为主，年龄层跨度较大，适合多阶层的消闲、会友、外出、购物等休闲活动，是使着装者具有亲和力的服装风格。

民族型风格汲取中西方民族、民俗服饰元素。中式借鉴中国传统服饰如唐装、旗袍及少数民族服装的形式要素。西式则以外国民族服装为灵感来源，如波希米亚风格、日耳曼民族风格、俄罗斯民族风格等具有复古气息的服装风格。

优雅型风格具有较强女性特征，讲究细部，强调精致，做工考究，注重细节，

① 上海针织一厂. 缝纫机电子控制自动启动 [J]. 针织工业, 1976, (4): 35-38.
② 谢家泽. 电脑绣花机 [J]. 纺织消息, 1986, (8): 10.
③ 祁凡. 服装粘合衬用粘合机 [J]. 粘合剂, 1989, (3): 36-38.
④ 毛立辉. 跨界设计: 一种新锐的生活态度 [J]. 中国服饰, 2012, (11): 21.
⑤ 冯旭敏. 服装感性类型风格形象特征及文化元素构成分析 [J]. 国际纺织导报, 2012, 40(1): 66-68, 70-72.
⑥ 闫超超. 分析高级时装设计中的混搭风格 [J]. 艺术科技, 2019, 32(5): 166.

装饰较女性化，兼具时尚感，较成熟。

中性型风格削弱女性特征，借鉴男装设计元素，以潇洒、利落的效果为主，有一定的时尚度。

前卫型风格运用具有超前性的流行元素，不对称结构与装饰较多，对于各种造型要素均有使用，但在数量、尺寸、位置上更为夸张，有异于常规服装的结构与装饰变化。

轻快型风格轻松、明快，适合年轻女性日常穿着，具有朝气和活力，活泼可爱。

服装的风格一般变化不大，但服装每年的流行款式和装饰等不尽相同。正所谓："年年岁岁花相似，岁岁年年服不同。"时尚其实是一个相对的概念。几十年前流行过的服装款式、风格、颜色和装饰等，可能会在服装设计师们的改造下重新流行起来。

服装设计师们每年会对各种类型的服装风格进行一定的修改或调整，再运用不同的面料、颜色和装饰进行搭配，打造时尚元素，经由时装周发布会的模特展示，形成流行风，引领服装时尚。研究表明，欧美设计师常借助前沿的流行趋势、前卫的设计思想，将现代服装设计与中国的汉族服饰元素进行融合创新。他们在保留传统汉族服饰特色的基础上，添加了个性化、合理化、流行化的设计元素，对推广和复兴汉族服饰文化起到一定作用。[①]另据调查，消费者对全球消费文化的接受度直接影响其对中式服装的态度，但没有显著影响消费意向；中式服装实用性预期对其消费意向的影响最为显著；消费者对国内外品牌认可度差异不明显，容易对国内品牌形成积极的态度；消费者更倾向以简洁含蓄的方式应用中式元素。[②]

2.2.4　服饰的功能用途个性化

传统服装的功能和用途相对单一，主要是蔽体遮羞、防寒保暖、防潮、防晒和防尘护肤。但在工业社会中，服饰的功能和用途趋于多元化和个性化。[③]这一方面是工业化的要求，另外一方面又是工业化产生的后果。

我们知道，现代社会与工业化的机器大生产相联系，工业化的批量生产不仅要求生产技术的标准化，而且要求员工着装规范化、统一化。因此，无论是在生产车间、服务窗口，还是其他一些面向公众服务的机关单位，我们都可以看到员工统一着装。

与此同时，我们也可以看到，人们在工作之余，会从事家务、体育健身或其他的休闲活动，会有不同的着装需求。因此，除通勤工作制服外，人们还有居家服、运动服、休闲服以及一些特殊场合下的服装（如婚礼服、丧礼服、演出服、舞蹈服等），以满足人们的个性化需求。

---

① 路晶晶，王付宏. 汉族服饰款式造型元素现代设计的时尚表达 [J]. 纺织学报，2020, 5(2): 150-155.
② 邢乐，梁惠娥，刘传兰. 中式服装消费意向的影响因素 [J]. 纺织学报，2017, 38(3): 155-161, 167.
③ "现代服装产业技术"课题组. 服装：高性能、多功能满足个性化需求 [J]. 中国纺织，2015, (6): 99.

从本质上讲，这其实是人们通过着装的变化区分工业化规制的流水作业时间和个人生活时间的一种方式。"未来服装设计师的任务，是在服装式样受到一定社会性和功能性制约的条件下，在批量生产的同时探索尽可能多的艺术表现手段，充分满足服装的个性化需求，以实现每个人特有的精神需求与时代感。同时必须把本民族的优秀传统与国际的先进设计构思有机地融为一体，做到相互借鉴，适应世界潮流。"①这是有道理的。毕竟，越是民族的，就越是世界的。世界各民族的服饰文化相得益彰，世界服饰才会更加璀璨夺目。

2.2.5　本节小结

值得注意的是，在工业化的现代生活当中，服饰的选择不仅仅出于防寒保暖、防潮、防晒、防尘护肤的生理需要，也包含着蔽体遮羞、修身美体、满足审美情趣等心理需要。因此，它其实在很大程度上反映着人类社会的文化偏好。

> **知识拓展与链接：**
>
> 　　20世纪末，国际时装界青睐起东方风格来，东方的古典与恬静，东方的纯朴与神秘，开始成为全球性的时尚元素。随着中国在世界地位的提高，穿上华服已经成为海内外华人自豪的象征。中国的女性自然而然地穿起了中式袄，很多男人也以一袭中式棉袄为时尚。如今的华服，并不完全是纯正的中式袄褂，很多女式华服已经时装化——上身是一件印花或艳色棉布镶边立领袄，下身配牛仔裤和一双最新流行款式的皮鞋，既现代又复古。
>
> 　　……服装质地的丰富大大满足了服装造型多变的需求，而对不同面料的偏好，似乎也被越来越多的中国人视作某种生活态度的流露——环保主义者拒绝皮草和羊绒制品，休闲爱好者钟情纯棉质地，亚麻产品特有的飘逸感则被赋予了高贵神秘的意味，而丝绸则为富贵与传统的形象代言。
>
> 　　20世纪业已证明是迄今最具时尚意识的世纪，高销售量的服装、配饰、化妆品市场与日益强大的传媒业的发展，使越来越多的人得以走近时装、欣赏时装、以时装为美。时装已构成了大众理解并乐于投资的一种生活方式。
>
> 　　——华梅：《中国服饰》，北京：五洲传播出版社，2004年版，第150-152页。

2.3　现代服饰及文化偏好

2.3.1　现代生活中的文化与服饰

我们刚才已经谈到，现代生活与工业社会相联系。工业化和标准化规制了人

---

① 程启，荀秉志. 现代服装流行趋势［J］. 天津纺织工学院学报，1987, (4): 116-122.

们的着装，同时也影响了人们对服饰文化的认知。

在现代生活中，服饰承载着文化，文化又反过来规制着服饰。我们的日常活动时间分为工作时间和非工作时间，因此，人们的着装在一天之中会经历多种轮换。"不把工作带回家"是人们重要的工作理念和生活方式，但对多数企业员工而言，准时上下班有时会变成一种理想或奢望。虽然到了下班时间，但手头工作还没做完，是留下来加班，还是把可以带回家的工作带回家去加班？这其实是一个两难问题。

另外，随着网络办公的兴起，一些白领足不出户，在家办公，着装当然也就随心所欲。

值得注意的是，无论是把工作带回家，还是在家办公，它们其实都混淆了工作和生活的时空边界，也使得原本具有明显时空区分的服装模糊了自己的时空边界。这也正是对标工业化的现代生活的新态势。

实际上，服装还具有空间象征意味。人体是前后、两侧四个面和胸、腰、臀的曲线组成的占有一定空间的特定的立体形象。服装是依附于人体而存在于一定的环境、空间里的立体形态。服装是处在一定环境中的可视形象，自然环境、社会环境或生活环境的改变，都会引起服装相应改变。否则，就会显得服装与环境不协调。例如，在现代建筑的人造空间环境里和在自然保护区的自然环境里，服装的空间形态应当有所区别，以达到服装与环境的协调。否则，就如同穿西服或晚礼服在海滩戏水，或穿比基尼泳装听学术报告一样，使得衣着与环境在空间上失调。

随着时间推移、科技进步和生活水平的提高，人们倾向运用服装材料、造型、色彩的时代感和服装的长宽高及时间等四维空间变化来设计服装。例如，一些老年妇女喜欢穿宽松、大花而艳丽的裙衫，以隐去日渐衰老的体态和试图挽回渐行渐远的青春；青少年偏爱穿紧身、偏灰的单色套装，以求展露萌发的青春和追寻即将到来的成熟风采。[①]

2.3.2 人类的服饰存在文化偏好吗？

我们知道，服饰起源于人类适应自然环境变化的生理需要，而后才不断融入审美因素。东西方不同的自然生态环境和文化传统影响着人们的服饰文化偏好。

有人说，中式服装像平面绘画，西式服装则像立体雕塑。这种感觉大体是对的。为什么？因为中式服装着重表现两维效果而非侧面结构设计。西式服装强调三维效果，适合人体结构特点和人体运动规律，既合体又实用，因此，受到西方各国人们的普遍青睐。

中西方服装的审美文化存在较大差异。中国文化起源于大陆文明，在服装上

---

① 赖涛. 试论服装的空间感 [J]. 南昌职业技术师范学院学报, 2000, (1): 36-39.

具有"原体"意识。另外，中国文化是一种隐喻文化，偏重抒情性，追求服装构成要素的精神寓意和文化品位，强调均衡、对称、统一的服装造型方法，以规矩、平稳为美。

中式传统服饰的美学特点，反映了中华民族的审美心态和文化征貌。中国人受儒释道互补的美学思想影响，重视情理结合，以理节情，追求闲适、平淡、中庸，追求超出形体的精神意蕴。因此，中式女装严密包裹人体，使人难窥其详，增加了神秘感；中式男装严整修长，洋溢着中和之美。

西方文化起源于海洋文明，文化本能比较开放，易于融合外域服装文化，善于表现矛盾、冲突，在服装构成上强调刺激、极端的形式，以突出个性为荣。它是一种明喻文化，重视造型、线条、图案、色彩本身的客观美感，以视觉舒适为第一，崇尚人体美，重视展示人体的性差异，不忌讳表现性感。西方古典服装模式是表现女性的第二性征，如露颈、露肩、露背、露半胸，以紧缩腰围和垫臀来表现女性曲线。现代服装模式是以简约的形式表现人体的自然身形，以短露和紧身为现代时髦。

中国文化忽视"性"的存在，服装不表现人体曲线，不具备感官刺激要素，宽衣博带，遮掩人体，表现的是一种庄重、含蓄之美。当然，随着改革开放的深化和全球化进程的加快，中西服饰文化出现了相互借鉴和融合的趋势。

2.3.3　本节小结

本节我们讨论了现代生活中的服饰与文化，分析了人类服饰中存在的文化偏好和中西服饰文化的差异及走向问题。

知识拓展与链接：

服饰既是民族文化的历史发展，又是理解人类大文化的一条渠道；服饰既是民间生活的风俗事象，又是探求人的生活习尚和深层心理的一条线索。中国谚语中有"入乡问俗"的说法，旅游者初次访问一个城市或乡村，首先映入眼帘的是房屋建筑等固置的物质外貌，其次就是当地人活跃的着装形象。不必通过语言去介绍，旅游者便可从着装形象（人及服饰）上，观察该地区的风俗民情，并从宏观方面思考该地区的大文化背景。

——华梅：《服饰民俗学》，北京：中国纺织出版社，2004 年版，第 3 页。

2.4　文化偏好及美容文化

2.4.1　什么是文化偏好？

偏好是一种活动倾向，它是指消费者认为某些物品重要，并愿意为此付出溢价。一定的偏好，会导致重复的行为发生。

文化偏好是相对于个人爱好或癖好而言的，它是消费者在共同文化环境影响下所形成的认识倾向。或者说，由于群体的共同价值观作用，而产生对某一事物的共同追求。

文化偏好与人们的风俗习惯、价值观、道德、宗教等密切相关。人们的文化偏好体现在日常生活的方方面面。例如，穿衣、饮食、住房、交通，以及购买商品时的色彩、数字、利益等方面的偏好。

文化偏好不同于生理性偏好，它来自文化的长期刺激或影响，形成在购买行为中的独特认识倾向。文化偏好本身具有以下特点：

1）普遍性。它是某个文化圈或群体共同的心理反应，是由许多人表现出来的、一个消费者群体的共同行为倾向，因而具有普遍性。

2）差异性。不同范围或亚文化圈层的消费者，他们的文化偏好差别较大。

3）稳定性。与文化影响相关，文化偏好也具有历史性、稳定性。

4）强制性。文化偏好由各个群体强加给各自的成员，因而具有一种明显的必然性和强制性。

知识拓展与链接：

从现在来看，以奶食品为主的民族与以稻米为主食的民族的分布，从东北到西南，似乎有一条斜线把他们分开，而从东北的朝鲜族地区到云南和西藏南部，恰好形成一个上弦新月形。以奶食为主的民族基本分布在北方，而以稻米（古代主要是糯米）为主食的民族基本上分布在南方，"北奶"和"南糯"可以概括中国少数民族的饮食特点。而在这两种地区的交界地带，则有在奶中加煮谷米的"奶粥"吃法。

——李炳泽：《多味的餐桌：中国少数民族饮食文化》，北京：北京出版社，2000年版，第41页。

2.4.2　美容及其文化偏好

顾名思义，美容就是美丽的容颜。这是一种静态的文化表述。实际上，美容还可以作为一种行动实践或社会行为，即整形美容。

常言道，女为悦己者容。美容似乎是女性的专利，其实不然。许多男性也加入了美容的行列。那么，美容究竟有哪些文化偏好呢？

首先，医疗技术的进步和时尚杂志、电视、电影等视觉传媒文化工业的发展，催生了白领阶层对明星偶像的崇拜和对明星衣着、服饰、容颜的效仿。

知识拓展与链接：

千百年来，全球各地的人群一直在设法装饰人体本身——采用文身、穿刺、割礼、缠足等方式，甚至改变颅骨的形状。为了达到这些目标，现代医疗科技提供了一整套全新的外科手术。

随着医疗逐渐成为一个大的产业，很多外科医生已经加入美容产业，以开发人类学家纳德尔（Laura Nader）所说的"标准化"体型。她关注妇女的身体，并注意到"在特定文化环境内看起来自然的身体形象"。例如，在美国的文化环境内，隆胸并不是件奇怪的事情；而在某些南非国家，女性的割礼和缩阴术（也被称为女性生殖器损毁）也不被认为是值得大惊小怪的事。

很多女性主义作家区分"美国妇女主动选择隆胸，而非洲妇女迫于教化才实施身体整形"，并认为年轻女性是在特定环境才如此。但实际上妇女的隆胸何尝不是美容产业综合体作用的结果呢？

——［美］威廉·A.哈维兰（William A.Haviland）、［美］哈拉尔德·E.L.普林斯（Harald E.L.Prins）、［美］达纳·沃尔拉斯（Dana Walrath）等：《人类学：人类的挑战（第14版）》，周云水、陈祥、雷蕾等译，北京：电子工业出版社，2018年版，第350页。

其次，在现代社会中，人总是像物一样被把握和判断。我们通过一个人的衣着服饰、学历出身、简历去迅速审视他、接受他或者否定他，这实际上是对人赤裸裸的物化和标签化，这种认识人、判断人的方法和程序遍布在现代社会体制之中的方方面面。

法国思想家、社会学家居伊·德波在其名作《景观社会》中断言："在现代生产无所不在的社会当中，生活本身展现为景观的巨大堆积，所有的直接存在，都转化为一个表象。"也就是说，在当今这个生产和传媒高度发达的社会里，我们不是通过活生生的真实体验和直接接触去认识和把握这个世界的，而是通过像电视节目、商品广告这样的表象来认识这个世界的。

最后，在现代社会中，消费者关于美的认知、关于美的追求、关于美的欲望，无不受到整形美容业和大众传媒的引导操控，这种复杂的引导和操控即是一种微妙的权力机制。正是这种权力机制，隐匿地支撑着当今的商业广告、明星模特、文化名人在公共舞台上进行炫目的表演，进而成为一种难以察觉的文化意识形态，笼罩着整个后现代世界。

整形美容也可以被视为一种创造快感的方式。日常生活柴米油盐，上班下班两点一线，绝大多数现代人的生活内容和经历体验都十分安全，但是有些人会觉得有些重复和无聊。出于对美好生活的向往和追求，具备一定经济基础的爱美之人，便试图通过整形美容来展现自己的美好形象和生活品质，这当然是无可厚非的。毕竟，爱美之心人皆有之，而且对美好生活的向往，也是人之常情。

20 世纪 90 年代，随着经济快速发展和医疗技术的日益成熟，整形美容渐渐进入我国大众视野并融入人们的生活中。整形美容是由整形外科衍生而来的一项新的分支学科，结合解剖学、形态学等学科，通过外科手术矫正和修复体表组织器官畸形和缺损，达到恢复与改善畸形部位功能、使形态正常的医疗目的。但是，如果过度整形美容，它所带来的危害也是不容忽视的。从伦理角度看，过度整形美容造成的危害包括整形美容者生命健康权益受到损害、主体性丧失、身份认同困难等方面的问题。①这应该引起人们的重视。

2.4.3　本节小结

人类社会是具有文化偏好的。文化偏好是消费者在共同文化环境影响下所形成的认识倾向，它具有普遍性、差异性、稳定性和强制性等特点。现实社会中的整形美容是文化偏好的重要表现。其原因，是人们对美的偏好和追求。

> **知识拓展与链接：**
>
> 一项开拓性隆胸手术，可以"按照古希腊女性雕塑的理想身体尺寸，精心测量并标注乳房的准确尺寸，在水平与竖直位置准确定位"。应美容市场的需求，现在的整形外科生意火爆，而且隆胸手术在全球迅速扩张。
> ——［美］威廉·A.哈维兰（William A. Haviland）、［美］哈拉尔德·E.L.普林斯（Harald E. L. Prins）、［美］达纳·沃尔拉斯（Dana Walrath）等：《人类学：人类的挑战（第 14 版）》，周云水、陈祥、雷蕾等译，北京：电子工业出版社，2018 年版，第 350 页。

2.5　美体、美食的文化偏好

2.5.1　美体及其文化偏好

（1）美体、曲线、肌肉与健身

形体美不美，不仅取决于人们的视觉感官，而且和人们对美的理解和判断标准有关，也与人们的文化偏好有关。何以见得呢？在现代社会中，"美"的身体是可以塑造出来的。除了医学整形，还可以通过标准化的健身训练来实现。因此，在高度发达的城市社会中，不乏健身场馆、健身器材和健身教练，甚至随处可见。

---

① 刘彩凤，刘镇江. 过度整形美容的伦理探析［J］. 中国医学伦理学，2019, 32(9): 1174-1178.

肚皮舞、瑜伽等健身舞蹈颇受青年女性青睐，跑步、推拉举重等运动则受到城市男性白领的喜爱。这一切，其实都是工业时代"生产"美体的结果。

（2）自我美体与他者感知：人靠衣装？

2019 年 3 月底，一则美国男生的母亲对女性不着紧身衣服的建议引发网友关注和热议。据《环球时报》2019 年 4 月 1 日报道，美国印第安纳州的圣母大学（University of Notre Dame），一所本科教育稳居全美国前 20 的顶尖学府，因一场关于"紧身裤问题"的争论上了热搜。该大学的一位男生的母亲玛丽安·怀特（Maryann White）在校方媒体上发表了一篇实名文章，抨击该校女学生们穿紧身裤（leggings），引起男生的"不适"①。这篇文章招来许多女生的反感和批评，甚至一些男生也穿紧身裤来力挺女生们。这些身穿紧身裤的女生认为，紧身裤可以凸显自己的身材和曲线美感，是自我美体的选择，与他人无关，况且又没有法律规定不能穿紧身裤。那位男生的母亲认为，女生穿紧身裤会引起男生的性幻想或冲动，会给男生带来"干扰"。这个事例说明，不同的人站在不同的立场，对美的感知和解读可能不同，甚至截然相反。

（3）医学整形美体：美的"权利"谁做主

现代医学比过去发达。由于经济条件改善和物质生活水平的提高，人们对美容美体也越来越重视。因此，美容医院在我国一些大中城市不断增多。但是，在工业化和流水线作业的现代社会中，你的身体你能够做主吗？如果能的话，你能够在多大程度上做主呢？实际上，你能够在医学美体上做主的"权利"是相当有限的。你可以决定自己身体的哪个部位进行整形，甚至要求美容医生把你整成什么样子，但是，你却无法决定美容医生怎么整，用什么医用材料给你整。即便有几种材料供你选用，那也不过是供你选用价格不同的工业产品填充到自己的身体里面而已。至于美容医生的整形过程，也不过是医学工业化流程在整形对象身上的实施罢了。从这个意义上说，你的"美"的权利是有限的，也是相对的。整形美容医生在你身上"整"出来的"美"，是刻板的、机械的，也是工业化的。

（4）身体亦"政治"：美的"权利"何在

在现代社会中，人们对身体之美的感知有时带有一定的"政治"意味。为什么呢？尽管人们对"美"的感知带有主观判断，但在工业化中，美与不美似乎又是带有一定的标准的。比如说，在模特行业中，模特的身高、三围、面孔等，身材比例是否符合"黄金分割"，以及走步的律动、神韵和眼神等，似乎都有一个基本的标准。但是，在现代工业社会中，究竟由谁来决定我的身体美不美呢？我该不该整形呢？我又该如何整形美体呢？诸如此类的问题，不仅涉及美的感知，而且关涉自己身体美的"权利"实现。因此，现代社会中的美体也存在着一定的"政

---

① 佚名. 这也成了罪？美国母亲狠批女生穿紧身裤，网友纷纷发图反击！［EB/OL］.（2019-03-31）［2019-06-10］. https://world.huanqiu.com/article/9CaKrnKjqPU.

治"意味。①毕竟，公共话语中的"美"与"丑"是被规训的。作为当前流行的身体规划，减肥、健身不仅改变身体的外观，还重塑了身体的秩序，将身体塑造为失去了政治功能的"纯粹的能指"，身体由此成为一种空壳化的存在。与此同时，减肥、健身塑造了一种"无差别的身体"，并将身体以资本化的方式改造。这种身体观已成为当下大众文化的典型征候，即追求感觉直观而却拒绝追问身体的真实处境。②

知识拓展与链接：

女性主义研究者努力想打破那些限定妇女能力、构建标准化形体、决定什么是女性之美的控制范式。《我们的身体，我们自己》（波士顿妇女健康小组）引导妇女认识她们自己的身体是实施权利的场所。像拉科夫和雪儿的《脸面的价值：美的政治学》，以及娜奥米·沃尔夫的《美丽神话：怎样用美丽形象反对妇女》这样的作品，都希望把妇女的思想从整形产业和时尚杂志对美的构建中解放出来。另外也有人讨论过：西方美女模型是如何影响那些特别容易接受广告对自己形象设计的族群成员的。选择是一种幻象，因为对品味的重新建构不可避免地与消费组织的转变联系在一起。

——［美］威廉·A.哈维兰：《文化人类学（第十版）》，瞿铁鹏、张钰译，上海：上海社会科学院出版社，2006 年版，第 502 页。

2.5.2　美食及其文化偏好

（1）何为美食？视觉、味觉还是感觉

何谓美食？这个问题其实不好回答。因为不同的人可能会有不同的答案。比方说，有的人觉得臭豆腐是美食，虽然它闻起来"臭"，但吃它的时候却很"香"；有的人则认为，臭豆腐闻起来就这么"臭"，吃起来怎么可能会"香"？究竟是"臭"还是"香"，真是仁智互见，莫衷一是。

所谓的"香"或"臭"，是相对的，不是绝对的。你所认为的"臭"，可能是别人的"香"，反过来说，你所认为的"香"，可能别人却认为"臭"。这种味觉文

---

① "身体政治"来源于西方学者阿图·弗兰克（Artu Frank）和米歇尔·福柯（Michel Foucault）等人的研究。阿图·弗兰克认为，人的身体在制度、话语和肉身组成的等边三角形的交叉点上形成。他从控制、欲望、他者联系和自我关联四个维度划分出了"规训的身体、控制的身体、镜像的身体（消费）和交流的身体（认知）"。福柯从前两种身体概念出发，认为政治和道德方面的规范和制度往往把身体分割成"公众"和"私人"两大部分，权力和知识关系通过对身体变成认识对象来干预和征服人的肉体，在各式各样的规训与惩罚技术后面体现着某种权力效应、某种知识指涉和某种机制功效，亦即人的身体是被驯服和惩戒的（参见米歇尔·福柯《规训与惩罚：监狱的诞生》，刘北成、杨远婴译，北京：生活·读书·新知三联书店，1999 年版）。葛红兵、宋耕的《身体政治》（上海三联书店，2005 年版）探讨了身体与文学的关系问题，进一步引发了国内学者对身体、文化、政治之间不同维度的思考和分析。

② 杨毅. 减肥、健身与身体的政治［J］. 文化研究，2018,(4): 262-273.

化，是有地域性的，也是带有文化偏好的。尽管美食是带有地域性和文化偏好的，但美食之所以能够称为美食，应该也是有一定的标准的。这个标准是什么呢？不外乎色、味、香、型、艺等方面。

具体说来，第一是美食的色泽鲜艳，让人一看就有食欲，即所谓"秀色可餐"；第二是美食的味道鲜美，所谓八珍玉食，其味无穷，回味悠长，酥脆香口，入口即化，唇齿留香，爽滑酥嫩，味道香醇，肥而不腻，辣而不燥，鲜嫩多汁，等等；第三是美食的香味迷人，诱人垂涎，所谓芳香四溢，沁人心脾，香气逼人，香飘十里，醉迷万家；第四是美食的造型美观，犹如艺术珍品，让人望眼欲穿，却又不忍动筷，如龙凤呈祥、肝胆相照、夫唱妇和、步步高升、四季花开、鸿运当头、金玉满堂、欢聚一堂等充满寓意的词语，作为菜名进入了新年团圆饭的菜谱，厨师更是通过食物造型传递出人们对美好生活的向往；最后是美食的烹饪加工充满艺术韵味。

出生于 18 世纪的法国政治家、美食家布里亚-萨瓦兰认为："天地万物都是生命，而生命需要进食。动物吃饲料，人吃饭，但是只有有思想的人才懂美食。民族的命运取决于其实现温饱的方式。"①世界各地饮食艺术风格迥异，各具其美。"意大利美食如文艺复兴雕塑，法国美食如古典绘画，日本美食如俳句短语，中华美食如山水画、古诗词，例如，中国顺德美食这种区域特征显著的饮食艺术，则如岭南画派、岭南诗词的代表作。"②顺德美食在物质创作、心理体验、精神寄予等方面充满艺术特质，在粤菜体系中有其特色和美。

（2）美食之美：色、味、香、型、艺俱佳的地域和民族差异

美食之美，在于色、味、香、型、艺俱佳。不过，所谓色味香型艺俱佳，也是有地域和民族差异的。为什么呢？原因很简单，不同的地域文化和民族文化涵造了不同的饮食文化及其美食。

由于我国各地气候、地形、历史、物产及饮食风俗等的不同，经过漫长历史演变而形成了一整套自成体系的烹饪技艺和风味，鲁、川、粤、苏、浙、闽、湘、徽共同构成全国八大地方菜系。中国人发明了炒、烧、煎、炸、煮、蒸、烤、凉拌、淋等烹饪方式，又向其他民族学习了扒、涮等方式，制作了各种丰富多彩的菜肴。

我国少数民族的美食也十分丰富。蒙古族的烤全羊和奶制品，回族的清真面食，藏族的酥油茶，苗族的酸味食品，傣族的牛肉和猪肉干巴、菠萝饭和香竹糯米饭，白族的凉拌生皮，壮族的五色糯米饭和各种形状的粽子，瑶族、侗族的油茶，高山族的米酒，朝鲜族的泡菜、冷面和年糕，赫哲族的特色鱼类美食，鄂伦

---

① 让·安泰尔姆·布里亚-萨瓦兰. 厨房里的哲学家［M］. 周小兰, 罗颖娴, 译. 广州: 广东旅游出版社, 2016: 5.
② 李炳聪. 顺德知味｜顺德美食的艺术画像［EB/OL］.（2019-04-17）［2019-04-19］. https://baijiahao.baidu.com/s?id=1631066739436901618&wfr=spider&for=pc.

春族的手把肉，鄂温克族的马奶酒，等等，都是民族菜肴中的特色美食。

知识拓展与链接：

在饮食方面，喜欢速食速简餐也可以看作是青年文化的特色之一。在工业社会里速食或速简餐是普遍被接受的餐饮方式自不待言，但是青年人的特别喜爱，似是当作一种喜爱的行为方式而不是一种迁就事实的办法，近日麦当劳的震撼，年轻人占食客中主要成分应是一个好例子。青年人的喜欢速食，可以说是不拘形式的特点，配合直截了当的行为，崇尚简洁，直接行动，甚至急速达成目的心态之表现。

——李亦园：《人类的视野》，上海：上海文艺出版社，1996年版，第136页。

（3）好吃与吃好：美食文化偏好的想象与实践

美国人类学家马文·哈里斯在其著作《好吃：食物与文化之谜》①中对印度人不吃牛肉，犹太人和穆斯林不吃猪肉，欧美人不吃昆虫，亚洲人难消化牛奶、黄油和奶油等饮食偏好进行了解释，认为肉食能够比植物性食物更高效地满足人类对于营养的需求。人们所吃的肉、鱼、禽类和奶制品，富含了人类身体所需的、植物性食物所缺少的维生素和矿物质。也就是说，肉食比素食更容易喂饱人们，也更容易让人们吃好。但是，为什么不同国家、不同地区、不同民族的肉食也会存在偏好呢？

知识拓展与链接：

当印度人拒绝吃牛肉，犹太人和穆斯林痛恨猪肉，还有美国人想都不敢想要吃狗肉时，人们从这些现象中可以意识到，在消化生理学的背后会有什么因素在发生作用，使人确认什么是好吃的。这种因素便是特定人群的美食传，是他们的饮食文化。

——［美］马文·哈里斯：《好吃：食物与文化之谜》，叶舒宪、户晓辉译，济南：山东画报出版社，2001年版，第2页。

马文·哈里斯认为，世界上的食谱差异主要是因生态的限制和不同地区存在的饮食文化不同所导致。人类的食物之谜可以从营养的、生态的和收支效益的角度进行解释。例如，肉类食谱通常出现在人口密度相对较低、不需要土地或不适宜农耕的地区；素食菜谱则容易出现在人口密度高、食物生产技术不足以供应动物肉食的地区。

马文·哈里斯将"自然科学"与"人文科学"相结合，运用生理学、病理学、

---

① 马文·哈里斯. 好吃：食物与文化之谜［M］. 叶舒宪，户晓辉，译. 济南：山东画报出版社，2001.

精神医学、药学、营养学、农学、畜牧学、生物化学、遗传学等各学科资源来解释食物与文化、社会、自然之间的关联。这在他的《母牛·猪·战争·妖巫：人类文化之谜》一书中均有论述。[①]在马文·哈里斯看来，从印度人对母牛的热爱，到南太平洋岛屿土著人频繁不断的冲突；从北美印第安人的冬季赠礼节，到欧洲历史上曾经流行过的妖巫，任何文化现象都根植于现实社会的土壤之中，都有其客观的现实基础。换言之，人类的好吃和吃好，都不过是美食文化偏好的想象和实践而已。

（4）美食与食补：食物的医学、经济学、政治学和社会学

在刚才提到的《好吃：食物与文化之谜》中，马文·哈里斯详细分析和讨论了印度的牛肉禁忌、以色列人禁食猪肉、法国等欧洲国家喜欢吃马肉、美国人不吃马肉却钟情牛肉等现象，认为美国人热衷牛肉而冷落马肉其实掺杂了政治、经济等因素。他强调，人们对于某种食物的选择，既有经济因素的考量，同时也是一个国家、一个地区、一个民族的自然环境、社会环境、文化、政治等因素的综合作用的结果。

知识拓展与链接：

从文化观的立场而言，西洋人的喜爱牛肉仍然是有相当主观的癖好。在西方人的观念中，牛肉象征男性的壮健，喜欢吃牛肉正是喜爱这种壮健的象征，其间虽说没有直接滋补的效用之意，但却也有"性征"的含义在，与中国式的"饮食男女"实有异曲同工之妙。

——李亦园：《人类的视野》，上海：上海文艺出版社，1996 年版，第 174 页。

总体上看，人们对美食的定义体现了不同国家、不同地区、不同民族或族群对于人与自然、人与社会、人与自我的文化理解或解释。无论是食材本身，还是刀工、佐料、火候、造型等烹饪技术，或者食用方式等，都充满文化意味。它实际上是一个国家或地区、民族或族群文化协商的结果。食物美不美，或者能否成为美食，不仅仅是舌尖上的美味那么简单，它还蕴藏着视其为美味佳肴的人们对它与自然、它与社会、它与食客内心需要的三个层次和美的深度理解与追求。

食补的医学意义非常明显，至少在中国民间传统饮食和中医文化那里得到了充分体现。无论春夏还是秋冬，也不管天南还是地北，中国一年四季的饮食都颇为讲究，甚至在现代工业技术加工基础上开发出精美的即食的工业食补美食来。超市里的龟苓膏、清补凉、王老吉、加多宝、凉粉等，琳琅满目，一应俱全。

---

① 马文·哈里斯. 母牛·猪·战争·妖巫：人类文化之谜 [M]. 王艺，李红雨，译. 上海：上海文艺出版社，1990.

　　然而，由于中国民间流传着"吃啥补啥"的观念，一些人想通过食用奇珍异食、山珍海味、飞禽走兽等野生动物来滋补身体，使得一些野生动物捕猎者和不法商家铤而走险，贩卖和销售野生动物，加剧了动物源性病毒或细菌传播的危险。为此，全国人民代表大会常务委员会在 2020 年 2 月 24 日审议通过了《关于全面禁止非法野生动物交易、革除滥食野生动物陋习、切实保障人民群众生命健康安全的决定》，明确提出严厉打击非法野生动物交易、全面禁止食用野生动物，从制度上防范非法交易和滥食野生动物"食补"可能带来的病毒疫情传播的公共卫生风险。这是十分必要的，也有助于食源性疫情防控。

2.5.3　本节小结

　　本节我们讨论和分析了美体、美食的文化偏好及其表现等问题，对文化偏好背后的政治、经济、社会等成因也做了简单的分析。希望通过这些问题的讨论和分析，能够帮助大家进一步理解人类的美容、美体、美食的文化偏好问题。

知识拓展与链接：

　　在今天的世界里，所有的战乱与纠纷，大半都由于种族冲突所致，人类学家加入能对这个世界有所贡献，就在于提供与异民族相处之道，这种"道"加入能为世人所体会，放弃他们对别人的偏见，世界的繁荣安乐才有预期的可能。

——李亦园：《人类的视野》，上海：上海文艺出版社，1996 年版，第 18 页。

2.6　食品、饮食及安全问题

2.6.1　食品、饮食与安全

　　食品就是人们的食用之品，或者说是食用的物品，即"食物"。不过，食品和食物的内涵还是有差异的。它们的差异究竟表现在哪里呢？

　　食品和食物均可供人们食用，但它们适用的语境不太一样。食品一般是指经过现代工业加工过的可以食用的物品；食物则泛指各个时代可以食用的物品，它不一定经过现代工业加工，纯手工打造也是可以的。

　　至于饮品，一般是可供人们饮用的食品。经过机器压榨的各类果蔬汁液，还有那些瓶装、罐装或听装的饮料或酒水等，都属于饮品。饮品虽然不是传统意义上以饱腹为目的的食品，"但是饮料具有提供机体能量、营养，尤其是愉悦感的基本功能。因此，饮料应该属于典型的流体食品。在管理上，饮料行业也归属食品工业"①。

在现代工业社会中，纯天然的食品、饮品弥足珍贵，备受人们喜爱。但是，工业加工的食品却充斥市场。食品安全问题，也越来越受到人们的关注。为什么呢？原因很简单，现代社会中的食品加工存在着不可忽视的安全问题。下面，对此进行简单的分析。

2.6.2　现代食品的安全问题

我们之前已经谈到，现代生活与现代工业社会相适应，它是以机器大生产为标志的。这种以机器大生产为标志的工业社会，刺激着人们对物质的追求和实现经济利益最大化。在这个过程中，食品的安全问题不容忽视。

现代工业社会中的食品加工中的安全问题可能主要来自以下几个方面：

首先，食品生产商为了降低成本，可能在食材选用方面保持最低合格标准，而非优质标准；加工、包装、储藏、运输等环节合格达标，但不一定达到优质标准。这种"合格"即"安全"，"安全"即"合格"的思想观念和行动实践，稍有不慎，就会出问题。另外，一些生产商为了改善食品口感、味道、色泽，可能违规增加食品添加剂；为了延长保质期，一些不良商家可能过量使用防腐剂；为了美化外观而使用了增白剂或漂白剂；等等，都有可能增加食品的不安全因素。换句话说，现代科学技术的发展，为人类食品的加工提供了技术支撑。但是，一些食品加工者为了降低成本和追逐利润，可能只求产品合格而非优质，甚至生产不合格的食品。食品的安全问题，值得重视。

其次，经销商或零售商在售卖食品的过程中，可能也会存在安全问题。例如，一些经销商或零售商有时低价促销快过期的食品和饮品，有的甚至涂改生产日期，销售快过期或变质的产品。这无疑也增加了食品的不安全因素。

再次，一些市民为了节约生活成本，可能会食用一些买时未过保质期，但买回家后因长期储藏而过期变质的食品，也会造成食品安全问题。

最后，现代工业社会给人们生活带来便利的同时，也带来了紧张、焦虑，一些人为此购买保健食品甚至以保健食品代替日常生活食品而影响身体健康，这是值得注意的。

很多消费者容易把食品的质量和安全混为一谈，往往把食品的质量好坏等同于食品安全与否。食品质量主要包括食品的物性、营养和感官等方面的品质，有显性质量（如形状、颜色、质地、包装等）和隐性质量（如成分、结构、营养等）之分。食品质量可以通过视觉评判、感官分析和仪器测量来评价。有些食品因包装、储藏、运输等造成外观变形或标签损毁，但并不影响食品的基本功能和食用安全。根据食品对人体可能造成的伤害范围，可将食品安全问题分

---

① 陈建设. 关于食品的几个基本概念［J］. 食品科学, 2019, 40(4): 3-4.

为物理安全（食品加工、包装、流通等环节混入异物）、化学安全（食品中含有因食物链或非法添加剂导致的安全问题）、微生物安全（食品中含有致病性微生物引起的安全问题）和过敏安全（食品中的某些特殊成分不耐受而产生病理性反应）四大类型问题。[①]

2.6.3　本节小结

食品与食物的内涵不同，与安全关系密切。以机器大生产为标志的工业社会，刺激着人们对物质的追求和实现经济利益最大化。在这个过程中，食品的安全问题来源广泛，生产、运输、储藏、销售等环节管理不当，都有可能产生现代食品安全问题。

知识拓展与链接：

工业化食物生产可以被定义为大规模的商业，涉及批量食物生产、加工和销售，而这主要依赖节省劳动力的机器。工业化的食物生产有着深远的经济、社会和政治意义，由于这些意义互相交织，仍然有未被了解的方面。如今生产食物的大公司拥有大片土地，在这片土地上庄稼被批量生产并用机器收割，肉食动物也被集中饲养。这些庄稼和动物一起在收获（宰杀）之后被加工、包装、高速运送至机场，提供给城市人口食用。

——［美］威廉·A.哈维兰（William A. Haviland）、［美］哈拉尔德·E. L.普林斯（Harald E. L. Prins）、［美］达纳·沃尔拉斯（Dana Walrath）等：《人类学：人类的挑战（第14版）》，周云水、陈祥、雷蕾等译，北京：电子工业出版社，2018年版，第447页。

2.7　工业社会中的快餐及文化解读

2.7.1　快餐与工业社会

快餐的出现，是现代社会生活节奏加快的直观反映。在现代工业社会中，人们生活的时间让渡于机器大生产的工业生产时间。

围绕着"流水作业"的时间，人们穿梭于工作单位和家庭之间，几乎很少有时间做饭，特别是城市中的白领，他们早上大多拎着早餐去上班，中午在写字楼里叫外卖，晚上回到住处随便吃些零食或宵夜，这似乎成了他们日常生活的"标配"。这不是因为白领不喜欢美食，或者是他们为了保持苗条身材少吃或不吃食

[①] 陈建设. 关于食品的几个基本概念［J］. 食品科学, 2019, 40(4): 3-4.

物，而可能是因为没有足够的时间和精力去烹饪，只能快速而简单地应付自己的用餐问题。

这其实也是工业化的一个直接后果，那就是：机器快速运转，时间非常紧张，人们步履匆忙，餐饮草草应付，不为一日三餐，只图事业发展，哪顾得上自己健康不健康！这种以牺牲健康为代价的快节奏、快餐饮的生活方式，实际上是工业化的生产方式在现代生活中的反映。

知识拓展与链接：

美国人喜好白肉，导致类似鸡腿肉的"黑肉"在美国严重过剩……一只普通的 3 千克的"雏鸡"被密西西比鸡肉工厂拿着最低工资工作的墨西哥移民宰杀后，会到哪里去？……它的腿上了莫斯科的餐桌，然而最后胸脯肉会来到美国人的餐桌上，或是国际航线的菜单上。其他部分呢？一只冷冻的翅膀装进了运往韩国的大集装箱；另外一只到了西非。内脏（脖子、心脏、肝和胃）运到了牙买加用来煮汤。多余的脂肪在得克萨斯的一个实验性精炼厂转化成了生物柴油。

——［美］威廉·A.哈维兰（William A. Haviland）、［美］哈拉尔德·E. L. 普林斯（Harald E. L. Prins）、［美］达纳·沃尔拉斯（Dana Walrath）等：《人类学：人类的挑战（第 14 版）》，周云水、陈祥、雷蕾等译，北京：电子工业出版社，2018 年版，第 449 页。

2.7.2　文化视野中的快餐

近年来，随着经济全球化的深入发展，麦当劳、肯德基等"洋快餐"也进入中国的大中城市，并且受到不少青少年朋友的青睐。

快餐之所以"快"，是因为食材本身已经是半成品或成品，顾客下单后只需简单拼装加热或加冰即可。

至于快餐的营养价值，可能已经不是顾客关注的重点。顾客可能心的是快餐何时送达、快餐贵不贵、快餐好不好吃等问题。无论是本土快餐，还是外来的洋快餐，都是适应社会快速发展的现实需要。自从快餐进入我们的生活以来，我们的生活节奏明显加快。"整个社会就像一台快速运转的机器，每件事都是速食。"[①]这种说法虽然有些夸张，但"都市快节奏"似乎已经难以停缓下来。

工业化催生了餐饮行业"快餐化"或社会的"麦当劳"化。正如美国学者批评的那样："麦当劳化不仅影响到餐饮业，也影响到教育、工作、医疗、旅游、休闲、饮食、政治、家庭，事实上影响到社会的每一个方面。各种迹象表明，

---

① 韩成栋. 速食时代 [J]. 现代交际, 2002, (8): 53.

麦当劳化已成为一个无情的过程，横扫世界上那些看来无以渗透的各种机构和部分。"①社会的快速、快节奏和高效运转，客观上要求现代工业社会实现人机同步。这样，食物的营养和价值，让位于现代社会工作忙碌、时间紧张的现实需要。需要说明的是，无论是中式快餐，还是洋快餐，快餐本身已构成现代生活的一种文化标志。

2.7.3　本节小结

快餐是现代社会生活节奏加快的直观反映，也是工业化的一个直接后果。无论是本土快餐，还是外来的洋快餐，都是适应社会快速发展的现实需要。快餐本身已构成现代生活的一种文化标志。

知识拓展与链接：

考虑到快速上升的相关疾病（包括中风、糖尿病、癌症和心脏病），世界卫生组织将肥胖界定为一种世界性的疾病。对于生活在机器已经解放了体力劳作和其他人类活动的社会中的个体来说，吃太多是非常不利于健康的，这也就帮助解释了为什么在一些工业社会和后工业社会中，超过一半的人都是超重的。

肥胖的盛行并不单独在于吃得太多，缺乏锻炼。一个主要的因素是高糖量和脂肪的大众市场食品。例如，日本的饮食习惯与美国有很大差异，日本的肥胖人数只占总人口的 3%，而美国的肥胖率在成人中高达 36%，在 2～19 岁的人群中达到 17%。……肥胖问题甚至在一些发展中国家也变得很严峻，尤其是将饮食转变到依赖于加工食品和罐装快餐的地区。

——［美］威廉·A.哈维兰（William A. Haviland）、［美］哈拉尔德·E.L.普林斯（Harald E. L. Prins）、［美］达纳·沃尔拉斯（Dana Walrath）等：《人类学：人类的挑战（第 14 版）》，周云水、陈祥、雷蕾等译，北京：电子工业出版社，2018 年版，第 660-664 页。

2.8　现代食品的文化偏好

如何从文化偏好的角度去看待现代食品？这是一个仁者见仁、智者见智的问题。

---

① 乔治·里茨尔. 社会的麦当劳化：对变化中的当代社会生活特征的研究 [M]. 顾建光，译. 上海：上海译文出版社，1999：1-2.

2.8.1　现代食品的科技偏好

随着科技的发展和进步，出现了越来越多的现代科技农业产品，例如，"瘦肉精"、催长剂等添加剂的滥用，使得现代食品从源头（食材）上就已存在不安全因素。

科技其实是一把双刃剑，科学、合理地使用科技，才会造福人类，改善人们的生活；反之，则会危害社会。因此，应该倡导健康、科学的科技观，发展绿色、环保、可持续发展的生态农业，从源头上保障现代食品安全。

2.8.2　现代食品的工业偏好

科学技术的发展，为我们深度加工、运输和储藏食品提供了技术保障。但是，由于各国食物的地方标准、国家标准和国际标准不尽相同，食品加工的技术标准和卫生标准就会存在一定的差异，食品安全的系数也就不尽相同。

前些年出现的奶粉中三聚氰胺超标，以及"苏丹红"事件等，想必大家都不陌生。为何要使用这些食品添加剂？除技术便利外，还可能与人们的文化偏好有关。不同国家、不同民族存在着不同的文化偏好，他们在进口或出口的工业食品选择上就会表现出不同的行为取向。

2.8.3　现代食品的多元文化偏好

常言道：一方水土养育一方人；靠山吃山，靠海吃海。那么，不靠山、不靠海的人们又食用什么呢？

在过去交通不发达、食物产量低下的时代，人们多数情况下是"靠天吃饭"。因此，在人们的民俗信仰中，会出现祈求风调雨顺、五谷丰登、六畜兴旺、年年有余的习俗活动。

这些民俗信仰根植于农耕社会，又随着工业文明的到来而融入工业社会，并以异化的方式存在于工业社会当中。例如，在已经高度城镇化的珠江三角洲地区，原来的农民朋友早已"洗脚上楼"，不再耕田，而是"耕楼"。什么意思呢？就是出租自家物业，通过收房租的方式，换取土地延伸出来的收益。他们从原来的农民变成现在收租的业主，成了"包租公（婆）"。他们的生产方式改变了，生活方式也慢慢地发生改变。但他们的文化心理显然没有随着他们的生产、生活方式同步改变。最明显的例子，莫过于他们在传统的岁时节庆中依然去祭拜他们庭院门前安置的土地神明。这些现象说明，农民心理和农耕习俗，并没有随着现代工业社会的到来而立即衰微，而将残存相当长的时间。

同样地，基于乡土社会发展起来的饮食文化仍然带有浓郁的地域性、民族性和族群差异性。例如，同样是喝茶，广州人发展出"吃早茶"的茶文化，它与成都人喝茶就是喝茶的休闲活动是不一样的。

　　广州人的"早茶"还有许多点心小吃，茶不是主角，而是配角。广州人"吃早茶"不仅是为了会友聊天，有时更是为了"谈正事"，把办事和餐饮接待有机结合起来，既节约了时间，又不失礼节，充分体现了广州人高效、务实、勤俭、节约的文化性格。因此，广州人"吃早茶"，吃的是点心等美食，喝的是茶水，谈的是生意合作等正事，散发出来的却是浓浓的、务实的广州文化。

　　除了在宾馆酒楼"吃早茶"的茶文化，广州还有老字号的手工制作的凉茶，如黄振龙、金葫芦等；也有经工业化加工的老字号凉茶，如王老吉、加多宝、和其正、徐其修等。

　　近年来，各种奶茶也流行起来，如都可、益禾堂、一点点、特思乐、贡茶等，深受青少年群体的喜爱，甚至成为他们日常生活的一部分。走在大街小巷，你会发现，传统手工凉茶、工业加工的凉茶和新式奶茶，各得其所，满足了不同群体的偏好。

　　还有一个例子，可以反映人们对现代食品的文化偏好：东南亚、南亚地区的人们喜欢咖喱风味的食品，但是，泰国的咖喱食品和印度、日本的咖喱食品还是有差异的。究竟存在哪些差异呢？总的来说，泰国咖喱清香多变、印度咖喱浓香重辣、日本咖喱口味偏甜。

2.8.4　本节小结

　　综上所述，我们在现代社会中看到了不同国家、不同地区、不同民族的食品存在着一些文化偏好。科技化、工业化、多元化贯穿着现代食品从食材生产到食品食用的全过程。

知识拓展与链接：

　　食品安全追溯体系是食品安全风险管理的关键措施和重要手段，是助力全链条食品安全的有效工具。全链条食品安全追溯体系不仅是帮助消费者把握食品"前世今生"的现代信息化技术，更是各级政府和食品安全监管部门实现精准监管，防控各种食品安全风险，应对食品安全事故和突发事件的一个重要武器。

　　——张守文：《把握食品的前世今生——论建立全链条食品安全追溯系统提高监管效能（下）》，《中国市场监管报》2020年8月13日，第005版。

2.9　公共卫生的文化理解

2.9.1　卫生、公共卫生与健康

（1）卫生

卫生是一个源于现代医学特别是西方医学的概念。虽然中国古代也有"卫生"一词，但其含义不尽相同。中国古代的"卫生"，一般是"守护生命，卫其健康"，即"养生"的意思。

"卫生"这个词最早出现于《灵枢》中，《庄子·庚桑楚》也有"卫生"一词："南荣曰：殊愿闻卫生之经而已矣。"晋代李颐在《庄子集释》中将"卫生"解释为："防卫其生，令合其道也。"宋代《南华真经新传·庚桑楚篇》说："卫生者，卫全其生也。能卫全其生，则生所以长存。"这样的"卫生"观念泛指个人养生之道，及社会大众追求健康的行为。有人认为，中国传统文化语境中的"卫生"大致包含养生、医药医疗、卫生保命、保卫生灵等含义。

现代医学意义上的"卫生"一般是指为增进人体健康，预防疾病，改善和创造合乎生理、心理需求的生产环境、生活条件所采取的个人的和社会的卫生措施，包括除害灭病、讲卫生。如今，"卫生"一词一般是指讲究清洁、预防疾病和有益于健康，讲究卫生对于人们生理健康和心理健康具有重要意义。

（2）公共卫生

如果说"卫生"还具有传统文化的观念影响，那么，"公共卫生"则完全是现代医学的范畴了。在现代医学中，"公共卫生"主要针对社区或者社会的医疗措施，如疫苗接种、健康、宣教、卫生监督、疾病预防和疾病控制，以及各种流行病学手段等，它有别于在医院进行的、只针对个人的医疗措施。因此，"卫生"和"公共卫生"的含义不同。但是，它们都与人类健康关系密切。

（3）健康

健康是相对于疾病而言的，人们对健康的不同认识，形成了不同的健康文化。1946 年 7 月 22 日签订于纽约、1948 年 4 月 7 日正式生效的《世界卫生组织组织法》明确指出："健康是身体、精神与社会的全部的美满状态，不仅是免病或残弱。"因此，健康实际上是人的生理、心理和社会适应三种状态的有机统一。

如此看来，现代健康应该是现代工业时代的人们的身体和心理的健康与现代工业社会适应的完美状态。如果状态不完美，则不能称之为健康。

2.9.2　现代公共卫生的文化偏好

我们在前面谈到，现代生活与现代工业社会相适应，并以机器大生产为标志。那么，工业社会时代的公共卫生是不是存在文化偏好？又会存在哪些文化偏好呢？

首先，我们可以从生理卫生和健康的角度去分析。在现代工业社会中，个人的生理卫生习惯可能会影响公共卫生防治问题。例如，2003年8月，尼日利亚有人毫无根据地宣称，接种口服脊髓灰质炎疫苗（oral poliomyelitis vaccine，OPV）不安全，而且会导致儿童成年后不育。这导致了尼日利亚北部两个州停止接种OPV，其他州接种OPV的比例也大大下降。脊髓灰质炎病例在尼日利亚北部大暴发，波及了该国其他多个以前没有脊髓灰质炎病例的地区。这次大暴发最终导致尼日利亚成千上万的儿童瘫痪，并且导致该疾病向其他19个无脊髓灰质炎病例的国家传播。

其次，疾病的国际性蔓延，使得全球公共卫生安全前所未有地依赖国际合作。但是，各国的民族习俗和文化传统不同，会影响全球公共卫生的防治行动和效果。例如，许多西方人喜欢吃牛肉，如果一个国家或地区暴发疯牛病，那么，这种食源性疾病就会沿着食物链的快速传播，威胁公共卫生安全。

再次，随着现代社会交通发展，人们旅行机会增加，感染性疾病发生快速传播的机会也随之增加。据估计，当今全球每年有数十亿航空旅客。一个地区的疾病暴发或者流行，对另一个地区造成严重影响，可能只需要几小时的时间。

根据世界卫生组织2020年9月3日的新闻报道，刚果民主共和国埃博拉病毒疫情地理蔓延范围持续扩大。截至2020年9月1日，11个卫生区的36个卫生分区报告发生110例病例（104例确诊，6例疑似），包括47例死亡（病死率为43%）。2003年出现的SARS病毒和2019年底至2020年初出现的新型冠状病毒肺炎疫情（COVID-19）的流行和传播速度也非常快，而且COVID-19对人类社会的健康和生命安全的影响比SARS病毒更大。世界卫生组织进行风险评估后认为："自2020年初以来，世卫组织没有获得足够的埃博拉资金，目前正在动用应急资金来支持流行病学和公共卫生干预。现行COVID-19疫情进一步加大了获得资金和人力资源的难度，给国家卫生系统带来了更多负担。COVID-19对监测和进行常规公共卫生活动造成的干扰风险，可能会危及该国迅速遏制这些埃博拉病例再现的能力。截至2020年8月29日，刚果民主共和国已报告1044例COVID-19病例和258例相关死亡。"[①]

最后，滥用抗生素造成细菌耐药、极端气候变化、突发的化学和放射事件等都会对公共卫生造成不良影响。很多地区在控制感染性疾病上取得的成绩往往受到抗生素耐药问题的严重影响。广泛耐药结核病现已成为一个严重的公共卫生问题。另外，腹泻、医院内获得性感染、疟疾、脑膜炎、呼吸道感染和性传播疾病甚至艾滋病中也产生了不同程度的耐药性。

《国际公共卫生条例（2005）》认为，人类的行为、人类对环境的影响，以及

---

① 佚名. 埃博拉病毒病：刚果民主共和国［EB/OL］.(2020-09-03)［2020-09-30］. https://www.who.int/zh/emergencies/disease-outbreak-news/item/ebola-virus-disease-democratic-republic-of-the-congo.

一些突发的化学和放射事件（包括工业事故、自然现象），都有可能威胁公共卫生安全。2001 年美国炭疽邮件、2003 年 SARS 事件及 2006 年科特迪瓦大规模倾倒有毒化学废物等均是 21 世纪新出现的威胁公共卫生安全的事件。

专家预测，最有可能威胁公共卫生安全的事件是再一次的流感大暴发。另外，战争、冲突也会对公共卫生造成不良影响。例如，1975～2002 年安哥拉内战导致了马尔堡出血热的流行。1994 年卢旺达内战后，刚果民主共和国发生了霍乱大流行。1994 年 7 月，有 50 万～80 万难民越过边境到刚果民主共和国寻求庇护，在他们到达后的 1 个月内，接近 5 万难民死于霍乱和痢疾。唯一的水源被霍乱菌污染、居住条件差、卫生状况差都是疾病如此迅速传播，造成多人感染的原因。1948 年 4 月 7 日，《世界卫生组织组织法》正式生效，标志着世界卫生组织成立。如今社会关注的空气和水的质量、疫苗和药物究竟是安全还是有害等，背后都有世界卫生组织所制定的相关技术指南支撑。但是，全球日趋复杂的公共卫生问题，对世界卫生组织提出了更加严峻的挑战。

2019 年底至 2020 年暴发的世界性的 COVID-19 超出了人们以往的认知。2020 年 9 月 23 日，世界卫生组织、联合国、联合国儿童基金会等发表的联合声明指出："COVID-19 是历史上第一次大规模使用技术和社交媒体来保证人们安全、知情、有生产力和保持联系的大流行疫情……我们呼吁会员国制定和实施管理信息疫情的行动计划，包括促进及时向所有社区，特别是高风险群体，传播基于科学和证据的准确信息；在尊重言论自由的同时，防止和打击错误和虚假信息的传播。"[①]只有这样，才有利于疫情防控。

病毒无国界，人类的生命健康休戚与共。在全球化日益发展的今天，没有一个国家可以在一些重大公共卫生问题上得以幸免。因此，世界各地的人们需要克服文化偏见或偏好，共同做好世界性的公共卫生防治工作，携手创建文明、健康、和乐、有序的康乐社会。

2.9.3　本节小结

卫生、公共卫生内涵不同，但均和健康关系密切。现代公共卫生是现代工业时代的人们的身体和心理的健康与现代工业社会适应的完美状态。健康无国界，世界各国各地区的人们需要克服文化偏见或偏好，共同做好世界性的公共卫生防治工作，才能切实打造文明、健康、和乐、有序的康乐社会，共同构建和而不同的人类命运共同体。

---

① 佚名. 管理 COVID-2019 信息疫情: 促进健康行为，减轻错误和虚假信息的危害［EB/OL］. (2020-09-23)［2020-09-30］. https://www.who.int/zh/news-room/detail/23-09-2020-managing-the-covid-19-infodemic-promoting-healthy-behaviours- and-mitigating-the-harm-from-misinformation-and-disinformation.

2.10 饮食偏好及成因

2.10.1 什么是饮食偏好？

关于饮食偏好的问题，不同的人可能会有不同的看法。这是不难理解的，因为不同的人生活在不同的环境当中。不同的自然环境、社会环境和文化环境，会塑造出不同的社会群体或个人，甚至同一环境下也会塑造出不同的个体。这可能主要是个体后天习得的文化或习惯差异所致，表现在饮食上，就是人们常说的"萝卜青菜，各有所爱"。例如，广西百色市 12 个县（市、区）中，聚居着壮族、汉族、瑶族、苗族、回族、彝族和仡佬族 7 个民族，其中壮族约占总人口的 80%，其余各民族约占总人口的 20%，形成了以壮族文化为主体，其他多个民族文化相互依存的地域文化特点，少数民族文化绚丽多姿。在漫长的历史进程中，桂西地区形成了极具地方特色的饮食文化，那里的人们对野生食用植物情有独钟。[①]

因此，我们可以这样来理解饮食偏好，饮食偏好是指人们在长期的饮食过程中形成的对某种或某些食物的加工、制作、食用或饮用的带有倾向性的爱好，它是自然环境和社会、文化环境共同影响的结果。

2.10.2 人为什么会有饮食偏好？

人们常说：千里不同风，百里不同俗。一个地区、一个国家、一个民族或族群饮食习惯的形成，应该是多种因素影响的结果。那么，到底有哪些因素影响着人们的饮食偏好呢？概括起来，不外乎自然环境和社会文化等因素。下面，我们进行简单的讨论和分析。

首先，我们来看看自然环境是如何影响人类的饮食偏好的。

我们知道，在人类社会的早期，人们过着采集、渔猎的原始生活。进入文明社会以后，随着人类对植物的人工栽培和对动物的驯化及人工饲养，人类的食物逐渐丰富起来。

在过去科技不发达、基本上"靠天吃饭"的情况下，不同地理环境、不同季节和气候条件下的物产是不太相同的。久而久之，人们就逐渐形成了具有地域特色的饮食偏好。

一般来说，在以往科技不发达、交通运输和储藏不便的地区，人们的饮食及其结构更容易受当地自然环境和粮食、作物以及家畜等的影响。也就是说，在相当长的历史时期内，人们的饮食习惯和偏好是受当地的自然环境所影响的。

---

① 苏仕林. 桂西壮族文化与植物多样性保护的关系 [J]. 植物资源与环境学报, 2014, 23(2): 107-113.

　　自然环境影响人类饮食偏好的另外一个例子，就是生活在低温和寒冷地区的人们，比生活在气温较高或热带、亚热带地区的人们更喜欢面食、肉类和白酒，菜肴的味道也更浓重一些，而南方沿海地区的饮食会显得相对清淡。但是，在南方一些闷热、湿润地区，人们也食用一些祛湿的食物，如花椒、红椒、尖椒、胡椒等调料，或者在汤里添加薏米等具有祛湿功效的食物。

　　其次，人们的饮食习惯和偏好还受当地的日常生活方式和社会环境的影响。

　　我们知道，人们在征服自然和改造自然的过程中，会形成不同的生产方式和生活方式。一般来说，产量高、容易种植或养殖的东西，更容易成为人们餐桌上的食物，而那些产量低或不易养殖的东西可能在重要的年节习俗活动中才会食用。例如，在南方的主要粮食（大米）中，传统的糯米产量一般都会低于杂交水稻的产量。因此，在日常生活饮食中，人们一般会食用杂交水稻的大米，而在传统的节庆或祭祀活动中才会使用糯米。这是环境影响作物收成，进而影响人类饮食偏好的结果。

　　在不同的社会文化环境中，人们对食物的认识是不太一样的。根据人类学家的观点，人们会对自己生活于其中的世界进行分类、命名并赋予其意义。

　　英国人类学家道格拉斯在她的名著《洁净与危险——对污染和禁忌观念的分析》中，从《圣经》和日常生活中人们对于"洁净"与"污秽"的理解入手，利用象征分析手法剖析人类的思维特点，并关注象征秩序与社会秩序的对应。她认为，在各社会文化系统中，洁净与污秽是更大的分类系统中的一部分。污秽是社会规范和秩序的违背，它意味着危险，意味着跨越不该跨越的界限所造成的恐惧。而污秽（危险）的清除，即禁忌的产生、仪式的举行、犯罪的惩处是重新确立原有秩序、维系社会规范的手段。因此，吃"洁净"的食物，不吃"污秽"的食物，就成了社会秩序的象征和表达。

　　但是，究竟哪些食物"洁净"，哪些食物"污秽"，不同国家、不同民族的认知是不太一样的。对于许多民族或族群来说，动物的内脏是不"洁净"的，因而是不能食用的。但是，有的人群却认为动物的内脏特别好吃，动物的血液也不错，不能浪费。有的人群甚至生吃某些动物的热血。还有的人喜欢吃鱼生，有的人则认为鱼生是不卫生的，他们认为芥末除了可以刺激鼻腔之外，并不能真正地杀死鱼生的细菌，常吃鱼生可能会感染华支睾吸虫等多种鱼源性寄生虫，导致肝细胞坏死，诱发肝硬化和肝癌。

　　俗话说：食在广州。这既说明广州的饮食文化发达，又隐喻了广州人的饮食无所禁忌，什么东西都可以做成美味，但同时也增加了很多饮食潜在的致病风险。

　　最后，人们的饮食偏好还受当地饮食传统习俗的影响。

　　食物不同，烹饪方式方法和色味香型也不同，甚至食用的时间、空间都有偏好。比如，有的人喜欢蒸，有的人喜欢炒，有的人喜欢焖，还有的人喜欢炸、卤、炖等，烹饪方法五花八门，层出不穷。再如中国人的口味，北方地区偏咸，江浙沪地区偏甜，珠三角地区清淡爱喝汤，中部地区（湖南、重庆、四川等）爱吃辣，还有一些地区爱酸麻。

据研究，人们的饮食偏好可能与疾病的发生存在相关性。油炸和烧烤类食物大多集中在北京周边和东北等高纬度地区，海南南部地区的人也偏爱烧烤，广东地区的人群对油炸和烧烤类食物同样"情有独钟"；"甜党"主要集中在沿海地区，北方地区对甜食的喜爱也很突出；"麻辣水煮党"以四川为首，分布差异不大。对油炸和烧烤的偏爱将导致高体质指数、高血压以及糖尿病的高发生率，这两类食物还和空腹血糖以及餐后血糖异常升高有关。甜食摄入量高与糖尿病发病率升高、空腹血糖异常升高有关。由于辣椒素可以降低空腹血糖水平，同时保持胰岛素水平，爱吃辣的程度与糖尿病发病率、空腹血糖和餐后血糖水平呈现反比关系。但是，肠胃功能较弱的人群，食管黏膜易受刺激，如果过量偏麻辣饮食会影响肠道菌群，增加肠胃负担，诱发上火、腹泻或便秘。另外，煎、炸的烹饪方式并不健康，煮、炖方式更健康。[①]如此看来，饮食偏好也可能还与人们的身体机能有一定的关系。

2.10.3　本节小结

饮食偏好是自然环境和社会、文化环境共同影响的结果，它是人们在长期的饮食过程中形成的对某种或某些食物的加工、制作、食用或饮用带有倾向性的爱好。自然环境、社会文化和烹饪方式等因素，都不同程度地影响着人们的饮食偏好。

知识拓展与链接：

"辣"是一种与众不同的味觉感受，研究发现，辛辣食物所导致的血压升高、心率加快等现象会使人上瘾。爱吃辣的人通常带着一股痛快劲儿，做事迅速果断，为人热情，脾气火爆，想到什么就说什么，坚持自己的想法。

爱吃又甜又咸、甜中带苦等"另类"口味的人，一般性格内向，喜欢独来独往，思维缜密，深藏不露，看上去有些冷漠孤傲，不好接触。

素食主义者多数性格内敛，喜静不喜动。喧嚣的人际圈子会让他们感觉不自在。

爱吃涮锅、烧烤等肉类食物的人则通常比较活跃，与不同的人都能交谈甚欢，在人际圈中总能让自己引人瞩目。

——李苏：《饮食偏好与性格特点》，《文摘报》2014年01月11日，第03版。

[①] 谢开飞，曹佳奕，陈旻. 饮食偏好与疾病的发生密切相关 [J]. 中国食品，2020, (15): 138-139.

2.11　人类的饮食偏好及其解读

2.11.1　人类有哪些饮食偏好？

有人说，广州是美食的天堂。但是，人们对美食的理解是有差异的。有人认为是美食，另外一些人可能并不这么认为。

由于认知和口味不同，城市里的酒店、餐馆就会提供各种不同风味的菜肴，并根据当地人的习惯微调。例如，广州地区不同餐馆、酒楼将川菜、湘菜的辣度进行了微辣、中辣和重辣的细分，如果顾客点餐时没有说明辣的喜好程度，服务员一般会询问和标注，以便厨师操作。

不仅中国人有饮食偏好，外国人同样也有饮食偏好。表 2-1 反映了部分国家的饮食偏好情况。此外，世界各地、各国、各民族的饮食习惯和偏好还有很多。

表 2-1　部分国家的饮食偏好

国家	饮食偏好
韩国	不喜欢羊肉、香菜、苦味蔬菜或麻辣食物；除面包和蛋糕外，少有发面蒸煮的食物；不爱放醋、糖或花椒，但喜欢大蒜等食物
日本	不喜欢辣，不爱吃动物内脏；口味以清淡、咸鲜为主
泰国	不喝热茶，忌讳牛肉和海参；不喜欢酱油，不吃红烧菜肴；偏爱腥鲜酸辣和刺激性强的味道；禁止食用狗肉和野生动物
新加坡、马来西亚	穆斯林不食猪肉、贝壳类食物；不饮酒；视左手为不洁，忌用左手传递食品
印度尼西亚	居民多为穆斯林，不食猪肉；不饮酒；一般不食带骨或刺的食物；忌用左手传递食品
澳大利亚	一般不爱辣味，喜欢酸甜；不吃海参
意大利	喜欢比萨；各种面类食物（如葱卷、馄饨、通心粉、炒饭等）当菜用，不作主食；喜欢用叉子把通心粉卷成团放入口中，而不用餐刀切断，也不用匙子把通心粉送入口中
法国	喜欢吃肥辣的猪、牛、羊肉和各种香肠、虾、鱼、蛋、禽、牡蛎、蜗牛以及颜色鲜艳的蔬菜；烹调中喜欢用大蒜、香草、番茄、丁香等做配料，爱喝清汤
德国	喜欢猪肉和猪肉制品；吃面包时喜欢用猪油；吃猪肉时配软烂的白菜；喜欢非全熟或生牛肉；喜欢炸、烤、炒、煮马铃薯；不喜欢吃鱼或深红色的食物
俄罗斯	口味偏甜、咸、酸、辣；比较重油；既爱喝烈酒、热汤，也喜欢冷食
英国	注重饮食质量，口味清淡、鲜嫩；讲究喝茶，早上喜欢"被窝茶"和点心；午餐和晚餐通常为两菜一汤，以牛、羊、鸡、鸭等肉品搭配点心、水果和果汁咖啡等，以及午后茶点
美国	用油少，菜清淡，量少而精；不喜欢辣、味精、狗肉；喜欢鲜嫩、焦香、酸辣；讲究喝茶、茶点和饼干；用餐时忌打翻盐瓶和发生碰响声
加拿大	爱吃牛肉、鸡鸭、蜗牛、海鲜等食物；口味偏甜，菜肴鲜嫩，必备葡萄酒；用餐时不饮啤酒和其他饮料；不喜欢刺多的淡水鱼

资料来源：佚名，《五彩缤纷的饮食习惯：世界各国餐桌巡礼》，《广西粮食经济》2002 年 3 期，第 46-47 页。

2.11.2　如何看待人类的饮食偏好？

由于人们的饮食偏好受到各国、各地区不同自然环境、社会环境和文化习俗等多重因素的影响，我们应该抱持文化多元和文化宽容的态度去看待不同的饮食文化，这样才能理解"他者"，自我反思，才能保护人类饮食文化的多样性，也才能达致我国已故的著名社会学家、人类学家费孝通先生所说的"各美其美，美人之美，美美与共，天下大同"①的世界人文景象。1990 年，费孝通先生在展望人类学的前景时，曾提出人类学要为文化的"各美其美，美人之美，美美与共，天下大同"做出贡献。2000 年前后，他在反思全球化的影响后提出了"和而不同"的观点，并把"和而不同"视为实现"各美其美，美人之美，美美与共，天下大同"的重要手段或路径。从"美美与共，天下大同"到"美美与共，和而不同"的提出，反映了费孝通先生晚年对自己一生的文化探索、思考和总结。这种尊重文化多样性、包容文化差异性的文化理念，可为我们分析人类的饮食偏好提供有益的借鉴和参考。

2.11.3　本节小结

从本节的讨论中，我们再次看到了食作为人类文化的主要载体之一而散发出来的无穷魅力，也进一步说明了"我们吃的是文化""我们的吃穿都在自己编织的文化世界里"。

2.12　现代饮食偏好与身体健康

2.12.1　现代饮食偏好的主要特征

在现代工业社会中，尽管不同地区、不同国家、不同民族的饮食习惯和偏好可能会有所不同，但他们应该都具有现代工业社会的一些基本特征。概括起来，这些特征主要包括以下几点。

（1）追求养生，但可能会矫枉过正

从现代医学的角度看，不合理的饮食结构是导致心血管疾病和肥胖症的重要诱因。为了保持苗条的身材和降低心血管疾病的患病风险，有的人群，特别是一些女性，除了做有氧运动外，还节食或者素食。但是，对于素食的偏好，可能也会带来一些健康问题。

从理论上讲，素食中包含除维生素 B_{12} 以外的人体所需要的全部营养，但其

---

① 费孝通. 创建一个和而不同的全球社会：在国际人类学与民族学联合会中期会议上的主旨发言 [J]. 思想战线, 2001, 27(6): 1-5, 16.

前提是，素食的种类和摄入量都能达到要求。如果只吃胡萝卜、白菜等素食，可能会缺乏多种微量元素和优质蛋白质，引起贫血等全身性系统疾病。反之，如果只吃动物性肉类食品而不吃或者少吃蔬菜、瓜果，则可能加重心脏负担，造成饱和脂肪过多，导致高血压、冠心病等疾病。因此，对于高危人群或追求健康的人而言，营养学家和医生的建议通常是：①素食和荤食搭配，多吃高不饱和脂肪酸食物（鳕鱼、坚果等）和可溶性膳食纤维食物（苹果、葡萄、柑橘、燕麦、糙米、豆类、蔬菜等），甚至生洋葱等。②选择全麦、高纤维、低糖、低脂、低盐的食物，每天至少摄入 5 种不同的果蔬。③每天喝够 6～8 杯水（含无糖咖啡、茶，以及低脂牛奶）；每天摄入果汁不超过 150mL。④每天吃两次鱼肉，少吃红肉和加工过的肉质食品。

（2）经常食用工业加工过的"垃圾食品"

如今，膨化食品、碳酸饮料、奶茶等，深受青少年群体喜爱。超市里琳琅满目的膨化食品，如饼干、蛋黄派、薯条、薯片，以及巧克力和氢化奶油蛋糕等，长期食用，对人的身体健康，可能是不利的。另外，方便面、火腿肠、培根、午餐肉等即食或只需简易加工的熟食成品，也不宜经常食用，以免影响健康。

（3）现代饮食偏好带有一定程度的代际影响

众所周知，人们的饮食习惯不是一两天形成的，而是长期的、从小就开始慢慢形成的。一般来说，父母的饮食偏好会影响孩子的饮食偏好，甚至祖辈的口味也会影响后代的口味。这可能主要与隔代抚养孩子有关。

中国青少年研究中心的一项调查发现，偏爱甜食、喜欢油炸食品和经常喝饮料，已经成为第二代独生子女三大不健康的饮食偏好。这与他们父母（第一代独生子女）的饮食偏好有关。

2.12.2　现代饮食偏好影响身体健康

我们知道，人体需要多种营养成分的供给。若饮食偏好无法供给人体所需要的营养，则容易出现健康问题。例如，中国第二代独生子女喜欢甜食、油炸食品和饮料。这三大食品是工业社会洋快餐的标准配置，它们基本上是工业化、标准化的加工产品，营养供给有限。长期如此，容易导致营养不良。医学研究发现，喜欢吃糖或甜食的人，近视患病率可能会增加。因此，青少年应该少吃糖或甜食。

另外，一个人的饮食偏好，可能在 7 岁以前就形成了。如果从小养成好的饮食习惯，那么，成年以后的慢性病可能就会减少很多。

目前，肥胖已经成为全球性的一种不健康的现象。根据世界卫生组织的估计，全球有超过 10%成年人患有肥胖症,每年有 280 万人死于与肥胖相关的疾病。1975年以来，世界肥胖人数已增长近三倍。2016 年，18 岁及以上的成年人中逾 19 亿人超重,其中超过 6.5 亿人肥胖;超过 3.4 亿名 5～19 岁儿童和青少年超重或肥胖,其流行率从 1975 年的 4%大幅上升到 2016 年的 18%以上。[①]世界多数人口所居住的国家，死于超重和肥胖的人数大于死于体重不足的人数。而超重或肥胖的根源在于高热量的垃圾饮食偏好。当然，超重或肥胖是可以预防和控制的，根本的办法就是不吃或少吃高热量的食品，限制来自总脂肪和糖的能量摄入，增加水果、蔬菜、豆类、全谷类及坚果的食用量，并通过定期运动（儿童每天 60 分钟，成人每周 150 分钟）等方式，加强人体的新陈代谢。

近年来，越来越多的人喜欢生食或半生食的蔬菜沙拉、生鱼片等。其实，生吃蔬菜，营养未必全面；生吃肉类和海鲜，不仅营养吸收率低，而且安全风险高，食源性疾病如寄生虫病容易发生；生吃有机食品，也可能会感染食源性大肠杆菌、沙门氏菌等细菌或病毒。

很多人认为食物越新鲜越好，刚挤出来的牛奶就直接饮用。但是，过于新鲜的牛奶中含有抗生素、黄曲霉毒素等，直接饮用可能会导致人体产生抗药性，甚至有致癌风险。很多豆类蔬菜（如刀豆、扁豆、四季豆等）中含有植物凝集素，生食会中毒，引起恶心、呕吐、腹痛、腹泻等症状，严重时甚至危及生命。有机食品同样也会使用有机农药，如果清洗不干净，或者直接生吃，也会带来隐患。有些有机蔬菜用动物排泄物来替代化肥，可能会沾染大肠杆菌、沙门菌等，未经煮熟生食的话可能导致食源性疾病。[②]

2.12.3　本节小结

本节讨论了现代社会饮食偏好的主要特征，以及饮食偏好与健康的关系等问题。在现代工业社会中，不同地区、不同国家、不同民族的饮食习惯和偏好可能会有所不同。若饮食偏好无法全面供给人体所需要的营养，则容易出现健康问题。

知识拓展与链接：

与工业品的制造过程不同，食物的生产过程并非机械化的制造过程，其有着自身的生长规律和培育过程。即便科技能够人为合成出许多农业品中所包含的人体必需元素，这也并不意味着人类可以重新组合出一个符合自然生长条件的生命体。那些用乙烯催熟的西红柿，虽然看起来还是同样一种食品，然而这种概念却只停留在了表面上。从这个角度来说，农业生产的内在规律与工业生产大相径庭，机械化的生产方式也并不能按照人们的思维惯性那般套用在食品的生产过程中。

农业生产与工业生产最根本的不同，就在于农业生产的对象和最终产品都

---

① 佚名. 肥胖和超重［EB/OL］.（2020-04-01）［2020-05-10］. https://www.who.int/zh/news-room/fact-sheets/detail/obesity-and-overweight.
② 罗斌，吴萍. 生食是健康还是危害？［J］. 保健与生活，2019,(2): 58.

是生命物，而工业生产的对象与最终产品都是非生命物。而近代以来运用到农业领域的科学技术，是起源于工业领域的科学技术或科技范式向农业领域进行的推广。将解决非生命物的科技简单地移植到生命物领域当中，必然造成工业化技术在农业领域的失灵，食品安全问题也就不可避免了。

农业活动和工业生产内在的本质不同，也就决定了两种生产方式之间的差异。建立在分工化、专业化、标准化、市场化基础上的工业化生产方式，之所以能成为引发工业革命、导致生产率持续增长的生产方式，就是因为这种生产方式最大限度地发挥了工具创新与科学技术的进步作用。然而，同样的生产方式在农业生产领域不仅在提高生产率上的作用是有限的，还会留下众多"后遗症"。

——李少卿：《"工业食品"后遗症》，《21世纪商业评论》2011年第7期，第97-101页。

3 住和行：人类社会的文化实践

3.1 居住选址的文化反思

3.1.1 居住选址的文化内涵

在现代工业社会中，人们对于居住地址和环境的选择有着不同于传统的习惯和偏好。

我们知道，在相当长的时期内，人们对居住地的选择是受制于自然环境的。例如，在中国传统农耕社会中，人们一般会选择便于农业生产劳动且有水源，而且通风采光比较好的地方建造房屋。中国古人在长期的生产生活实践中形成了具有丰富内涵的居住文化，反映到居住选址上，就是中国民间流行的"风水堪舆学说"。这种"学说"的核心是强调"藏风得水"。

中国民间流行的"风水"观念和实践，其实最初是一种朴素的相地技术，即环境选择技术。后来，由于融入了周易八卦、阴阳五行等而变得神秘起来，成为至今在中国民间社会仍然有影响和市场的"风水堪舆"文化。

实际上，这些所谓的"风水"，是中国独特的地理环境、气候条件影响人们选择居住环境的结果。中国北面、西面、西南面三面为山，东面是大海，这种"山环水抱"的地理环境和全国多为春秋昼夜温差大、干旱少雨，夏季高温闷热，冬季寒冷的大陆性季风气候条件，使得古代中国人逐渐形成了居住选址的文化：背风向阳，靠近水源，却又避开低洼易潮之地，利用山地的高低起伏遮挡冬季的寒冷北风。因此，在后有靠山，前方远处有案山，左右两侧也有低于后山的山岭相护的平坦开阔的地带，比较容易看到中国传统的村落。如果这个村落还有一条河流从左到右环绕流过，就更容易成为中国民间的"风水宝地"。中国传统农耕社会中的居住选址其实在一定程度上是人与自然和谐的反映。良好的生态承载力、适宜的居住密度、充足的阳光、清新的空气、洁净的水和舒适的运动空间，共同构成了理想的居住选址要素。[①]

3.1.2 现代居住选址的多样性

在现代工业社会中，人们对自然环境的依赖程度有所降低，特别是在"寸土

---

① 张磊. 居住环境与健康［J］. 养生大世界, 2020, (6): 57-59.

寸金"的城市中，人们的居住选址更多考虑的是现实的经济因素和工作生活的便利程度。城市房价的高低、地段、公共配套服务设施和公共交通的便利性等，成为市民购房选址考虑的重要因素。"地铁通到哪，房价就涨到哪"似乎已经成为中国特大城市居住选址的一种标识。

城市建筑受制于城市土地的综合开发和高效利用，城市的房屋选址不可能像农村地区那样讲究"风水"，而是根据城市规划和城市建设用地性质，因地制宜地开发房地产资源。另外，由于现代工业社会能够较好地解决交通、水源、通风、采光、温度、湿度等问题，人们对自然环境和自然条件的依赖程度降低，使得人们对居住选址有了多样化的选择。这种多样化的现代居住选址主要表现在哪些方面呢？

首先，"可居"与"宜居"并存。对于大城市和特大城市的居民而言，拥有自己的房子"可居"，而不是租住别人的"宜居"住房，成为多数年轻人的期望、梦想和刚需。因此，在一些地理位置较偏，房屋坐向、楼层、房内空间布局等不太理想的楼盘，也会有人购买置业，成为按揭贷款的"房奴"。对于有改善型住房需求的人来说，他们对居住选址要求较高，他们对居住的自然环境、社会环境、文化环境等进行综合考量，追求的是高品质和高品位的生活。与其说他们是选择居住地址，不如说他们选择生活本身。高档住宅小区、独栋联排或复式别墅，成为城市中产阶层或富裕阶层人士的一种选择。

从某种意义上说，现代工业社会中的居住选址，实际上是社会分层的一种反映。"可居"和"宜居"反映着不同的生活态度和追求。

其次，城市和乡村共存。在欧美发达国家，生活富裕的人们宁愿居住在乡村别墅里，开车上下班，亲近大自然，而不愿意居住在喧嚣拥挤的城市里，成为"逆城市化"和返璞归真的重要表征。

中国的现代居住选址与欧美国家不同，由于中国城市特别是大城市、特大和超大城市的公共服务和配套设施更加集中和完善，"虹吸效应"更加明显。因此，越来越多的年轻人向往大城市。"宁要城里一张床，不要郊区一栋房"成为改革开放以来中国青年"用脚投票"、流入城市的生动写照。北京、上海、广州、深圳这些人口超千万的超大城市，至今依然城乡并存，满足不同社会阶层和社会群体的居住需要。

不仅中国的一线城市如此，亚洲其他国家的首都和特大城市也基本如此。例如，在东京、首尔、吉隆坡、曼谷等城市，不少人宁愿"蜗居"，也不愿意选择在乡下居住。这与欧美国家的情况不同。城市和乡村的社会、经济、文化结构固然存在差异，但无所谓好坏，只是人们的追求和体验不同而已。但是，在现代工业社会中，当人们的住和行、购和娱等密切关联起来的时候，城市和乡村的居住选址就不可避免地存在差异性和多样性了。

最后，传统与现代共融。在现代工业社会中，传统并没有完全被现代所取代，而是找到了存续的载体和契机。

3.1.3　小结：居住环境与文化选择

本节讨论了现代居住选址的文化内涵和它的多样性问题。通过前面的讨论，我们发现，不同时代、不同社会、不同空间的居住选址虽然存在着多样性和不同的文化表达，但它们都无一例外地指向了人对自然环境的选择。只不过，人们在现代居住环境选择中更加突出社会环境和文化环境的因素。可以这么说，人们对居住地的选择是自然环境和社会、文化环境选择等要素叠加的结果。西方"逆城市化"的乡村居住选址和东方或亚洲的城市集聚所表现出来的不同的住地选择，应该是不同文化选择的结果。

但是，无论哪一种选择，都再次说明了"我们居住在文化空间里"这一事实。希望通过这些问题的讨论和分析，能够帮助大家进一步认识人类社会的文化实践问题。

知识拓展与链接：

　　许多人类学家认为新居住模式与金融或商业经济的出现相关。他们认为，这种模式可能出现在当人们能够将自己的劳动与产品出售换为金钱时，他们能够自己购买住处，而不需要依靠亲属。实际上，新居住模式倾向发生在有金融和商业交换的社会中，没有金融的社会当中夫妇则更多地与亲属共同或邻近居住。因此金融的出现，占据了新居的部分比例，金钱使得夫妇能够独处生活。然而，这一事实并不能很好地解释他们缘何如此选择。商业社会中的夫妇能够独立的原因之一，也许在于相关的工作需要身体活动或社会流动。或许夫妇更愿意远离亲属居住，是因为他们希望避免部分人际之间的紧张关系，以及与近亲住在一起产生的需求。但为何夫妇在拥有金钱之后，更愿意独立居住，其中的具体原因仍不得而知。

　　——［美］卡罗尔·恩贝尔（Carol R.Ember）、［美］梅尔文·恩贝尔（Melvin Ember）：《人类文化与现代生活：文化人类学精要（第 3 版）》，周云水、杨菁华、陈靖云译，北京：电子工业出版社，2016 年版，第 285 页。

3.2　居住文化的现代解读

3.2.1　现代人的居住理念及其变迁

在上节内容中，我们讨论了居住选址问题。我们知道，居住选址要解决的是"住哪里"的问题。接下来，我们要讨论的是"怎么住"的问题。

对于中国人来说，住房是人生的一件大事。在中国传统的家庭观念中，四世同堂曾一度被视为中国传统居住模式的典范，不仅象征家庭和睦，而且隐喻着家族兴旺。父严母慈、兄友弟恭、妯娌和顺、子孙满堂等，往往成为人们羡慕的家庭相处模式。

中国传统的家族文化给中国人的居住方式注入了太多的功利色彩。大家族式的居住方式比较适合于流动性不太强的传统农耕社会，但不适合流动性强的商业社会和工业社会。特别是在城市社会中，人们的居住理念已经发生明显的变化，也可以说是社会变迁在居住领域的一个反映。

那么，现代人的居住方式和理念究竟发生了哪些变化呢？

首先，"游牧一族"频繁换"巢"。现在的年轻人经常"跳槽"和变换工作地点而成为"游牧一族"，出于工作便利的需要，他们频繁换"巢"，更换住处。这与大多数年轻人是租房居住而不是买房子住的居住状况相适应。他们认为，房子是一种日用品，就像毛巾、牙膏和肥皂，把它们并列在一起，你就会找到自由。他们宣称：40 岁以前不必买房，可以去租房。因为租到的不仅是房子，还是一种崭新的生活方式。

其次，重新组合，"袋鼠"回"巢"。如今，许多已经独立的独生子女纷纷回到父母的身边，过起新"袋鼠"生活。他们把新房子买在父母身边，隔条街，隔栋楼，或者干脆同楼不同层，不是直接入住而是住在父母家旁边，既可以互相照应，又不妨碍各自生活。

再次，家外有家，努力筑"巢"。如今，不少人都有两套以上的房子。他们认为，"1+1"是新世纪的一种理想生活模式，即城里有一套住房，便于工作；郊外也有一套住宅，供周末和节假日度假使用。不少年轻人既喜欢城市喧嚣，也喜欢郊外的宁静和清新的空气。

最后，一些年轻人还崇尚酒店式公寓的新型居住观念。虽然有着"酒店式的服务，公寓式的管理"，酒店式公寓本质上还是酒店，但它自由方便，而且价格相对较低，有居家的格局和良好的居住功能；配有全套家具与家电，能够为客人提供酒店的专业服务。这种将传统的酒店服务与现代公寓的硬件设施相结合，以居家自助服务为主，酒店式服务为辅，为现代人提供温馨、舒适、自由的居住环境，能够满足各行业人群的不同需求，受到年轻人的喜爱。

3.2.2　现代人的居住模式

在现代社会中，城市往往是文明的标志。20 世纪 90 年代，我国城市居民的居住模式基本上是按照城市"居住区—居住小区—居住组团"的层级结构进行设计的。2003 年以后，人们开始探索"城市—住宅—居民"的新型居住模式，并在交通组织、公共设施、绿化系统和停车系统等方面强调人与城市环境的和谐。①

现代城市人居模式强调要做城市的主人，坚守都市生命线，并在此基础上注重环保与生态、兼享都市与自然的全新生活，不必远离都市，不必走近郊野，不必蜗居在都市的心脏部位，也不必生活在都市的边缘地带。现代都市的丰裕便利与世相繁华，以及大自然的清纯与清新，都是生活中不可或缺的一个组成部分。这是目前城市人居的顶级模式。

房地产界曾经出现过几种潮流的城市人居理论，如城市郊区化、新都市主义、新自然主义等。相对而言，在都市和乡村自然中寻找其最佳结合点是比较适合人居的居住新模式：亲近都市，亲近自然，忙于工作，享受生活。

3.2.3　小结：在都市与自然之间选择

本节我们讨论了现代人的居住理念及其变迁，以及现代人的居住模式等问题。都市和乡村不是互不相容，而是可以有机结合的。现代人主张亲近都市、亲近自然的居家模式，有利于把工作与生活，物质、精神与情感结合起来，更能够体现人类居住的价值、品位与进步。

知识拓展与链接：

云南的傣族建筑，展示了一种理论格式的规律性和雅致，足以与现代科学性的精确的建筑相比，有同样严格的推理，并且表现了更大程度的文化完整性。人们在传统社会的社会生活，是有逻辑性和有理性的组织，与他们的文化价值相适应。在现代社会，我们可能不相信有神灵存在，但是对那些相信有神灵的社会，这些神灵表示了真实的人类社会自身的各种社会关系，这些社会里的其他活动也是以这些关系为基础的。我们因此不应该基于我们的"科学"的观点判断这些传统社会里一个人的价值观。

——高芸：《中国云南的傣族民居》，北京：北京大学出版社，2003年版，第152页。

3.3　交通工具的现代观察

3.3.1　交通工具的发展演变

（1）古代交通工具

在古代社会中，人类的交通工具相对简单，主要是借助人力、畜力、水力等

---

① 何禾, 石文华. 新型居住模式初探 [J]. 城市, 2011, (7): 35-38.

自然力发展起来的。例如，在陆地行走的交通工具有牛车、马车、骆驼等。

人力车主要有人力脚踏三轮车、手拉车、手推车以及中国人所熟悉的轿子等。至于水路的交通工具，常见的有手工撑船、划桨的木船、筏子等，所谓"击水楫舟"，即为写照。

在自给自足的自然经济时代，人们的交通工具较为单一，不仅相对落后，而且耗时费力，难以满足人们日益增长的社会需求。

（2）现代交通工具

随着蒸汽机和电气技术的发明和应用，现代工业社会的交通工具越来越发达，也日益影响着人们的社会生活。充斥大街小巷的，是各式各样的汽车、火车等蒸汽、电气助力车。而在广大乡村小镇，人力车、畜力车或借助自然水力的舟筏等水上交通工具，仍是交通主力。总的看来，现代交通工具动力的变化改变了通行的空间范围和时间长短。现代交通的机械动力代替了古代交通对于人力、畜力及自然力的依赖，机械性使得交通运行速度大幅提高、旅程耗时大为缩减，现代交通的时间意义在增速中愈发明显。这种时间特性的实现从表面看是基于现代交通工具的直接使用，但其内在则是现代时间参与构建的结果。现代时间是抽离生命的量化时间，是远离生活的均质时间，是疏离具体的抽象时间。现代交通和现代时间共同强化了现代性本身。[①]

（3）当代交通工具

与古代或现代的交通工具不同，当代交通工具主要以电子信息、人工智能和新能源等为主要标志，它追求的是快速、便捷、舒适和节能环保，既是生活需要，有时又是社会地位和身份的象征。

如今，飞机、高铁、轻轨、大巴、快艇、轮船等已成为人们旅行的主要交通工具；公交车、地铁、私家车、电动车、自行车等则构成了城市的立体交通体系，人们可以根据自己的意愿和需求灵活选择交通工具。

从古代、现代到当代的交通工具发展演变中，我们容易察知技术进步引发了交通工具的变革，而且也不难感知交通工具对于社会生活的影响。

3.3.2　现代交通工具的类型、特点和价值

（1）公路交通工具的类型、特点和价值

对于大多数内陆国家或地区而言，公路交通仍然是不少人的理想选择。公路的交通工具主要是汽车，可以自驾车，也可以搭乘大巴。在道路选择上，因人而异，既可以选择高速公路，也可以选择一般公路。

一般来说，单程少于 200 千米的行程，自驾出行较为合适；单程 200～400 千米，选择大巴可能较好；500 千米以上的行程，选用其他的交通工具可能比较

---

① 姚晓霞，孙大鹏. 现代交通中的现代时间 [J]. 浙江社会科学，2019, (3): 90-94, 158.

理想。当然，这样的行程划分是相对的，主要考虑的是司机长途开车容易疲劳而可能导致交通事故。

公路交通路网发达，交通工具种类丰富，交通成本可能高于铁路但低于航空，而且出行较为便利，是不少民众外出通行的首选工具。但是，这种交通工具的交通事故也相对多一些。总体上看，在陆地上，公路交通工具仍是主要的交通方式。

首先，汽车是目前世界上数量最多的代步工具。

其次，汽车通行较为灵活，具有其他交通工具难以比拟的优势。

最后，中国的汽车消费趋于大众化，汽车通行方兴未艾，难以在短时间内退出现代交通工具市场。这是值得关注的社会文化现象。

（2）铁路交通工具的类型、特点和价值

铁路交通工具主要有普通铁路、高速铁路、城际轻轨、地铁等，造价成本高，便利程度不如汽车，但交通运输安全性较高，而且出行成本一般低于汽车，较少出现拥堵情况，因而也受民众欢迎。

（3）航空交通工具的类型、特点和价值

航空运输类型单一。由于空域管制和成本高昂等，私人拥有飞机和个人专用航线的情况较少；飞机乘客多为公务人士、商务人士或游客。出行目的地达 500千米以上，人们一般会根据出行任务、时间成本和经济成本选择航空交通工具。航空出行在跨国和跨洲际的行程中有其优势，而且航空事故概率相对小一些，因此也受人们欢迎，有存在的价值和目标市场定位。

不过，近年来国际上出现的飞机失联和飞机被劫持事件偶有发生，也在一定程度上影响了人们对于航空安全问题的思考和出行选择。一些人甚至主张，出于安全考虑，不到万不得已，不要乘坐飞机。这种看法虽然有些片面，但也在一定程度上反映人们的交通工具选择态度。

（4）水路交通工具的类型、特点和价值

在沿江、沿海地区，水系发达，水路运输可能成为当地人主要的交通方式。水运主要包括海运和河运，甚至摆渡也成为人们出行的一种方式。

无论是海运，还是河运，其交通成本都可能是最低的，但它的速度也相对缓慢。对于那些考虑成本而又不赶时间的人们来说，水路运输工具应该依然是一种不错的选择。因此，水路交通仍有它存在的价值。

3.3.3　小结：在工具与价值之间选择

我们在本小节讨论了公路、铁路和航空的现代交通工具，简单分析了它们的类型和特点，也看到了不同交通工具存在的价值。这里涉及文化与人们的行动实践问题。

人们选择什么样的出行方式和交通工具，看似是各种成本博弈后的理性选择，实际上是一个国家、一个地区，或者说是一个民族、一个族群的文化规制的结果。交通工具的工具"理性"与乘坐什么样的交通工具更有"面子"的价值"理性"的博弈，使得人们的出行文化，呈现出不同的结果。

知识拓展与链接：

2020 年 6 月 1 日，中共中央、国务院印发《海南自由贸易港建设总体方案》（简称《方案》），明确提出实施高度自由便利开放的运输政策，实现运输来往自由便利，将海南自由贸易港打造成为引领我国新时代对外开放的鲜明旗帜和重要开放门户。

根据《方案》，到 2035 年，海南将实现贸易自由便利、投资自由便利、跨境资金流动自由便利、人员进出自由便利、运输来往自由便利和数据安全有序流动；到本世纪中叶，全面建成具有较强国际影响力的高水平自由贸易港。

《方案》明确，实施高度自由便利开放的运输政策，推动建设西部陆海新通道国际航运枢纽和航空枢纽，加快构建现代综合交通运输体系。

《方案》提出，建设"中国洋浦港"船籍港，简化检验流程，逐步放开船舶法定检验。在确保有效监管和风险可控的前提下，境内建造的船舶在"中国洋浦港"登记并从事国际运输的，视同出口并给予出口退税。对以洋浦港作为中转港从事内外贸同船运输的境内船舶，允许其加注本航次所需的保税油；对其加注本航次所需的本地生产燃料油，实行出口退税政策；对符合条件并经洋浦港中转离境的集装箱货物，试行启运港退税政策。

——王博宇等：《海南自由贸易港建设明确时间表路线图　运输政策高度自由便利开放》，中国交通新闻网，2020-06-05。

3.4　社会交往的当代反思

3.4.1　现代社会交往的新面相

（1）现代社会交往方式的变化

传统的社会交往，是人与人之间面对面的直接交往，是真实世界的彼此往来。

在现代工业社会中，由于人们从事不同的职业，"流水作业"的时间支配了包括人们社会交往在内的日常生活。随着电话、电报等现代通信工具的发明，人们的社会交往开始由传统的经常面谈慢慢转向电话交谈或电报留言。随着 20 世纪八九十年代手机、寻呼机的出现，语音通话成为社会交往的主要方式。

20 世纪 90 年代中后期，随着计算机技术和互联网的发展，网络社会交往成为新时尚。人们通过电子邮件以及后来的 QQ、微信等即时通信工具，在真实世界和虚拟的网络世界之间建构了各种各样的社会交往关系。加上智能手机的功能不断拓展，"一机在手，应有尽有"的海量信息为人们的社会交往和互动提供了便利。

照理说，现代即时通信工具的发展为人们的社会交往提供了强大的技术支撑，人们的社会交往应该越来越密切。但真实的情况却是，人们越来越喜欢用各种网络符号或表情包去回复朋友或网友，语言文字的规范表达和交流趋于减少。即便是现实社会中的亲朋好友聚会，人们也大多低头翻看自己的手机，通过人机对话与邻座或对面的好友亲朋进行无声的"交流"。此情此景，过去应该是见所未见，也闻所未闻的。这说明什么呢？说明现代社会交往方式发生明显变化。

（2）现代社会交往行为的变化

网络的出现和发展，对人类的日常社会生活产生了巨大的影响。

随着网络的逐步推广和普及，网络社会交往将呈现出向日常社会交往回归的趋势，逐步成为人类社会生活中的一个重要组成部分。不管网络生活有多么丰富多彩，也不论网民之间的交往信任程度有多么高，网络必须面对的一个现实就是同人类的日常生活之间的不可分割。由于网民同日常生活不可分离，网民的行动不可能一直脱离现实生活而在虚拟的网络空间中驰骋，其中多数人必将转到现实社会生活中来。[①]

实际上，决定我们生活状态走向的不是智能手机等高科技工具，而是我们自身的思维模式和处世态度。我们不应该在网络社会交往中渐行渐远，而应该有效地区分真实世界和虚拟世界，不能混同彼此。

在很长的历史时期内，人们往往是在"熟人社会"中活动，交往圈子很小；而当今社会的公共生活领域，则更像一个"陌生人社会"。人们在公共生活中的交往对象并不仅限于熟识的人，而是进入公共场所的任何人。科学技术的迅猛发展和社会分工的日益细化，使人们更多地在陌生的公共环境中与陌生人打交道。

（3）现代社会交往内容的变化

在微信功能不断拓展的今天，不少人打开手机的第一件事情都是浏览相关信息。下载和安装过各类 APP 的用户都知道，APP 会根据用户的浏览内容推送类似的相关信息。因此，浏览朋友圈和自己关注的公众号推送的信息，就构成了微信社会交往的主要内容。其结果就是我们花费在现实社会交往中的时间趋于减少，而花在聊天软件上的时间却越来越多。如今，不少人越来越沉迷于虚拟社交，这可能是源自内心对现实社交的深层恐惧，只有在虚拟网络中消解了自己的性别、外表、身份、地位，才敢在众人前展示和暴露自己的情感。这在一定程度上是对现实社交的恐惧和自我逃避。

---

① 童星, 等. 网络与社会交往 [M] . 贵阳: 贵州人民出版社, 2002.

3.4.2　现代社会交往的文化反思

（1）现代社交软件让人们的交往形式变得简单，但人们却不一定心灵共鸣

腾讯公司从 1998 年做社交软件到现在，它研发的 QQ 和微信，基本上已经垄断了国内社交领域的用户和流量。

2011 年，腾讯微信社交软件诞生，短短五年时间用户数量达到了 8 亿多。但是，现在有些人开始反思：微信曾让交流变得简单，唯独缺少的是真正的人与人之间的交流信息，人们的时间也开始被微信所占用。朋友圈刚出现时，用户为这个功能着迷，可以记录生活点点滴滴，可以让朋友知道自己的现在进行时，可以用无数的赞证明自己的人气和人缘。

如今，微信朋友圈，却成为微商展示场和行踪记录仪，你的一举一动都有可能曝光在整个社交场。微信用户主要通过生活叙事和微信消费来显露自己的阶层身份，通过设置边界对阶层进行积极区分，通过点赞、评论和转发，以及私聊与群聊形式的交往互动寻找、确认他们的归属感。与现实生活阶层认同不同的是，微信便于用户建立多元化的阶层认同，用户可同时穿梭于不同的阶层群体之间，在各个群体内寻找、确认自己的归属感。[1]微信中的朋友圈与现实社会中的朋友圈有共性，但差异更为明显。"熟悉"的"陌生人"和"陌生"的"熟人"是微信朋友圈人际关系的两种主要状态。基于互联网等现代通信媒介，"朋友"在微信场域中具有多重身份认同和身份建构。通过多样化的象征符号及其表达，微信朋友圈的即时互动和超地域性使其具备了现实朋友圈难以企及的社会资本动员能力和文化张力。微信红包、微信点赞、微言众听、微群讨论甚至微商广告等，构成了"互联网+"时代微信朋友圈的基本业态和常态。微信朋友圈的出现和流行，在某种程度上是文化与技术融合的现代性产物。作为文化与技术融合的当代社会交往媒介和载体，微信朋友圈已开始出现了一些后现代社会生活的端倪。[2]如今，有的人却觉得事与愿违。其原因是社交停留在表面，沟通并未真正从心灵开始。

（2）现代社会交往本质上是文化交流

人是社会交往的主体，但人又是文化的载体。因此，在现代社会生活中，人们的社会交往就转换成了文化交流。这种社会交往中的文化交流，应该是深层次的思想观念的交流，而非浅表的物质交换或行为表达。简便快捷的即时通信工具在文化的深度交流方面，似乎未能发挥其预期的效能。

（3）从社会交往文化到文化社交：全媒体时代的社会与文化的深度融合

社会交往文化是人们在长期的生产和生活实践中不断积淀形成的，规制着人们的交往实践和行为。在新媒体、自媒体高度发展的今天，人们的社会交往应该

---

① 杨桃莲. 微信朋友圈中阶层认同的建构 [J]. 当代传播, 2017, (4): 93-96.
② 廖杨, 蒙丽, 周志荣. 微信朋友圈: "互联网+"场域中的身份建构与文化表达[J]. 民族学刊, 2017, 8(5): 11-20, 97-101.

从以往偏物质和经济层面的交往，转入到文化交往的层面上来。我国已故的著名社会学家费孝通先生曾把文化交往形象地概括为："各美其美，美人之美；美美与共，和而不同。"这是很有见地的，它为全媒体时代的文化自觉提供了参考。

3.4.3　小结：在表象与实质之间抉择

在本节中，我们讨论了现代社会交往的多个方面和现代社会交往的文化反思等问题，分析了现代社会交往的本质及其实现路径。需要说明的是，现代交往工具的革新和日新月异的即时通信技术的进步，可以最大限度地缩短人们交往联系的时空距离，但不一定能够同步缩短"交往"对象彼此之间的心理距离和社会空间。毕竟，"工具"和"价值"不在同一范畴，正如物理意义上的时空距离与社会意义上的情感空间距离不可同日而语。"近在咫尺"，却"远在天涯"，即为写照。

知识拓展与链接：

　　历史和现实的例子告诉我们，人类文明发展史上，以流域交通体系为主要表现形式的交通走廊是文明交流与文化传播的重要途径，也催生文明的产生。这些流域交通体系以分水岭为节点和枢纽，以廊道为连接方式，在实现文化交流、推动文化传播方面，起到了不可替代的作用。

　　——田阡：《流域人类学导论》，北京：人民出版社，2018年版，第102页。

4　游和购：旅游时代的文化逻辑

4.1　旅游与旅游消费

4.1.1　旅游本质上是文化活动

（1）文化是旅游的灵魂

关于旅游和文化的关系，学者们做过许多研究，基本上认同文化是旅游的灵魂。为什么？

人们之所以暂时离开自己的常住地，到某个旅游目的地去旅游，肯定是有原因的。其中一个重要的原因，就是这个旅游目的地的某个景区、景点、景观吸引游客去观赏或体验。

但是，游客如何感知某个景区、景点、景观是否值得去参观或体验呢？其中就涉及旅游的相关知识。

大家知道，旅游景区、景点、景观是需要规划设计和开发的。而在规划设计和开发之前还需要普查旅游资源，并根据不同的指标体系评价旅游资源。然后根据核心旅游资源的丰度和品质，结合当地的地脉和文脉提炼旅游的主题概念和内涵，在此基础上规划设计景区、景点和景观，并把它整合到一个更大的旅游产品当中，加上旅游线路的设计和策划营销，吸引更多的旅客前来旅游。因此，无论是在开发前的资源普查、规划设计，还是开发中的景区、景点、景观设计或营造、线路设计，以及开发后的推介营销、经营等，实际上都涉及文化感知，是旅游规划者、开发者、经营者、从业者和游客共同感知的结果。从这个意义上说，旅游充满了文化韵味。

（2）旅游是游客的一场文化体验

从游客的角度来说，旅游的文化属性就更为明显了。去哪里旅游，怎么去，去多久，去看什么，等等，都是游客出游考虑的主要因素。

因此，旅游本质上是一种文化活动。游客暂时离开常住地外出旅游，实际上是以付费方式置换一场不同的文化体验和愉悦审美。

4.1.2 旅游消费的文化解读

随着人民生活水平的提高，出门旅游成了多数人提高生活质量和生活品位的一种方式。

总体上看，不少民众的旅游消费基本上还停留在粗浅层次，主要以城市观光和旅游购物为主。深度的文化旅游和参与式的体验旅游、探险旅游需求总体不足，国内不少游客的旅游方式较为单一，"到此一游""拍照留念"仍然是一些旅游的主要方式，以至于国内一些导游调侃部分游客："上车睡觉、景点拍照、回到家里啥也不知道。"这些话语虽然带有一些讽刺意味，但它在一定程度上反映了旅游消费的低层次性。

不仅如此，有的游客出境旅游的主要目的不是旅游，而是为了购物。这也在一定程度上反映了部分游客的旅游层次不高。虽然购物是旅游的衣食住行游购娱七大构成要素之一，但它应该是旅游派生出来的，而不应该成为旅游的主要目的和主体活动。换句话说，那种不以旅游为目的旅行购物，严格来说是不符合旅游的本质要求的。

值得注意的是，部分游客到境外旅游疯狂购物的消费行为也引发了国际社会的广泛关注，显示了中国游客的强劲消费能力。据报道，近十多年来，中国游客的出境旅游消费涵盖了珠宝首饰、名牌服装、化妆品、名表、字画等众多奢侈品，甚至日常生活用具等，也成为境外旅游购物的重要选项。

据研究，早在2011年，中国游客的海外奢侈品消费就已登上全球奢侈品消费亚军的宝座。[1]应该指出，中国游客在海外奢侈品市场的畸形消费是值得关注的。近年来，中国公民出境旅游增加明显。2018年中国公民出境旅游人数14 972万人次，比上年同期增长14.7%。[2]2019年中国公民出境旅游人数15 463万人次，比上年同期增长3.3%。[3]

如何从热衷于购物转向真正的旅游观光和深度旅游，并在旅游过程中保持良好的游客形象，显然是中国游客出境旅游应该学好的必修课。

4.1.3 小结：在游与购之间升华

本节我们讨论了旅游和旅游购物消费的相关问题，解析了部分游客出境旅游的畸形消费及其表现。透过对旅游消费的文化反思，希望大家能够进一步认识旅游时代的文化逻辑。

---

① 佚名. 中国富裕家庭增速快于他国登上奢侈品消费亚军［N］. 人民日报海外版, 2010-02-10(12).
② 财务司. 2018年旅游市场基本情况［EB/OL］. 中华人民共和国文化和旅游部官网(索引号：357A04-04-2019-48887), (2019-02-12)［2019-12-25］. http://zwgk.mct.gov.cn/zfxxgkml/tjxx/202012/t20201204_906481.html.
③ 财务司. 中华人民共和国文化和旅游部 2019年文化和旅游发展统计公报［EB/OL］. 中华人民共和国文化和旅游部官网(索引号：357A04-04-2020-48897), (2020-06-20)［2020-07-20］. http://zwgk.mct.gov.cn/zfxxgkml/tjxx/202012/t20201204_906491.html.

知识拓展与链接：

　　旅游人类学存在着旅游学与人类学交叉渗透的学理基础，旅游、旅游学与人类学之间存在着内在关联，多元文化并置、"地方性知识"和"文化互为主体性"原则构成旅游学与人类学交叉结合的方法论原则。

　　——廖杨：《旅游人类学：旅游学与人类学的交叉渗透》，《贵州民族研究》2004 年第 4 期，第 74-79 页。

4.2　网购、代购与海淘

4.2.1　经济全球化与跨境电商的兴起

　　（1）经济全球化与现代生活

　　进入 21 世纪以后，经济全球化高歌猛进，自由贸易大步流星，带来全球经济繁荣、财富激增、民众生活的普遍改善。

　　有关经济全球化的定义，目前尚无统一说法。国际货币基金组织在 1997 年 5 月发表的报告中说："经济全球化是指跨国商品与服务贸易及国际资本流动规模和形式的增加，以及技术的广泛迅速传播和世界各国经济的相互依赖性增强。"经济合作与发展组织说它是一个过程，"在这个过程中，经济、市场、技术与通信形式都越来越具有全球特征，民族性和地方性在减少"。美国学者罗伯特·吉尔平（Robert Gilpin）说它是"世界经济的一体化"。[①]

　　（2）经济全球化是人类社会科技进步和生产力发展的必然结果

　　18 世纪中期，蒸汽机的轰鸣声排山倒海，第一次工业革命到来，国际分工产生。英国曼彻斯特棉纺厂加工的已经是来自西印度群岛、南北美洲的棉花。英国棉布成为人类史上的第一个全球化商品。

　　19 世纪中后期，发电机、内燃机、生产流水线广泛应用，第二次工业革命——电气时代来临。汽车、飞机、电报、电话颠覆了人们传统的生活方式，"天涯若比邻"成为现实。工业、商业资本向全球扩张，不同国家的生产流通、消费环节更紧密地结成一张大网，催生了第一次经济全球化浪潮。1870～1913 年，全球贸易额实现翻番。但两次世界大战和大战之间的经济大萧条，使经济全球化进程遭受重挫。

　　20 世纪 70 年代以后，信息技术革命成为第三次工业和技术革命的核心，彻底改变了传统经济运行模式，催生了数字经济等新经济与社会发展形态。人们仿

---

① 钟轩理. 不畏浮云遮望眼：经济全球化趋势不可阻挡［N］. 人民日报, 2018-12-10(2).

佛生活在一个相互为邻的"地球村"。

1970～2017年，以2010年不变价美元计算，全球GDP总量从不足20万亿美元升至80万亿美元。同期，人均GDP从5 185美元升至10 634美元。全球贸易额在GDP中的占比由26.72%升至2017年的56.21%。直接投资净流出从130.4亿美元升至1.525万亿美元。1981～2013年，全球贫困人口比例已经由42.3%下降至10.9%。而全球85%的人口预期寿命可达60岁，是100年前的两倍。①

目前，人工智能、大数据、量子信息、生物技术等新一轮科技革命和产业变革正在积聚力量，催生大量新产业、新业态、新模式，给全球发展和人类生产生活带来更多新变化。"我们要抓住新技术、新产业、新业态不断涌现的历史机遇，营造有利市场环境，尊重、保护、鼓励创新。"②特别是要建立适合中国又能引领世界发展的产业链、供应链、价值链、创新链等多链协同的新模式和新机制，促进国内经济大循环和国内国际经济的双循环。

（3）跨境电商的兴起

跨境电商是指分属不同关境的交易主体，通过电子商务平台达成交易、进行电子支付结算，并通过跨境物流送达商品、完成交易的一种国际商业活动。它基于网络发展，具有全球性、匿名性、无形性、即时性、无纸化、快速化等特点。我国跨境电商主要分为企业对企业（即B2B）和企业对消费者（即B2C）的贸易模式。

《2015年中国网络零售市场数据监测报告》显示，2015年中国跨境电商交易规模为5.4万亿，同比增长28.6%，其中跨境出口交易规模达4.49万亿，跨境进口交易规模达9 072亿，主要跨境进口电商模式有平台模式、闪购模式、直运平台模式、自营模式、C2C代购模式等九大模式。中国跨境电商的进出口结构比例中出口电商占比83.2%，进口电商占比16.8%。③

在2020年1月14日的国务院新闻发布会上，中国海关总署副署长邹志武说："2019年我国跨境电商等外贸新业态继续保持蓬勃发展态势，其中通过海关跨境电商管理平台进出口达到1 862.1亿元，增长了38.3%。市场采购方式进出口5 629.5亿元，增长了19.7%。两者合计对整体外贸增长贡献率近14%。"④

4.2.2 网购、代购和海淘成为现代生活的一部分

（1）网购

对于网购，相信大家并不陌生。许多人都有过网上购物的经历和体验。我们

---

① 钟轩理. 不畏浮云遮望眼：经济全球化趋势不可阻挡［N］. 人民日报, 2018-12-10(2).
② 习近平. 习近平谈治国理政：第三卷［M］. 北京：外文出版社, 2020：474.
③ 佚名. 2015年跨境电商交易5.4万亿［J］. 市场瞭望, 2016, (5)：18.
④ 高飞. 2019年跨境电商零售进出口总值1862.1亿元增长38.3%［N］. 电商报, 2020-01-14.

先来看看网购的发展历程。

中国第一宗网络购物发生在 1996 年的 11 月，购物人是加拿大驻中国大使贝祥，他通过实华开公司的购物网点，购进了一只景泰蓝"龙凤牡丹"。1999年前，中国互联网的一些工程师就开始建立 B2C 网站，致力于推动中国网购的发展。1999 年底，互联网发展高潮来临，国内诞生了 300 多家从事 B2C 的网络公司。2000 年，这些网络公司增加到了 700 家。但随着纳斯达克（National Association of Securities Dealers Automated Quotations，NASDAQ）指数的下跌，到 2001 年人们还有印象的只剩下三四家。随后网络购物经历了一个比较漫长的"寒冬时期"。

2007 年是中国网络购物市场快速发展的一年，无论是 C2C 电子商务还是 B2C电子商务市场交易规模都分别实现了 125.2%和 92.3%的快速增长。2007 年中国B2C 电子商务市场规模达到 43 亿元；2007 年中国 C2C 电子商务市场交易规模达到 518 亿元。2018 年，中国电子商务服务业继续保持稳步增长态势，市场规模再上新台阶，全年电子商务服务业营业收入规模达 3.52 万亿元，同比增长 20.3%。随着电子商务服务业发展的进一步成熟，营业收入增速逐渐放缓，但仍高于 2018年规模以上服务业企业营业收入增速 8.9%。[①]图 4-1 直观地反映了我国近年家电网购渗透率的变化。

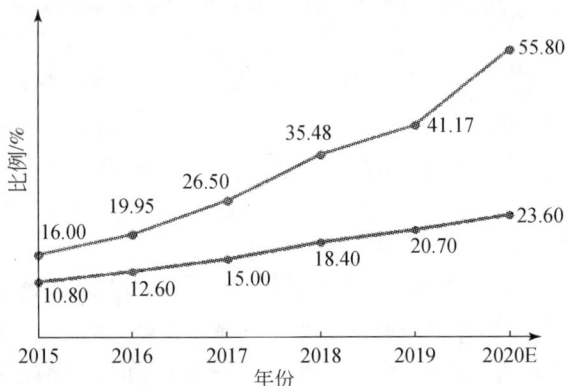

图 4-1　我国近年家电网购渗透率与网购平均渗透率比较

资料来源：中国电子信息产业发展研究院：《2020 年第一季度中国家电市场报告》，电子信息产业网，2020-04，http://www.cena.com.cn/special/2020dyjdjdsc.html。上线为网上零售额占家电市场零售总额比例，下线为实物商品网上零售额占社会消费品零售总额比例

与此同时，网民们也养成了网购的消费习惯。2020 年 9 月 29 日中国互联网络信息中心发布统计报告显示，截至 2020 年 6 月，我国网民规模达 9.40 亿，较

---

① 佚名. 2018 年中国电商代运营市场规模达到 9 623 亿元, 预计今后几年 B2C 与 C2C 市场交易规模差距会进一步拉大 [EB/OL] . (2019-07-02) [2020-04-30] . http://www.chyxx.com/industry/201907/754348.html.

2020 年 3 月增长 3 625 万，互联网普及率达 67.0%，手机网民规模达 9.32 亿。我国网民规模相当于全球网民的 1/5。互联网普及率约高于全球平均水平 5 个百分点。城乡数字鸿沟显著缩小，城乡地区互联网普及率差异为 24.1%，2017 年以来首次缩小到 30% 以内，网络扶贫作为扶贫攻坚的重要手段，已越来越多地被网民所了解和使用。网上外卖、在线教育、网约车、在线医疗等数字服务蓬勃发展，用户规模分别达 4.09 亿、3.81 亿、3.40 亿和 2.76 亿，占网民整体的比例分别为 43.5%、40.5%、36.2% 和 29.4%，在满足网民需求的同时也为服务业的数字化发展提供了助力。①随着 5G 时代的到来，网购将会变得更加日常。

（2）代购

代购是指通过中介机构或者代购者，从国外网站、商场、商店购买商品，直邮、转运或由个人带回商品的一种消费方式，中间商或者代购者会收取一定的佣金。海外代购往往涉及信誉问题，因此需要谨慎。

海外代购虽然商品相对便宜，但也存在诸如信用风险、税收流失和外汇管理等难题，因此，2019 年 1 月 1 日正式实施的《中华人民共和国电子商务法》，对代购行为进行了规范。

（3）海淘

海淘，就是在海外网站上购物，通过互联网搜索海外商品信息，完成商品的在线支付，通过国际快递在海外购物网站上交货，或者代表转运公司接收商品，然后把商品运回国内。海淘的付款方式一般是付款交割（如网上信用卡付款、贝宝账户付款）。

海淘与代购的主要区别是购买方式和是否收取佣金的差异。网络信息和物流业的发展，使得海淘也在提速。2020 年"6·18"快递提速超过 30%，全国 300 多个城市消费者享受到了小时达、半日达和当日达服务，甚至海淘也出现了半日达。②

4.2.3 小结：在线上线下与海内海外之间选择

在本节中，我们讨论了经济全球化和跨境电商的兴起问题，也介绍了网购、代购和海淘等现代购物方式。互联网信息技术的发展加速了经济全球化进程，电子商务由此兴起。无论是国内还是国外的网上购物，或者是国（境）外的代购，都已成为当代信息社会中网民生活的一部分。对于"宅男"或"宅女"而言，网络化生存和生活已经成为他们联系社会的主要方式。社会信息化和互联网、物联网将会重构和型构人们的生产及生活。

---

① 中国互联网络信息中心. 第 46 次中国互联网络发展状况统计报告［R］. CNNIC 中国互联网络信息中心, 2020: 1-52.

② 王洋. 配送更快 品类更多 海淘悄然生变［N］. 消费日报, 2020-06-17(A4).

4.3　全球化与文化的跨境流动

4.3.1　出境旅游：文化跨境流动与文化全球化

（1）出境旅游：文化的跨境流动

随着经济社会的发展和人们生活水平的提高，出境旅游逐渐成为人们休闲生活的一种选择。近年出现的"世界那么大，我想去看看"的网络语言迅速"走红"，也让不少网民"走心"，其实反映了人们出境旅游的现实需求。

中国旅游研究院、携程旅游集团联合发布《中国游客中国名片，消费升级品质旅游——2017 年中国出境旅游大数据报告》显示，2017 年中国公民出境旅游突破 1.3 亿人次，花费达 1 152.9 亿美元，比 2016 年的 1 098 亿美元增长了 5%。保持了世界第一大出境旅游客源国地位。从某种程度上说，出境旅游已成为衡量中国城市家庭和年轻人幸福指数的一大标准。

在出境旅游的过程中，旅游目的地通过旅游景区、景点和景观展示着当地的文化，或者说，是当地人对自然、人文或遗址等不同旅游资源的认知、规划、开发和利用，游客通过观光、游览或体验来感知旅游目的地的自然景观或历史人文景观。这是一种跨文化的旅游体验，旅游目的地的文化和游客自身的文化通过出境旅游活动实现了文化的跨境流动和全球交流。这实际上是经济全球化伴生文化全球化的结果。

（2）出境旅游与文化全球化

出境旅游带来的文化全球化不是某种文化的单向度输出或输入，而是多种文化的冲突、调适和协商。许多国家或地区为了迎接中国游客的到来，都不同程度地在旅游策划、旅游产品（线路）、旅游宣传、旅游营销等方面融入了中国文化的相关元素，特别是在春节等中国传统节日期间，许多国家都竞相营造中国人熟悉的文化氛围，以至于部分中国游客怀疑自己究竟是不是在国外，仿佛置身国内。这是国外旅游目的地主动适应中国游客的文化的结果。作为文化的载体之一，游客的跨境流动促进了文化全球化发展。根据世界旅游组织的预测，2010～2030 年全球国际游客将保持年均 3.3%的增长速度，并在 2030 年达到 18 亿人次。[①]如此规模的跨国旅游，无疑会推动文化的全球流动和传播。文化全球化当然也就不可避免，除非闭关锁国不让外国游客到来。

---

① UNWTO. Tourism towards 2030–Global overview ［C］. Madrid: UNWTO 19th General Assembly, 2011: 10.

4.3.2　民族旅游工艺品：民族文化商品化、在地化和全球化

（1）作为民族文化商品化的旅游工艺品

在旅游的过程中，相信大家都有过购买旅游工艺品的经历或体验。人们可能不一定会去思考旅游工艺品的民族文化属性，而是觉得这个旅游工艺品不错、有纪念意义或价值等。

实际上，旅游工艺品虽然是一个小物件，但它却承载着旅游工艺品设计者、开发者、制造者和销售者对旅游目的地文化代表性的理解：究竟什么样的旅游工艺品才能代表当地标志性的文化？特别是在民族地区，究竟什么样的旅游工艺品最能代表当地的民族文化？这其实应该是旅游工艺品设计者、开发者、销售者和游客多个维度的文化协商，也可以说是民族文化商品化的一种方式和结果。旅游工艺品是在旅游业发展中产生的一种新产品，它是民族文化的重要载体，它的本质内涵是民族文化商品化。文化、技术与民族生境，构成了旅游工艺品开发与民族文化商品化的内在关联。[①]

（2）在地化和全球化：民族旅游工艺品的发展趋势

人们常说：越是民族的，就越是世界的；或者说，既是民族的，也是世界的。这就是说，民族与世界虽然不同，但是它们却又彼此关联。

民族旅游工艺品也是这样，它既具有"在地化"特点，也有全球化特征。何以见得？

一是旅游工艺品往往取材于当地，是当地民族审美、艺术、思维、习俗等文化与全球先进技术的有机结合。仅有民族"文化"而技术粗糙的旅游工艺品是没有"卖点"的，只有先进的技术和精良的制作工艺配以独特的民族文化，这样的民族旅游工艺品才有价值和卖点，也才更受游客的青睐和旅游纪念品市场的欢迎。从这个意义上说，民族文化的"在地文化"在旅游工艺品器物上的凝聚和反映，具有明显的"在地化"特征。旅游工艺品背后蕴含着民族或族群的文化认同。[②]

二是民族"文化"全球化。这个全球化，不仅表现在全球的技术、全球的潜在市场，也表现在民族文化通过旅游工艺品的销售而走向世界。通过工艺品的形式，搭建了游客与目的地之间的文化交流平台。

4.3.3　小结：文化在旅游中流动

本节我们讨论了出境旅游与文化流动及文化全球化问题，分析了民族旅游工艺品与民族文化商品化、在地化和全球化的关系。希望这些讨论和分析，能够帮助大家进一步认识旅游时代的文化逻辑问题。

---

① 廖杨. 旅游工艺品开发与民族文化商品化 [J]. 贵州民族研究, 2005, (3): 134-141.
② 廖杨. 象征符号与旅游工艺品中的民族文化认同 [J]. 民族艺术研究, 2006, (2): 39-44.

5 娱和乐：消费时代的文化表达

5.1 娱乐与社会变迁

5.1.1 娱与乐：消费时代多样化的文化表达

（1）娱、乐与娱乐的含义

我们对娱乐并不陌生，但是，如果要精确地界定娱乐的概念，恐怕也不太容易。《说文解字》中说"娱"："乐也，从女吴声。"[①]

在古代文献记载中，既有"娱""乐"分用的现象，也有"娱""乐"合用的情形。例如，王羲之《兰亭序》中说："仰观宇宙之大，俯察品类之盛，所以游目骋怀，足以极视听之娱，信可乐也。"

《史记·廉颇蔺相如列传》："赵王窃闻秦王善为秦声，请奏盆缻秦王，以相娱乐。"这里的"娱"或"乐"主要是指欢愉快乐或欢乐的意思。此外，"娱乐"还有快乐有趣的活动之意。例如，《北史·齐纪中·文宣帝》："或聚棘为马，纽草为索，逼遣乘骑，牵引来去，流血洒地，以为娱乐。"当然，也有"乐娱"连用的情形。例如，汉代焦赣《易林·无妄之蛊》载："骖驾蹇驴，日暮失时。居者无忧，保我乐娱。"这里的"乐娱"指的是"欢欣"的意思。

古代"娱"字又通"悟"，即"领悟"。"娱"是一种领悟之后的情绪；"乐"在甲骨文中是成熟的麦子的意思，所以娱乐是领悟之后的感受和成熟之后的喜悦。在现代社会中，文化与技术的结合，使得娱乐的内容和方式更加丰富多彩。特别是在当今的信息社会中，消费的便利化、即时化、定制化、网络化和全球化，已成为消费时代和消费社会的主要特征。

消费时代的消费主要是通过互联网和信息技术来达成的，信息流量就成为消费社会的关键所在。在流量为王的消费时代中，产品的流通、交易、服务等，都依赖于信息网络。因此，流量为王成为当下信息消费的响亮口号。这种信息消费，使得娱乐的内容和方式更加丰富多彩。

（2）消费时代多样化的文化表达

从物质和产品的角度看，消费时代的物质产品消费不仅注重产品质量，而

---

① 许慎. 说文解字: 附检字 [M]. 北京: 中华书局, 1963: 262.

且更加注重购物者的购物体验。无论是实体店、产品展销店、体验店还是网购或海淘，愉悦、新奇或者有意义的购物经历或体验，都已成为消费者关注的重要内容。

从消费的内容构成上看，精神层面的消费特别是娱乐方面的信息消费已成为消费者的新宠儿，甚至超过人们的物质消费。从消费的方式方法上看，信用消费、分期支付和电子支付等，已成为人们消费的新时尚。从消费的形态上看，理性消费与非理性消费、合理消费和不合理消费等边界趋于模糊并因人而异。

5.1.2 消费时代的娱乐变迁

（1）从娱乐过渡到"娱乐至死"

消费时代是工业社会的产物，它是一个倡导消费主义的时代。这个时代的消费不同于一般时代的消费。就娱乐消费而言，消费时代的娱乐消费往往带有"狂欢"的意味。有人认为，在消费社会中，娱乐信息化、大众化和扁平化，似乎已成为现代社会的一种普遍现象。通过智能手机，人们就可以在网络世界里消费自己喜欢的信息，并通过这些信息达致自己所要的物质、精神世界。这在农业社会和工业社会早中期是难以想象的。一些消费者整天沉溺于手机游戏，"手不离机，机不离手"，甚至在手机游戏中耗费青春，或者沉浸在短视频中，"娱乐至死"。这是值得警惕的。

（2）从娱乐大众到"娱乐自我"

有人曾经探讨过我国当代的娱乐转向问题，认为我国经历了从娱乐文化被否定、被改造的时代，到娱乐文化被肯定、被张扬的时代，出现了从娱乐原罪化到娱乐无罪化、从娱乐精英化到娱乐平民化、从娱乐政治化到娱乐商业化三大变化，出现了价值取向多元、自我愉悦追求、商业利益驱动和表现形式通俗四大特征。在这样的泛娱乐化时代，我们无法用"是非对错"这种二元对立的标准来衡量传播形态所塑造的娱乐文化的好坏，而应该认识到消费时代娱乐文化的内容和形式都发生了变迁。这是信息、技术和文化商品化的结果。

"互联网+"时代的全媒体、自媒体释放了消费时代的大众消费活力，也使得娱乐的内容和形式趋于多元化、平民化、草根化和快捷化，引发了由大众走向自我的自娱自乐和"娱乐自我"的消费变迁。

（3）从内容完整到信息碎片

消费时代娱乐变迁的第三种变化是娱乐内容的完整化变为信息的碎片化和内容的片段化或微型化。这一方面是手机流量的影响，同时也与人们快节奏的工作方式有关。人们上下班搭乘公共交通或工作休息的片刻时间，阅读网络作品或观看手机视频，娱乐一下，放松身心，已成为城市年轻人的普遍行为和生活方式。"低头族"和人机对话，是消费时代娱乐变迁在年轻人生活中的真实反映。

5.1.3　小结：娱乐在消费中变迁

本节讨论了娱与乐及娱乐的含义，分析了消费时代多样化的文化表达和消费时代的娱乐变迁等问题。希望本节讨论，能够帮助大家进一步认识消费时代的文化表达问题。

知识拓展与链接：

消费型社会，是以消费为主导的社会，代表的是生产与消费之间的一种新型关系，即消费在整个社会制度安排中处于优先地位。其主要特征是：在经济层面上，以创新和服务为基础的第三产业构成了经济的主体；在社会层面上，以专业化为特征的社会中产阶层构成了社会的主体；在制度层面上，收入增长与分配、社会保障制度构成了社会政策的主体。历史唯物主义认为，保持生产与消费之间的平衡始终是经济规律的基本要求。19世纪以来，随着工业化程度的不断提升、世界市场日趋饱和，西方工业社会生产与消费之间的失衡逐渐加剧，最终导致全球性经济危机频发。20世纪上半叶，先发国家进行了经济社会领域的系列变革，使生产与消费之间重新获得新的平衡，生产型社会逐渐向消费型社会转型。20世纪下半叶，消费已成为先发国家发展的主导因素，消费的本质变化决定了不同时期消费型社会的基本特征。

进入21世纪，先发国家对消费型社会的局限性进行了深刻反思，积极探索建立趋于共享、重视简约的新型消费社会。2018年我国消费对国内生产总值的贡献率为76.2%，已经开始向消费型社会转型。

——范锐平：《加快建设中国特色消费型社会》，学习强国四川学习平台，2019-06-17。

5.2　消费文化与文化消费

5.2.1　消费文化与文化消费的概念

（1）消费文化

何谓消费文化？简单地说，消费文化就是消费时代或消费社会的文化。也有人主张，消费文化实际上指的是消费主义文化。

无论如何理解消费文化，它都是与消费时代、消费社会和消费主义相联系的。消费文化具有以下几个方面的特征。

1）消费文化是消费社会的产物，讨论消费文化须以消费社会为前提。

2）消费文化把文化变成商品，按市场逻辑行事。

3）消费文化取消了商品与艺术品的分野，商品艺术化、艺术商品化成为消费社会的一种主要趋势。

4）消费文化的核心内容之一是消费主义，并与享乐主义关系密切。

5）消费文化的重要功能在于刺激人的感觉，激发人的想象，再形成消费观念。因此，时尚、情调、格调、符号价值等，成为人们消费的主要内容。

（2）文化消费

那么，文化消费又该如何理解呢？

文化消费通常是指用文化产品或服务来满足人们精神需求的一种消费，它主要包括文化、教育、娱乐、体育、健身、旅游观光等方面。

在知识经济条件下，文化消费被赋予了新的内涵，文化消费呈现出主流化、高科技化、大众化、全球化的特征。

在社会学家看来，文化是一个不断被创造和生成的过程。文化消费是一个社会行为，永远都受社会脉络与社会关系的影响，人们在文本与实践的消费中，也在创造文化。因此，文化消费绝不是文化创造的终结，而是刚刚开始。从某种意义上说，文化消费过程其实也是文化的创制过程。

文化消费的历史可以追溯到 20 世纪 50 年代末期至 60 年代初期。当时，欧洲与美国首度出现相对来说足够富裕的劳动大众，有能力不再具是照顾"需要"，而是从"欲望"的角度去进行消费，电视、冰箱、汽车、吸尘器、出国度假等逐渐成为常见消费品。此外，劳动大众开始利用文化消费的模式去关联自己的认同感。

5.2.2　消费文化与文化消费的关系

（1）消费文化为文化消费提供精神源泉

消费文化兴起于 20 世纪二三十年代的美国大萧条时期，20 世纪五六十年代扩散到西欧、日本等地。它主张追求消费的炫耀性、奢侈性和新奇性，追求无节制的物质享受、消遣与享乐主义，以此求得个人的满足，并将它作为生活的目的和人生的终极价值。它是西方国家进入消费社会后所出现的消费文化最初形态。

20 世纪 70 年代以后形成的后现代消费文化则是早期现代消费文化的延伸和发展。尽管消费文化的出现是经济、社会、文化因素共同作用的结果，但现代媒体在传播与建构消费文化中发挥了重要作用。

在符号价值的意义高于使用价值、物质消费转化为意识形态意义的美学消费的鼓动下，基于消费文化的文化消费在西方发达国家迅速发展起来。这种文化消费也影响到改革开放之后的中国社会。不少年轻人还没有接触现代化和高级消费社会之前，就已经根据美国、韩国和日本等地的电影、电视剧或各种时尚杂志，建立了关于消费主义的想象和向往，他们开始根据电影、电视和时尚杂志的形象重新包装自己。可见，消费文化驱动下的文化消费影响是多么深广。

（2）文化消费为消费文化提供获得幸福感的路径

文化消费活动作为一种典型的非物质追求活动，其发展、成熟、规模的扩大决定于生产力的发展、剩余产品规模的大小以及居民收入水平的提高。

在消费文化中，广告、流行出版物、电视、电影文化等，提供了大量风格化的躯体形象。身体被商品化，躯体被认为是快乐的载体。于是，工业化的技术规制了整形、美容、美体等技术标准，唯美的消费文化又使得整形、美容、美体充满躯体意象。人们在身体消费中获得快感和"幸福感"。但这其实是现代传媒引导并操纵消费者欲望和趣味的结果，也暴露出消费社会享乐主义的道德观。

随着信用或信贷消费的出现，花未来的钱，及时行乐和享受，成为第二次世界大战以后西方大众消费者时髦的消费生活方式。卢卡奇认为，消费文化是一种肯定文化，它为社会提供一种补偿性的功能，它提供给异化现实中的人们一种自由和快乐的假象，用来掩盖现实中的真正缺憾。幸福被等同于消费，幸福的"大小"取决于物品的"大小"。①这种消费主义实际上是一种意识形态，消费主义主张的物化现象是人类社会生活中的一种非正常的异化状态。马克思原本寄望于人们在未来的社会中消除异化状态，以实现人的自我完善和自我发展，或者说，人的本质力量能够在对象化的劳动产品中得以实现。但在消费社会中，人的创造力早已从生产领域转移到消费领域，人们的自我实现主要体现在对各种有形或无形的商品的消费中，而不再体现在劳动产品中。②消费果真能给人们带来自由与幸福吗？西方马克思主义者的回答是否定的。他们认为，在当代资本主义社会中，人们的消费也是受控制和被操纵的。从表面上看，只要有钱就可以随心所欲地消费，但实际上，人们不过是根据厂商意图和广告引导来消费而已。人们在消费领域中消费是不自由的。这无疑揭穿了消费"幸福"的美丽谎言。

（3）文化消费与消费文化互为表里

文化消费一方面要满足的是消费主体的精神需要，使主体感到愉悦、满足；另一方面又要满足主体所需要的精神文化产品或精神文化活动。这两方面的需要，都由消费文化所影响和规制。因此，消费文化是文化消费的内核，文化消费不过是实现消费文化的手段和方式，二者互为表里。网络直播的兴起，体现着"微时代"媒介技术对日常生活的渗透。在"奇观化"和"镜像化"的呈现中，它滋生了网络亚文化的"拟像共同体"，也预示着一种多方面消费文化的形成。在此过程中，技术的泛滥与符号的增殖使得拟像的狂欢进一步放大了情绪的互动，更将主播的身体抽离于自然的意义，使其在一种"情感劳动"的消费模态中被赋予了规训性的审美话语和商品般的价值层级。这种消费文化的形成不仅体现为符号差异与象征资本之间所产生的交换与互惠，也表征着"生存性消费"向"享受性消费"

---

① 卢卡奇. 历史与阶级意识 [M]. 汉译世界学术名著丛书. 北京: 商务印书馆, 1999.
② 李辉. 卢卡奇的物化理论: 兼论其对消费文化的影响 [J]. 山东师范大学学报（人文社会科学版），2007, (2): 69-73.

的时代转位，其背后涉及的是一种"消费资本化"的驱动和运作。[①]

5.2.3 小结：消费是一种文化表达

本节讨论了消费文化和文化消费的含义，分析了消费文化和文化消费的关系等问题。希望本节内容的讨论，能够帮助大家进一步认识消费时代的文化表达问题。

知识拓展与链接：

2020 年春节期间，数字出版企业掌阅的用户活跃度比往年同期提升了 20%～30%。掌阅文学 CEO 王良说："通常春节期间，除了网络游戏的用户活跃度会上升之外，网络文学、音乐、视频等行业的用户点击率和活跃度都会下降一点，因为大家要走亲访友、聚会聚餐。但今年与网络相关的文化产品的用户活跃度都在提升。"据了解，与疫情相关的科普类图书尤其受到欢迎，掌阅推出的抗击疫情专题在客户端、微信等多渠道的点击率超过 1 亿次，《新型冠状病毒肺炎防治手册》等电子书位于热榜前列。
——张贺：《开放内容、多元体验　文化消费有了更多可能》，《人民日报》，2020-03-09。

5.3　广告、信息与消费

5.3.1　广告、信息与消费的关系

（1）广告与信息

在现代生活中，广告和信息无处不在，而且关系密切。一般来说，广告是信息的载体，信息则是广告的主要内容构成。另外，信息的有效传递需要广告的效果来实现，但是广告可信与否不在于广告本身，而在于广告信息真实与否。广告主和广告受众对于固定信息的不同解读，导致了广告主发出的信息和受众接收信息的差异。

（2）广告与消费

在现代社会中，人们的消费或多或少地受商品广告的影响。广告信息包括商品信息、劳务信息、观念信息等。它除了向广告受众传递商品信息，还传递着观念信息。请名人代言广告是许多广告公司的常见做法，这主要是利用名人知名度

---

① 吴震东. 技术、身体与资本："微时代"网络直播的消费文化研究[J]. 西南民族大学学报（人文社科版），2020, 41(5): 170-177.

高及其效用心理。

在自媒体和全媒体时代，广告更是无处不在，深入到人们日常生活的每个领域。通过微信、QQ 等即时通信技术，广告信息已成为现实生活的一部分。可以说，广告刺激消费，消费又反过来推动广告的发展。

（3）信息与消费

信息消费是消费时代的一个突出特征。在消费社会中，信息扮演着十分重要的角色。人们消费什么、如何消费、去哪里消费等，其实都与信息消费息息相关。有人认为，消费时代是信息为王的时代。谁控制或拥有了流量，消费自然就流向谁。因此，许多商家店铺都免费提供 Wi-Fi，主要的目的就是通过信息消费吸引消费者的到来。

（4）广告、信息与消费

消费社会的种种现象表明，广告、信息与消费之间存在着较强的逻辑关联。通过广告和信息，商品的生产者、流通者、经销者和消费者构成了信息流的生产者和消费者。广告信息和商品信息、价格信息、销售信息等，构成了消费社会波动性、非线性的信息传递。

5.3.2　广告、信息与消费的实质

改革开放 40 多年来，中国广告业基本上是伴随着中国工业化、现代化的发展而发展的。从 1978～1983 年的破冰与萌芽、1984～1991 年的"野蛮成长"、1992～2001 年的升级与竞争，到 2002～2012 年的繁荣发展，再到 2013 年之后的转型升级与全球引领[①]，中国的广告、信息与消费已步入新时代，进入信息消费新常态。

刚才我们已经谈到，在消费社会中，人们更多地关注商品的符号价值、文化精神特性与形象价值，追求无节制的物质享受、消遣与享受。受此影响，消费时代的广告信息也不可避免地投向这些符号化、标签化的消费需求。可以这么认为，消费时代的广告、信息与消费是消费社会价值取向的反映，实质上是现代工业社会向后工业社会的过渡。

5.3.3　小结：消费是一种符号象征

本节我们讨论了广告、信息和消费的关系，分析了消费社会中广告、信息和消费的实质问题。在现代社会中，广告其实是一种信息消费。在后现代社会中，广告不仅仅是一种信息消费，广告消费还成为消费社会的一种符号象征和价值隐喻。希望本节内容的讨论，能够帮助大家进一步认识消费时代的文化表达问题。

---

① 黄升民，赵新利，张驰. 中国品牌四十年：1979—2019 [M]. 北京：社会科学文献出版社，2019.

知识拓展与链接：

中国商业联合会近期发布通知，要求由该会下属媒体购物专业委员会牵头起草制定《视频直播购物运营和服务基本规范》和《网络购物诚信服务体系评价指南》等两项标准。这是行业内首定全国性标准，将于2020年7月发布执行。

据商务部统计，2020年第一季度，全国电商直播超过400万场，网络零售对消费的促进作用进一步提升。"直播带货"既有电视购物的节目形式，也有网络购物的邀约信息，还有广告代言的表现存在，产业链条比较复杂，网络主播、内容发布平台、产品供应企业等相关参与者缺乏明确的管理标准和监管机制。

据介绍，通过制定实施两项标准，有利于引领和规范我国直播购物和网络购物行业的发展方向，杜绝直播行业乱象、重塑行业生态，提升新零售行业的技术管理水平，维护广大消费者利益。

——杜海涛：《直播带货将有新规　将于7月发布执行》，《人民日报》，2020-06-09。

5.4　人工智能时代的娱乐与消费

5.4.1　人工智能时代的娱乐

在后现代社会中，人工智能（artificial intelligence，AI）已越来越显示其作用和效能。它不仅能够实现语音交互，而且还可以模仿明星的声音。

人工智能将触及娱乐行业的方方面面，即使是家长与小朋友的睡前故事传统节目。Novel Effect 公司创建的语音交互内容，会随着家长的声音"召唤"出活灵活现的视觉效果，比如当家长读《野兽国》（*Where the Wild Things Are*）时，会随时出现一个书中描绘的全息影像。通过交互式全息技术，可以为阅读内容创建音频互动的形象，家长们可以使用这些交互式的"音频书"让孩子们直接在床上看到故事中的角色和场景。总之，AI 在娱乐领域的运用将会给人们带来更好的互动和模仿。每当你和 AI 一起玩、聊天或者通过 AI 增强设备做出决定时，它们会更好地理解如何通过自己的行为或内容选择来娱乐你。

有人说：娱乐是生产力发展的真正力量。而我们的娱乐相较于其他方面，正在或已经交给了 AI。例如，有人让 Siri 用抖森的声音跟自己聊天、播报天气和提示交通信息，或为自己订机票和选择餐厅。但是，我们知道 AI 永远不能替代真正的抖森。

5.4.2　人工智能时代的消费

在消费社会中，网购已成为新时代下人们的主要购物方式。从用户体验角度看，人工智能很大程度上改变了消费者的习惯，通过无人化和智能化技术，如智能搜索、语音助手、无人超市等，使用户购物体验更佳。当然，也存在着不止在购物方面的应用场景受限以及在情感上带给消费者的违和感等瓶颈之处。

在人工智能的引导下，人们的购物和消费出现了新的时代特征：一是购物范围更广，可以在全球网购；二是货币电子化；三是根据不同的客户需求精准定制生产，快递到家；四是不同国家的产品购置不存在语言沟通、货币兑换等难题。

总之，人工智能时代的消费将更个性化、更便捷、更趋向于顾客的心理需求和消费体验。目前，人工智能支持的应用已经遍及面部识别、语言翻译及语音助手等我们日常生活的多个领域。随着这些消费应用程序的出现，越来越多的企业开始应用人工智能，这进一步促进了创新和生产力的提升。同时，它也对人们的工作和生活产生了深远影响，简单重复的工作和需要长时间高度专注的工作将逐渐由智能机器人去完成，其他职业的需求也会随着技术发展而逐渐变化。没有知识、没有技能、没有创意的人，未来"无工可打"，将成为现实。

5.4.3　小结：人工智能化还是智能人工化？

本节我们讨论了人工智能时代的娱乐和消费问题，希望本节内容的讨论能够帮助大家进一步认识消费时代的文化表达问题。

知识拓展与链接：

承载大数据、人工智能、物联网、区块链等技术的云计算，依托算力、数据、算法这三个关键要素，与5G、新一代自动化技术聚合发展，产生聚变效应和辐射效应，是推动物理世界数字化转型、传统企业上云、各行各业数字化转型升级的数字基础设施。

简言之，云计算底座承载大数据处理和人工智能算法，通过5G触达人们手中的智能端，完成云网端一体的大闭环，共同构成一个万物智能的世界。

作为新一代数字技术集大成者，工业互联网是数字技术与传统工业技术的"叠加"与"融合"。未来，工业互联网在技术、架构、模式、生态等方面都将升级、迭代或是重构。

——刘松：《数字化生产生活新图景》，《人民日报》，2020-04-28。

6　嫁和娶：人类社会的婚姻家庭

6.1　是嫁还是娶 VS 不嫁不娶？

6.1.1　婚姻与家庭

（1）婚姻与家庭的含义

不同学科对婚姻和家庭有着不同的理解。中国古代汉语中"婚"和"姻"有其独特含义。

《说文解字》释"婚"："妇家也，礼娶妇以昏时；妇人，阴也，故曰婚。"①又说"姻"："婿家也，女之所因，故曰姻。"①因此，在中国古代社会中，"人约黄昏后，女因男而来"通常成为人们婚姻嫁娶的写照。《辞海》将"婚姻"解释为男女双方建立夫妻关系。②

马克思主义认为，婚姻是男女两性之间的一种社会关系，其性质、特点和发展变化由经济基础决定。社会主义社会实行一夫一妻制度，男女双方的地位和权利义务平等，互相扶养，赡老育幼。

对于"家庭"，《辞海》将其定义为"由婚姻、血缘或收养而产生的亲属间的共同生活组织"。狭义的"家庭"指一夫一妻制个体家庭（单偶家庭）；广义的"家庭"泛指群婚制出现以后各种形式的家庭（如血缘家庭、亚血缘家庭、对偶家庭和一夫一妻制家庭等）。③

（2）婚姻与家庭的关系

在传统的社会中，婚姻和家庭的关系密切。一般来说，婚姻是家庭产生的前提，家庭则是婚姻关系缔结的结果。

随着生产力和生产关系的发展，人类的婚姻家庭会表现出不同的特点。在社会主义制度下，人们的婚姻家庭形式表现为一夫一妻制婚姻家庭，夫妻在家庭中地位平等，互敬互爱，相互扶助，共尽育幼养老的责任和义务。

（3）现代婚姻与家庭

在传统的社会中，婚姻和家庭相对稳定。我国已故的著名社会学家、人类学

---

① 许慎. 说文解字: 附检字（卷一二下）[M]. 北京: 中华书局, 1963: 259.
② 辞海编辑委员会. 辞海 [Z]. 1999年版缩印本. 上海: 上海辞书出版社, 2000: 1335.
③ 辞海编辑委员会. 辞海 [Z]. 1999年版缩印本. 上海: 上海辞书出版社, 2000: 1236.

家费孝通先生曾经把父—母—子（女）的三角关系看作是婚姻家庭结构稳定的重要模型。

在现代工业社会中，人类的婚姻和家庭关系随着社会的流动和财富的增加，出现了新的家庭形式。

一是传统的生育观念趋于多元，出现了不孕不育式的丁克家庭。

二是未婚先孕、非婚生子和单亲家庭开始为人们所接受。

三是家庭形态多样化，出现了单亲家庭、非婚同居家庭、再续家庭、丁克家庭、空巢家庭、核心家庭、联合家庭等不同的家庭形态。

四是现代医学技术的发展，使得通过人工授精等方式繁衍后代成为可能，导致婚姻未必成为建立家庭的必要条件或前提。

五是欧美一些国家的同性恋婚姻家庭，冲击着人类的传统婚姻家庭形式。

六是日本等科技发达国家智能机器人的发明和普遍应用，使得"跟机器人结婚"成为少部分思想前卫的日本人的念想。果真如此的话，人类婚姻家庭的概念和社会伦理将会被赋予新的时代特征和文化内涵。

此外，日本放送协会（NHK）电视台节目组通过调查发现，在城市化、高龄少子化等背景下，日本社会中所谓"无缘者"（没有亲人、与他人没有关联）人数众多，他们在孤独中死去，死后尸体无人认领。[①]

6.1.2　现代婚姻的嫁娶方式

（1）是嫁还是娶？

在传统的中国社会中，男娶女嫁被视为男女双方婚姻关系缔结的文化表达。这实际上是父权制社会的文化遗存。它突出地表现在婚后出生的子女的取名上，究竟是随父亲姓氏还是母亲姓氏。取姓于父，男娶女嫁无疑；如随母姓，则是男嫁女娶（俗称上门女婿或"倒插门"）。

姓氏源于宗族，孩子姓氏的取舍，实则反映不同的宗族观念和诉求。特别是在计划生育年代，孩子数量少，孩子的姓氏取名牵动着不少家长、家庭甚至宗族的心。为什么呢？

原因很简单，孩子的姓名虽然只是一个符号，但是，它却关乎着夫妻双方的家系传承。同为独生子女，他们婚后所生的子或女，是两个独生子女家庭的希望所在，自然希望孩子跟随自己的姓氏。因此，第二代或第三代独生子女的孩子的姓氏问题，就成为部分独生子女婚后的一个心结。令人欣慰的是，随着我国二孩政策的实施，两个孩子分别跟随父母姓氏，似乎解决了这个问题。从某种意义上说，独生子女的姓氏问题反映着是嫁还是娶的婚姻关系缔结方式。

现代社会人们流动性强，年轻人的独立性也比较强，他们有时远离父母，在

① 严蕾. "无缘社会"困扰日本 [J]. 恋爱婚姻家庭（下半月），2020, (4): 33.

陌生的城市里打拼和成家。这容易造成"不嫁不娶"的现代婚姻方式。

（2）不嫁不娶

这种"不嫁不娶"，主要是就婚姻双方的居住方式而言的。传统的男娶女嫁的婚姻居住方式主要表现为从夫居，"不嫁不娶"，意味着夫妻双方在远离各自父母的陌生城市里共同经营着"小家"。有时甚至出现女方父母购置婚房，婚后孩子跟随父姓的现象。这种婚姻关系的缔结，表面上看是从妻居和从父姓，实际上是"不嫁不娶"或"半嫁半娶""既嫁又娶"的反映。这种嫁娶方式的变化，是我国经济社会转型和人口结构变化的结果，也是我国城市房价高在年轻人婚姻家庭生活中的表征。

6.1.3 小结：在变与不变之间选择婚姻和家庭

本节我们讨论了婚姻、家庭的概念，婚姻和家庭的关系，现代婚姻家庭的变化，以及现代婚姻嫁娶方式的变化等问题。

从本节内容的讨论中，我们看到了婚姻家庭的观念、形式甚至内容等方面都发生了一些变化。同时，我们也看到了婚姻和家庭仍然是维系人类社会合法性关系和亲属关系的主要方式。正是在这样的"不变"中有"变"，"变"中有"不变"的社会发展进程中，人类对自己的婚姻和家庭进行了抉择。希望本节内容的讨论，能够帮助大家正确认识人类社会的婚姻家庭问题。

知识拓展与链接：

在南亚的大部分地区，一个人会跟来自相同种姓或阶层的人结婚。许多父母仍然坚持他们孩子的婚姻应当被安排好。但这样的情况有所改变。想象一下在英国的南亚年轻人如何安排他们自己的婚姻。

媒人渐渐被网站、聊天室，以及网络上的个人广告所取代。通过电信网络相识的伴侣可能会安排一次面对面的会面，被称为"南亚速配"；他们同意会面并交谈——仅仅只是短短的 3 分钟——在一家餐厅或酒吧，接着他们继续发展。这些参与者，年龄都在 20 岁左右，出身中产阶级，都认为自己非常时尚。他们怡然自得地协调着东西方的行为举止。对于美国的南亚人而言情况也是如此吗？

——［美］卡罗尔·恩贝尔（Carol R. Ember），［美］梅尔文·恩贝尔（Melvin Ember）：《人类文化与现代生活：文化人类学精要（第 3 版）》，周云水、杨菁华、陈靖云译，北京：电子工业出版社，2016 年版，第 262 页。

6.2　聘礼嫁妆的现代流变

6.2.1　聘礼与嫁妆

（1）聘礼的含义

中国是礼仪之邦，自古讲究婚姻礼数。中国古代婚姻六礼（纳采、问名、纳吉、纳征、请期、亲迎）中的"纳征"亦称纳币，即男方家以聘礼送给女方家。这是中国古代人"订婚"的主要手续之一。

（2）嫁妆的含义

嫁妆亦称"陪妆""妆奁（lián）"，一般是指妇女在结婚时带到她丈夫家里的结婚用品和财物，如房子、车子、衣被、家具及其他生产和生活用品等。由于各地、各民族的风俗习惯不同，其所准备的嫁妆也不相同。

（3）嫁妆与聘礼的关系

我们知道，聘礼为夫家所送，嫁妆为娘家所送。嫁妆与聘礼关系密切，不少家庭为了给出嫁的女儿置办嫁妆，除了亲家送的聘礼外，自家还贴现不少。有的人比较宠爱自己的女儿或者为了面子，嫁妆有时是聘礼的数倍。中国传统的"礼尚往来"的习俗文化，在现代婚姻的聘礼和嫁妆方面也就比较明显地体现出来了。

不仅如此，国外也有类似的习俗。例如，在人口较多的印度，嫁妆和聘礼也成为普通家庭的不小负担，一些家庭更是害怕生养女儿。《印度时报》称，印度的传统习俗认为，新娘嫁妆中的黄金越多，婚后生活越富足。尤其是在看重这一习俗的喀拉拉邦地区，一次婚礼需要的黄金多达 400 克，新郎一家会想方设法索要更多黄金。一些父母为了给女儿置办嫁妆，不得不卖房、借贷，重"金"打造嫁妆。[①]即便进入 21 世纪，印度的陪嫁之风依然久刹不止。[②]这可能会导致男女性别比例失衡，进而引发严重的社会问题。

6.2.2　现代聘礼和嫁妆的流变

在中国传统社会中，男耕女织通常被视为农耕社会的理想生产和生活模式。因此，聘礼和嫁妆一般都会或多或少地带有"农（牧）"特征。聘礼和嫁妆都带有一定的实物性质。例如，除钱款之外，中国南方地区的农作物种子、谷米甚至一些生产工具，北方地区的牛羊等牲畜，等等，往往也成为嫁妆的一部分。

---

① 章鲁生. 嫁女成本高　印度家长"抢新郎"[J] . 东西南北, 2014, (12): 66-67.
② 薛克翘. 当前印度的陪嫁之风 [J] . 当代亚太, 2002, (5): 60-64.

在现代社会中，工业化和城市化的发展，使得原来的聘礼和嫁妆形式发生了变化。这不仅表现在聘礼和嫁妆的数量增多，而且也表现在不同时期的嫁妆内容的差异上。

在新中国成立初期至改革开放之前，人们的经济状况不太好，聘礼和嫁妆自然也就相对简单，甚至半斗米就解决了。20世纪七八十年代，手表、缝纫机和自行车成为中国人结婚的"三大件"；20世纪90年代，彩电、冰箱和摩托车成为新的"三大件"，此外，还有金银玉镯等。进入21世纪以后，住房、汽车和钻戒等，开始成为人们聘礼和嫁妆的主要内容。

从新中国成立至今70多年的发展变化中，我国大部分地区的聘礼越来越多，嫁妆也越来越钱财化，有些家庭甚至将十多公斤的黄金首饰直接戴在新娘身上，颇有炫富意味，这也再次说明工业化刺激了人们对物质的追求。

6.2.3 小结：礼物的流动与婚姻家庭文化的传承

本节我们讨论了聘礼、嫁妆的含义，嫁妆和聘礼的关系，以及现代婚姻中的聘礼和嫁妆流变等问题。

从本节内容的讨论中，我们看到了聘礼和嫁妆实际上是一个礼物的流动问题，也是一个婚姻家庭文化的传承问题。希望本节内容的讨论，能够帮助大家进一步认识人类社会的婚姻家庭问题。

知识拓展与链接：

在许多社会中，尤其是那些以农业为基础的社会，女子结婚时往往随身带着嫁妆。嫁妆是父母财产中女子的那一份，不是她父母去世时传给她，而是在她结婚时分给她。这并不意味着，她保留婚后对这份财产的控制权……在美国，一种形式的嫁妆是新娘家支付婚礼费用的习俗。

——[美]威廉·A. 哈维兰（William A. Haviland）、[美]哈拉尔德·E. L. 普林斯（Harald E. L. Prins）、[美]达纳·沃尔拉斯（Dana Walrath）等：《人类学：人类的挑战（第14版）》，周云水、陈祥、雷蕾等译，北京：电子工业出版社，2018年版，第491页。

6.3　人口流动与跨国婚姻

6.3.1　人口流动

（1）人口流动的含义

人口流动是指人口在地区之间所做的各种各样短期的、重复的或周期性的运动。

（2）人口流动的类型

根据人口流动的时间，可以把人口流动划分为以下几种不同的类型。

1）长期人口流动。它是指离开户口登记地 1 年以上，在外寄居，而户口仍留在原地的人口流动。

2）暂时人口流动。它是指离开户口登记地 1 天以上、1 年以下，在外寄居或停留，而户口仍在原地的人口流动。

3）周期性人口流动。它是指有规律的定期离开户口登记地和返回户口登记地的人口流动。

4）往返性人口流动。一般指早出晚归、不在外过夜的人口流动（如城市职工的上下班等），又称为钟摆式人口流动。

5）跨国人口流动。它主要指人口在不同国家之间进行的跨国流动，主要形式有劳务输出、出国探亲和缔结涉外婚姻三种。

6.3.2　跨国人口流动与跨国婚姻

随着我国改革开放的发展，中国人的婚恋观念变得更加宽容与开放，跨国婚姻近年来有所增加。尤其值得一提的是，在中国的大城市里，跨国、跨民族甚至跨种族伴侣的人数增加较为明显。

根据中华人民共和国民政部数据，2017 年我国有十万对涉外及港澳台的结婚登记。据美国有线电视新闻网报道，2012 年中国有 53 000 对跨国配偶登记结婚，而"中国大陆在 1978 年没有登记任何的跨国婚姻"[①]。

随着世界经济、科技和文化的发展，人类婚姻似乎出现了全球化。据了解，上海涉外婚姻中的境外人士几乎覆盖了全世界，涉及除南极洲以外的所有大陆。其中，日本人最受上海人的青睐，占境外人员总数的 39.6%；其他相对集中的国家和地区是美国（9.1%）、澳大利亚（6.1%）、加拿大（3.9%）。[②]

由于各国文化底蕴、历史传统、家庭观念的差异，跨国婚姻中的夫妻忧虑和

---

① 佐伊·墨菲. 中国跨国婚姻，因爱而生［N/OL］. 甘文凝，译. 环球时报，2013-10-25.
② 佚名. 中国当前的跨国婚姻现象［EB/OL］.（2013-09-18）［2015-04-29］. http://www.bblhls.com/art/view.asp?id=765030234881.

风险可能会更多一些。这主要由于跨国婚姻者在国外的身份不稳定、对当地的法律不熟悉，以及在语言沟通、文化、观念、习俗等方面都不占据优势，可能会因地域差别和文化差异（价值取向、歧视）而出现婚姻危机。不同文化背景下的夫妻二人可能会产生语言交流、风俗习惯、价值观等方面的障碍。

当然，不是所有的跨国婚姻都会出现问题。很多跨国婚姻组成的家庭也是很温馨幸福的。需要说明的是，跨国婚姻和国内婚姻一样，需要履行正常的、合法的登记手续，只是涉外婚姻的登记手续相对烦琐。

无论国内婚姻还是跨国婚姻，一般都少不了亲人的祝福和礼物的赠送。礼物及其承载的婚礼文化，会随着跨国婚姻的人口流动而流动，并在代际间不断传承下去。

6.3.3　小结：礼物的流动与婚姻家庭文化的传承

本节内容我们讨论了人口流动和跨国婚姻问题。跨国婚姻不仅会引起人口的跨国流动，而且会带来礼物和跨国婚姻家庭文化的代际传承。希望本节内容的讨论，能够帮助大家进一步认识人类社会的婚姻家庭问题。

知识拓展与链接：

全球大规模的移民、现代科技和许多其他因素，也影响到了婚姻、家庭和家户的跨文化镶嵌。例如，通过光缆和卫星实现的数字通信方式，已经改变了个人在浪漫恋爱中如何表达性吸引和性占有的方式。

如今，地方的、跨文化和跨国的爱情关系通过互联网而开花结果。许多在线公司提供约会和相亲服务，允许个体发布个人资料，并在有担保的网络环境下寻找恋爱的对象或未来的配偶。这项服务亦吸引了在族群或宗教方面的离散个体，去寻找与其个体、族群或宗教背景相匹配的人。例如，当今印度的婚恋网站也用于包办婚姻的目的，让父母上传孩子的视频资料，在屏幕上筛选潜在的求婚者，并安排合适的相亲。

社交媒体也允许人们对有关被禁止的欲望或亲密关系通过私下用短信联系，去追求传统上被禁止的关系——比如在印度传统穆斯林社区内年轻未婚男女之间跨越种姓等级的交往。

——［美］威廉·A. 哈维兰（William A. Haviland）、［美］哈拉尔德·E. L. 普林斯（Harald E. L. Prins）、［美］达纳·沃尔拉斯（Dana Walrath）等：《人类学：人类的挑战（第 14 版）》，周云水、陈祥、雷蕾等译，北京：电子工业出版社，2018 年版，第 497-498 页。

6.4　现代社会的特殊"婚姻"

6.4.1　同性恋"婚姻"及其对人类婚姻家庭的影响

（1）何谓"同性恋"？

简单地说，同性恋是指只对同性别的人产生爱情和性欲而对异性不感兴趣的性取向。那些具有同性爱恋或同性吸引取向的个体被称为同性恋者。根据同性爱恋或吸引对象不同，同性恋可分为男同性恋和女同性恋两种类型，前者简称"男同"，后者简称"女同"。

性取向和性愉悦有关，但同性恋不等于同性性行为。在特殊境遇下，一个异性恋者可能会与同性发生性行为，一个同性恋者也可能会与异性发生性行为。性取向是一个复杂的问题。一些科学家、心理学家、医学专家曾对人类的性取向做过相关研究。美国心理学协会发表的一篇文献认为：长期的实验记录证明，同性恋是无法被"矫正"的，性取向无法改变。

我国生命科学家饶毅认为：同性恋有基因参与，不过目前并不清楚究竟哪些基因影响了人类的性取向。"当然，注射性激素会影响性向，而性激素不仅改变性向，而且改变其他性行为，也改变与性相关的一些形态特征。并未证明性激素相关的基因变化是导致人类同性恋的原因。"①科学地认识同性恋问题而不"视而不见"或"讳疾忌医"，应该是现代文明社会的基本态度和道德立场。

（2）同性恋"婚姻"

同性恋"婚姻"（same-sex marriage），是指同性之间的"婚姻关系"。同性恋"婚姻"的支持者将其称为婚姻平等或平等婚姻。这种婚姻形态，可能意味着现代婚姻多元化的发展趋势，满足了同性恋者的结婚需求。从 2001 年荷兰成为世界上首个实现同性婚姻合法化的国家至 2019 年，近 20 年时间里，全球 36 个国家或地区将同性婚姻与民事结合视为合法化。②但是，同性婚姻在我国目前是不被官方认可的（台湾地区除外），民政部门对同性别的"婚姻关系"不予登记。

2019 年 12 月 20 日上午，在全国人大常委会法工委第三次记者会上，全国人大常委会法工委发言人岳仲明表示，《民法典婚姻家庭编（草案）》三次审议稿征求意见过程中，有意见认为，同性婚姻合法化应该写入《民法典婚姻家庭编》。此前，2019 年 10 月召开的全国人大常委会会议曾三审《民法典婚姻家庭编（草案）》。岳仲明表示，此次审议之后，2019 年 10 月 31 日至 11 月 29 日，《民法典婚姻家庭编（草案）》通过中国人大网向社会公开征求意见，"共收到 198 891 位社会公

---

① 饶毅. 欲解异性恋，须知同性恋 [J]．科学文化评论, 2012, 9 (5): 63-74.
② 苗洪. 您如何看有意见建议"同性婚姻合法化"写入民法典[EB/OL]. (2020-05-07)[2020-06-30]. http:// bbs.tianya. cn/post-news-390036-1.shtml.

众网上提出的 237 057 条意见和 5 635 封群众来信。意见主要集中在完善近亲属的范围、修改可撤销婚姻的撤销机关、进一步完善夫妻共同债务、同性婚姻合法化等方面"。①

（3）同性恋"婚姻"对人类婚姻家庭的影响

2006 年 3 月 6 日，在美国洛杉矶，我国导演李安凭借一部反映同性恋的电影《断背山》获得奥斯卡最佳导演奖。在此时的北京，也有一个同性恋话题引人关注：2006 年 3 月 3 日，正在参加全国政协十届四次会议的著名社会学家、全国政协委员李银河向大会正式提交了《同性婚姻提案》。中国作为世界上人口最多的国家，官方一直没有关于同性恋发生的数据和一般性取向者的对照数字，但学界估测中国国内同性恋者约有 4 000 万人。这意味着，我们身边每一百人中可能就有 2～3 人或更多的人愿意选择同性为伴侣。在这个庞大的数字背后，是一个不容忽视的群体。②

有学者对北京、上海、沈阳、天津、西安、成都等地不同年龄阶段的男同性恋群体的观察和访谈发现，男同性恋群体发展出三种特殊的婚姻形态：婚外有"婚"、两个儿子的"婚姻"、男同女同形式婚姻，这是同性爱欲与异性恋一夫一妻制协调和结合的结果。我国没有承认同性婚姻，男同性恋群体的策略性实践及其背后隐含的文化性适应与潜在的异性恋框架值得关注。

同性恋者的"婚姻"不能带来传统婚姻所倡导的家庭人口的增长，因此，同性恋者的"婚姻"及其组成的"家庭"很难为传统世俗社会所认可。虽然工业时代的机器化、智能化可以在一定程度上辅助解决人类社会的劳动力短缺的问题，但是人工智能毕竟难以完全取代人类自身的存在。

6.4.2 机器人"婚姻"及其对人类婚姻家庭的影响

（1）何谓机器人"婚姻"？

近年来，随着人工智能技术的发展，一些人对机器人似乎很感兴趣，人类能否与机器人"结婚"的问题也曾一度成为社会关注的焦点。

所谓机器人"婚姻"，是指人类与高度智能化的机器人"结婚"。机器人的"人"化还有漫长的道路要走，但是，一些人工智能专家已经乐观地预估人类可以在 2045 年或 2050 年跟机器人"结婚"。当然，这种"婚姻"并不是传统意义上的异性婚姻。机器人并非真人，只是智能化的机器而已。但是，"人机婚配"的结果不仅"雷人"，而且也颠覆了人们对现实婚姻家庭的认知。果真如此，"人机婚配"将改写人类婚姻家庭历史。

---

① 王姝. 全国人大常委会法工委发言人：有意见建议"同性婚姻合法化"写入民法典［N］. 新京报, 2019-12-20.
② 佚名. 我国首查同性恋人群基数［EB/OL］. (2004-08-19)［2005-01-15］. http://news.sina.com.cn/c/2004-08-19/16113439105s.shtml.

（2）"机器人婚姻"对人类社会的影响

机器人伦理是科技伦理研究的一个新领域。与人类关系比较密切的情侣机器人将引发与传统的婚姻伦理、性伦理相冲突的一系列问题，包括如何看待人与情侣机器人之间的爱情，情侣机器人的地位与权利问题，以及与情侣机器人之间的性关系是否道德，是否可以虐待情侣机器人，等等。对这些问题的回答及其解决，需要哲学家、科学家、制造商与使用者共同面对，从而使机器人更好地为人类服务。

在机器人应用越来越广泛的今天，机器人可能引发的种种伦理问题也日益紧迫地摆在人们的面前。但是，机器人只是人类的一种重要辅助工具，它并不能完全取代人。

可以预见，如果人与机器人的"婚姻"得到许可，那么，人类自身终将走向毁灭。

6.4.3　小结：在"和而不同"的婚姻家庭文化中认识社会

本节我们讨论了现代社会的特殊婚姻形态——同性恋"婚姻"和机器人"婚姻"。这是一个充满争议的话题，也是现代科技发展对人类现代婚姻家庭生活提出的重大挑战。希望通过本节内容的讨论，能够帮助大家在"和而不同"的婚姻家庭形态中进一步认识人类社会的婚姻家庭问题。

知识拓展与链接：

在喜马拉雅山的雷布查人，如果一个人吃了未被阉割的猪的肉将被认为会变成同性恋者。同时，雷布查人否认他们当中存在同性恋行为，并且对这种行为感到厌恶。或许因为很多社会否认同性恋存在，在有约束的社会中，同性恋行为很少被外界知道。在自由的社会中，同性恋的类型和普遍性的态度是不一样的。在一些社会中，同性恋被接受但被限定于特定的时间和特定的人。比如，在美国西南部的巴巴哥人，那里有"农神节的夜晚"，在那里同性恋的性取向可以表达。巴巴哥人还有很多男性异性装扮衣着癖者，他们穿着女性的衣服，做女性常做的家务，如果他们未婚就可能有男性来访。女性没有同样表达的自由。她们可以参加神农节晚会，但是要经过她丈夫的允许，不存在女性异性装扮衣着癖者。

——［美］卡罗尔·恩贝尔（Carol R. Ember），［美］梅尔文·恩贝尔（Melvin Ember）：《人类文化与现代生活：文化人类学精要（第 3 版）》，周云水、杨菁华、陈靖云译，北京：电子工业出版社，2016 年版，第 245 页。

7 老和病：人类社会的养老关爱

7.1 现代社会转型中的养老问题

7.1.1 社会转型的现代性

（1）何谓社会转型？

简单地说，社会转型就是社会结构、经济形态和文化价值观念等发生深刻变化，转变为另一阶段的过程。新中国成立以来，中国经历着一场史无前例的社会转型，社会转型促使中国在各方面都发生了重大变化，民生改善体现在从贫困社会向小康社会的转变，体制创新体现在从社会管理向社会治理的转变，公平正义体现为从金字塔型社会向橄榄型社会的过渡，对美好生活的向往体现为从生存型消费向发展型消费的转变。①

（2）社会转型的内容

社会转型的具体内容包括结构转换、机制转轨、利益调整和观念转变等方面。

从中国经济体制上讲，它具体表现为 20 世纪 80 年代以来从计划经济体制向市场经济体制的转变。从社会结构上说，它包括中国社会阶层结构、社会组织结构、家庭结构、就业或分工结构、收入分配结构和消费结构等方面的转变。从社会形态上看，它主要表现为从传统社会向现代社会、从农业社会向工业社会、从工业社会向信息社会转变。在社会转型时期，人们的行为方式、生活方式、价值体系都发生明显的变化。

（3）现代社会转型的现代性

在现代社会转型过程中，现代性主要表现为工业时代流水作业的时间取代传统农耕社会的自然时间，机器化的批量生产方式取代手工限量的生产方式，标准化、模型化和刻板化取代个性化，组织、协同、高效取代个体、分散、低效，自由、民主、平等、正义的人本价值取代封建专制、不平等、不公正等现象。

---

① 孙凤. 70 年来中国社会转型的"四个向度"[J]. 人民论坛, 2019, (29): 35-37.

7.1.2　现代社会中的养老问题

（1）传统家庭养老模式难以为继

在工业社会之前，家庭养老是人类社会的主要养老方式。传统的家庭养老保障通过纵向的代际传承方式将财富从上一代人向下一代人进行实物转移，这种财富的代际转移方式在资本市场缺失、工业化出现之前几乎是唯一可行的养老保障模式。

在西方国家，当人口老龄化问题还未出现、养老未成为重要的社会问题被提出之前，家庭养老模式一度占据主流。欧美等发达国家中选择居家养老模式的老年人总占比为80%左右，中国、日本和新加坡等亚洲国家，基本上以家庭养老为主。但是，随着人口结构转型和劳动人口日益减少，传统的家庭养老模式也趋于难以为继。据报道，发达国家5%~15%的老年人选择了机构养老模式，其中北欧为5%~12%，英国大约为10%，美国大约为20%。①此外，不同国家或地区还发展出社区养老、迁徙养老、以房养老、互助养老、医养结合等多种养老模式。

改革开放以来，我国工业化和城镇化的发展速度快，乡—城人口迁移规模大，以及计划生育政策的实施，加剧了社会人口结构的变化。例如，家庭规模小型化，"空巢"化与"少子"化家庭增多，代际交换时间与空间距离拉大，弱化了传统家庭养老模式的保障功能。

据预测，2050年我国80岁以上高龄老年人口将达到8 300万人。从2015到2035年，中国老年人口将从2.12亿增加到4.18亿，占比提升到29%。这意味着，2012年五个人养一个老人，2030年两个人养一个老人，2050年一个人就得养一个老人！与此同时，我国失能和失独老人数量还不断增多。据测算，2010年我国独生子女总量约为1.5亿人，预计2050年将达到3.1亿人。随着独生子女人数总量的增多，因独生子女死亡所产生的中国失独家庭数量也在激增，2010年达到84.1万户，2020年突破100万户。②如此庞大的老年人数量和独生子女政策形成的特殊人口结构和劳动力结构，使得传统的家庭养老模式难以为继。

（2）未富先老对养老模式提出了新挑战

判断老龄化社会的国际通行标准有两个：一是1956年联合国认定的一个国家或地区65岁及以上老年人口数量占总人口比例超过7%；二是1982年维也纳老龄问题大会认定的60岁及以上老年人口比例超过10%。我国2000年第五次全国人口普查时，两个标准均满足，意味着自1999年底起，我国已正式进入老龄化社会，迄今已20年。③

我国不仅是世界上老龄人口数量最多的国家，也是全球老龄化速度最快的国

---

① 杨云帆. 国外养老模式的经验和启示［N］. 学习时报, 2015-03-09(A15).
② 马瑾倩. 立遗嘱的年轻人［N/OL］. 新京报网, (2019-07-12)［2019-12-10］. http://www.bjnews.com.cn/news/2019/07/12/602682.html.
③ 韩维正. 今天, 我们如何养老［N］. 人民日报海外版, 2018-07-09(10).

家。目前我国每年老年人口的增长率在 3.5% 左右。从成年型社会到老龄化社会，法国用了 115 年，美国用了 60 年，日本也用了 30 多年，而中国只用了 18 年。更重要的是，发达国家在进入老龄化社会时，人均 GDP 为 5 000～10 000 美元，而中国 1999 年底的人均 GDP 仅为 850 美元。[①] 由于我国老龄化形势严峻，2016 年 7月，民政部和国家发改委印发了《民政事业发展第十三个五年规划》，提出了更为具体的养老服务体系目标，即"全面建成以居家为基础、社区为依托、机构为补充、医养相结合的多层次养老服务体系"。

在未富先老、传统家庭养老模式难以为继的情况下，我国养老面临着缺少经济保障、生活照料、精神慰藉和失独失能等难题。

（3）个人、社会、国家的协同养老

在"养儿防老"已不现实的情况下，我们靠什么来养老呢？有人说，要靠老伴、老窝、老底、老健、老友、老来俏和老来乐来养老。当然，这更多是从老龄人自身的条件来说的。

事实上，养老问题不仅仅是公民个人的事情，也是国家和社会应尽的责任和义务，多方协作才能解决得更好。"中国式养老"需要政府及社会协同配合。[②] 在国家和社会不能为公民个人完全兜底的情况下，公民个人的养老更有赖于个体的健康。在通货膨胀和货币贬值的情况下，公民个人"储蓄金钱不如储蓄健康"似乎不乏道理。

7.1.3 小结：在社会变迁中认识"老有所养"

养老是人类社会的永恒话题。本节我们讨论了社会转型及其现代性，以及现代社会转型中的养老问题。在社会变迁中认识"未富先老""老有所养"等问题，可以更好地理解生活的本质和意义。希望通过本节内容的讨论，能够帮助大家进一步认识人类社会的养老等问题。

知识拓展与链接：

随着一个国家老年人口的增加，未来照料老年人的责任已经越来越令分析学家们担心。这一问题在西欧和日本尤为严重，他们 65 岁以上老年人的比例最大。

——［美］詹姆斯 M. 汉斯林（James M. Henslin）:《走进社会学：社会学与现代生活（第 11 版）》，林聚任、解玉喜译，北京：电子工业出版社，2016 年版，第 302-303 页。

① 韩维正. 今天，我们如何养老［N］. 人民日报海外版，2018-07-09(10).
② 佚名. "中国式养老"需要政府及社会协同配合［EB/OL］. (2016-05-05) ［2017-03-07］. http://district.ce.cn/newarea/roll/201605/05/t20160505_11241986.shtml.

7.2　人口结构变动与养老文化

7.2.1　人口结构及其变动

（1）何谓人口结构？

人口结构又称人口构成，它是指全国或某一地区一定时期内人口构成状况，反映着一定地区、一定时间人口总体内部各种不同质的规定性的数量比例关系。它具有相对的稳定性，一般随着时间的推移及经济发展而有所变化。

（2）人口结构的类型和特征

按人口过程的特点及运动方式，可将人口结构分为人口自然构成、人口社会构成和人口地域构成三部分和其他若干种类。其中，自然构成还可分为年龄构成、性别构成等；社会构成可分为民族构成、文化构成、宗教构成、阶级构成等；地域构成则可以分为城乡构成、区域构成等。尽管人口有着性别、年龄、居住地、民族、阶级、文化、婚姻、职业及宗教信仰等标志，但就其性质特征而言，人口结构类别具有自然性、社会性和地域性等特征。

（3）人口结构的变动

年龄和性别是人口结构各因素中最基本、最核心、最重要的因素，人口结构中影响最大的就是年龄结构和性别结构。理想的年龄结构应符合"人口低增长和长寿命"特征，理想的性别结构应符合"同年龄的男女性别人数相等或相近"特征。

人口结构不仅受自然环境的影响，而且还受一个国家或地区经济社会和地域文化的影响。例如，在一些重男轻女思想严重的农村地区，人们偏好男孩，男女性别比例可能会偏高；而在城市当中男女性别比例基本持平，有时可能出现女性高于男性的情况。此外，人们的生育偏好可能还受宗教文化等因素的影响。2010年，第六次全国人口普查数据显示，我国 20 岁至 29 岁的男性人口总数为 1.148 4 亿人，同年龄段女性为 1.135 8 亿人，两者只差 126 万人，整体比例趋于均衡。但是，到了 2013 年，我国人口已经出现新的变化趋势，人口结构已严重失调，人口结构性矛盾也日益显现，影响人口可持续发展，已成为当前及今后较长时期人口发展的主要矛盾和制约经济社会发展的关键因素。

当前，我国人口结构性的矛盾突出表现在"少子"化严重、总和生育率低、人口老龄化，需要从全局和战略的高度未雨绸缪，及时对人口战略和政策做出战略性抉择，进一步完善人口与经济社会政策，统筹解决人口问题，促进民族后代可持续发展，维护粮食安全，确保经济社会可持续发展。

7.2.2 人口结构变动中的养老文化

（1）"富""老"变化的养老文化

近年来，有关"富"和"老"的关系问题，经常成为人们讨论的话题。我国的养老文化也随着"富"和"老"关系的变化而不同。

1999 年后，我国开始进入老龄化社会。当时，我国人均 GDP 大致处于全球"后三分之一"，而老龄化率已接近世界"前三分之一"，"未富先老"的特征十分明显。城乡老年人中，只有 1/4 享有社会化养老保障；全国总人口中，只有 1/30 的人拥有医疗保险；贫困人口中，只有 1/13 的人被纳入政策性的兜底保障。[①]

如果以 65 岁及以上人口占总人口比重 7%、世界银行高收入门槛水平的不变价人均 GDP、人口老龄化与经济发展协调指数（AECI）±50 为三条标准，可以将"富–老"关系协调程度按从低到高顺序依次划分为"未富先老""富而过老""未富偏老""边富边老""未富不老""富而轻老""富而不老"七种类型。这七种类型，实际上都反映了我国现代人口结构的变动。应对这七种不同的老龄化社会类型，形成了"老而不富"→"且老且富"→"富而不老"的文化走势。

（2）"未来已来"的养老文化

近年来，养老驿站、医养结合、智慧养老等概念和模式的出现为养老事业开辟了新成长目标。自 1979 年开始实施计划生育到 2016 年全面放开二孩政策，在长达 38 年的时间里，我国经历了人口从爆发式增长到断崖式下跌的过程。

当 2019 年的新年钟声敲响的时刻，"10 后"已是儿童向少年迈进，"00 后"更是步入青年。而"90 后"已是"叔叔""阿姨"，"80 后"已成为"老前辈"，"70 后"更是晋级成为"爷爷""奶奶"了。于是，人们纷纷感慨："老了""真的是老了""一晃就老了"。这真应了那句话：未来已来，别说无奈。

毋庸置疑，我国的老龄化及养老所面临的问题，是人口结构变动的产物。但是，这不是简单的抚养比问题，而是人口素质和劳动生产率提升的问题。解决方法绝非提升人口出生率那么简单。原因在于，如果只是低素质人口的逆向增长，整个国家和民族的人口素质就会降低，劳动生产率的提升就难以实现，尊老、敬老、爱老、养老的文化自然也就难以形成和发展。因此，在未来已来的养老文化中，高素质人口出生率、抚养比和 AI 人工智能的发展是关键。

7.2.3 小结：在"变"与"不变"中认识养老问题

本节我们讨论了人口结构及其变动对养老问题的影响。希望本节内容的讨论，

---

① 顾严. 暂别"未富先老"，养老挑战依然严峻［N］. 中国经济导报, 2018-07-05(6).

能够帮助大家进一步认识人类社会的养老问题。

知识拓展与链接:

作为世界上最大的发展中国家，中国面临的人口老龄化及其养老保障问题的重要性显得格外突出，而中国的经济结构及其特殊的经济转型决定了中国人口老龄化及其养老问题的"重中之重"是中国农村人口的老龄化及其养老问题。

中国农民群体的角色多样性与收入的多渠道，甚至不稳定性都对农村养老保障问题构成了强有力的约束与挑战……为了满足广大老年人更丰富多样化的养老需求，家庭养老保障、集体养老、个人养老以及社会救济养老等多样化的组织制度模式都应该受到鼓励和支持，这意味着中国农村养老保障制度建设必定是一个多层次和多样化的复杂结构……

我国农村养老保险的制度目前正处于起步和探索阶段，各种经验模式不仅具有鲜明的地区特色，而且对不同角色或职业的农民群体也存在显著的差异。没有任何一种经验模式可以简单地在其他地区乃至全国进行推广。

——梁鸿、赵德余，等:《人口老龄化与中国农村养老保障制度》，上海:上海人民出版社，2008 年版，第 294-298 页。

7.3　失独老人与医疗养老保障

7.3.1　失独老人及其养老问题

（1）何谓失独老人?

顾名思义，失独老人指的是失去独生子女的老年人。家中唯一的子女不幸离世，这样的家庭被称为失独家庭。与空巢老人不同，失独老人无法期待已经死亡的子女回家，只能期盼这个国家和社会给他们多一些保障与关爱。

（2）失独老人的养老问题

失独养老和一般养老的最大区别，是失独老人家庭缺乏一般家庭所具备的子女辈对老人的孝敬和关爱，缺乏晚辈所能给予的亲情维系和心灵慰藉。失独老人可能配偶尚还健在，但他们所拥有的可能也只是彼此的相互守候和照顾。或者可能也仅仅是拥有自己已经失去的独生子女的子女，构成祖孙或外祖孙的特殊家庭关系。这样的家庭如何养老? 这是人们普遍关心的问题。

有的研究者认为，可拿"三无"老人做参照，当前"三无"老人、农村"五保"老人均由政府供养，采取分散与集中的方式解决这部分人的生活。①

失独老人是一类特殊的群体，而且失独家庭有增多趋势。2013 年中国社会科学院发布的《中国老龄事业发展报告（2013）》指出，中国将迎来第一个老年人口增长高峰，2013 年老年人口突破 2 亿大关。在 2025 年之前，老年人口将每年增长 100 万。同时，劳动年龄人口进入负增长的历史拐点，劳动力供给格局开始发生转变。2012 年中国失独家庭已超百万个，每年新增 7.6 万个失独家庭。②失独家庭与老龄化因素叠加，更加剧了失独失能老人养老问题的复杂程度。这是值得关注的。

7.3.2　失独老人的医疗养老保障

（1）失独老人容易因病致贫

全国政协的调查结果显示，50%的失独老人患有高血压、心脏病等慢性疾病；患有癌症、瘫痪等的有 15%；60%以上患有抑郁症，其中一半以上曾有过自杀倾向；因家庭发生重大变故，50%的失独家庭经济困难，月收入在 1 200 元以下；20%的失独家庭靠低保生活。③失去孩子后，失独老人们变成了游离在社会外的"特殊群体"。害怕与人沟通，神经变得脆弱而敏感，工作也难以为继。我国还没有从国家层面建立对失独老人的抚恤、养老、意外伤害和医疗保险等专项安抚制度。

独生子女去世后，父母容易自行封闭，精神濒临崩溃；而子女伤残的家庭则容易陷入经济困境。据调查，因子女伤残求医治病而导致家庭返贫的比例达 50%以上。④同时，他们的养老也是难题，因为现有的养老院、敬老院绝大多数属私营且收费昂贵。在较长的一段时间内，看病难、看病贵成为我国基本医疗保障领域面临的突出问题。

（2）失独老人养老和医疗保障的基本路径

针对我国部分失独家庭收入单一，难以承担养自身的养老费用；公办养老院严重不足，民办养老院费用过高，失独老人难入院养老；缺乏家庭温暖，空虚和孤独，难以得到心理慰藉等状况，需要从政策、组织和经济等方面精准施策，纾解失独老人的医疗养老困境。

一是加强政策支持，制定或修订相关法律法规，建立自助养老、居家养老、社区养老等养老模式，切实帮助失独老人解决养老难题。

二是提倡文明家风，进一步调整人口生育政策，积极支持和鼓励适龄男女生

① 周尧，李欣，车丽. 我国每年新增失独家庭 7.6 万个 寺院成养老选择 [EB/OL]. (2012-09-29) [2018-10-15]. http://finance.people.com.cn/insurance/BIG5/n/2012/0929/c59941-19155549-2.html.

② 佚名. "失独"家庭亟待精神赡养 [EB/OL]. (2013-05-13) [2018-10-15]. http://www.wenming.cn/wmpl_pd/shzt/201305/t20130514_1223799.shtml.

③ 廖君，周莹珣，吴晓颖，等. 老无所依?走近中国失独家庭 [EB/OL]. (2012-07-18) [2018-10-15]. http://www.banyuetan.org/chcontent/sz/szgc/2012718/55652.shtml.

④ 晓程. 百万家庭破裂了 [J]. 当代工人（C版），2012, (5): 10.

育两个孩子，倡导支持和鼓励失独父母收养孩子，从心理上排解老人孤寂，从根本上减少失独老人产生。

三是加强组织扶持，建立针对失独老人的专门养老和保障机构或部门，通过政府购买社会工作服务等方式，开展失独老人的心理疏导和精神康复等活动，使失独老人老有所依、老有所养。

四是加强经济救济，不断提高失独老人救助扶助标准，努力改善失独家庭的经济状况。

五是加强社区医院智能化建设，推进传统居家养老向自助养老、居家养老、社区养老+智慧医疗养老等医养结合养老模式的转型。

7.3.3　小结：如何让失独老人能够"乐养"？

在本节中，我们讨论了失独老人及其养老问题，讨论了失独老人的医疗养老保障路径。希望通过本节内容的讨论，能够帮助大家进一步认识人类社会的养老问题。

7.4　空巢老人与医养结合

7.4.1　空巢老人及其面临的问题

（1）何谓空巢老人？

顾名思义，空巢老人一般是指子女离家后的老年人。他们没有子女照顾、单居或夫妻双居，一般分为三种情况：一是无儿无女无老伴的孤寡老人，二是有子女但与其分开单住的老人，三是儿女远在外地，不得已寂守空巢的老人。

当子女由于工作、学习、结婚等原因而离家后，独守空巢的中老年夫妇因此而产生的心理失调症状，称为家庭空巢综合征。

空巢现象是一个全球性难题，发达国家独居及夫妇空巢的家庭比例高达70%～80%。随着我国逐步进入老龄化社会以及城镇化建设的加快，今后空巢老人将越来越多，空巢期也会明显延长，老年人面临的问题将更加趋于严峻。这是我国人口结构变化和社会转型的产物。

（2）空巢老人面临的主要问题

空巢老人面临的主要问题包括以下几个方面。

1）生活照料。由于子女长期不在身边，年纪大和体弱多病的空巢老人的日常照料和服务成为一个主要问题。目前我国的专业化养老服务水平不高，既缺乏专业的管理公司，又缺乏专业的养老护理员，只能靠空巢老人自己照顾自己。

2）社会保障。目前我国农村的养老保障水平普遍不高，空巢老人可能需要通过自己劳动挣取生活费用，偏远山村更是如此。城市的空巢老人的生活状况可能相对好一些，他们一般有房、有独立经济能力、有单独的生活空间，生活质量相对较高。

3）精神慰藉。空巢老人的子女不在身边，生活比较孤单。空巢老人时常表现出的症状是心情郁闷、沮丧、孤寂，食欲减低，睡眠失调，平时愁容不展，长吁短叹，甚至流泪哭泣，常有自责倾向，认为自己没有完全尽到做父母的责任，有对不起子女的地方。另外也有责备子女不够孝顺的倾向，觉得子女对父母不孝，只顾自己的利益而让父母独守空巢。数据显示，空巢老人中存在心理问题的比例达到 60%，达到疾病程度，需要医学关注、心理干预的空巢老人，比例占到 10%～20%。[1]调查显示，社会针对老年人的电视节目少、健身娱乐设施不足，导致老年人的精神生活贫乏，加之空巢老人社会活动减少、子女关怀不够，容易引发精神疾病。[2]这些问题带有普遍性，是现代社会转型和社会变迁的一种反映。

7.4.2　医养结合的空巢老人养老保障

（1）空巢老人需要医养结合

养老、看病是老人必须面对的话题。由此出现了医养结合的养老服务新模式。所谓"医"，是指康复、保健、医疗、疾病诊治和护理以及临终关怀等一系列服务。"养"则包括生活照护、精神心理及文化活动服务等。为此，养老机构和医疗机构应该在社区中无缝对接，真正实现"有病治病，无病康养"。2009 年，上海建工医院创办了核定床位 180 张的上海建阳养老院，形成了"小病不出门（养老院），大病不出院（建工医院）"的医养结合服务特色。2013 年，上海建工医院与上海建峰职业技术学院合作创办了核定床位 230 张的上海建峰护理院，与上海建工医院建立会诊和转诊机制，突出医护结合服务特色。上海建工医院、建阳养老院、建峰护理院 3 家医疗养护机构各有优势，又互相帮衬、协同发展，提供了解决老年人养老、医疗、护理的实践模式。[3]政府应加快社区照料服务的发展，通过政策引导，鼓励市场化运作，吸引更多人参与医养结合的养老服务工作。

（2）加大力度培养医务社会工作人才

人口老龄化是世界性问题，对人类社会产生的影响持久而深刻。医学院校应该加大力度培养既懂医学知识，又熟悉长者社会工作的高级专业人才。非医学院校的社会工作专业，要与医学院校和社区医院合作，聘请医学专家和医护人员授

---

① 徐治. 空巢老人需要重视心理健康 [J]. 康颐, 2019, 74(10): 69.
② 杨洁，陈文. 我市户籍老人有近一半空巢　六成有心理问题 [EB/OL]. (2012-10-19) [2020-05-10]. http://www.cnxz.com/newscenter/2012/2012101972056.shtml.
③ 佚名. 上海建工医院：社区医疗与养老无缝对接 [EB/OL]. (2017-03-01) [2017-12-30]. http://www.rmzxb.com.cn/c/2017-03-01/1370741.shtml.

课，实现社会工作实务与医疗护理的深度融合，将养老护理人才培养纳入卫生人才发展规划，加快培养老年服务管理、医疗保健、护理康复、营养调配、心理咨询等专业人才，才能更好地满足老龄社会特别是空巢老人的需要。

（3）空巢老人更需制度"暖巢"

由于我国传统文化的影响和现实条件的制约，空巢老人更需从制度上进行"暖巢"。中共十九大提出，要"积极应对人口老龄化，构建养老、孝老、敬老政策体系和社会环境，推进医养结合，加快老龄事业和产业发展"①，进一步弘扬中华民族敬老、养老、助老的美德，完善居家养老机制，全面构建以居家为基础、社区为依托、机构为支撑的空巢老人安全关爱服务体系，有效预防空巢老人意外死亡后无人发现的事件发生，实现老年人老有所养、老有所乐、老有所医。"我国已经进入老龄化社会。让老年人老有所养、老有所依、老有所乐、老有所安，关系社会和谐稳定。"要"大力发展老龄事业，让所有老年人都能有一个幸福美满的晚年"②。政府和社会组织应大力推进居家养老模式，即以社区为平台，整合社区内各种服务资源，为空巢老人提供助餐、助洁、助浴、助医等服务。

（4）推行"互联网+医养结合"的空巢老人养老服务

随着互联网技术的发展，"互联网+医养结合"的空巢老人智慧养老服务已经成为现实。

如今，越来越多的养老机构与医疗机构合作建立医疗网络信息平台。他们应用互联网、物联网、云计算、人工智能、可穿戴设备等新技术，建立"互联网＋健康医疗""人工智能＋健康医疗"服务，完善支付和信用、健康管理与促进体系，推广在线医疗服务新模式。通过智能镜分析用户日常健康数据，检测体重、睡眠质量、脂肪率、水量、骨量、血压、体温等人体的微小数据，进而分析数据，生成检测报告与建议，全方位关注身体健康数据。与此同时，通过发展老年电子商务、老年互联网金融、老年互联网教育等新业态，为空巢老人提供老年人常见疾病跟踪监控、定位、紧急呼叫、网上购物、远程情感关怀、远程文娱、远程文艺交流等各类服务。这样，通过"互联网+医养结合+居家养老"的多维联动，让智慧养老解决空巢老人的养老问题。

7.4.3　小结：如何让失独老人能够"乐养"和"安养"？

本节我们讨论了空巢老人及其医养结合和智慧养老等问题，希望通过本节内容的讨论，能够帮助大家进一步认识人类社会的养老问题。

---

① 习近平. 习近平谈治国理政: 第三卷［M］. 北京: 外文出版社, 2020: 38.
② 习近平. 习近平谈治国理政: 第三卷［M］. 北京: 外文出版社, 2020: 345.

知识拓展与链接：

社会保险最能体现自保与他保相结合、公平与效率相结合等现代社会保障事业运行的原则，适合市场经济的需要，更为广大投保对象所接受。当然，享受社会保险是有严格的条件限制的，养老、医疗、失业、生育、工伤、残障、死亡、家属津贴等项目皆然。不符合相应条件的成员，则只能通过社会救助实现生存保障。随着社会从传统向现代的转型和市场经济的发展，符合与接受社会保险的成员将愈益上升，并成为社会成员的主体，接受社会救助的对象将愈来愈少（当然亦不会完全消失）。至于社会福利，像"福利国家"所实行的那样，属于高层次的社会保障内容，运行中尚有一系列问题未能得到解决，最根本的是它妨碍了经济效率的实现，西方国家目前正针对庞大的福利体系进行改革。鉴于此，我国社会保障体系的未来走向，不能以"福利国家"为目标，而只能以社会保险为核心。

——李迎生：《社会保障与社会结构转型：二元社会保障体系研究》，北京：中国人民大学出版社，2001年版，第193-194页。

8 生和死：人类社会的终极关怀

8.1 生命观及其现代转变

8.1.1 生命观

（1）生命观的含义

简单地说，生命观就是人们看待生命的态度、原则和立场。恩格斯从辩证唯物主义的观点给生命下了一个科学的定义：生命是蛋白体的存在方式。这种存在方式本质上就是蛋白质和核酸的复合体。生命的本质是蛋白体的同化作用和异化作用的对立统一和矛盾运动。生命过程是蛋白体不断自我更新、自我复制、自我调节的过程。蛋白体的同化与异化和不停地跟外界进行物质、能量、信息的交换是生命存在、发展的基本条件和根本动力。蛋白体内部的同化和异化、遗传与变异的矛盾运动，即新陈代谢、自我繁衍是生命发展的根本规律。①这样的定义概括了从最简单的生命到人类生命的根本特征。

从人类历史发展整体看，生命观反映了人类社会的文明程度和人类对自身的认识程度。越在人类社会早期，人们对生命观的认识就越模糊。随着现代医学技术的发展和生命科学研究的进步，人类对生命起源问题的探寻也不断取得新进展。

（2）马克思主义的生命观

马克思主义认为，生命观是致力于实现人的整体性生命存在的一个完整的理论架构，是自然生命、社会生命和精神生命"三位一体"的整体性生命观。它涉及生命存在和生命发展等一系列根本性问题，具有多种需求的生命需要、资本主义私有制导致的生命异化和通过实践手段进行的生命解放等特点。②

马克思主义生命观的形成与确立大致经历了四个阶段，并涵括了人的生命存在的四个层次：第一阶段是在《德谟克利特的自然哲学和伊壁鸠鲁的自然哲学的差别》时期，以"人的自我意识具有最高神性"为理性坐标的生命存在；第二阶段是在《1844年经济学哲学手稿》时期，以"自由自觉的感性对象性活动"为内在根据的生命存在；第三阶段是在《关于费尔巴哈的提纲》时期，以"社会关系

---

① 中共中央马克思恩格斯列宁斯大林著作编译局. 马克思恩格斯文集 [M]. 第九卷. 北京: 人民出版社, 2009: 37-150.
② 杨利利. 马克思生命观的理论意蕴及当代启示 [J]. 阴山学刊, 2019, 32(4): 72-77.

的总和"为现实表现的生命存在；第四阶段是在《德意志意识形态》时期，以"具体的生产生活方式"为辩证逻辑的生命存在。①马克思的生命观从整体性存在角度确证了人的生命意义和价值，构成了马克思独特的生命内涵和生命意蕴。②③

8.1.2 现代生命观的转变

在古代社会中，由于人们对生命等自然现象了解不深和医学技术不够发达，人们对生命的看法和态度往往带有一定的神秘色彩，进而形成一套自成体系的生命礼俗文化。例如，不少国家历史上都存在过交感巫术求子习俗。

在传统的农耕社会中，子女往往是家庭劳动力的主要来源。因此，生育子女便构成了不少国家或地区婚姻家庭的一项任务。中国古代社会曾经盛行的"不孝有三，无后为大"的宗法观念，成为妇女婚后多年未能养育男性子嗣被休弃的首要缘由。能否生育或者生男生女是夫妻双方的问题，中国古代社会将此问题归咎于女方是不恰当甚至是完全错误的。

在现代社会中，随着科学技术的发展和医疗卫生条件的改善，人们对生育及其文化有了更多、更深的认识。主要表现在以下几点。

首先，人们已经能够科学地认识到能否生育或生男生女是夫妻双方共同作用的结果，而不只是女方的事情。这已被现代医学所证明。

其次，优生优育已经成为人们的普遍追求。因此，婚前进行医学检查已经成为现代社会的新风尚。这也是现代社会文明在人类自身再生产中的一个重要体现。

最后，由于传统观念的影响，一些人利用现代医学技术，人为干扰人类生命的自然孕育。这是违背自然规律的，也是违法的。例如，一些人利用 B 超对孕妇进行胎儿的性别鉴定，或者使用一些药物改变精子或卵子结构使其双胞化，等等，都属非法行为。

8.1.3 小结：生命观在社会变迁中转变

本节我们讨论了生命观以及现代社会中的生命观转变等问题，分析了现代科技对于生命观的影响，希望能够帮助大家进一步认识人类社会的终极关怀问题。

知识拓展与链接：

个人、家庭和社会是三种并立而又相互区别的价值。这三种价值所涉及的范围是从小到大排列的。在传统社会和现代社会中，这三种价值重要性的排序是不同的。

① 张懿, 夏文斌. 马克思生命观形成与确立的历史考察 [J]. 东南学术, 2019, (5): 72-79.
② 张懿, 夏文斌. 论马克思的生命观对西方生命哲学的三重超越 [J]. 广东社会科学, 2018, (2): 68-74.
③ 张懿, 夏文斌. 马克思生命观的历史、理论与现实 [J]. 青海社会科学, 2018, (5): 72-80.

在传统中国社会中，家庭的价值最重，个人和社会较轻；在现代中国社会中，这三种价值的轻重排序在一些人那里正在发生变化。

——李银河、郑宏霞：《一爷之孙：中国家庭关系的个案研究》，上海：上海文化出版社，2001 年版，第 179 页。

8.2　现代养生与中医文化

8.2.1　养生与养生文化

（1）何谓养生？

养生原指道家通过各种方法颐养生命、增强体质、预防疾病，从而达到延年益寿的一种医事活动。养即调养、保养、补养之意；生即生命、生存、生长之意。

现代意义上的"养生"指的是根据人的生命过程规律主动进行物质与精神的身心养护活动。也可以说，养生就是保养五脏，使生命得以绵延。

（2）养生文化

养生文化是指人们在长期的生活实践中所创造的有关养护身体、生命的物质文化和精神文化。其中，有关养生的理论典籍和实用方法，是养生文化的主要内容。我国的养生文化源远流长，有着数千年的历史，在秦汉以前就已形成了基本的理论思想与方法体系，并在发展过程中融合了自然科学、人文科学和社会科学诸多因素，集中华民族数千年养生文化于一身，在世界养生文化中占有重要地位。

在我国先秦时期的诸子百家当中，老子、庄子轻形重神，认为"气道合，身不朽，长生不老"；认为"人法地，地法天，天法道，道法自然"。

作为我国医学成就的重要代表，《黄帝内经》更是提出了整体健康、顺应自然、摄情养志、形神兼修、重在预防的养生思想，强调"不治已病治未病"。

汉朝时期，《淮南子》提出了养生经世、报德终年的"体道"养生思想，强调形、神、气"三位一体"。可见，先秦至秦汉时期，中国古人养生注重内外兼修，形神俱备，通过行气、服食、导引等方法，强调德性双修，对我国传统养生文化影响很大。

（3）现代养生文化

现代社会是工业社会，工业社会对人类社会生活的影响是广泛而深刻的。除了产品丰富、经济发展之外，工业社会也给人类带来紧张、焦虑、不安、拜金、物欲膨胀等负面影响。另外，工业时代的科技伦理问题也成为人们担心的一个问题。因此，绿色、环保、低碳成为人们追求的目标，心态、饮食、运动、睡眠、理疗、药物等，成为现代人养生无法回避的重要难题。绿色、有机、简朴、休闲、亲近自然、放松身心、放飞灵魂等，已经成为现代养生文化的标志。

8.2.2 现代生活中的中医养生

（1）中医文化中的养生思想

中医是我国的传统医学，从最早的《黄帝内经》《神农本草经》到《伤寒杂病论》《脉经》《诸病源候论》，再到明代著名医学家李时珍于 1578 年写成的《本草纲目》，都是我国古代中医发展的经典著作。中医养生是通过各种方法颐养生命、增强体质、预防疾病，从而达到延年益寿的一种医事活动。中医养生的目的是预防疾病，治未病，因而重在强调整体性和系统性。

从思想上看，中医养生主张：未病先防、未老先养；天人相应、形神兼具；调整阴阳、补偏救弊；动静有常、和谐适度。因此，对于不同的人和不同的季节，中医都有不同的养生要求。

中医认为对于男性来说，养生根本在于养肾护肝。在中医文化中，肾主水，肝主木，水生木，因而肾乃肝脏之本。因此，中医提倡养肾要侧重在养精蓄锐，要求寡欲、节劳、息怒、戒酒、慎味。

对于女性来说，中医则强调补气养血，适当运动，气血平稳则经络相通，百病不存；心情舒畅，郁气自解，身心自然俱佳。

对于老年人来说，由于身体机能相对退化，养生方式方法也有所讲究，不贪精白米面，不贪脂肪肉类，不贪坚硬食物，避免积食或低血糖，不贪热食快食，不贪杯饮酒。

中医强调，人的五脏（心、肝、脾、肺、肾）六腑（小肠、大肠、胆、胃、膀胱、三焦）相互配合，五脏为主，六腑为辅，才能共同完成人体的各种功能。由此出现了人体五脏六腑的表里关系：肝与胆相表里，心与小肠相表里，脾与胃相表里，肺与大肠相表里，肾与膀胱相表里。另外，中医文化还受五行相生相克和子午流柱等观念的影响。①

（2）现代养生中的中医文化

1）健身养生。健身器材本身是工业产品。人们利用健身器材进行体育锻炼，是城市居民尤其是年轻人常见的养生方式。无论是为了健美还是为了减肥，其实都是为了达到传统中医养生文化所主张"形神兼修"的形体美感。因此，健身养生倍受城市青年人青睐。

2）食补养生。现代生活节奏很快，速食和膨化食品增多，给人们身体健康带来许多不利的影响。中医食疗根据季节变化而补给，可为工业时代的养生提供借鉴。一年四季，春生、夏长、秋收、冬藏。春天是万物复苏的季节，是养生的最

---

① 例如，肝胆属木、心和小肠属火、脾胃属土、肺和大肠属金、肾和膀胱属水，"火生土"（心功能正常，可使脾胃功能正常），"金生水"（肺功能好，则肾正常），等等。子时（23:00—01:00）胆经旺，丑时（01:00—03:00）肝经旺，寅时（03:00—05:00）肺经旺，卯时（05:00—07:00）大肠经旺，辰时（07:00—09:00）胃经旺，巳时（09:00—11:00）脾经旺，午时（11:00—13:00）心经旺，未时（13:00—15:00）小肠经旺，申时（15:00—17:00）膀胱经旺，酉时（17:00—19:00）肾经旺，戌时（19:00—21:00）心包经旺，亥时（21:00—23:00）三焦经旺。

佳时机。中医认为，春养于肝，夏养于心，秋养于肺，冬养于肾。所以，春天进补，重在养肝，宜选用较清淡、温和且扶助正气、补益元气的食物，同时还应根据不同的体质来调养。

夏天进补，重在养心，应该以清补、健脾、祛暑、化湿为原则，一般以清淡的滋补食品为主。

初秋食物，宜减辛增酸，以养肝气；中秋炎热，应多吃新鲜少油的食品和含维生素和蛋白质较多的食物。晚秋时节，应多吃富含蛋白质、镁、钙等营养素的食物，这样可以有效地预防心脑血管疾病的发生。

现代医学认为，冬季是一年中最寒冷的季节，万物处于封藏状态，是一年中最适合饮食调理与进补的时期。俗话说"三九补一冬，来年无病痛"，这是有一定道理的。

冬季进补，注意养阳，以温补为主。形体偏瘦、性情急躁、易于激动者，应以"淡补"为主，禁食辛辣；形体丰腴、肌肉松弛者，忌食寒湿、冷腻、辛凉之物；脑力工作者，宜多吃富含蛋白质、维生素和微量元素的食物。

3）清心静养。工业社会本质上是物质的社会、消费的社会，它刺激着人们对财富和身份地位的追求，给人们带来贪婪、焦虑、不安浮躁和急功近利等负面影响，需要人们进行心理调适，节欲保精，淡泊名利，调息养气，清心静养。

8.2.3　小结：现代社会中"养生""养身"还是"养心"？

本节我们讨论了养生和养生文化，以及现代生活中的中医养生等问题，从中医文化整体观角度分析了现代工业社会中的养生、养身和养心的均衡和谐问题。希望通过本节内容的学习和讨论，能够帮助大家进一步认识人类社会的生死问题。

知识拓展与链接：

传统文化一向将个人有机体看作是一个小宇宙，因此也以阴阳对立的观念来解释小宇宙的均衡和谐，而表现这阴阳对立现象最明显的就是食物中的"冷"与"热"的观念，以及其延伸的"进补"观念的普遍流行。

……这样的阴阳冷热观念起源甚古远，所以不但影响中国人的食物药物观念、食物习惯、烹调方法，同时也与中医药联系在一起，而成为中国人日常生活中最重要的一个特征，不仅在国内至为普遍，在海外中国人社会也因物质供应的富足而更为流行起来。

　　　　　　——李亦园：《人类的视野》，上海：上海文艺出版社，1996 年版，第 152 页。

8.3 死亡文化及其城乡差异

8.3.1 死亡与丧葬文化

（1）何谓死亡？

临床医学上的死亡，通常是指人的延髓处于深度抑制和功能丧失状态，各种反射消失、心脏停搏、呼吸停止和脑死亡。民间认为的死亡更多关注呼吸是否停止，即是否还有"气"。这其实是不科学的。因为呼吸暂停，但人的脑功能不一定停止。因此，不能以呼吸有无来判断一个人的生死。死亡是生存的反面，它意味着丧失生命或生命终止、生存停止。

美国的一项研究表明，当人类心脏停止跳动时，大脑还会继续运作。换言之，人类大脑会意识到自己已经死亡这个事实。

据了解，我国传统上一直以心跳呼吸停止、反射消失作为判定死亡的标准，即通常所说的"心死亡"。但近年来，脑死亡开始逐渐被社会接受，是指全脑功能包括脑干功能不可逆的终止。人体的呼吸中枢位于脑干，如果脑干发生结构性破坏，会直接导致呼吸功能停止，无论采取何种医疗手段都无法挽救患者生命。目前，全球已有100多个国家和地区正式承认脑死亡，但在我国尚未立法，仍存争议。

（2）丧葬文化

丧葬总是和死亡相关联。不同国家、不同地区、不同民族，在不同的时空中可能会形成不同的丧葬文化。

我国各地各民族的丧葬习俗不尽相同。这种不同，既有历史文化的影响，也有宗教信仰文化的规制。我国未全面实行尸骨火化的殡葬改革之前，"入土为安"成为土葬文化的基本表达。"入土为安"的土葬一般包括停尸、择日、报丧、招魂、送魂、净身、入殓、吊唁、哭丧、出殡、下葬等仪式过程。信仰伊斯兰教的少数民族的土葬，则受伊斯兰文化的影响；过去信仰天主教或基督教的信教群众的土葬也有别于中国传统的土葬习俗。此外，我国一些民族历史上还存在过火葬、水葬、树葬、悬棺葬、崖葬和二次葬等丧葬方式。

（3）我国现代丧葬文化的变迁

新中国成立以后，国家为了节约土地，杜绝疾病蔓延，规定除部分信仰伊斯兰教的少数民族外，其余一律采用火葬。因此，人死后尸体被送往殡仪馆冰冻存放。殡仪馆会根据死者家属的要求，设置灵堂，为死者举行遗体告别仪式和追悼会，随后用"专用车"把遗体送到火葬场，经大火焚烧后化为骨灰。死者家属可以把骨灰放入骨灰盒保留，也可把骨灰撒入大海或用于植树等，回归大自然。

8.3.2　中国城乡的死亡与丧葬文化差异

（1）20世纪90年代以来中国城乡居民主要疾病死亡率的变化

2015年的《中国心血管报告》数据显示，我国心血管病的死亡率近年来持续走高，大幅高于肿瘤、呼吸疾病、损伤等病症。2014年农村心血管病死亡率为295.63/10万，城市心血管病死亡率为261.99/10万，心血管病占居民疾病死亡率在农村为44.60%，城市为42.51%。农村心血管病死亡率从2009年起超过并持续高于城市水平。

由于城乡二元经济、社会、文化等结构的影响，我国城乡居民的死亡文化也表现出较为明显的差异。

（2）中国城乡居民的死亡与丧葬文化差异

1）乡村居民对"死"的认知基本上还停留在传统的"死"的认知（即"断气"或"呼吸停止"），城市居民对"死"的认知则更符合临床医学的"心死亡"，部分居民越来越接受"脑死亡"的说法。

2）乡村居民仍然受到"入土为安"传统思想的影响，即便死者遗体火化，死者亲属也仍然倾向将骨灰坛埋入土中；城市土地等资源稀缺，墓地单位价格甚至超过城市居民住宅的单位面积价格，因此，部分城市居民纷纷感慨"死不起"。有的城市居民干脆委托墓园存放管理，每年清明节"借"出来拜祭后再"归还"墓园存放。由于墓园是公共空间，在公共空间中进行"私人祭拜"，使得传统的丧葬祭祀习俗也趋于简化。

3）乡村社会对非正常的意外死亡较为忌讳，如果在家外或村外死亡，死者遗体一般是不能抬进家里或村里的，而是在家外、村外处理好之后安葬，否则会被视为不吉利。城市居民则没这么多"讲究"。当然，随着乡村火化等殡葬习俗改革的推行，骨灰安放和处置可能与传统"入土为安"的土葬习俗有所不同。不过，这葬俗变化本身，也是现代工业化影响的结果。或者说，这是工业化在中国现代城乡丧葬习俗变迁上的反映。

（3）选择与尊严：中国城乡居民面对死亡的文化选择

受中国传统孝文化的影响，子女或晚辈对长辈的孝顺有时也表现在对身患重疾的父母或长辈的治疗态度上。

对于身患重疾的父母或长辈来说，子女或晚辈到底是变卖家产、竭尽所能甚至举借巨债为其频繁治疗，"折腾"病人，还是听从病人的意见，进行"保守"治疗甚至放弃治疗呢？这个问题如今越来越引起人们的关注和理性思考。

有的患者子女明明知道即使花费重金巨款也难以治愈重疾或绝症患者，但是由于"孝"的观念而"明知不可为而为之"，终究也是回天乏术，"人财两空"。重疾或绝症患者在接受手术或治疗的过程中可能也倍感身心俱痛，苦不堪言。患者子女只从自己尽孝的角度要求医生"过度医疗"，但是他们有没有考虑过患者自身的意愿？患者也有选择的权利。如何让重疾或绝症患者有尊严地治疗或离去，这是现代社会中的一道难题。

生存权是最基本的人权。死亡权是不是也是人的一项基本权利呢？一个身患重疾或绝症的患者有没有权利决定自己应该治疗还是放弃治疗？应该采取哪种治疗方式呢？患者与子女之间虽然有亲属关系，但涉及生命权利的问题，还是要尊重当事人的意见，如果当事人希望保守治疗，子女就不能只考虑自己尽孝而为患者"过度医疗"，如果患者声明放弃治疗，那么患者子女也应该顺从其意，而不能"死马当作活马医"。这才是文明社会的气质。

值得注意的是，2013 年，北京生前预嘱推广协会（LWPA）在创办于 2006 年的"选择与尊严"（Choice and Dignity）公益网站的基础上成立。该网站是中国（除港澳台外）第一家推广"尊严死"的公益网站，它推广"尊严死""生前预嘱"理念，使"生前预嘱"文本《我的五个愿望》具有可实施性和可操作性，使公民能够真正通过"生前预嘱"实现"尊严死"。该协会主张：在不可治愈的伤病末期，放弃抢救和不使用生命支持系统。让死亡既不提前，也不拖后，而是自然来临。在这个过程中，应最大限度尊重、符合并实现本人意愿，尽量有尊严地告别人生。毋庸置疑，这是我国社会的一大进步。

8.3.3 小结：死亡文化的不同时空差异及其表达

本节我们讨论了死亡和丧葬文化，以及我国城乡的死亡文化差异等问题。希望通过本节内容的学习和讨论，能够帮助大家进一步认识人类社会的生死问题。

8.4 不同文化中的死亡观

8.4.1 中国传统文化中的死亡观

传统文化与文化传统不同。前者强调从古至今流传下来的文化，后者则是强调文化形成过程中的源头及其流传过程中的此消彼长或混融。就中国传统文化而言，它是指中国历史上形成的以儒家思想为核心，并经历代儒学家们不断改造而绵延至今的文化。从春秋战国时期的"百花齐放"到汉代董仲舒"罢黜百家，独尊儒术"，再到魏晋南北朝时期儒、释、道"三教合一"，并经隋唐、宋元、明清时代的发展，中国传统文化实际上包含了儒家思想、道家思想和佛教思想在内的"百家思想"。儒家思想不是宗教，但有的人却把它视为"宗教"或者"类宗教"。宗教处理的是人与神的关系，而儒家思想更多地涉及人与人的关系。

（1）儒家思想中的死亡观

儒家思想认为，死亡是一种自然现象，对人的生死问题应该超脱一些。《论语·颜渊》中即有"自古皆有死,民无信不立"之言,也有"死生有命,富贵在天"的表述。

孔子在回答其弟子子路"死事如何"之问时说:"未知生,焉知死?"他强调关心生而不必想到死,求知生而不必求知死。儒家"亚圣"孟子也说:"夭寿不二,修身以俟之,所以立命也。"他强调人们不必过于关注和计较寿命之长短,致力于一己之修身立命就好。孟子还提出"正命"与"非正命"的观点,"尽其道而死者,正命也;桎梏死者,非正命也"。他主张为自己的道德理念和信念而死,而不应因逆道非道而死。

从总体上看,儒家也未偏离生而喜、死而悲的情感套路。《论语》记载,颜渊死,孔子深叹:"天丧予!天丧予!"感到痛苦万分。

从个体生命来说,人的生命只有一次,人死而不能复生,因而儒家非常注重和讲究对死者的哀思和丧祭。儒家讲孝道:"事死如事生,事亡如事存,孝之至也。"儒家认为应当视已故的先人如同仍活着一般。受此影响,人们往往把丧事当作大事来操办。《孟子·离娄下》:"养生者不足以当大事,惟送死可以当大事。"这样,"当大事"就成为儒家"事死如事生"的一种文化标志和行动实践。

(2)佛教的死亡观

众所周知,佛教强调轮回。佛教看淡生死,看破无常。"死,是人生的一件大事。佛教认为:生、老、病、死,人之常情,死并非生命的结束,只是另一场轮回的开始,故说'生死一如',要我们看淡生死,进而看破无常。"[1]信仰佛教的人同样存在生死问题。星云大师说,"信仰佛教并非就没有生死问题,而是要人看破生死!生和死如影随形,不仅凡人生了要死,死了再生,生生死死,死死生生,生死不已",信仰佛教的人"一样有喜怒哀乐,一样有生死问题"。[2]"死亡不足惧,面对死亡,要顺其自然,要处之泰然。"[3]"人出生时,就注定死是必然的结果,所以人之生也,都要死亡,又有何可喜?人之死也,如冬尽春来,又有何可悲?生死一体,生了要死,死了再生,生生死死,死死生生,循环而已。"[4]这种生死观,正是佛教轮回永生思想的反映。

(3)道教的死亡观

道教是我国的本土宗教,产生于东汉末年,追求长生不老,认为人们只要善于养生,则可以成仙,从而长生不老。

道教主张生死同质。老子说:"人法地,地法天,天法道,道法自然。"[5]在老子看来,人和自然万物的生死变化都来自阴阳二气的结合,"道生一,一生二,二

---

① 星云大师. 人间佛教语录: 中册 [M]. 台北: 香海文化事业有限公司,2008: 236.
② 星云大师. 人间佛教语录: 中册 [M]. 台北: 香海文化事业有限公司,2008: 244.
③ 星云大师. 人间佛教语录: 中册 [M]. 台北: 香海文化事业有限公司,2008: 251.
④ 星云大师. 人间佛教语录: 中册 [M]. 台北: 香海文化事业有限公司,2008: 253.
⑤ 陈鼓应. 老子注译及评价 [M]. 北京: 中华书局,2016: 159.

生三，三生万物。万物负阴而抱阳，冲气以为和"①。此外，道教又主张生死必然和死生一体，与"道"合一，进而达致死而不亡的理想境界，具有"乐死""善死"的美学意境。

总之，面对死亡问题，道教不是用自然规律来自我安慰，或是寻求精神层面上的不朽来减轻死亡带来的焦虑，而是相信人可以利用智慧参悟出世间造化运转的道理，可以摄取天地循环流转的力量，逆转生命的结局。

虽然道教提倡的"长生久视，羽化登仙"的生死观念只是一种虚幻的想象，但它包含着一种热爱生命、充实生命、升华生命和超越生命的意涵。②道教的"入世"与佛教的"出世"形成鲜明对比，道教的"生死异途"和佛教的"三世轮回"也不同。就生死来说，道教和佛教、基督教等宗教不同之处在于，道教的神仙世界跟我们所在的这个世界是统一的，从这个世界到那个世界去可以是一个自然生命的延续，而不需要一个死亡的过程。道教的生死观植根于对生命的渴望以及对人世间的挚爱，希望能够长存人间，体现了中华民族追求人生幸福的现世主义态度。由于儒、佛、道思想在魏晋南北朝时期出现"合流"端倪，中国传统的生死观也受到影响。

8.4.2　西方宗教文化中的死亡观

基督教认为死亡是人类生命的必然过程。基督徒认为，死亡是一段人生旅程，不是人生的幻灭，更不是人生的终结。

基督教视死为"新生"，这种"生"不是"轮回式的再生"，而是从今生过渡到天国、从暂时过渡到永恒、从异土过渡到故乡的"生"。

《圣经》论述人的死是土（身体）归于土，灵归于赐灵的上帝。人身体的本质是土，来自土必须归土，这是尘世肉身的回归，灵魂来自上帝却要归回到赐灵的上帝，这是灵魂的返乡。但是，基督教的"回归"或"归回"与佛教的"轮回"是不同的。

实际上，任何一种宗教都力图回答人存在的终极性问题，即关于死亡的问题。据研究，基督教对于死亡问题的答案建立在希腊哲学和希伯来信仰基础之上。基督教神学认为，无论是身体死亡，还是灵性死亡或永远死亡，其实都是罪的必然结果，但耶稣基督却以自己的死亡去打破死亡对人的权势，并以基督教神学的方式诠释基督教的生死观。③

---

① 陈鼓应. 老子注译及评价 [M]. 北京: 中华书局, 2016: 225.

② 赵博超. 道教的生死观 [N]. 中国社会科学报, 2018-03-20(4).

③ 宗晓兰. 死亡是生命的终结吗?——简论基督宗教的死亡观[J]. 西南民族大学学报（人文社科版）, 2015, 36(9): 81-87.

8.4.3　小结：人神关系在生命历程中的文化表达

本节我们讨论了死亡和丧葬文化，对不同时空当中的死亡文化及其差异也做了简单的分析。希望本节内容的讨论，能够帮助大家进一步认识人类社会的生死问题。

知识拓展与链接：

老病并不可惧，可惧的是少壮不努力，等到老病时带着空白的一生随着草木腐朽；死亡也不可悲，可悲的是生前不知奉献社会，等到临死才带着满腔遗憾，迈向不可知的未来。

——星云大师：《人间佛教论文集（上册）》，台北：香海文化事业有限公司，2008年版，第698页。

---

9 孝和祭：人类文化的时空差异

9.1 孝文化及其现代变迁

9.1.1 中国传统的孝文化

中国是一个讲究孝道的国家。有关孝的思想观念及其行动实践，都构成了中国传统孝文化的基本内容。正所谓"百善孝为先""孝乃善之本"。据学者们研究，孝文化萌芽于尧舜时代，《史记·五帝本记》曰："舜二十岁以孝闻名。"中国二十四孝"孝感动天"篇记述，舜孝顺父母，友爱兄弟。尧帝知舜仁孝，便以女嫁之。汉代以孝治天下，孝悌成为做人的行为规范。

秦汉时期，《孝经》继承和发展孔子、曾子和孟子等儒家孝道思想，成为儒家孝道文化的集大成者，对中国传统孝文化产生了十分重要的影响。

《孝经·开宗明义》提出："夫孝，始于事亲，中于事君，终于立身。"它十分明确地将行孝与"事君"结合在一起，把"事亲"与"事君"混同起来，"事君"成了孝道的不可或缺的内容，这是孝进一步政治化的表现。

此外，《孝经》把孝分为"五等之孝""天子之孝""诸侯之孝""卿大夫之孝""士之孝""庶人之孝"，分五章讨论，体现了孝道的不同层次。

总体上看，《孝经》思想的主题或最大特点是孝的泛化、政治化，甚至神秘化。《孝经》将以孝治天下描绘成一幅诱人的图景，"先王有至德要道，以顺天下，民用和睦，上下无怨"。《孝经·孝治》指出，假若能够以孝治天下，便会得到"万国之欢心""百姓之欢心"，达到"天下和平"、灾害不生、祸乱不作的地步。这部不足两千字的《孝经》，多次讲到"治"和"顺"，行孝道，就能"治天下""顺天下"，这是有其深刻的历史背景的。

我们知道，春秋战国时期进入了我国思想史上的"轴心时代"，人们的思想文化多元，出现了所谓的"礼乐崩坏"的局面。秦以武力统一六国之后，一反西周奴隶制下的礼乐文明，在统治思想上推行法家学说，企图以法的精神建立新的社会秩序，结果却空前激化了社会矛盾，很快走向了灭亡之路。西汉统治者总结秦亡的教训，经过一段时间的摸索和酝酿，终于选择了以儒家思想为主干，同时兼采各家思想的适用部分作为自己的统治思想，其中"以孝治天下"是其思想的重要组成部分。这样，孝就被纳入封建道德体系中，开始成为封建家长制专制统治的思想基础。这时的孝已越出了家庭伦理的范围，成为中国传统社会在经济、政治、文化生活中具有贯通性、统领性的道德意识。

在"家国同构"的中国古代社会中，孝文化成为宗法制度的重要内容。西汉以后，我国的封建孝道并无太大变化。从孝观念的历史演变过程中，可以看出，我国的孝文化经历了从祭祀祖先的宗教伦理到家庭伦理，再到政治伦理的转变过程。在这个过程中，孝观念的内容在不断蜕变，其中不合理因素愈来愈多、消极因素被引向极端。这是值得人们注意和反思的。

9.1.2 孝文化的现代变迁

有的人说，中国传统的孝文化主要与农业社会相联系，现代工业社会中的孝文化由于人们生产、生活方式转型而发生了变迁。这种变迁主要表现在以下几点。

（1）养亲和敬亲方式方法发生变化

传统孝观念不仅要求子女对父母尽心奉养，更强调子女对父母要有敬爱之心。例如，《论语·为政》中说："今之孝者，是谓能养。至于犬马，皆能有养；不敬，何以别乎？"

在现代社会中，子女虽然仍然敬爱自己的父母，但那些不在父母身边工作和生活的人总觉得自己尽孝不够，有时逢年过节也没回家看望父母，只是电话或视频问候，觉得自己亏欠父母太多。

当然，也有一些独生子女自幼受到长辈过度溺爱，他们虽然已经长大成人，但不愿意出去工作或者不能吃苦耐劳，而待在父母家中"啃老"，自己不赡养父母，反而需要年迈的父母供养自己，何来养亲和敬亲呢？

（2）顺亲和谏亲因家庭和父母与子女的关系不同而不同

传统孝道要求听从父母的话，按父母的意志办事，凡事以父母的标准为标准。否则，就是忤逆父母和不孝的表现。

在现代社会中，由于社会开放程度高，人们的价值观念趋于多元，在一些家教不严和过度溺爱孩子的家庭当中，和父母争吵、顶撞父母等行为，也时有发生。有些年轻人较为自私，只考虑自己的个人感受，有时谩骂或殴打自己的父母或长辈。这是十分不孝的，甚至是违法犯罪的行为。

（3）传宗接代为个人情感心理所取代

传宗接代观念是中国古代报答、安慰父母的一种方式和尽孝的情结。《孝经·圣治》中说："父母生之，续莫大焉。"生养男孩被看作是古代婚姻的主要目的。"不孝有三，无后为大"的思想观念在中国古代社会中酿成了不少家庭悲剧。

在现代社会中，人们的婚姻家庭观念发生了变化，结婚的主要目的因人而异，但更多的是追求自己的爱情和幸福，更倾向满足当事人的情感和心理需要，而不一定是传统的生儿育女的生理需要。因而，丁克家庭、晚婚甚至不婚主义等，在一些思想开放的青年人当中拥有一定的"市场"。

但是，从社会的发展和人口的再生产的角度看，晚婚、不婚或丁克家庭等，会带来一个国家、地区或民族人口减少等问题。这是值得思考的一个现实问题。如何平衡个人与家庭、社会、国家的"忠孝"问题，需要全社会给予更多关注。

（4）丧亲、祭亲趋于简化，立身、立功、显父母，在我国现代社会中依然盛行

在我国传统孝文化中，非常重视丧事和祭祀。《中庸》："事死如事生，事亡如事存，孝之至也。"《吕氏春秋·孝行览》也说："养可能也，敬为难；敬可能也，安为难；安可能也，卒为难。"可见，中国传统的孝观念是非常重视"事死"的。曾子将丧亲、祭亲之孝概括为"慎终追远"。慎终是父母死亡的丧葬行为，追远是父母死后的祭祀礼仪。可见，子女表达丧亲之孝的形式就是丧葬和祭祀，也就是说父母或长辈去世后要举行葬礼和祭礼。

除"事死"重孝外，中国传统孝观念不仅要求子女立身，而且在立身的基础上要立德、立言、立功。《孝经·开宗明义》说："扬名于后世，以显父母，孝之终也。"子女们寒窗苦读，跻身仕途，求取功名，为的是秉承父志，善继善述，实现父母对子女的希望。《中庸》："夫孝者，善继人之志，善述人之事者也。"这说明，光宗耀祖，光大宗门，是传统孝道对子女在家庭伦理范围内的最高要求。

在现代社会中，由于人们横向的地理空间流动和垂直的社会流动增强，子女有时和父母生活在不同的城市，或者生活在同一城市的不同社区，工作和生活都较为忙碌，没有太多的时间陪伴和照顾父母，父母去世后一般丧事和祭祀从简。但是，对于现代社会中的大多数父母来说，子女读个好大学，找到一份好工作，和一个"门当户对"的人结婚（找个好的归属），仍然是不少父母对子女的期望，真是"可怜天下父母心"。这是我国现代孝文化变迁中"不变"的主要表现。

9.1.3　小结：传统孝文化的现代表达

本节我们讨论了我国传统的孝文化，以及我国现代社会中的孝文化的变迁等问题，对孝文化的"变"与"不变"的表现做了简单梳理。希望通过本节内容的学习和讨论，能够帮助大家进一步认识人类文化的时空差异问题。

知识拓展与链接：

子孙无有穷尽，永远享保宗庙世祀，是与立言、立功、立德一并被中国人视为不朽的。在对下一代更下一代的子孙期待里，存留的皆是人伦世俗的种种道德、政治、修养的要求，是因为这种种要求而成立的终极价值目标。几千年来，中国人的文化实践，大都没有超过这些不朽的范围。
　　　　——李向平：《死亡与超越》，上海：上海文化出版社，1997年版，第132页。

知识拓展与链接:

在农户门前禾场上有晃动的幡, 在禾场的一个角落摆着十多个花圈, 在院子里搭着高大的凉棚: 明显是有人去世, 正在办丧事, 但从禾场中正在搭台表演电声乐的场面以及音乐声中一点也看不出来……整个现场, 除了一些人脸上木然的表情, 就是一些人嘻笑和期待的表情, 没有人脸上写有悲伤……

带着不可思议我们回到住的地方。办丧事如何办得像喜事? 如何看不出一点悲伤? 中国传统中的确是有人年龄大了去世是好事, 所谓 "白喜事" 的说法, 但死人终究是一件不好的事情, 是伤心伤感的一个家庭甚至一个亲友体系的重大转折点, 如何可以用这么欢快的音乐, 还是电声乐队? 我们问所在镇镇委书记, 他不是沭阳人。他说这种办丧事的方式在沭阳已有 10 来年了, 那化妆的年轻姑娘当然不是哭的, 她们要唱。唱什么? 唱 "妹妹你大胆地往前走"。在丧事上唱这样的歌, 书记也认为实在荒唐, 又不可理解。这种荒唐的事情因为一直如此, 当地人倒是很习惯了。村民因此如看戏一样去看办丧事时请来的电声乐队的表演。

——贺雪峰:《新乡土中国》, 桂林: 广西师范大学出版社, 2003 年版, 第 17-18 页。

9.2　中西方祭祀文化的差异

9.2.1　中国传统的祭祀文化

我国是一个统一的多民族国家, 各民族在长期的发展过程中形成了丰富多彩的文化。

祭祀作为文化的重要组成部分, 它在中华各民族社会中的表现不尽相同。但是, 中国传统的祭祀文化, 仍然是有其基本特征的。我们首先来了解什么是中国传统的祭祀文化。

简单地说, 中国传统祭祀文化就是中国历史上形成的, 以儒家孝文化为内核, 杂糅了其他思想流派并经历代儒学家们不断改造而绵延至今的祭祀文化。我们可以从祭祀对象、祭祀场所、祭品、祭祀方法及礼仪等方面进行讨论和分析。

（1）中国传统的祭祀对象

根据文献的祭祀, 我们可以知道, 中国传统祭祀对象相当庞杂, 既有宗教信仰的对象和自然界的各种 "神秘力量", 也有人间亡魂或已故的祖先, 还有 "天上人间" 或 "人间天上" 的各路神仙, 甚至民间所谓的阴曹地府中的怪力乱神, 也赫然在列。其原因, 是中国传统信仰体系复杂。

我们知道, 在中国传统信仰体系当中, 既有圣贤明君或才华绝伦、武艺超群的历史名人被民间当作神明来崇拜，也有佛教、道教的神灵系统，儒家思想、佛教和道教"三教合一"在魏晋南北朝时期出现了端倪，并在后来的历史发展中有所强化，使得中国传统的祭祀对象多元化和复杂化。

（2）中国传统的祭祀场所

在中国传统文化中，祭祀是礼俗文化的重要内容。在家国同构的文化中，国家是家庭、宗族的无限放大，国君是最大、最高的"宗族长"。

在中国传统社会中，祭祀是国家、宗族、家族和家庭都十分重视的礼仪。"国之大事，在祀与戎。"把祭祀放在保家卫国之前，作为头等大事来对待，可见祭祀在中国古代社会中处于何等重要的地位。受中国传统宗法文化的影响，中国古代的祭祀场所因主持祭祀的人的社会地位不同而不同。

中国古代祭祀等级界限严格，有"神不歆非类，民不祀非族"之说。天神地祇只能由天子祭祀，诸侯大夫可以祭祀山川，士庶人则只能祭祀自己的祖先和灶神。从天地、山川到祖先灶神祭祀对象的区分，也反映了宗法文化影响下的中国古代天子、诸侯大夫到士庶人祭祀的等级差异和祭祀空间场所的不同。天坛、地坛、平地、宫庙、祠堂、坟墓等，都成为中国传统祭祀的主要场所。

（3）中国传统的祭品

祭品指的是祭祀用品或物品。中国传统的祭品因祭祀对象不同而不同。在中国传统宗教祭祀活动中，祭品的生熟状态往往象征神灵角色的大小。

在中国古代社会中，人们常用牲血来祭天，用生肉来祭祖宗，用半熟的肉来祭山川草泽，而用熟肉来做一献的小祭。中国古人偏爱食用肉嫩的幼牲，并用这种喜好类比神灵的嗜欲，认为用肉嫩的牛犊来祭天表示以诚信为贵。因此，周代祭祀天地用的牛，牛角如蚕茧一般小，而祭祀宗庙的牛，则牛角大到可用手握住，即用祭牲的小大来类比祭祀对象的尊卑。

人类学家李亦园先生认为，台湾民间宗教祭祀通常用"生"或"熟"的祭品来表示祭祀者和被祭者关系的亲疏，祭品越"生"，关系越疏远；反之，关系则越熟。具体来说，拜"天公"或祭孔子时的全猪全羊都未经烹煮，都是生供，含有对祭拜对象一种遥远关系的意义；而祭祀妈祖、关帝、王爷、千岁等一般神明时，其祭牲在祭供之前都稍加烹煮，但不真正煮熟。这些都是表示对"天"下的各种神祇较下一等的敬意，同时也因祭品稍加烹煮而表示关系较为密切，与不问世俗事的天帝有所差别。供奉祖宗的祭品，则不但要煮熟，有时还加以调味，明确表示祖宗与其他神灵有异，属于"自家人"范畴，完全以家常之礼对待，带有亲昵的敬意。此外，还用"全整"和"部分"来区分尊卑程度。一般来说，"全"或"整"的祭品表示最高的敬意和隆重，而"部分"或祭品块子越小表示尊敬或隆重的程度越低。①对于冥制和香火等祭品，不同的神明和祖先等也有不同的

---

① 李亦园. 人类的视野［M］. 上海: 上海文艺出版社, 1996: 291-292.

讲究，见表 9-1。

表 9-1　　中国民众对不同神明使用不同的祭品

神灵		神		鬼	
		天	神明	祖先	小鬼
冥纸		金纸		银纸	
		天金，盆金	寿金，割金	大银	小银
祭品	形状	完整	大块	小块	小块
	是否烹调	生	半生	煮熟，调味	普通熟食
香火	形式	盘香	三枝	二枝	一枝
	分香与否	无	分香，割香	分香	无

　　资料来源：李亦园：《人类的视野》，上海：上海文艺出版社，1996 年版，第 292 页。

（4）中国传统的祭祀方法和礼仪

　　根据文献的祭祀，中国古人对不同的祭祀对象采用不同的祭祀方法。例如，祭祀天帝、日月等神明，一般采用燔烧方式。《周礼·春官·大宗伯》中就有"以实柴祀日月星辰"的记载。

　　祭祀地神一般使用灌注方式。《周礼·春官·大宗伯》说："以血祭祭社稷。"《礼记·郊特牲》："灌以圭璋，用玉气也。既灌，然后迎牲，致阴气也。"此外，中国古人祭水神使用沉投，祭山神使用悬投等。这些不同的祭祀方式，反映了中国古代人对于人我和物我的理解。

9.2.2　西方的祭祀文化

　　西方的祭祀文化与中国传统祭祀文化不同。这种不同不仅表现在祭品上，而且也表现在其根源性的宗教信仰和实践当中。

　　中西方祭品的最大不同，或许应该是中国人喜欢用食物拜祭，西方人更倾向用鲜花到墓地去探访和追思。有一个有趣的故事：1935 年，英国著名的人类学家拉德克利夫-布朗到北京燕京大学访问，有一次他由燕京大学一位年轻的助教陪同去村落考察。他发现有一户人家的厅堂里摆满了祭祀祖先的食物。他感到十分好奇，就问陪同的那位年轻助教："你们中国人是不是真的相信祖先的灵魂会来吃这许多的祭品？"那位年轻助教反问英国教授："你们英国人是不是真的相信你们的祖先会闻到献于他们墓前的花香？"[①]这个有意思的对话，反映了中西方祭品的象征意义。"在西方的世界里，人是不完美的，他们需要借助于一个完美的神来约束人的生活和行为，这是西方的超自然观念；中国人的世界里，人是可以完美的，所以那些行为近乎完美的人就被崇拜为神，以便作为人们的典范，这是我们的超

───────────

① 李亦园. 人类的视野 [M]. 上海:上海文艺出版社, 1996: 293.

自然观念。在我们的超自然世界里，神与鬼必须共同存在的，假如没有鬼，就不能衬托出神的完美性，但是我们的鬼不像西方的撒旦，那是与宇宙并存的，我们的鬼却都是人死后变成的。"①这种人—神—鬼的不同观念，实际上反映了中西宇宙观的差异。

在根源性祭祀文化的影响因素中，中国的传统祭祀文化更多受中国传统礼制的影响，而且越到底层社会，越表现出非制度化宗教（即民间宗教习俗）的影响；而在西方社会中，制度化的宗教文化体系对其祭祀文化的规制作用较为明显。

9.2.3　小结：中西祭祀文化不同

本节我们讨论了中国传统祭祀文化的概念、祭祀对象、祭祀场所、祭品、祭祀方法和礼仪等内容，简单分析了西方祭祀文化不同于中国传统祭祀文化的表现及成因。希望通过本节内容的学习和讨论，能够帮助大家进一步认识人类文化的时空差异问题。

知识拓展与链接：

在现代西方社会中，宗教是什么状况呢？它与人类学家对北美印第安人宗教的描述奇怪地相似。印第安人已皈依基督教，但他们古老的前基督教的宗教却没有被根除。基督教是这种古老宗教的外表，在很多方面彼此混为一体。在我们本身的文化中，一神教、无神论和不可知论都是依在一些宗教之上的一层薄壳，这些宗教在很多方面比印第安人的宗教更"原始"，纯粹是偶像崇拜，也就与一神教的基本教义更不相容。我们崇尚权力，成功和市场权威只是一种集体的、有效力的现代偶像崇拜；但在这些集体形式之外，我们还会发现另外一些形式。如果我们撕去现代人的外表，就会发现许多已经个人化的原始宗教。其中一些被称为精神病，但也可以按照各自的宗教名称称作：祖先崇拜，图腾崇拜，拜物教，仪式主义，洁癖，等等。

我们现在还能看到祖先崇拜吗？事实上祖先崇拜是我们社会中最广泛的原始崇拜，即使我们像精神病学家那样称为对父母的精神固著，其表征是改变不了的。让我们看一个祖先崇拜的案例。一位漂亮且有才华的女画家十分依恋父亲，她拒绝与任何其他男子有密切交往，一有闲暇就陪伴在父亲身边；他是一位举止文雅但相当乏味的绅士，早年丧妻。她向别人描述的父亲与真人大不一样。父亲死后这位女画家自杀了，她留下遗嘱要求埋葬在父亲身边。
——［美］埃利希·弗洛姆：《精神分析与宗教》，贾辉军译，北京：中国对外翻译出版公司，1995年版，第21页。

---

① 李亦园. 人类的视野［M］. 上海：上海文艺出版社, 1996: 293-294.

9.3　"互联网+"的网祭文化分析

9.3.1　网祭："互联网+"时代祭祀文化的新形式

顾名思义，"网祭"就是网络祭祀的简称，它与传统的祭祀方式不同，它不需要到现场去祭拜，而是在互联网上开辟祭祀空间，模拟现实的祭拜现场进行虚拟的拜祭形式。这种互联网拜祭方式，目前一般以公共祭祀为主。例如，为革命英烈和其他已经去世的重要公众人物在其诞辰或去世之日进行网祭。网祭一般由公益组织或热心网友发起，参与者以年轻人居多。

值得注意的是，近年来出现了网祭的另外一种变异形式——"代人扫墓"或"代人哭坟"。互联网技术和即时通信工具的发展，催生了许多新业态和商业模式。其中，代人扫墓或哭坟值得关注。

对于一些定居国外或常年在外打拼而没有时间回家乡扫墓的人来说，通过网上付费请人代为扫墓或哭坟，一方面可以免除自己返乡亲自扫墓的辛劳，另一方面又可以表达自己的哀思。因此，大概在 2012 年前后，代人扫墓或哭坟在我国一些地方兴起。与此同时，也出现了其他相关祭祀方式。

1）音乐祭祀——播放逝者生前最喜爱的歌曲，表达对其缅怀之情。

2）鲜花祭祀——用逝者生前最喜爱的鲜花祭扫，或参加各公墓组织的"鲜花换烧纸"活动。

3）植树祭祀——通过植树祭奠故人。

4）洗墓祭祀——清洗墓碑表达思念。

5）家庭追思会——将逝者生前的照片、录像资料制作成光盘，组织家庭成员观看，进行回忆。

6）社区公祭——专职礼仪师进驻社区，由社区组织辖区居民敬放过世亲属遗像、果品、气球等，逝者家属宣读祭文，公祭群众敬献鲜花。

7）网上祭祀——通过互联网表达对已故亲人的哀思。

8）放飞思念——社区组织居民开展放飞白气球、放飞思念的活动。

此外，一些城市的民政部门近年来也倡导和鼓励市民采用网祭、社区公祭、音乐追思等现代祭祀形式，不放烟花爆竹，少烧香蜡纸烛，多用鲜花祭扫。这对于网祭和"互联网+"时代的祭祀文化创新发展来说，有其积极作用。

9.3.2　如何看待网祭文化？

网祭文化近年刚刚兴起，人们对其褒贬不一。如何看待网祭文化，或许是一个仁者见仁、智者见智的问题。

对于常年定居国外或因年老行动不便而无法亲自到墓地或陵园祭奠已故亲人

的人们来说，通过互联网方式付费请人代劳或许是一种不得已的做法。人们对此是能够理解和支持的。但是，也有人认为，别人是无法代替自己尽孝的，特别是请人哭坟会显得虚情假意，根本传递不了家人之间的亲情。一些承接"代人扫墓"等业务的店家也明确表示不开办"代人哭坟"业务。

对于近年来出现的"代人扫墓"或"代人哭坟"等网祭文化持保留态度的人，基本上是思想比较传统的人。他们认为，孝道是中国人应该恪守的基本道德。一个人如果连最基本的孝道都不尽的话，你还希望他能遵守什么道德规范呢？虽然说尽不尽孝很大程度上是个人的事情，但它基本上也反映着一个人的"德行"。

实际上，不管你是亲自去墓地或陵园祭拜，还是网上祭拜，或者通过互联网委托他人或专业机构代为扫墓等，都不过是祭拜的方式不同而已，更关键的其实还是祭拜和尽孝的心意。是真心祭拜和怀念已故的亲人，还是虚张声势做给别人看的？这只有当事人自己心里最清楚。

其实，尽孝的最好时机是亲人健在的时候，尽可能陪伴其健健康康、快快乐乐、开开心心过好每一天，而不是等到亲人过世之后才尽孝。生前不孝死后孝，这种逻辑肯定荒谬至极，是不值得倡导的，而且也背离了中国传统的孝道精神。

现代社会是工业社会。工业社会的一个基本特点就是，商品可以付费交换和消费。网祭及其延伸出来的诸如"代人扫墓""代人哭坟"等异化形式，反映了祭祀文化商品化的发展趋势。对此，我们应该辩证地看待和分析，简单地肯定或者否定，都无法准确地进行解读。

9.3.3 小结：祭祀文化的超时空表达

本节我们讨论了"互联网+"时代的网祭及其延伸出来的"代人扫墓""代人哭坟"等现代祭祀文化，并对如何看待网祭文化做了简单分析。希望通过本节内容的学习和讨论，能够帮助大家进一步认识人类文化的时空差异问题。

知识拓展与链接：

今年的特殊情况推进了网上祭祀的发展和普及。在网上完成献花、上香、写悼词等一系列祭祀流程，打破了时间和地域限制，随时随地都能对已逝亲人进行追思，让网上祭祀彻底火了。

数据显示，清明节期间，线下祭祀人员大幅减少，儋州逾 125 万人次网上祭祀，到公墓实地祭祀的市民大幅减少，比去年同期减少八成；广州逾十几万人次参与网上祭拜；沈阳开展网上祭祀 9 413 人次……

与之相对应的是网络祭祀企业数量的增长，据了解，目前全国共有从事网络祭祀相关企业 60 家，仅 2019 年就新增网络祭祀相关企业 19 家，占企业总数的 31.7%。全国网络祭祀相关企业中注册地在广东省的数量居首位，共 16 家，湖北省和福建省分别以 9 家和 5 家数量位居第二和第三。

其中，作为新兴网络祭祀平台的思念堂，一经推出就引起巨大反响。思念堂官方公布的大数据显示，清明节当天该平台用户访问量突破 30 万。

这些数据无一不证明着人们对网络祭祀的接受度在不断提高，参与度也直线上升。相比传统祭祀方式，网络祭祀更便捷、高效。还是以思念堂为例，注册账号、填写被纪念人基本资料，只用两三分钟就可以完成纪念堂的创建，这里可以永久保留逝者生前的影像资料，还可创建逝者生平简介，用户在平台上能够为逝者献花、电烛、留言祈祷等。人们还可以转发给亲友或分享到朋友圈，让散居各地的人们随时随地祭奠，以表达对已故亲友的思念之情。

此外，在思念堂平台，用户可以建立家族祠堂，并分享给亲友共同祭奠，还可以在名人纪念堂，对逝去的伟人、学者、科学家等进行祭奠，思念堂为用户提供多种选择。

在国家倡导绿色祭祀、文明祭祀的当下，网络祭祀平台的出现恰逢其时，人们的接受度也越来越高，未来发展值得期待。

——驱动中国：《网上祭祀彻底火了，未来发展值得期待》，网易新闻，2020-05-03。

10 "地球村"：人类"文明冲突"与文化交融

10.1 工业文明与文化

10.1.1 工业文明与工业社会

简单地说，工业文明就是以工业化、机器化、标准化、"流水作业"占主导地位的一种现代社会文明状态。

与传统农业文明相比，工业文明的内涵更加丰富，主要表现为城市化、法治化、民主化、社会阶层流动性增强、教育普及、消息传递加速、非农业人口比例大幅度增长、经济持续增长等。

在工业社会中，由于机器生产率的提高和标准化的产品的量化生产，同质化或同质性成为工业文明区分农业文明的重要标志。统一的市场、统一的语言文字，普遍的社会流动和平等，无处不在的标准化，等等，都是同质化的具体表现。从这个意义上说，工业社会是一个同质的社会，农业社会则是一个有着许多异质的亚文化的不同质的社会。

由农业社会进入工业社会，科学技术的发展发挥了重要的推动作用。但是，科学技术是一把"双刃剑"。它在给人类创造美好生活的同时，可能也会给人类社会带来一些负面的影响。关键是人类如何在确保生态文明的基础上，利用科学技术更好地改善民生和服务社会。

工业文明早期曾造成环境污染、资源浪费、贫富差距扩大等问题。这些问题现今在一些发展中国家依然存在。有关工业革命、科学技术及其现代性的问题，已经引起人们的普遍关注和讨论。

当前，西方发达国家已经进入后工业时代，它们从 20 世纪 70 年代就开始反思工业化的后果。我国目前还处于工业化的进程当中，这就要求我们要吸取西方发达国家的经验教训，在工业化道路上尽可能少走弯路，以期更早进入信息文明时代。换句话说，工业社会的科学技术应该"文明"使用，应该造福社会而非"祸害"于民。

工业社会有其自身的发展逻辑。但是，技术进步不应导致人类"文明"的退步，而应相得益彰。

10.1.2 工业社会的文明"冲突"

工业社会是否存在文明"冲突"？这是一个值得深入思考的问题。

（1）物质文明与精神文明的"冲突"

任何一个国家和社会都离不开物质文明建设和精神文明建设。工业时代本质上是一个追求物质的时代，不仅工厂开动的机器消耗原材料以生产出更多更好的产品，人们也不断地消费着新鲜出炉的工业产品。在"物欲"膨胀的时代，人们对精神层面的追求可能会有所减低。这就不可避免地导致物质文明和精神文明的"冲突"，有些人可能还会出现精神层面的道德滑坡。

（2）工业文明与生态文明的"冲突"

相对于传统农业来说，工业创造的财富和价值更高一些。因此，工业强国、工业强省、工业富市、工业富县的工业文明，就会驱动着人们对于工业创造的价值和财富的追求。

一些地方政府在优先发展工业的情况下，出台相关优惠政策或措施，加大力度招商引资，发展工业，有时甚至把一些高耗能、高污染的外资或外地企业引入本地区，后因监管不力，导致企业环保不达标，或者企业为了降低环保成本而偷排乱排未经处理的废气、废水等，严重污染或破坏了生态环境。这种以牺牲环境为代价的工业发展之路，直接挑战了人类社会的可持续发展。

（3）全球化与人类命运共同体的"冲突"

全球化首先在经济层面展开。它要求资金、资源、产品、市场等经济要素的全球配置。其结果，是导致"多元一体"的世界经济和"一体多元"的人类文化的"冲突"。人类共同生活在同一个星球——地球上，既不能"民至老死，不相往来"，只谈"民族化"而否认"全球化"；也不能只讲"全球经济一体化"而不谈人类命运"共同体"。

人类学的常识告诉我们，经济、政治嵌合于文化是人类社会的基本命题。面对日益发展的跨国公司和地缘经济、地缘政治的挑战，在参与全球协同治理的过程中构建人类命运共同体已成为世界各国各民族面临的紧迫任务。"当前，世界多极化、经济全球化、文化多样化、社会信息化深入发展，人类社会充满希望。同时，国际形势的不稳定性不确定性更加突出，人类面临的全球性挑战更加严峻，需要世界各国齐心协力、共同应对。"[①]这种应对，既需要经济和科技力量，更需要文化文明力量。只有深化人类文明的交流互鉴，才能真正共建人类命运共同体。

10.1.3 小结：工业时代的文化与文明走向

本节我们讨论了工业文明与工业社会，以及工业社会中的文明"冲突"等问

---

① 习近平. 习近平谈治国理政：第三卷 [M]. 北京：外文出版社，2020：465.

题，对工业时代的文化和文明走向也做了简单的分析。希望通过本节内容的学习和讨论，能够帮助大家进一步认识人类社会的文明"冲突"和文化交融问题。

知识拓展与链接：

西方实用主义的和善于分析的世界观从与现代科学及其在技术中的应用相结合而获取新的力量。一个方程似乎正在形成：如果一个社会要取得物质和经济的发展，它就必须接受并恰当地利用现代技术；如果它要掌握现代技术，就必须接受西方的理性主义的实用主义的文化。这个方程式似乎令人信服；它影响了世界上绝大多数领导人的思想。但这个方程式是否完全正确是另外一回事。

对这个方程式来说，重要的是假设技术与文化之间的特殊组合。最新的技术被认为是最需要的技术：这些技术确保最高的生产率，并决定每个国家在世界经济中竞争的能力，作为在国民经济中创造财富的源泉，这些技术被假定为全部社会经济发展的基础。因为这些技术主要是西方文化的产物，所以人们相信，掌握这些技术的使用，需要西方式的思想和行为。

……产生于西方科学合理性的新技术并不是产生这些技术的文化的唯一工具，这些技术的利用并不局限于在西方世界产生的发展目标。但是，由于一切方式的发展都认为需要依靠对新技术的利用，而对新技术的利用则需要西方式思想和针对目标所做的准备，于是一种文化所特有的合理性和经验主义便传遍了全世界。其结果是，一种具有强大一致性冲击力的技术文明的出现威胁着世界文化的多样性。地方文化面临一种必须履行的责任：或者接受西方的文化并利用新技术，或者保持自身的传统而消失在历史中……

但是，西方理性主义—经验主义文化和利用新技术这个方程式并不是放之四海而皆准的。就西方世界来说，精心搞出新技术的文化就是利用这些技术的文化，这可能是确实的，至少是合乎逻辑的。但是，对于其他文化来说，这就不确实了：在这些文化中，新技术有助于提出完全不同于那些标准的社会经济发展目标的目标。没有哪种技术不可避免地局限于某种特定的思想和行为方式，局限于达到某些特定的目标。

——［美］欧文·拉兹洛：《联合国教科文组织国际专家研究报告：多种文化的星球（第2版）》，戴侃、辛未译，北京：社会科学文献出版社，2004年版，第226-227页。

10.2　信息文明与文化

10.2.1　信息与信息文化

（1）信息的概念

一般认为，信息是指音讯、消息、通信系统传输和处理的对象，泛指人类社会传播的一切内容。

作为科学术语，"信息"最早出现在哈特莱（Hartley）1928年撰写的《信息传输》一文中。20世纪40年代，信息的奠基人香农（Shannon）给出了信息的明确定义。1948年，香农在题为《通信的数学理论》的论文中指出："信息是用来消除随机不定性的东西。"这一定义被人们看作经典性定义，并被不断地加以引用。

（2）信息文化

信息文化产生并形成于信息时代。它是以信息技术广泛应用于社会生活为主要特征而形成的新的文化形态。从构成上看，信息文化大体上有四种不同的构成方式。

作为物质形态的信息文化和作为社会规范的信息文化是广义信息文化的物化基础，作为行为方式的信息文化和作为精神观念的信息文化则是广义信息文化的理性分析。因此，有人倾向把作为行为方式的信息文化和作为精神观念的信息文化看成是狭义的信息文化。除具有文化的一般特征外，信息文化还具有如下四个方面的特性。

首先，数字化、全球化体现了信息时代的物质文化特征。

其次，虚拟性、交互性体现了信息时代的行为文化特征。

再次，开放性、自治性、自律性成为信息时代制度文化的特色。

最后，信息交流自由、平等、共享的理念正逐渐演化为信息时代精神。

在信息科学日益发达的今天，信息的重要性不言而喻，它对社会乃至整个人类都产生了重大的影响。可以说，信息文化构成了人类历史上第三次重大的科技腾飞，它将发挥越来越强大的作用。

10.2.2　信息社会与信息文明

（1）信息社会

信息社会是以电子信息技术为基础，以信息资源为基本发展资源，以信息服务性产业为基本社会产业，以数字化和网络化为基本社会交往方式的新型社会。

在这个信息化的社会中，信息成为比物质和能源更为重要的资源，以开发和利用信息资源为目的的信息经济活动迅速扩大，并逐渐取代工业生产活动而成为国民经济活动的主要内容。因此，以计算机、微电子和通信技术为主的信息技术革命，就构成了社会信息化的主要动力源泉。

（2）信息文明

由于信息技术在资料生产、科研教育、医疗保健、企业、政府管理及家庭中的广泛应用，它对人类社会和经济发展产生了巨大而深刻的影响，从根本上改变了经济业态和商业模式，以及人们的生活方式、行为方式和价值观念。因此，信息文明可以看作是一种新型的、要素叠加的文明形态，它既有物质文明的特点，又具有精神文明的特征。

信息文明使得人类社会表现出一些新的特点。

首先，信息成为重要的生产力要素，它和物质、能量一起构成社会赖以生存的三大资源。

其次，在信息社会中，科技与人文在信息知识的作用下结合得更加紧密，知识成为基本要求。

最后，信息社会的经济以信息经济、知识经济为主导，它有别于以工业经济为主导的工业社会。

当然，信息文明也有其自身待解决的问题。这些问题主要包括以下几点。

1）信息污染，如信息虚假、信息垃圾、信息干扰、信息无序、信息缺损、信息过时、信息冗余、信息误导、信息泛滥、信息不健康等。

2）信息侵权，如知识产权侵权和侵犯个人隐私权，"人肉搜索"等。

3）信息犯罪，如黑客攻击、网上"黄赌毒"、网上诈骗、窃取信息等。

4）信息侵略，如信息强势国家通过信息垄断和大肆宣扬自己的价值观，用自己的文化和生活方式影响其他国家，开展"颜色革命"等。

总之，信息社会的文明其实也是一把"双刃剑"。文明的好或坏，不在于"剑"本身，而在于用之人。伴随着信息技术的发展，信息化和全球化已成为当代世界经济不可逆转的大趋势，应该主动应对，趋利避害，才能促进信息文明的健康发展。

10.2.3 小结："地球村"里的信息

本节我们讨论了信息、信息文化的概念和特点，分析了信息社会和信息文明的发展等问题，对信息文明的特点和负面影响也做了简单的分析。

希望通过本节内容的学习和讨论，能够帮助大家进一步认识人类社会的文明"冲突"和文化交融问题。

知识拓展与链接:

　　现在数十亿人通过电子、光纤、数字通信科技相互连接。有约 1 000 个卫星在距地面 400 至 3.5 万公里的高空绕地飞行。其中有约 560 个是专供通信的卫星,其他的作为军用、科研、气象观测卫星在运行。其中还包括 24 个全球定位卫星(GPS),距地 1.6 万公里。无线通信设备通过大批量生产的轻型移动通信设备——电话、电视、电脑,所有的信息都被引入这个小小的设备中,持续即时地将全球数十亿人联系在一起。

　　……

　　人类越来越密切相互接触的政局是全球人员、产品和观念的流通,现代的大众运输和通信传媒让这些事情成为可能。这也导致了文化间很多外在的一致性,形成蔚为壮观的盛景,人类的未来会成为单一同质的全球文化。世界范围内,人们已经越来越多地共享着相同的娱乐,看和听很多相同的世界新闻,吃着相同的快餐,穿着同款的衣服,玩相同的运动,随着同样的音乐起舞,以少数通用语言进行交流……

　　现代电子数字科技的深远影响力创造了一个全球传媒环境,在个体和社会如何看待他们在世界的位置中扮演着重要角色。与广播和电视一道,互联网成为现在世界大众交流的主要渠道。通过光纤、信号塔、绕地通信卫星传输的全球信息流通,已经几乎全部数字化,并发生在被称为"全球传媒"的新无限文化空间中。

　　近些年,企业的力量通过传媒扩张变得强大。在过去的 20 年中,全球商业传媒的发展,由少数美国大企业(例如通用电气、时代华纳、迪士尼)控制了电视、互联网和其他媒体,还有广告产业,这些跨国公司深刻影响着世界范围内上亿普通人日常的观念和行为。

　　——〔美〕威廉·A.哈维兰(William A.Haviland)、〔美〕哈拉尔德·E.L.普林斯(Harald E. L.Prins)、〔美〕达纳·沃尔拉斯(Dana Walrath)等:《人类学:人类的挑战(第 14 版)》,周云水、陈祥、雷蕾等译,北京:电子工业出版社,2018 年版,第 645-657 页。

10.3　宗教文明与文化

10.3.1　宗教文化与宗教文明概述

　　宗教是人类社会的特殊文化现象,是人类传统文化的重要组成部分,它影响到人们的思想意识、生活习俗等方面。宗教本身以信仰为核心,同时它又是整个社会文化的组成部分。

（1）宗教文化

作为文化现象的宗教，有其自身的文化体系和发展规律。

从广义上看，凡是涉及宗教的一切文化都属于宗教文化。狭义的宗教文化仅指宗教自身的文化体系，如宗教思想、宗教观念、宗教经典、宗教教义、宗教情感、宗教神职人员和信徒、宗教活动场所及建筑、宗教仪式、宗教道德、宗教习俗等。总之，宗教文化是一个相对宽泛的概念。宗教文明的内涵则相对集中。

（2）宗教文明

长期以来，人们对文化与文明的区别和联系存在不同的认识。

一般认为，文明是相对静止的，文化则是富于流动的；文明是文化长期积淀的结果，但不是所有的文化都能积淀成为文明。

从这个角度来看宗教文化，可以认为，宗教文明是人类文明的一种类型，它是宗教在其长期的发展过程中不断适应社会需要并积淀下来的，有利于社会和平、安定、和顺的宗教文化的结晶。是否"结晶"或能否"结晶"，是宗教文明和宗教文化的最大区别。

"结晶"化的宗教文明不像流动的宗教文化那样易于变动，因而成为人类文明的一种类型，只不过它带有浓厚的宗教色彩。

10.3.2 宗教文明"冲突"与交融共生

（1）宗教文明"冲突"还是融合？

在美国著名的政治学家塞缪尔·亨廷顿看来，世界各大文明之间是冲突的。亨廷顿所提出的"文明冲突论"实际上是宗教文明的"冲突"论。

实际上，亨廷顿只看到了世界宗教文明的"冲突"而忽略了不同文明之间的交融与共生。

从我国各大宗教的发展情况来看，儒家思想和佛教、道教在魏晋南北朝时期已出现了"三教合一"的端倪。此后尽管发展时有反复，但是，儒、释、道的"合流"成为历史发展趋势。唐宋时期传入我国的伊斯兰教也经历了"中国化"的发展历程，形成了西北地区伊斯兰教的门宦制度。明清时期，一些信仰伊斯兰教的回族学者还运用儒家经典诠释《古兰经》，出现了"以儒诠经"的伊斯兰教"中国化"实践。

明清时期，基督教传入中国时，曾出现过"礼仪之争"。由于基督教的教规与中国传统的敬天祭祖等习俗和偶像崇拜格格不入，因此基督教在华传教基本上难以成功。近代中国历史上的教案频发，似乎为基督教文明与中华文明的"冲突"提供了注脚。但是，以儒家文明为核心的中华文明其实具有强大的开放性和包容性。

20世纪20年代，中国基督教出现的"本色化"运动，反映了中华文明与基督教之间是可以融合的，而不只是"冲突"。中国宗教的发展历史表明，世界上各大宗教文明之间不一定是"冲突"的，反而可能融合。是"冲突"还是融合，其实取决于宗教文明之间的对话和交流。

"全球化为宗教界带来新的生命力，拉近了信仰之间的距离，传统的信仰模式面临解构，新形态的信仰模式应运而生。在不同信仰通过现代科技文明的带动下，东方与西方、传统与现代、神圣与世俗都被放置在同一时空中产生碰撞，不同宗教、信仰间的对话、交流成为可能，而且是必要的。"①这表明，宗教界和学术界在宗教对话和交流的重要性方面已经形成基本共识。

（2）宗教圆融共生

宗教和顺、圆融的关键是不同宗教之间和不同教派之间要积极开展宗教对话和宗教交流，求同存异，彼此包容。

一切正常的宗教都是劝人行善，教导信众做一个对国家、社会、家庭有用的人。在这一点上，各宗各派都是一致的，只不过实现路径、方法和对教义的理解可能有所不同。这就需要宗教对话和交流，在此基础上，实现宗教的圆融共生。此外，还需要积极引导宗教与社会主义社会相适应，"积极践行社会主义核心价值观，弘扬中华文化，努力把宗教教义同中华文化相融合"②；"在'导'上想得深、看得透、把得准，做到'导'之有方、'导'之有力、'导'之有效"②。只有这样，才能更好地实现宗教圆融和人类社会的和谐共生。

10.3.3　小结：宗教文明在"冲突"中圆融共生

本节我们讨论了宗教文化和宗教文明的概念，分析了宗教文明如何在"冲突"中圆融共生等问题。希望通过本节内容的学习和讨论，能够帮助大家进一步认识人类社会的文明"冲突"与文化交融问题。

10.4　和而不同的文化星球

10.4.1　人类文化的多样性

多样性是人类文化的一个重要表征。和自然生态环境一样，人类的文化生态也具有多样性。为什么呢？

理由其实很简单。从文化的圈层结构来看，由外到内的人类文化依次是物质文化、行为文化、制度文化和精神文化。③

---

① 释了意. 觉醒的力量：全球宗教对话与交流 [M]. 北京：宗教文化出版社，2010: 2.
② 习近平. 习近平谈治国理政：第二卷 [M]. 北京：外文出版社，2017: 301-302.
③ Yang L, Li M. Cultural understanding of global governance: a perspective of religious culture [J]. *Advances in Applied Sociology*, 2018, 8(5): 359-365.

　　处于最外围的物质文化与自然生态环境密不可分。因此，人类的物质文化自然也就具有自然生态环境的多样性特征。

　　由物质文化向文化内核行进的第二层次的文化是行为文化。人类的行为文化受其社会制度等约束，不同社会制度规制下的行为文化自然也就表现出不同的文化特征，其文化多样性自然也就不言而喻。

　　至于制度文化和精神文化的多样性，那就更不必多说。制度文化是精神文化的形态化或外向投射。有什么样的精神文化，就有什么样的制度文化和它相适应，反之亦然。俗话说得好："一方水土养育一方人"，"一种米养出百种人"。这非常清楚地说明了人类文化的多样性。

　　此外，由于文化的历史性、地域性和民族性、时代性等多重因素的影响，不同国家、不同地区的文化存在较大差异，甚至同一国家或地区的不同民族、不同国家或地区的同一民族、不同时代的同一民族或者同一时代的不同民族，等等，都会存在较大的文化差异。

10.4.2　和而不同的文化未来

　　和而不同是全球化时代最为耀眼的文化图像。尽管现代社会的工业化、标准化会带来一定程度的表面"趋同"，但是，这并不意味着人类文化的同质化或一体化。相反，全球化所带来的表面趋同实际上刺激着人们对"自我"和"他者"的文化感知和认同。其结果，是导致人们对"自我"文化的强调和复兴，以使自己及其所属群体能够屹立于世界民族之林。

　　2000 年前后，我国著名的社会学家、人类学家费孝通先生思考 21 世纪的人文世界和文化发展走向时，将他自己早年提出的"各美其美，美人之美，美美与共，天下大同"的论断，修改为"各美其美，美人之美，美美与共，和而不同"。当然，费孝通先生是把"和而不同"看作实现"天下大同"的重要手段和路径的。这是很有见地的。应该说，费孝通先生修改后的这十六个字，更加客观、全面地展望了人类社会的文化未来及其发展走向。

　　经济全球化带来的直接后果，是世界各国、各地区、各民族的交往交流更加频繁，但文化的真正交融还任重道远，和而不同仍然是人类未来发展的方向。这就给人们提出了一个值得珍视的发展命题：和而不同的文化究竟是全球化的动力还是阻力？

10.4.3　小结：多种文化的星球与和而不同的人文世界

　　本节内容我们讨论了人类文化的多样性，以及和而不同的文化未来等问题。希望通过本节内容的学习和讨论，能够帮助大家进一步认识人类文明的"冲突"与文化交融问题。

知识拓展与链接：

　　要使当今社会的多样性与一种新水平的统一性平衡起来，这从文化意义上来说是个最大的挑战。文化不仅是其中的一个因素，而且是其决定性的特征。归根结蒂，区别一个社会与另一个社会的不仅仅是金钱或自然资源的财富，而且并首先是它的人民的价值观念、积极性和创造力。一个民族能够建立现代工业、发展高技术，逐渐形成一个消费社会；另一个民族能够迅速地赶上它，第三个却采取了抵制态度，寻求其他的发展道路，这种情况主要并不是气候和地理位置所决定的，也不能用经济因素来充分加以解释。其原因在于文化，在于各不相同的明确特征，在于不同的思维方法和组织每个人和每个社会的生活方式。墨西哥城世界会议指出，与那种以国民生产总值为标准来衡量的经济增长过程比较起来，发展过程的内涵要复杂得多，丰富得多，广泛得多。的确，"只有当它建立在每个社会独立意志的基础之上，只有当它真实地表明它的基本特性时"，发展才能证明是有效的。

　　寻求和平，寻求理解，寻求团结，寻求统一，最终是寻求一种多样性的和谐协作。因为多样性与统一性都是由文化决定的，人们的追求也只能通过文化上的对话和合作来实现……

　　通过对话和合作，各种各样的文化和文化上多样化的社会正在有意识有目的地为促进一个整合的局面打好基础。它们的成功将取决于各个方面的相互尊重和它们在平等地位上合作的意愿。各种文化无所谓谁好谁坏；它们是多样的，它们的多样性是至关重要的。

　　——［美］欧文·拉兹洛：《联合国教科文组织国际专家研究报告：多种文化的星球（第2版）》，戴侃、辛未译，北京：社会科学文献出版社，2004年版，第7-9页。

11 结论：生活乃文化，文化即生活

11.1 工业文化与现代生活

现代社会是基于工业技术发展起来的社会。工业技术及其文化体系已深深地渗透于现代生活的每个领域。无论人们喜欢不喜欢，也不管人们愿意不愿意，适应工业技术的现代文化体系都在深刻地支配着世界各国各地人们的现实生活。

从本书前面几章所讨论的话题和内容上看，应该不难理解"生活乃文化，文化即生活"的基本内涵。

需要强调的是，工业技术及其文化体系所要求的机器化、模型化、标准化、流程化、批量化、市场化乃至全球化，已经完全支配了人们的衣、食、住、行、游、购、娱、婚、丧、生、老、病、死、葬、祭等生活领域。现代社会中的人们想要摆脱这些领域中的技术控制，实际上已不可能。

在现代生活中，人们看似有很多选择，其实并没有多少选择。因为你所能够选择的，都是现有技术或新兴技术生产出来的产品。即便是现代农业特别是设施农业，基本上也带有浓厚的工业化特征。

从作物育种到栽培耕种，从防虫除害到增产增收，再到采收加工和运输储藏，哪一项不是现代农业技术的运用和支持？至于现代产业化的家禽畜牧产业，那更是现代农业技术推广运用的结果。可以说，良种、良法、良技的"三良"技术构成了现代农业产业体系的重要基石。作为解决民生最重要工程（饮食）的农业行业尚且如此，其他行业如服装、医疗、交通等行业自不待言。

因此，现代生活是由工业技术所建构的生活，生活的方式和方法都不可避免地受到工业文化的规制。越到工业社会的后期，人们受到工业技术及其文化的影响越明显。

到了信息社会，绝大多数人的工作和生活已经越来越无法摆脱对互联网技术和即时通信技术的依赖。但问题的关键在于，在现代社会生活中，是技术服务于我们，还是我们服务于技术而成为技术的"奴隶"？技术是一把"双刃剑"，我们应该相信技术，但是不应该迷恋或迷信技术；技术应该为人服务，而不应该成为奴役人们的工具。抱持这样的理念和思想，我们对现代社会中的技术、文化与生活应该会更有信心，也可能会生活得更精彩。

11.2　文化的时空差异和非线性表达

文化在其发展演变的过程中存在着时空差异和非线性的表达方式。

文化本质上是历史性的，文化反映历史多于反映现实社会，反过来说，文化反映现实社会少于反映历史。也就是说，文化本身是带有更多的历史基因的。因此，文化在时间上是存在历时性的差异的。这种历时性的差异表现为文化变迁，而文化的空间差异则表现为文化变异。

在现代社会中，文化在世界各国各地的时间和空间有差异性。这种差异性主要与工业化的发展进程有关。

一般情况下，工业化起步越早、发展越成熟的国家或地区，工业文化对现代生活的影响程度越深。但是，在一些后发的工业化国家或地区，工业文化对当地人们生活的影响也有可能是跳跃式的，即非线性的影响。

从本书前面几章讨论的话题和内容上看，工业技术及其文化对当地人们生活的影响都不同程度地反映出非线性的特点。相对而言，现代工业技术及其文化对人们的衣、食、住、行、游、购、娱等生活领域影响较深，而对婚、丧、生、老、病、死、葬、祭等领域的影响不一，体现出工业文化在现代生活中的非线性影响。

11.3　小结：文化即生活是现代生活的基本命题

我们从工业、技术与社会的维度讨论工业文化与现代生活，做了人类学的文化解读。

文化本身纷繁复杂，现代生活却又包罗万象。但在工业社会和信息社会中，"文化即生活，生活乃文化"构成了现代生活的基本命题。

知识拓展与链接：

通过在一个特定文化变异及其假定的理由之间已经发现的大量跨文化关联性，我们得以去努力理解文化变迁。所有的文化都随着时间变迁，变异是微分变化的产物。因此，我们看到的变异是变迁过程的产物，而那些变异已经发现的预测因素可以说明变迁的原因和方式。

——［美］卡罗尔·恩贝尔（Carol R. Ember）、［美］梅尔文·恩贝尔（Melvin Ember）：《人类文化与现代生活：文化人类学精要（第3版）》，周云水、杨菁华、陈靖云译，北京：电子工业出版社，2016年版，第65页。

后　记

2002年6月博士毕业以后，我在广西师范大学先后开设过人类学与现代生活、中国—东盟的民族宗教与旅游概观等通识类公选课程和旅游人类学、历史人类学等本科生选修课，以及经济人类学、宗教人类学、旅游人类学专题，民族学人类学理论与方法、民族学人类学民俗学经典著作选读等硕士研究生课程，在人类学的相关课程教学中不停耕耘。

2008年10月从兰州大学民族学博士后流动站出站后，我到华南农业大学工作，继续开设人类学与现代生活等通识类公选课程。由于学科专业发展需要，我先后主讲过社会调查理论与方法、田野调查与社会实践、文化人类学、民族社会学、文化社会学等本科生课程和公共管理质性研究方法、MPA社会研究方法等公共管理硕士研究生课程，在多学科的交叉渗透中不断丰富对社会制度、社会行为等文化现象的理解和认识。

2012年初，由我所主讲的人类学与现代生活公选课被遴选为学校A系列课程，成为在校大学生毕业前应该选修的人文素质通识课程之一。同年7月，我主编的《人类学与现代生活》教材出版，12月被评选为广东省优秀社会科学普及作品，我本人也被评为全国优秀社会科学普及名家。此后，我便萌生了从人类学的文化维度系统解读现代生活的想法。

2013年是中国大学的慕课元年，国内一些名校名师开始建设和推出慕课。我也开始以人类学与现代生活课程和教材为基础，筹划建设一门全新的有关现代生活文化分析的课程。2015年7月，我参加了智慧树在线教育公司在广东清远举办的东西部高校联盟慕课培训会，同年底申报了学校首批慕课建设项目——现代生活的文化解读并获得立项资助。由于原来的人类学与现代生活课程属于专题式的校级和广东省级精品视频公开课，是按精品课程模式建设的，并不符合慕课的特点和要求。因此，我决定拓展和重组教学资源，建设全新的慕课（立项为2018年广东省在线开放课程建设项目），但其难度超出自己的想象。几经周折，终于在2019年国庆节后上线智慧树在线教育平台。与此同时，我与科学出版社签订了教材出版合同，但把视频内容转化成文字教材又是一道难关，它们的表达差异实在太大。

本教材的编写分工如下：前言和第1、2、6、7、9、10、11章由廖杨负责编写，第3、4、5、8章由蒙丽负责编写，由廖杨负责统稿。

　　目前，本教材已正式完稿。感谢华南农业大学本科生院（原教务处）各位领导同事对本课程建设和教材出版提供的帮助和支持，感谢科学出版社领导和编辑为本书顺利出版所做的努力！另外，还要特别感谢华南农业大学外国语学院陈喜华副教授领衔的翻译团队（包括张欢、李志英、龙昱琼和美国的 Eliot Wycoff 等老师）对本书英文文稿的译校和润色。由于时间仓促和水平有限，书中难免存在不足之处，敬请读者朋友批评指正。

廖　杨　谨识

2021 年 6 月于羊城

Chapter 1 Modernity, Modern Life and Cultural Interpretation

1.1 Modernity and Modern Life

1.1.1 What Is Modernity?

Modernity is a concept relative to the concept of *tradition*. What is the difference between *modernity* and *tradition*? Of course, different people may have different answers.

From the perspectives of production and life, the characteristics of *modernity* are obvious:

1) Traditional manual production has been replaced by machine production;

2) Time for personal life is given away to serve the industrialized "flow operation";

3) Large-scale machine production and industrialization, standardization, marketization, and profitability constitute the standard configuration of modern society, while time, money and efficiency constitute the main variables of modern life.

1.1.2 What Is Modern Life?

By definition, modern life is connected with modernity and modern society. Compared with the traditional, self-sufficient farming life and handicraft social life in the natural economic era, modern life is adaptive to large-scale machine production in an industrial society.

In other words, modern life refers to the life having a connection with the industrial society. So what are the characteristics of modern life? Firstly, modern life time is dominated by the production or working hour of "flow operations" in an industrial society. Secondly, modern living space is restricted by the space of industrial society. Thirdly, the content of modern life is affected by the types of industrial products. Finally, the quality of modern life is influenced by multiple factors such as the quality of industrial products, market prices and social environment.

1.1.3   Preliminary Interpretation of Modern Life

Modern life is all-encompassing and very complicated. Different people may have different understanding of modern life, and of course they will also have different lifestyles.

As we all know, modernity is connected with industrial society. Large-scale machine production and flow operations are the main characteristics of the production mode of industrial society. Objectively, the large-scale production of machines on this assembly line requires standardization and modeling. For example, standardized technology, standardized production lines, standardized price mechanisms, standardized sales channels, standardized time periods, standardized space design styles (factories, warehouses, shopping malls, direct stores, experience stores, etc.).

The lifestyle that is compatible with this standardization, modeling, and industrialization is modern life, which is completely different from a traditional lifestyle based on natural economy marked by self-sufficiency. Therefore, it is easy to find that people's daily life involves clothing, food, housing, transportation, travel, shopping, entertainment, marriage, funeral, birth, death, sickness, aging, burial, offering, etc., all of which bear an imprint of industrialization.

In modern life, people seem to have many choices, but in fact, that is not the case. Although many people like doing DIY, but this activity is actually restricted to self-design and self-made works due to limited time, space and standardized industrial materials. Doing DIY is essentially a departure from the modern lifestyle, and to a certain extent it can also be seen as a self-return to traditional life. Tradition and modernity are relative, not absolute. Culture has played a very important role in the transition from traditional life to modern life.

1.1.4   Summary

In this section, the meaning of modernity and modern life was discussed, and the main characteristics and basic dimensions of modern life were explained. We hope that through the discussion in this section, students can deepen their understanding of modernity and modern life so that they can lay a good foundation for a further study in the following chapters.

Further Exploration and Links:

Cultural values and attitudes can hinder or promote progress, but their role has been largely ignored by governments and development agencies. I believe that incorporating factors that change values and attitudes into development policies, arrangements and planning is a very meaningful way to ensure that in the next 50 years the world will not experience poverty and injustice which have trapped the majority of poor countries and unfortunate ethnic groups in the past 50 years.

—Samuel Huntington, Lawrence Harrison. *Culture Matters: How Values Shape Human Progress*, Translated by Cheng Kexiong. Beijing: Xinhua Publishing House, 2002: 24.

Suggested Reading:

Culture Matters: How Values Shape Human Progress is a book edited by the famous contemporary political theorist and thinker Huntington. This book demonstrates and expounds the broad and profound influence of culture in various aspects, including culture and economic development, culture and political development, culture and gender, culture and American ethnic groups, Asian crisis and situation changes, answering how cultural values have shaped human progress.The academic proposition that "culture is the mother of system"put forward by Etonga Mangel in this book can be regarded as the finishing touch of this book.

—Quoted from the editor's preface of the Ivy League Translation Series.

1.2   The Relationship Between Culture and Modern Life and Its Interpretation

1.2.1   Culture and Its Relationship with Modern Life

What is culture? According to incomplete statistics, there are as many as two to three hundred cultural concepts. Different people may have different understanding of *culture*. From the perspective of anthropology, everything marked by human activity pertains to culture. Therefore, it is reasonable to say that culture is the product of human activities. In other words, culture refers to all human activities.

What we eat is culture; what we wear is culture; what we live is culture; what we travel is also culture. We live in a world of cultures. Different countries, different regions, and different ethnic groups have formed different cultures through the long-term interaction with nature, with other people, and with themselves, thus constructing varied humanistic worlds and diverse "cultural planets". The cultural landscapes featured by harmony in diversity constitute the basic cultural image of the contemporary world.

Culture is the gene of society, which is historical in nature. Culture reflects history more than it reflects real society, or in other words, culture reflects real society less than it reflects history, as culture provides a bond for a society. Without the bond of culture, there would be no community or organizational unit in society. Therefore, special significance can be found in the analysis of modern life from a cultural perspective.

Culture is closely interrelated with life: life is culture; culture is life. Life and culture complement each other both externally and internally, whose relationship is between being concrete and abstract. Culture is the "glue" of society and the "spice" of life. A society without culture will be in a mess for it cannot function normally and effectively.

1.2.2　How to Explain Modern Life from a Cultural Perspective?

What are the analytical perspectives of culture? In different disciplines, there are different analytical perspectives on culture. In most social sciences and humanities disciplines, culture is understood in narrow sense and merely treated as spiritual things, for instance, spiritual culture. However, such understanding is incomplete even if institutional culture extended from spiritual culture is involved. The reasons are as follows.

From an anthropological perspective, culture is actually an organic whole, either in terms of "division of culture" (material culture and spiritual culture), the "rule of thirds" (material culture, spiritual culture, and behavioral culture), or the "quadruple" (material culture, behavioral culture, institutional culture, and spiritual culture). By making a cross-sectional dissection of culture, we can find the circle structure of culture from outside to inside: material culture→behavioral culture→institutional culture→spiritual culture.[①]

---

① Yang L, Li M. Cultural understanding of global governance: a perspective of religious culture[J]. *Advances in Applied Sociology*, 2018, 8(5): 359-365.

Clothing, food, housing, transportation, travel, shopping, entertainment, marriage, funeral, birth, death, sickness, aging, burial, and offering: all of these constitute the basic areas or dimensions of life in modern society, covering cultural material, behavioral level, institutional level and spiritual level. In modern society, the secular space and the "sacred" space of life are not diametrically opposed, instead, they are relatively opposed. The time limit of spatial isolation depends on the cultural needs of the local society (group). Therefore, we need to analyze modern life as a whole. "The real difference between anthropologists and other onlookers is that they think about what people do in terms of the culture of the subject."[1] The holistic, relative and comparative views of culture constitute an effective perspective for the cultural interpretation in modern life.

1.2.3   Summary

In this section, the relationship between culture and modern life was analyzed; the basic fields, the analytical perspectives of cultural interpretation in modern life, and the logical connection between modern life and cultural interpretation were discussed. With relevant knowledge of cultural anthropology, we hope to help students look at social life and create a better life.

Further Exploration and Links:

The batik craftsmanship of Chinese ethnic costumes has been recorded in detail in the Song Dynasty of China. It is recorded in *Lingwai Dai Da* written by Zhou Qufei, Guilin *Tongpan* in Song Dynasty:

"The Yaos use blue pigment to dye cloth to make markings. These markings are very fine. It uses two pieces of wood, carved into fine flowers to sandwich the cloth, and the molten wax is poured into the hollow, and then the board is taken. The cloth is thrown into various blue dyes. If the cloth is affected by blue, the cloth will be boiled to remove the wax, so it can be imprinted with very fine spots, which is very impressive."

—Zhou Qufei. *Proofreading and Annotation of Lingwai Dai Da*. Beijing: Zhonghua Book Company, 1999: 224.

---

① 约翰·奥莫亨德罗. 像人类学家一样思考 [M]. 张经纬, 等, 译. 北京: 北京大学出版社, 2017: 16.
John Omohundro. *Thinking like an Anthropologist* [M]. Translated by Zhang Jingwei, et al. Beijing: Peking University Press, 2017: 16.

Suggested Reading:

Thinking like an Anthropologist was compiled and published by John Omohundro, an outstanding professor in the Department of Anthropology, State University of New York, Potsdam, USA. Each chapter is carefully organized by focusing on a key issue, and related field stories reveal potential problems, challenges and consequences encountered by anthropologists in this field. Through personal field experience, the author vividly demonstrated the core concepts and probed into problems faced by anthropologists, which helps students to master the methods of anthropological research on human behaviors and concepts. In addition, students will have an opportunity to read this book and keep thinking like an anthropologist in either local or exotic culture environments.

Chapter 2   Clothing and Food: Cultural Preferences in Human Society

People cover their bodies with clothing and regard food as their prime want. To keep ourselves alive, we have to dress and feed ourselves. However, when we are living in today's industrialized society, clothing and food are not only the basics for maintaining our survival, but also reflect our cultural preferences in human society to a large extent.

2.1   The Meaning and Origin of Clothing

2.1.1   The Meaning of Clothing

Yifu (clothing) is a noun in modern Chinese. It generally refers to things that people wear to cover the body or protect themselves against cold, wind, moisture, sunburn, and dust. However, in ancient Chinese, the two characters of *yi* and *fu* were ever given different meanings. In the Han Dynasty, Xu Shen defined *yi* and *fu* in his *Shuowen Jiezi*: "*Yi* is what people wear to cover their bodies. The clothes worn on the upper part of the body are called 'yi', and those worn on the lower part of the body are called 'chang'. The shape of this character resembles the shape of one character of 'ren'(human) overlapping other two characters of 'ren'. Any character related to clothing will take the character of 'yi'as its component. "[1] Regarding the interpretation of *fu*, as explained in *Shuowen Jiezi*, *fu* means use. Another explanation of this character is that *fu* refers to the horse on the right side of the carriage for the convenience of the carriage turning to the right. "zhou" and "ren" are used as the components of the character *fu* in ancient Chinese[2].

---

① 许慎. 说文解字: 附检字（卷八上）[M]. 北京: 中华书局, 1963: 170.
Xu Shen. *Shuowen Jiezi* (with check characters)[M]. Volume 8, upper part. Beijing: Zhonghua Book Company, 1963: 170.
② 许慎. 说文解字: 附检字（卷八上）[M]. 北京: 中华书局, 1963: 176.
Xu Shen. *Shuowen Jiezi* (with check characters) [M]. Volume 8, upper part. Beijing: Zhonghua Book Company, 1963: 176.

According to *Cihai*, the definition of *yi* is similar to that of *yifu*: "In ancient China, *yi* referred to the clothes worn on the upper part of the body and *chang* referred to those worn on the lower part of the body"[①]. The word of *Yishang* is recorded in *Book of Songs*, in which one of the poems described the panic of people's wearing "yi" as "chang" and "chang" as "yi" when they are asked to work early in the morning before dawn. This shows that people in ancient China already had a clear distinction between the upper and lower clothes at the latest of the Warring States Period in China.

It can be seen that in the context of ancient Chinese, *yi* and *fu* did have different meanings. As for the use of *yifu* as a word by combining characters of *yi* and *fu*, this practice was only popular since modern times of China.

2.1.2   The Origin of Clothing

Scholars have different views on the origin of clothes or clothing. Generally speaking, theories on its origin include adaptation-to-climate theory, human-body-protection theory, talisman theory, symbolism theory, aesthetics theory and shame theory. From the very basics, clothing should be created as a result of human adaptation to the natural environment.

According to the research of modern science, it is found that human beings have undergone climate changes since the birth of humans. Especially as early as in the Quaternary Ice Age, humans began to cover themselves with animal furs to keep out the cold and stay warm. Changes in the climate and environment have promoted the creation of human clothing at the very beginning when people kept warm by putting on leaves and animal skin wraps. The origin of ancient Chinese costumes is "a gradual and dynamic development process in which human beings discover nature, overcome difficulties from nature and conduct the transformation of nature. It is a continuous process from simple to complex, from physiology to psychology, and from materials to culture, including constant upgrade, revolution and enrichment"[②]. In the primitive society, human evolution was more supported by natural physiological adaptation than by social adaptation. "Therefore, the origin of clothing is more based on practicality. However, due to the extremely wide distribution of humans and huge variations between the climate, natural geographical conditions, and environments from place to place, clothes invented in primitive tribes from different regions all appeared in their

---

① 辞海编辑委员会. 辞海 [Z] . 1999 年版缩印本. 上海: 上海辞书出版社, 2000: 2306.
   Cihai Editorial Committee. *Cihai* (1999 edition)[Z]. Shanghai: Shanghai Lexicographic Publishing House, 2000: 2306.
② 贾玺增. 中国服饰艺术史 [M] . 天津: 天津人民美术出版社, 2009: 1.
   Jia Xizeng. *History of Chinese Costume Art*[M]. Tianjin: Tianjin People's Fine Arts Publishing House, 2009:1.

special forms. In the cold-temperate regions, human beings put on animal skins or leaves very early in order to defend against the cold. In the tropical regions, although the problem of keeping out the cold does not exist, there are other factors that endanger human survival."[①] "The appearance of clothing is the result of changes in human body structure and physiological organs during their evolution from apes to humans in order to adapt to the needs of nature."[②] Climate adaptation theory and human body protection theory may be the best theories to reflect the real origin of human clothing in ancient times. Doctrines such as talisman theory, symbolism theory, aesthetics theory, and shame theory are the research results gained after human beings entered a civilized society.

Culture is an important symbol that distinguishes humans from animals. However, culture is defined by its circle structure. To speak of the cultural structure in a broad sense, the "dualistic" culture is composed of the material culture in the outer circle, and the spiritual culture in the inner circle. The "ternary-structured" culture is composed of the material culture in the outer circle, the spiritual culture in the inner circle and the behavioral culture falling in between. The "quaternary-structured" culture is composed of the material culture, behavioral culture, institutional culture and spiritual culture from the outside to the inside. Humans have both biological and social attributes, with biological attributes being inherent and social attributes derived or evolved. In this sense, the origin of clothing should be the result of satisfying human adaptation to the natural environment, especially to the climate change. After all, the physiological needs to adapt to changes in the natural environment are far more important than the psychological needs, and are more in line with the characteristics of the primitive society.

2.1.3　Summary

Yifu in modern Chinese is a noun. But *yi* and *fu* in ancient Chinese had different meanings. The combination of *yi* and *fu* to be used as *yifu* is not a common practice until after the modern times. The origin of clothing should be the result of human adaptation to the natural environment, especially to the climate change.

---

① 戴争. 中国古代服饰简史 [M] . 北京: 中国轻工业出版社, 1988: 2.
　Dai Zheng. *A brief history of ancient Chinese costumes*[M]. Beijing: China Light Industry Press, 1988: 2.
② 朱和平. 中国服饰史稿 [M] . 郑州: 中州古籍出版社, 2001: 52.
　Zhu Heping. *Draft of Chinese Clothing History*[M]. Zhengzhou: Zhongzhou Ancient Books Publishing House, 2001:52.

Further Exploration and Links:

Although the costumes of Chinese ethnic groups are very different from region to region, they often retain the traditional styles of ancient Chinese costumes, reflect many primitive cultural imprinting, and show us the development of ancient human costumes. They are the "living fossils" for us to better understand and prove the reality of early human costumes. We have discovered the origin and evolution principles of clothing: it originated from human's sheltering from wind and rain and defending against nature; it assists in sexual exaggeration or avoiding sexual attraction between opposite sexes; it develops in the enlightenment of nature, and prospers as a means of showing off one's wealth.

——Yang Changguo. *Symbolization and Symbols*: *Chinese Ethnic Costume Culture*. Beijing: Beijing Publishing House, 2000:6.

2.2   Main Features of Modern Clothing

As we just mentioned, modern society is often associated with the machine and the assembly line production in industrial society. Therefore, clothes in modern society actually evolve as a result of industrialization. This change is mainly manifested in the following aspects.

2.2.1   Diversified Fabric Materials of Clothes

Most of the fabrics of traditional clothing are made locally from local natural plants and processed by hand. For example, the cultivation of mulberry silkworms, spinning and weaving in traditional Chinese farming society are basically pure natural. Even some fabrics are processed by wax printing technology, with the raw materials of the fabrics being mainly natural minerals or plants.[1]

In modern society, due to the advancement of industrial technology and the general improvement of aesthetic appreciation, the fabric materials of modern clothing are no longer limited to the simply processed animals skins, plants or minerals from nature. Instead, some materials or fabrics made by chemical synthesis have appeared in the market, such as artificial fibers, glass fibers, copper ammonia fibers, metal fibers, polyester, artificial leather, and so on. These new materials together with traditional

---

① 戴争. 中国古代服饰简史 [M] . 北京: 中国轻工业出版社, 1988: 8-21.
　　Dai Zheng. *A brief history of ancient Chinese costumes*[M]. Beijing: China Light Industry Press, 1988: 8-21.

materials such as cotton, linen, silk, wool, and leather, constitute a diversity of fabric materials for clothing in modern society.[1][2]

2.2.2   Refined Manufacturing Process of Clothing

The production process of traditional apparel is relatively simple, mainly relying on manual measurement, manual cutting of fabric, and hand stitching by using sewing needle and thimble hoop. And to deal with different fabrics, different types of needles are used. For example, No. 7 to No. 9 needles are used for silk and other fine fiber fabrics; No. 4 to No. 5 needles are used for making buttonholes or sewing buttons; No. 6 to No. 8 needles that are neither thick nor thin are used for general wool. In addition, some traditional garment decoration techniques such as bordering, inlay, piping (also called *Kun*), swinging cloth, and making a Chinese frog will consume us a long time, adding difficulties to the large-scale production.[3]

The batch cutting for modern apparel (also known as industrial cutting), machine sewing, special process sewing and electric ironing processing, the production process has provided us with a more standardized and refined production process. Even for the production of a single-piece tailor-made garment, the production process has become more elaborate. In the 1950s, in addition to manual spreading, trolleys or reciprocating electric spreaders began to be put into use. In the 1980s, a microcomputer was used to control the automatic spreader, which can automatically cross the front and back or single-sided spreading, automatically trim the edges, and even count.[4]

In terms of cutting methods, computer-controlled automatic cutting machines appeared in the late 1960s. From the perspective of sewing technology, in addition to high-speed lock-stitch sewing machines (referred to as lock-stitch machines), modern sewing machines are also equipped with multi-needle and multi-thread over-lock sewing machines (referred to as over-lock machines). As well as replacing manual bag opening, buttonholing, buttons sewing, pad-stitching, lining (combination of clothing and lining), sleeves installing, trousers waist installing, various special sewing machines

① 马新敏. 服装面料艺术再造的多元化 [J]. 纺织导报, 2012, (4): 92-93.
   Ma Xinmin. Diversified fabric materials of clothes[J]. *China Textile Leader*, 2012, (4): 92-93.
② 佚名. 传统面料如何多元化[EB/OL]. (2002-02-06)[2019-09-01]. https://www. tnc.com.cn/info/c-001001-d-61906. html.
   Anonymous. How to diversify traditional fabrics[EB/OL].(2002-02-06) [2019-09-01]. https://www.tnc.com.cn/info/c-001001-d-61906.html.
③ 李华麒. 从服装缝制工具的演变看手工制作的意义和作用 [J]. 武汉纺织大学学报, 2019, 32(1): 3-6.
   Li Huaqi. The handmade meaning and function from the evolution of clothing sewing tools[J]. *Journal of Wuhan Textile University*, 2019, 31(1): 3-6.
④ 程启, 苟秉志. 现代服装流行趋势 [J]. 天津纺织工学院学报, 1987, (4): 116-122.
   Cheng Qi, Gou Bingzhi. Fashion trend of modern clothing[J]. *Journal of Tianjin Institute of Textile Science and Technology*, 1987, (4): 116-122.

such as the pleating machine and the multi-function electronic sewing machine with automatic speed control and solid circuit were invented and put into use.[①]

In the 1980s, the industrial cameras and electronic computer monitoring were used to automatically identify the style of cutting, and a relatively more advanced automatic sewing system was invented to conduct transmission and automatic classification control. At the same time, advanced computerized embroidery machines were brought into the market, which can accomplish nine-color embroidery with 24 heads working synchronously, and are equipped with more than 10 decorative machines with two to twenty-five needles. They can create complex art patterns on the fabric, so as to further improve the production process of modern clothing.[②]

In addition, electric irons were more commonly used since the 1950s. In the late 1950s, China's first generation of "three-collar machine" was successfully developed and began to be used for the bonding and arc shaping of shirt collars. And a special bonding machine for bonding fusible interlining by hot pressing was invented in the United Kingdom. This type of bonding machine can complete rolling and flat pressing, with the time, pressure and temperature controlled.[③]For the ironing of semi-finished and finished products, steam ironing machines have been applied to complete complex processes such as moulding, inflation, multi-station rotation, etc. A suit of steam ironing equipment can be used to complete 12 types of final ironing including ironing sleeves, body, three-dimensional shaping and other 18 types of intermediate ironing, such as slitting and drawing, so as to bring the final product that is dry and matte with the pressing mark. The emergence of these new modern ironing equipment and new techniques has greatly improved the ironing quality of products.[④]

2.2.3 Modern Fashion Styles

The modern fashion styles are always imprinted with characteristics of the times. In general, there are eight major types of fashion styles, including the classic, sport, casual, ethnic, elegant, neutral, avant-garde and relaxing styles.[⑤]

---

① 上海针织一厂. 缝纫机电子控制自动启动 [J]. 针织工业, 1976, (4): 35-38.
   Shanghai 1st Knitting Factory. Automatic start of sewing machine electronic control[J]. *Knitting Industries*,1976, (4): 35-38.

② 谢家泽. 电脑绣花机 [J]. 纺织消息, 1986, (8): 10.
   Xie Jiaze. Computer embroidery machine[J]. *Textile News*, 1986, (8): 10.

③ 祁凡. 服装粘合衬用粘合机 [J]. 粘合剂, 1989, (3): 36-38.
   Qi Fan. Adhesives for clothing adhesive interlining[J]. *Adhesives*, 1989, (3): 36-38.

④ 毛立辉. 跨界设计: 一种新锐的生活态度 [J]. 中国服饰, 2012, (11): 21.
   Mao Lihui. Cross-border design: a cutting-edge attitude to life[J]. *China Fashion*, 2012, (11): 21.

⑤ 冯旭敏. 服装感性类型风格形象特征及文化元素构成分析 [J]. 国际纺织导报, 2012, 40(1): 66-68, 70-72.
   Feng Xumin. Analysis of clothing perceptual types, style, image characteristics and cultural elements composition[J]. *Melliand China* 2012, 40(1): 66-68, 70-72.

The classic style has the characteristics of traditional clothing. Being relatively mature, it is suitable for most middle-aged women and relatively conservative young women, and can be accepted by most women. This style is plain and simple, with invisible personalized features, and slightly weaker fashionable aesthetics, but it is a choice for a wide range of females who pay attention to the quality of the garments.

Drawing on sportswear design elements, the sporty style is filled with vitality. It mostly applies block surface division and strip division, zipper, trademark and other decorations. This kind of urban fashion style appeals to a wide range of customers.

The casual style brings us a relaxing, casual and comfortable wearing experience, and appeals to customers of various age groups. This style is suitable for daily activities such as relaxing oneself, meeting friends, going out, shopping, and so on, making people look friendly and accessible.

The ethnic fashion style draws inspiration from elements of Chinese and western ethnic and folk costumes. The Chinese style features the elements of traditional Chinese costumes such as Tang suits, cheongsams and other ethnic costumes. The western style features foreign national costumes, such as bohemian style, German national style, Russian national style and other retro styles.

The elegant style is characterized with strong feminine elements, delicate details, and exquisite workmanship. It is a more fashionable, mature, and gorgeous fashion style.

The neutral style weakens the feminine characteristics by drawing on the design elements of menswear. It aims to present the chic and neat effect. With a certain degree of fashion, it is a tough-looking and tasteful fashion style.

The avant-garde style features advanced popular elements, with application of more asymmetrical structures and decorations. Various modeling elements are also applied in this style but only exaggerated in quantity, size and position. It is a style with strong personality, which is different from conventional style in the structure and decoration.

The relaxing style features lively and vibrant elements, which is suitable daily wear for young women. It is a girlish fashion style replete with vigor.

Despite there is little change to these styles, the popular style will always vary from year to year. As the saying goes, "there are often different styles coming into fashion while there are similar flowers in bloom every year". Fashion is actually a relative concept. The styles, colors and decorations of clothing that used to be popular decades ago may return to fashion under the creative transformation of fashion designers.

Every year, fashion designers make certain modifications or adjustments to various types of clothing styles. They use different fabrics, colors and decorations to create new fashion elements for the born of a popular style, which are displayed by models at the Fashion Week. For instance, following the new trend, some European and American designers apply the cutting-edge design thinking to integrate Chinese Han clothing elements into modern design to create the new fashion style. By retaining the characteristics of traditional Han costumes and adding individualized, rational and popular design elements, they play a certain role in promoting and reviving Han costume culture.[①] According to the relative survey, the cultural acceptance of global consumers directly affects their attitudes towards Chinese clothing, but does not completely affect their consumption intentions. The practicality of Chinese clothing is expected to have the most significant impact on their consumption intentions. Although consumers have developed similar degree of brand recognition for domestic and foreign brands, they tend to form a positive attitude towards domestic brands. Consumers are more inclined to choose the fashion style applying Chinese elements in a concise and subtle way.[②]

2.2.4　Individualized Functional Use of Clothes

There are relatively single purposes of the function and use of traditional clothing. They are mainly used to protect humans from cold, moisture, sun exposure, and dust, keep them warm, provide skin care, and cover up their embarrassment. But in the industrial society, the functions and uses of clothing tend to be diversified and individualized[③], which is not only required by industrialization, but also the consequence resulting from industrialization.

As we know, modern society is connected with the large-scale production by industrialized machinery. Industrialized mass production requires not only the standardization of production technology, but also the standardized and unified dress of employees in factories or enterprises. Therefore, no matter whether in the production workshop, service window, or some government offices serving the public, we can see employees in uniforms.

At the same time, we can also see that people are often engaged in housework,

① 路晶晶, 王付宏. 汉族服饰款式造型元素现代设计的时尚表达 [J]. 纺织学报, 2020, 5(2): 150-155.
Lu Jingjing, Wang Fuhong. The fashionable expression of modern design of the style and shape elements of Han ethnic clothing[J]. *Journal of Textile Research*, 2020, 5(2): 150-155.
② 邢乐, 梁惠娥, 刘传兰. 中式服装消费意向的影响因素 [J]. 纺织学报, 2017, 38(3): 155-161, 167.
Xing Le, Liang Hui'e, Liu Chuanlan. Influencing factors of Chinese clothing consumption intention[J]. *Journal of Textile Research*, 2017, 38(3): 155-161, 167.
③ "现代服装产业技术" 课题组. 服装: 高性能、多功能满足个性化需求 [J]. 中国纺织, 2015,(6): 99.
"Modern Apparel Industry Technology" Research Group. Apparel: high-performance, multi-function to meet individual needs[J]. *China Textile*, 2015, (6): 99.

sports or other leisure activities after work, with each of them having different dress requirements. Therefore, in addition to work uniforms, people also have home clothes, sportswear, casual clothes, and some special occasion clothing (such as wedding clothes, funeral dresses, performance costumes, dance clothes, etc.) to meet people's personalized needs.

In essence, this is actually a way for people to distinguish the time spent working for the industrial production from the time spent on personal life through the change of dress. Someone said, "The task of the fashion designer in the future is to explore as many artistic expressions as possible in mass production so as to create individualized fashion styles and fully satisfy people's spiritual needs and their need of trendy clothes when fashion styles are subject to certain social and functional constraints. At the same time, designers should achieve the organic integration of the national outstanding traditions with advanced international design concepts to follow the global trend with design ideas learnt from different cultures"[①]. This statement makes sense as the design will definitely be more popular globally when it is featured with more ethnic elements. What a dazzling and beautiful world it will be when the fashion cultures of all ethnic groups in the world complement each other.

2.2.5   Summary

It is worth noting that in the industrialized modern life, the choice of clothing is not only to meet people's physical needs of protecting them from cold, moisture, sun exposure, and dust, and providing skin care, but also their psychological needs of covering up embarrassment, body-shaping and improving aesthetic taste and so on. Therefore, the choice of clothing reflects people's cultural preferences in human society to much extent.

Further Exploration and Links:

At the end of the 20th century, the oriental style came into the spotlight of the international fashion industry. The elegance, peace, simplicity and mystery of the oriental style began to become the most trendy fashion elements in the world. With the rise of China, Chinese home and abroad are increasingly proud of being dressed in Chinese style. Chinese women begin to favor Chinese-style jackets, and many

---

① 程启，苟秉志. 现代服装流行趋势 [J]. 天津纺织工学院学报, 1987, (4): 116-122.
  Cheng Qi, Gou Bingzhi. Fashion trend of modern clothing[J]. *Journal of Tianjin Institute of Textile Science and Technology*, 1987, (4): 116-122.

Chinese men also believe it to be fashionable to wear Chinese-style padded jackets. Today, Chinese fashion is not just limited in the design of Chinese jackets but also reflected in various women's dresses. For many Chinese women, their clothes are so much in fashion that they are sometimes dressed in a printed or colorful cotton bordered and stand-collar jacket, matching jeans and a pair of leather shoes in the latest popular styles, which is so modern and retro.

...The increasingly enriched clothing texture greatly meets people's changing needs of fashion styles and their preference for different fabrics and reflects people's attitude towards life. For example, some environmentalists reject fur and cashmere products, leisure style lovers are fascinated about pure cotton texture, the unique elegance of linen products is endowed with a noble and mysterious meaning, and silk is the endorsement of wealth and tradition.

The 20th century has proved to be the most fashion-conscious century so far. The expanding markets of clothing, accessories, and cosmetics with increasing sales and the rapid development of media industry have enabled more and more people to approach fashion, appreciate fashion, and discover beauty in fashion. Fashion has become a kind of lifestyle that the general public understands and is willing to invest in.

—Huamei. *Chinese Clothing*. Beijing: China Intercontinental Press, 2004: 150-152.

2.3   Modern Clothing and Cultural Preferences

2.3.1   Culture and Clothing in Modern Life

As mentioned in the previous part, modern life is connected with industrial society. Industrialization and standardization have regulated people's dress styles, but also affected people's perception of clothing culture.

In modern life, clothing carries cultural perceptions, and culture in turn influences styles of clothing. The industrialized production distinguishes our daily activities in working hours from those in non-working hours. Therefore, we often change our clothes even a few times in a day. "Do not take work home" is an important work philosophy and lifestyle for people, but for most employees, commuting on time sometimes becomes an ideal or luxury. Although it is time for people to get off work, they will still be stuck in a dilemma about whether to work overtime or take work home if they have not finished it.

In addition, with the popularity of working online, some white-collars can work at home without leaving their homes. Of course, they can be dressed in any clothes as they please.

It is worth noting that the boundary between work and life in terms of the time and space will be blurred when people take work home or work at home. Therefore, the obvious space and time boundaries of fashion also begin to blur, which reflects the new trend of industrialized modern life.

In fact, clothing is also endowed with space image and connotation. The human body is a specific three-dimensional image that occupies a certain space composed of four faces on the front and back, and on both sides, and curves of the chest, waist, and hips. Clothing is a three-dimensional form attached to the human body and exists in a certain environment and space. Since clothing is a visual image in a certain environment, it will change with the change of the natural environment, social environment or living environment. Otherwise, the harmony will be broken between the clothing and the environment. For example, in the man-made space environment of modern buildings and the natural environment of nature reserves, the spatial form of clothing should be different to achieve the harmony between clothing and environment. On the contrary, if someone wears a suit or evening dress to play on the beach, or a bikini to listen to an academic report, the spacial balance between clothing and environment will be lost.

With the passage of time, the advancement of technology and the improvement of living standards, people tend to design their own looks by using trendy clothing fabrics, shapes, and colors as well as four-dimensional spatial changes including the length, width, height and time of clothing. For instance, elderly women in Europe and the United States like to wear loose, large-flowered and gorgeous skirts to hide their aging body and try to restore their fading youth. Teenagers prefer to wear tight-fitting, gray and monochromatic suits to reveal their budding youth and pursue the coming maturity.[①]

2.3.2   Are there Cultural Preferences for Human Clothing?

As we know, the origin of clothing is to meet human physiological needs to adapt to changes in the natural environment. Later, aesthetic factors are incorporated in the design and creation of clothes. The different natural ecological environment and

---

① 赖涛. 试论服装的空间感 [J] . 南昌职业技术师范学院学报, 2000, (1): 36-39.
    Lai Tao. On the sense of space in clothing[J]. *Journal of Nanchang Vocational and Technical Teachers College*, 2000, (1): 36-39.

cultural traditions of the East and West affect people's cultural preferences to their choice of apparel.

Some people say that Chinese clothes are like two-dimensional paintings, while western clothes are like three-dimensional sculptures. These statements sound reasonable since Chinese clothing displays the two-dimensional effect but ignores the side structure design and western-style clothing emphasizes the three-dimensional effect, fits the curves of human body and accords with the laws of human movement, therefore generally favored by people in western countries for being both fit and practical.

There is a big difference in the aesthetic cultures of Chinese and western fashion industry. Chinese culture originated from the continental civilization, which leads to a more stubborn "primitive" awareness in fashion industry in China. In addition, Chinese culture is a culture carrying subtle sentiment, with its art emphasizing lyricism. As a result, the spiritual meaning and cultural taste of clothing are considered as important components for its fashion design, with emphasis on the balance, symmetry, and uniformity of fashion style, and priority given to regularity of clothes.

The aesthetic characteristics of traditional Chinese clothing reflect the aesthetic mentality and cultural features of the Chinese nation. Chinese are influenced by the complementary aesthetic ideas of Confucianism, Buddhism and Taoism, and attach great importance to the combination of emotion and reasoning. Therefore, Chinese-style women's clothing often tightly wraps the human body, adding a sense of mystery, while the men's clothing is often custom fit and is full of the beauty of harmony.

Originating from marine civilization, western culture is relatively more open in nature. With a tendency to integrate foreign clothing culture, it is good at expressing contradictions and conflicts, favors stimulating and extreme fashion styles, and treats individuality as a priority. It is a culture filled with similes, which attaches importance to the objective aesthetic beauty of shapes, lines, patterns and colors. In the western culture, visual comfort is regarded as the first priority, the beauty of the human body is admired, the sexual differences of the human body are presented, and the expression of sexiness is never treated as a taboo. The western classical fashion designers often tend to express women's second sexual characteristics, such as showing their neck, shoulder, back, and half-chest to express the female curves by tightening the waist and cushioning the hips, while the modern style tends to present the natural shape of the human body in a simple form, with short and tight design regarded as fashionable.

2.3.3　Summary

In this section, we discussed clothing and culture in modern life, and analyzed people's cultural preferences in their fashion choices, the differences between Chinese and western clothing cultures and the future trend of their respective development.

Further Exploration and Links:

Clothing not only reflects the historical development of national culture, but also provides a channel to understand overall human culture. It not only tells us the local customs in people's civil life, but also gives us a clue to explore people's life habits and deep thoughts. There is an old saying in China: "Learn about the local customs whenever you arrive at a new place." When you visit a city or village for the first time, you will first see the physical appearance of houses and buildings, and then the dresses of the local people. From the dresses and images of local people, you will immediately learn about the local customs and traditions, and think about the overall cultural background in that area from a macro perspective before having any verbal communication.

—Hua Mei. *Costume Folklore*. Beijing: China Textile and Apparel Press, 2004: 3.

2.4   Cultural Preference and Beauty Culture

2.4.1   What Is Cultural Preference

Preference is one's tendency to do a certain activity, which means that one is willing to pay a premium for some items that consumers consider as very important to him or her and are willing to pay a premium for it. Certain preferences will lead to people's repetitive behaviors.

Cultural preference is relative to personal hobbies. It is a cognitive tendency formed by consumers under the influence of a common cultural environment. In other words, it occurs when the common values in a community drive people to have a common pursuit of something.

Closely connected with the traditions and customs, values, moral standards, and people's religious beliefs, cultural preferences are reflected in all aspects of their daily life. For instance, people's choices of clothes, food, housing and transportation means, and their requirements of certain colors, numbers, price and quality in the purchase of goods are often influenced by their cultural preferences to certain extent.

Cultural preference is different from physiological preference. It is the unique cognitive tendency in people's purchase behavior due to the long-term stimulation or influence of culture. Cultural preference itself has the following characteristics:

　　1) Universal. It is considered as a universal concept as it is a common psychological reaction in a certain cultural circle or group, and a common behavior tendency in a consumer group shown by many people.

　　2) Different. Consumers from different cultural groups or at sub-cultural levels differ greatly in their cultural preferences.

　　3) Stable. Similar to cultural influence, cultural preferences are also historical and stable.

　　4) Mandatory. Cultural preference is imposed on each member by various groups, so it has an obvious necessity and coercion.

Further Exploration and Links:

　　There seems to be a diagonal line from northeast to southwest separating ethnic groups that rely mainly on dairy products from ethnic groups that rely on rice as a staple food. Therefore, a winding crescent is formed as the line runs from the Korean area in the northeast of China to Yunnan and southern Xizang. The ethnic groups that mainly have dairy products basically live in the north, while the ethnic groups that eat rice (mainly glutinous rice in ancient times) live in the south. "Northern milk" and "southern rice" can summarize the dietary characteristics of Chinese ethnic groups. At the bordering areas of these two regions, there is a "milk porridge" diet of adding boiled rice to milk.

　　—Li Bingze. *A Multi-Taste Table*: *Chinese Ethnic Food Culture*. Beijing: Beijing Publishing House, 2000: 41.

2.4.2　Beauty and Its Cultural Preferences

　　As the name suggests, beauty refers to a beautiful face, which is a static cultural expression. In fact, beauty can also be used as an active practice or social behavior: plastic surgery.

　　"A girl will doll herself up for him who loves her." The plastic surgery seems always the choice of women, but in reality it has also been the option of many men. So, what are the cultural preferences for the plastic surgery?

　　Firstly, the advancement of medical technology and the development of visual media industry such as fashion magazines, television, and movies have spawned idol worship among white-collars and their copying of the clothing, apparel, and appearance of their idols.

Further Exploration and Links:

For thousands of years, people from all over the world have been trying to decorate the human body by tattoos, piercings, circumcision, binding feet, and even changing the shape of the skull. In order to achieve these goals, modern medical technology has offered a whole new set of surgeries.

As the medical industry continues to grow, more and more surgeons have entered the beauty industry to develop what the anthropologist Laura Nader calls the "standardized" body shapes. Laura Nader pays attention to women's bodies and realizes that "the body image looks natural in a specific cultural environment". For example, in American culture, breast augmentation is nothing but common choices, while in some South African countries, female circumcision and vaginal reduction (also known as female genital mutilation) are not considered to be bizarre.

Many feminist writers believe that "American women choose to receive the surgery of breast augmentation, while African women are just forced to have it done". However, maybe no one will deny that in fact women choose to have the breast augmentation surgery under the comprehensive influence of the beauty industry.

—William A. Haviland, Harald E.L.Prins, Dana Walrath, et al. *Anthropology: The Human Challenge* (14th Edition), Translated by Zhou Yunshui, Chen Xiang, Lei Lei, et al. Beijing: Publishing House of Electronics Industry, 2018: 350.

Secondly, in modern society, a person is always perceived and judged like an object. We tend to examine a person quickly through his or her clothing or the education he or she receives to, accept or reject him or her. This is actually an absolute materialization and labeling of people. Such methods of and procedures for knowing and judging people are found in all aspects of modern social systems and institutions.

Guy Debord, a French thinker and sociologist, once asserted in his masterpiece work *The Society of the Spectacle*: "In a society where modern production is omnipresent, life itself is shown as a huge accumulation of landscapes with all direct forms of existence transformed into a kind of vision." In other words, in today's society with highly developed production and media, we know and understand the world through watching TV programs and commercials instead of having real personal experiences and direct contact.

Finally, in the modern society, consumers' perception of beauty, pursuit of beauty, and desire for beauty are all guided and manipulated by the plastic surgery industry and mass media. This complicated guidance and manipulation is a subtle power mechanism. It is this power mechanism that implicitly supports the glamorous performance of today's commercial advertising, stars, models, political leaders, and cultural celebrities on the public stage, which then becomes an imperceptible cultural ideology influencing the entire postmodern world.

Plastic surgery can also be seen as a way to invent and create pleasure. In the daily life of common people, they are often busy with cooking in the kitchen or travelling between home and their workplace having a very safe experience of life. But some people may feel so bored about the repetitive lifestyle. Out of the desire for the pursuit of a better life, some people with certain financial foundation attempt to better present their beautiful images and improve the quality of life by receiving plastic surgery. This is a natural choice deserving our respect. After all, the pursuit of a better life is human nature.

In the 1990s, with the rapid economic development and the increasing maturity of medical technology, plastic surgery gradually came into the view of the public in China and integrated into people's lives. Cosmetology is a new branch subject derived from plastic surgery. It combines anatomy, morphology and other disciplines to correct and repair deformities and defects of the surface tissues and organs of human body through surgical operations, so as to restore the function and shape of the deformed human parts or to improve normal human parts. However, if one receives excessive plastic surgery, the harm it brings can not be ignored. From an ethical point of view, the hazards caused by excessive plastic surgery include the damage to the life and health rights of the plastic beauticians, the loss of subjectivity, and difficulties in identity.[①] It should arouse people's attention.

2.4.3 Summary

Cultural preferences are prevalent in human society. Cultural preference is the cognitive tendency formed by consumers under the influence of a common cultural environment. It has the characteristics of being universal, different, stable and mandatory. Plastic surgery in the real world is an important manifestation of cultural preferences due to people's preference to and pursuit of beauty.

---

① 刘彩凤, 刘镇江. 过度整形美容的伦理探析 [J]. 中国医学伦理学, 2019, 32(9): 1174-1178.
　Liu Caifeng, Liu Zhenjiang. The ethical analysis of excessive plastic surgery[J]. *Chinese Medical Ethics*, 2019, 32(9): 1174-1178.

Further Exploration and Links：

In a pioneering breast augmentation surgery, the doctor can "meticulously measure and mark the exact size of the breast, and accurately position it in the horizontal and vertical position according to the rational body size of ancient Greek female sculptures". In response to the needs of the beauty market, the current plastic surgery business is booming and breast augmentation surgery is expanding rapidly around the world.

——William A. Haviland, Harald E.L.Prins, Dana Walrath, et al. *Anthropology: The Human Challenge* (14th Edition), Translated by Zhou Yunshui, Chen Xiang, Lei Lei, et al. Beijing: Publishing House of Electronics Industry, 2018: 350.

2.5　Cultural Preferences for Body Shaping and Food

2.5.1　Body Shaping and Its cultural Preferences

(1) Body shaping, curves, muscles and fitness

The beauty of human body is not only based on people's visual senses, but also on people's understanding and standards of beauty. More importantly, it is based on people's cultural preferences. The reason is simple: in modern society, the "beautiful" body can be shaped. In addition to medical plastic surgery, it can also be achieved through standardized fitness training. Therefore, in a highly developed urban society, there are many fitness venues, fitness equipment and fitness coaches, and they can even be seen everywhere. Belly dance, yoga and other fitness dances are popular with young women, while treadmills, push-pull weightlifting and other sport are popular among urban male white-collars. All of these phenomena are actually the result of "production" of the beautiful body in the industrialized age.

(2) Self-beauty and perception of others: do people rely on clothing to look beautiful?

At the end of March 2019, the suggestion by an American mother that women should not wear tight clothes attracted a lot of attention online and heated debate. According to a report from *Global Times* on April 1, 2019, the University of Notre Dame in Indiana, with its undergraduate education ranking in the top 20 in the United States, went on a hot search because of a "legging problem" argument. The mother of a male student of the university, Maryann White, published a real-name article in the school media, slamming the leggings of female students of the university to cause "discomfort" for boys, leading to the scorn and criticism by many girls. Even some boys wore tights to support the girls.Those girls who wore tights thought that tights can highlight their figure and curvaceous beauty, and they are the choice of self-beauty and it has nothing to do with others. In addition, there is no legal requirement on whether or not girls should wear tights. But the boy's mother still believed that girls wearing tight pants would let boys have sex fantasies or impulses, which was a kind of "interference" to boys. This example shows that different people may have different, or even opposite perception and interpretation of beauty when they have different stands.

(3) Medical plastic surgery: who has the "right" to beauty

Modern technology in medical science is much more developed than before. Due to the improvement of economic conditions and the material living standards, people attach more and more importance to improving their looks and shaping their bodies. Therefore, cosmetic surgery hospitals are springing up in increasing numbers in some large and medium cities in China. However, in such a highly industrialized society filled with assembly line work, can you have a right about your own body? If so, to what extent can you make the decision? In fact, you often have very limited "right" to the cosmetic surgery on your body. You can decide which part of your body to be plasticized, and even ask the cosmetic doctor to shape your body in a certain way. However, you can't decide the doctor's surgery plan and what medical materials to be used. Even if there are several materials for you to choose, they are all industrial products with different prices. As for the procedure of the cosmetic surgery, it is nothing more than the implementation of the industrialized operation process on an object. In this sense, your right of asking for "beauty" is limited and relative. The "beauty" that the plastic surgeon "creates" on you is stereotyped, mechanical, and industrialized.

(4) What is our "right" of asking for beauty when the human body is attached with a "political" sense

In modern society, people's perception of the beauty of their body sometimes is attached with a certain sense of "political" meaning. The reason is simple. Although people's perception of "beauty" carries subjective judgments, they seem to have a certain standard for beauty and ugliness in industrialized society. For example, in the model industry, the height, measurements, face and waistline of a model should meet the "golden section" and the rhythm of his or her walking, charm and eye contact all should meet the basic standard. However, in the modern industrial society, who will decide whether my body is beautiful or not? Should I receive plastic surgery? How should I get it done? All of these similar questions are not only related to the perception of beauty, but also to the realization of the "right" to require beauty of one's body. That is why the human body in modern society also is attached with a certain "political" meaning.[①]After all, the "beauty" and "ugliness" in public discourse are disciplined. As the current popular means of body planning, keeping fit and working out will not only change the appearance of our bodies, but also reshape the order of our bodies. So the body can exist like an empty shell, which becomes a "pure signifier" that has lost its political function. At the same time, keeping fit and working out help create an "undifferentiated body" and transform the body in a capitalized way. This view of the body has become a typical symptom of current popular culture, which is people's seeking obvious visual changes on their bodies but refusing to learning about the real physical condition of their bodies.[②]

Further Exploration and Links:

Feminist researchers strive to break the control paradigm that limits women's abilities, sets up a standard for the body, and determines the beauty of women. In the book *Our Body, Ourselves*, Boston Women's Health Group guides women to exercise power on their own bodies. Works like Lakov and Cher in their work *The Value of Face: The Politics of Beauty* and Naomi Wolfe in her work *The Myth of Beauty: How to Use Beautiful Images Against Women* all hope to free women's mind from the fixed concept of beauty established by the beauty industry and fashion magazines. In addition, some people have discussed how those beautiful models in the west affect members of the ethnic group who are particularly receptive to the design of their own image by advertising. Choice is an illusion, because the reconstruction of taste is inevitably linked to the transformation of consumer organization.

—William A. Haviland. *Cultural Anthropology* (10th Edition), Translated by Qu Tiepeng, Zhang Yu. Shanghai: Shanghai Academy of Social Sciences Press, 2006: 502.

---

① "Body politics" comes from the research of Artu Frank and Michel Foucault. Artu Frank believes that the human body is formed at the intersection of an equilateral triangle composed of institutions, words, and flesh. He divided the "disciplined body, the controlled body, the mirrored body (consumption), and the communicative body (cognition)" from the four dimensions of control, desire, connection with the other, and self-relation. Starting from the first two concepts of the body, Foucault believes that political and moral norms and institutions often divide the body into two parts, "public" and "private". The relationship between power and knowledge intervenes by turning the human body into an object of cognition. Conquering the human body, behind various disciplines and punishment techniques, embodies a certain power effect, a certain knowledge reference and a certain mechanism effect, that is, the human body is tamed and punished (Michelle Foucault *Discipline and Punish: The Birth of the Prison*, Translated by Liu Beicheng and Yang Yuanying, Beijing: Life•Reading•Xinzhi Sanlian Bookstore, 1999). Ge Hongbing and Song Geng's *Body Politics* (Shanghai: Shanghai Sanlian Bookstore, 2005) explored the relationship between the body and literature, which further inspired Chinese scholars to think and analyze the different dimensions of body, culture, and politics.
② 杨毅. 减肥、健身与身体的政治 [J]. 文化研究, 2018, (4): 262-273.
   Yang Yi.Weight loss, fitness and the politics of the body[J]. *Cultural Studies*, 2018, (4): 262-273.

2.5.2　Food and Its Cultural Preferences

(1) What is delicious food? Is it decided by our vision, taste or feeling?

What is delicious food? This question is actually not easy to answer, because different people may have different answers. For example, for some people, stinky tofu is a delicacy and it tastes very "appetizing" when they are eating it although it smells "bad". However, others just doubt its savory taste because of its bad smell. Whether it is "smelly" or "savory" varies greatly among different people.

In fact, the definition of so-called "savory" or "smelly" food is relative instead of being absolute. What you think of as "smelly" food may be someone's "savory" food. Vice versa. This taste culture is often regionally effective and attached with people's cultural preferences. Although gourmet food is favored in different regional and among people with different cultural preferences, there should still be a certain universal standard of gourmet food, which is related to the color, taste, smell, presentation of the food.

In specific terms, firstly, the color of food often arouses people's appetite at the first glance, which is the so-called "eye candy". Secondly, it is the taste of food. In China, people often speak of the so-called "eight delicacies". They have fascinating taste that lingers for a long time. They are crispy and delicious, or quickly melt in your mouth, or are smooth and tender, or leave fragrance in your mouth, or are fat but not greasy, or spicy but not dry, or fresh and juicy and so on. Thirdly, the scent of food is so attractive and mouthwatering that its fragrance can spread ten miles, lingers in your mind even at night and favored by thousands of families. Fourthly, the presentation of food. They are like artistic treasures. People long for tasting it but are reluctant to raise their chopsticks. In the menu of the new year's reunion dinner, you will always discover a lot of lucky and meaningful names of food: prosperity brought by the dragon and the phoenix, treating each other with sincerity, harmony between the husband and wife, promotion step by step, four seasons of flowers, good fortune, treasures filling the home, sweetness for everyone, gathering together, etc. The chef also conveys people's aspiration for a better life through the presentation of food. Finally, the cooking process of gourmet is also full of artistic charm.

Brillat-Savarin, a French politician and gourmet born in the 18th century, believes that: "Everything in the world has life, and one needs food to sustain life. Animals eat fodder and humans eat food, but only humans who can think understand food. The destiny of a nation depends on the way its people have adequate food and clothing."[①]

---

① 让·安泰尔姆·布里亚-萨瓦兰. 厨房里的哲学家 [M]. 周小兰, 罗颖娴, 译. 广州: 广东旅游出版社, 2016: 5.
Jean Anthèlme Brillat-Savarin. *The Physiology of Taste*[M]. Guangzhou: Guangdong Travel and Tourism Press, 2016: 5.

The art of eating varies significantly from country to country, each with its unique charm. It is said that "Italian cuisine is like a Renaissance sculpture; French cuisine is like classic paintings; Japanese cuisine is like haiku phrases; Chinese cuisine is like landscape paintings or ancient poetry, and *Shunde* cuisine is a food art with distinctive regional characteristics, like the masterpieces of *Lingnan* paintings and the representative works of *Lingnan* poetry "[①]. The cuisine of *Shunde*, in Guangdong is full of artistic qualities in terms of material creation, psychological experience, spiritual entrustment, etc. It has its own characteristics in the Cantonese cuisine system.

(2) The beauty of delicious food: regional and ethnic differences in color, flavor and art

The beauty of delicious food lies in its beautiful color, savory flavor and delicate cooking art, which, however, varies greatly in different regions and ethnic groups. The reason is simple. Different regional cultures and national cultures contribute to different food cultures and their gourmets.

Due to different climates, topography, history, products, and eating customs, a series of cooking skills and flavors establish their own systems after a long-time historical evolution. There are eight major local cuisines in China, including Shandong, Sichuan, Guangdong, Jiangsu, Zhejiang, Fujian, Hunan, Huizhou cuisines. Chinese invented diversified cooking methods to stir-fry, braise, deep-fry, fry, boil, steam, roast, cold mix and leach food. They also learned the methods of grilling and shaving from other ethnic groups, and produced a variety of delicious dishes.

Ethnic groups in China also have very rich varieties of food. The Mongol people roast whole sheep and dairy products. The Hui people have Muslim pasta; Tibetans have buttered tea. The Hmong people love acidic food. The Dai people like to have smoked beef and pork, pineapple rice and sticky rice held in bamboo. The Bai people have cold-mix raw pork slice. The Zhuang people eat colored sticky rice and sticky rice dumplings in various shapes. There are also oil tea from Yao and Dong ethnic groups; rice wine from Gaoshan ethnic group; kimchi, cold noodles and rice cakes from Korean ethnic group; fish specialties from Hezhe ethnic group; hand-served mutton from Elunchun ethnic group; horse milk from Ewenke ethnic group, etc. They are all specialty cuisines among various ethnic groups.

---

① 李炯聪. 顺德知味 | 顺德美食的艺术画像［EB/OL］.(2019-04-17)［2019-04-19］. https://baijiahao.baidu.com/s?id= 1631066739436901618&wfr=spider&for=pc.
Li Jiongcong. Artistic portraits of Shunde cuisine[EB/OL].(2019-04-17)[2019-04-19]. https:// baijiahao.baidu.com/s? id=1631066739436901618&wfr=spider&for=pc.

Further Exploration and Links:

In terms of food, the preference for fast food and quick meals can also be regarded as one of the characteristics of youth culture. It goes without saying that fast food or quick meal is a generally accepted way of dining in the industrial society, but the special favor of these meals among young people seems to be a way of behavior rather than a way to accommodate the facts. Recently, foods of McDonald's are mostly favored by young people. It is a good example to show this kind of favor among young customers. The young people's preference for fast food can be said to be a straightforward behavior regardless of the forms of the action. They advocate simple food, take direct action to obtain it, and even achieve the goals quickly.

—Li Yiyuan. *Human Vision*. Shanghai: Shanghai Literature and Art Publishing House, 1996: 136.

(3) Tasty and healthy food: the imagination and practice of food culture preferences

American anthropologist Marvin Harris ever explained the reason why Indians do not eat beef, Israels do not eat pork, Europeans and Americans do not eat insects, and Asians have difficulty digesting milk and butter in his book *Delicious: The Mystery of Food and Culture*[①]. It is believed that eating meat can better meet human nutritional needs than plants. The meat, fish, poultry and dairy products people eat are rich in vitamins and minerals that are needed by the human body and are scarce in plant foods. In other words, meat is easier to feed people than vegetarian food, and it is more healthy for people. But why are there food preferences in different countries, regions, and non-ethnic groups?

Further Exploration and Links:

When Indians refuse to eat beef, Jews and Muslims hate pork, and Americans dare not eat dog meat, people can realize the factors behind the digestive physiology that make people confirm the standards of delicious food. This factor is the gastronomy of a specific group of people and their food culture.

—Marvin Harris. *Delicious: The Mystery of Food and Culture*, Translated by Ye Shuxian, Hu Xiaohui. Jinan: Shandong Pictorial Publishing House, 2001:2.

Marvin Harris believes that the difference in recipes in the world is mainly due to

---

① 马文·哈里斯. 好吃: 食物与文化之谜 [M]. 叶舒宪, 户晓辉, 译. 济南: 山东画报出版社, 2001.
Marvin Harris. *Delicious: The Mystery of Food and Culture*[M]. Translated by Ye Shuxian, Hu Xiaohui. Jinan: Shandong Pictorial Publishing House, 2001.

ecological constraints and the different food cultures that exist in different regions. The mystery of human food can be explained from the perspective of nutrition, ecology and income and expenditure. For example, meat recipes usually appear in areas where the population density is relatively low and land is not required or unsuitable for farming; vegetarian recipes are more likely to appear in areas with high population density and insufficient food production technology to supply animal meat.

Marvin Harris combines the researches of "natural science" and "humanities", and uses various disciplines resources such as physiology, pathology, psychiatry, pharmacy, nutrition, agronomy, animal husbandry, biochemistry, genetics to explain the connection between food and culture, society and nature. This was discussed in his book *Cows, Pigs, Wars and Witches*: *The Riddles of Culture*[①]. From the perspective of Marvin Harris, from the Indians' love of cows to the frequent and ongoing conflicts among the indigenous peoples of the South Pacific islands; from the winter gifting of the North American Indians to the witches that have been popular in European history, any cultural phenomena are rooted in the soil of the real society, and all have their objective realistic foundation. In other words, the delicious and healthy food for human beings are just the imagination and practice of food culture preferences.

(4) Delicious food and food supplement: the interpretation of food from medical science, economics, political science and sociology

In the *Delicious*: *The Mystery of Food and Culture* mentioned earlier, the anthropologist Marvin Harris discussed and analyzed in detail the taboos of eating beef among Hindu people, the banned pork-eating among Israels, the favor of eating horse meat in France and other European countries and Americans' love of beef but never eating horse meat. It is believed that some elements of political economy and other factors are involved in American's special favor of beef instead of horse meat. He insists that people's choice of a certain food is not only a factor of economic consideration, but also the result of the combined effect of various factors such as the natural environment, social environment, culture, and politics of a country, a region, and a nation.

Further Exploration and Links:

From the cultural perspective, westerners' favor of eating beef is a rather subjective preference. In western people's views, beef symbolizes the strength

---

① 马文·哈里斯. 母牛·猪·战争·妖巫: 人类文化之谜 [M]. 王艺, 李红雨, 译. 上海: 上海文艺出版社, 1990.
Marvin Harris. *Cows, Pigs, Wars and Witches: The Riddles of Culture*[M]. Translated by Wang Yi, Li Hongyu. Shanghai: Shanghai Literature and Art Publishing House, 1990.

of males. Western people love to eat beef just due to their desire for this strength. Although maybe there is not direct nutritional effect, the extra implication of strengthening the male sexuality shows no difference from the idiom of "the natural instincts of man" in Chinese cuisine culture.

—Li Yiyuan. *Human Vision*. Shanghai: Shanghai Literature and Art Publishing House, 1996: 174.

In general, people's definition of delicious food reflects the cultural understanding or interpretation of people and nature, people and society, people and their self-identity in different countries, regions, different ethnic groups or communities. No matter whether it is the food materials, or cooking techniques such as the skill of cutting up vegetables and meat, applying seasoning, controlling fire, setting up food presentation, or eating methods, etc., they are all replete with cultural significance. This definition is actually the result of cultural negotiation in a country or region, nation or ethnic group. Whether the food is delicious is not simply determined by its delicious taste on the tip of your tongue. On the contrary, it reflects people's in-depth understanding and pursuit of harmony at three levels, between the food and nature, food and society, food and the inner needs of diners.

The medical significance of food supplements is very obvious, which at least has been fully presented in the Chinese folk traditional diet and Chinese medicine culture. Whether it is in spring, summer, autumn or winter, or in the south or the north of China, Chinese are quite demanding about their diet throughout the year, and even have developed exquisite and ready-to-eat industrial food supplements on the basis of modern industrialized processing. If you visit a Chinese supermarket, you will be amazed at the dazzling and complete list of food, including the tortoise cream, nourient cool soup, Wanglaoji(a herbal tea brand), Jiaduobao(a herbal tea brand), bean jelly, etc.

However, due to the widely spread concept of "you are what you eat" in Chinese folks, some people want to nourish the body by eating wild animals such as exotic foods, seafood, wild animals, birds and beasts. The sale of wild animals exacerbates the risk of the spread of animal-derived viruses or bacteria. To this end, the Standing Committee of the National People's Congress on February 24, 2020 reviewed and approved the Decision on the Comprehensive Prohibition of Illegal Wildlife Trade, Elimination of the Abuse of Wild Animals, and the Effective Protection of the People's Health and Safety. The illegal wildlife trade and the comprehensive ban on the consumption of wild animals are specifically prescribed in the law, which systematically guard against the public health risks of the spread of the virus or epidemic due to illegal trading and eating of wild animals.

2.5.3   Summary

In this section, we discussed and analyzed the issues of bodyshaping, cultural preferences for delicious food and their corresponding presentations, and made a simple analysis of the political, economic, and social causes behind cultural preferences. It is hoped that through the discussion and analysis of these issues, you can further understand humans' cultural preferences for beauty, bodyshaping and food.

Further Exploration and Links:

In today's world, most of all wars and disputes are caused by ethnic conflicts. Anthropologists can contribute to the world by providing a way for different peoples to get along with each other. This kind of "Taoism" can help people from different countries in the world better understand each other and abandon their prejudice against others, increasing the possibility of prosperity and peace of the world.

—Li Yiyuan. *Human Vision*. Shanghai: Shanghai Literature and Art Publishing House, 1996:18.

2.6   Food, Diet and Food Safety Issues

2.6.1   Food, Diet and Food Safety

Food is what people eat, or the object for eating (or foods). However, there are differences in the meaning of food and foods. Where are the differences?

Both edible products and foods can be eaten by people, but they are used in different contexts. Edible products generally refer to edible items processed by modern industrial technology. Foods generally refer to items that can be eaten in various eras. They are not necessarily processed by modern technology, but hand-made food.

As for drinks, they are generally food that people can drink, including all kinds of fruit and vegetable juices squeezed by the machine, as well as those bottles or cans of beverages or drinks, etc. Although beverages are not food for satiety in the traditional sense, "Beverages have the basic functions of providing the body with energy, nutrition, and especially pleasure. Therefore, beverages should be the typical fluid food. In terms of management, the beverage industry also belongs to food industry"[①].

In the modern industrial society, pure natural food and beverages are very precious and favored by a lot of people. However, industrially processed food and diet are increasingly flooding into the market. Food safety and dining safety issues are also getting more and more attention. The reason is simple. There are safety issues that cannot be ignored in food and dining processing in modern society. We can give you a simple analysis of these issues.

2.6.2　Food Safety Issues in Modern Society

As we have already mentioned before, modern life is compatible with modern industrial society characterized by the large-scale production of machines to drive people's pursuit of materials and to maximize economic benefits. During this process, food safety issues originating from food and dining processing are topics we can never ignore in modern industrial society, which occur mainly due to the following reasons.

Firstly, in order to reduce costs, food and beverage manufacturers may maintain the lowest eligibility criteria in the selection of food ingredients rather than high-quality standards. The processing, packaging, storage, transportation and other links are qualified, but not necessarily able to meet high-quality standards. We need to be vigilant in holding this concept and taking relative actions based on the belief that "being qualified" equals to "being safe" and "being safe" equals to "being qualified", since problems may occur due to a little carelessness. In addition, some manufacturers may add food additives in violation of regulations in order to improve the taste and add color to foods and drinks, or some dishonest merchants may use excessive preservatives, whitening agents or bleaching agents in order to beautify the food appearance to extend their shelf life, which may increase the risk factors in food and beverages. In other words, the development of modern science and technology has provided technical support for the processing of human food and diet. However, in order to reduce costs and pursue profits, some food and food processors may only ask for qualified products rather than high-quality products, or even produce unqualified food products. Therefore, food safety issues deserve our high attention.

Secondly, there are also food safety issues during the process of selling food and drinks by distributors or retailers. For example, in order to gain greater profits, some distributors or retailers may secretly mix some unqualified or counterfeit products with qualified products in the sale of products. They sometimes promote foods and drinks

---

① 陈建设. 关于食品的几个基本概念 [J]．食品科学, 2019, 40(4): 3-4.
　　Chen Jianshe. Several basic concepts about food [J]. *Food Science*, 2019, 40(4): 3-4.

that are about to expire at low prices, and some even fake the date of production so that they can sell products that are about to expire or go bad. All these behaviors will undoubtedly increase the insecurity of food.

Thirdly, in order to save the cost of living, some citizens may purchase some foods that do not expire at the time of shopping at stores, but deteriorate due to long-term storage, which will also cause food safety problems.

Finally, while modern industrial society brings convenience to people's lives, it also brings tension and anxiety. It is worth noting that some people purchase health foods to relieve tension and anxiety and even replace regular foods we eat everyday with health foods, which will do harm to their health.

Many consumers tend to confuse food quality and food safety, and treat high-quality food as safe food. Food quality mainly refers to the physical properties, nutrition and sensory quality of the food. There are obvious quality elements (such as shape, color, texture, packaging, etc.) and hidden quality elements (such as composition, structure, nutrition, etc.). Food quality can be evaluated by visual judgment, sensory analysis and instrumental measurement. The appearance of some foods may be deformed or their labels damaged due to packaging, storage, transportation and other reasons, but the basic functions and food safety of the food are not affected. According to the range of possible harm caused by food to the human body, the scope of food safety can be divided into the following four areas: physical safety (foreign matters mixed in food processing, packaging, circulation, etc.), chemical safety (food contains safety issues caused by the food chain or illegal additives), microbial safety (safety problems caused by pathogenic microorganisms in food) and allergy safety (pathological reactions caused by intolerance of certain special ingredients in food).[①]

2.6.3 Summary

Food, diet and food safety are closely related, but their connotations are very different. The industrial society is featured by large-scale production of machinery that has stimulated people's pursuit of materials and maximized economic benefits. In this process, food safety problems come from a wide range of sources. Improper management of production, transportation, storage, sales and other links may cause food safety issues in modern society.

① 陈建设. 关于食品的几个基本概念 [J]. 食品科学, 2019, 40(4): 3-4.
   Chen Jianshe. Several basic concepts about food[J]. *Food Science*, 2019, 40(4): 3-4.

Further Exploration and Links:

Industrialized food production can be defined as the large-scale commerce, involving batch food production, processing, and sales, which mainly rely on labor-saving machines. Industrialized food production has far-reaching economic, social and political significance. Because these meanings are intertwined, there are still aspects that are not understood. Today, large companies that produce food have large amount of land where crops are mass-produced and harvested by machines, and carnivores are also intensively raised. As soon as they are harvested or slaughtered, these crops and animals are processed, packaged, and transported to the airport for consumption by the urban population.

——William A. Haviland, Harald E.L.Prins, Dana Walrath, et al. *Anthropology*: *The Human Challenge* (14th Edition), Translated by Zhou Yunshui, Chen Xiang, Lei Lei, et al. Beijing: Publishing House of Electronics Industry, 2018: 447.

2.7　Interpretation of Fast Food and Its Culture in the Industrial Society

2.7.1　Fast Food and Industrial Society

The emergence of fast food is an intuitive reflection of the accelerated pace of life in modern society. In the modern industrial society, the time people are supposed to spend on their private life yields to the time spent on the large-scale machine production.

Revolving around "assembly line production", people shuttle between work units and families, and almost have no time to cook. Especially for white-collars working in the city, most of them carry breakfast to work in the morning, order take-out in the office building at noon, and return to their place to eat some snacks or midnight quick meals. It seems to become the "standard" of their daily life. This is not because white-collars do not like delicious food, or that they have a reason to eat less or even not eat anything to keep fit, but they do not have enough time and energy to cook , so that they can only cope with their dining problems in a quick and simple way.

This is actually a direct consequence of industrialization. With the rapid running of machines and tight schedule of people, everybody is in a hurry. Having decent three meals in a day has become a luxury, as what people really care is only their career development. They can just rashly finish eating their meals, with little attention given to their health! This fast-paced, fast-food lifestyle at the expense of health is actually a reflection of industrialized production in modern life.

> Americans like white meat, which leads to a serious surplus production of "dark meat" similar to chicken thighs in the United States. ...Where will an ordinary 3kg chicken be after it is slaughtered by Mexican immigrants working at the minimum wage in a Mississippi chicken factory? ... Its thigh will be on a table in Moscow, and its breast meat will be served on a table in America or listed on the international airline menu. What about the other parts? One frozen wing will be loaded into a large container shipped to Republic of Korea; the others will go to West Africa. The internal organs (neck, heart, liver, and stomach) of the chicken will be transported to Jamaica to make soup. Excess fat is converted into biodiesel at an experimental refinery in Texas.
>
> —William A. Haviland, Harald E.L.Prins, Dana Walrath, et al. *Anthropology: The Human Challenge* (14th Edition), Translated by Zhou Yunshui, Chen Xiang, Lei Lei, et al. Beijing: Publishing House of Electronics Industry, 2018: 449.

2.7.2   Fast Food in Cultural Views

In recent years, with the deepening of economic globalization, McDonald's, KFC and other "foreign fast food" chain stores have also entered large and medium-sized cities in China, and are favored by many teenagers.

The reason why fast food is "fast" is because the ingredients themselves are already semi-industrialized products or finished products. After the customer places an order, they are simply assembled and heated or added with ice.

As for the nutritional value of fast food, it may not be the focus of customers. They may be more concerned about when fast food will be delivered, whether it is expensive, or whether it is tasty or not. Whether it is local fast food or foreign fast food, they both appear in order to adapt to the practical needs of rapid social development. Since fast food entered our lives, the pace of our lives has accelerated significantly. "The whole society is like a fast-running machine, with everything running like fast food."[1] Although this statement is a bit exaggerated, it seems difficult for the "fast-pace" urban life to slow down.

---

[1] 韩成栋. 速食时代 [J]. 现代交际, 2002, (8): 53.
Han Chengdong. The era of fast food[J]. *Modern Communication*, 2002, (8): 53.

Industrialization has induced the "fast-food" trend in the catering industry or the "McDonaldization" in our society. As criticized by American scholars: "McDonaldization not only affects the catering industry, but also affects education, employment, medical care, tourism, leisure, catering, politics, family, and in fact every other aspect of society. Various signs indicate McDonaldization has become a ruthless process sweeping through the various institutions and parts of the world that seem to be impenetrable."[①] The rapid, fast-paced and efficient operation of society objectively requires the synchronization of man and machine in a modern industrial society. In this way, the nutrition and value of food give way to the reality of busy work and tight schedule in modern society. It should be noted that whether it is Chinese fast food or foreign fast food, fast food itself has constituted a cultural symbol of modern life.

2.7.3　Summary

Fast food is an intuitive reflection of the accelerated pace of life in modern society and a direct consequence of industrialization. Whether it is local fast food or foreign fast food, they both appear in order to adapt to the practical needs of rapid social development. Fast food itself has constituted a cultural symbol of modern life.

Further Exploration and Links:

Taking into account the rising occurrence of related diseases (including stroke, diabetes, cancer and heart disease), the World Health Organization defines obesity as a worldwide disease. For individuals living in a society where machines have liberated physical labor and other human activities, eating too much is very unhealthy, which helps explain why in some industrial and post-industrial societies, more than half of people are overweight.

The prevalence of obesity does not lie solely in overeating and lack of physical exercises. A major factor is high-sugar and high-fat foods sold in the mass market. For example, the eating habits of Japanese are very different from those of Americans. The obese population in Japan only accounts for 3% of the total population, while the obesity rate in the United States is as high as 36% among adults and 17% among people aged 2-19. ...The problem of obesity has become

① 乔治·里茨尔. 社会的麦当劳化: 对变化中的当代社会生活特征的研究 [M] . 顾建光, 译. 上海: 上海译文出版社, 1999: 1-2.
George Ritzer. *The McDonaldization of Society: An Investigation into the Changing Character of Contemporary Social Life*[M].Translated by Gu Jianguang. Shanghai: Shanghai Translation Publishing House, 1999: 1-2.

severe even in some developing countries, especially in areas where its population feed on processed foods and canned fast food.

—William A. Haviland, Harald E.L.Prins, Dana Walrath, et al. *Anthropology: The Human Challenge* (14th Edition), Translated by Zhou Yunshui, Chen Xiang, Lei Lei, et al. Beijing: Publishing House of Electronics Industry, 2018: 660-664.

2.8   Cultural Preferences for Modern Food

The understanding of modern food from the perspective of cultural preferences varies from person to person.

2.8.1   Technology Preferences for Modern Food

With the progress of science and technology, more and more modern agricultural products have appeared. For example, the abuse of additives such as "clenbuterol" and growth promoters, has created unsafe factors from the food source(food ingredients) in modern society.

Technology is actually a double-edged sword. Scientific and rational use of technology will benefit mankind and improve people's lives. Otherwise, it will do harm to the society. Therefore, we should advocate a healthy and scientific outlook on science and technology, develop green, environmentally friendly and sustainable ecological agriculture, and ensure the safety of modern food from the source.

2.8.2   Industrial Preference for Modern Food

The development of modern science and technology has provided us with technical guarantee for the deep processing, transportation and storage of food. However, due to different local standards, national standards and international standards of food in various countries, there are certain differences in the technical standards and hygienic standards of food processing, as well as in the coefficients of food safety.

Until today, many people still remember the scandals of adding excessive addition of melamine in milk powder and applying Sudan red in spice sauces. Why do people use those food additives? In addition to technical convenience, it may also be related to people's cultural preferences. As people have different cultural preferences in different countries and ethnic groups, they will show different behavioral orientations in the choice of imported or exported industrial food.

2.8.3   Multicultural Preferences for Modern Food

As the saying goes, the water and soil in a place nurtures people who live there. People rely on their living environment to feed themselves, be it mountain or sea. So, what do people eat if they do not live near the mountains or the sea?

In the past time when transportation was inconvenient and food production was limited, people mostly "relied on weather conditions to feed themselves". Therefore, in traditional Chinese folklore, there are customary activities praying for good weather, good harvests, thriving domestic animals, and abundance of food every year.

These traditional folk beliefs in China are rooted in the farming society. With the advent of industrial civilization, it merged into the industrial society, and exists in the industrial society in the form of alienation. For example, in the already highly urbanized Pearl River Delta region, the used-to-be farmers have already "washed their feet and gone upstairs", as they are no longer engaged in farming work, but in "buildings work". What does that mean? Farmers rent their own properties to collect the rent, which is the extra benefit of using the land. They have changed from farmers to today's "landlords and landladies".

Their production methods have changed, and their lifestyles have slowly changed. But their cultural psychology obviously has not changed synchronously with their production and lifestyle. The most obvious example is that they still worship the land gods placed in front of their courtyards during traditional Chinese New Year festivals. All these phenomena indicate that the mindset of farmers and farming customs do not perish with the advent of modern industrialized society. On the contrary, they will still exist for a quite a long time.

Similarly, the food culture developed with the development of the rural society still has strong regional, national and ethnic differences. For example, to speak of drinking tea, Guangzhou people have developed a culture of "morning tea", which is different from the leisure activities of tea-drinking for Chengdu people.

When Guangzhou people have morning tea, Dim Sums(light refreshments) and snacks are also served at the same time. Here, tea does not play the leading role, but the supporting role. People in Guangzhou "have morning tea" not just for chatting with friends, but sometimes for "talking about business". They organically combine doing business with dining, which will not only save time but also not lack in etiquette. This kind of meeting fully reflects the highly-efficient, pragmatic, diligent and frugal cultural characters of Guangzhou people. Therefore, if people in Guangzhou "have morning tea", they eat snacks and other food, drink tea, and talk about business, which presents a spectacularly indigenous and pragmatic culture in Guangzhou.

In addition to the culture of "having morning tea" in the hotels or tea houses, Guangzhou also has well-established hand-made herbal teas brands such as *Huang Zhenlong*, Golden Gourd and so on. There are also industrially processed herbal teas brands, such as Wang Laoji, Jiaduobao, Heqizheng and Xu Qixiu.

In recent years, various milk teas have also become popular, such as CoCo, Yihetang, Yidiandian, Tesile, Gongcha, etc., which are favored by a large number of young people and even have become part of their daily lives. Walking in the streets and alleys, you will find that traditional handmade herbal tea, industrially processed herbal tea and new-style milk tea all have a place in the market to meet the preferences of different groups.

There is another example that can reflect people's cultural preferences for modern food. For example, people in Southeast Asia and South Asia like curry-flavored food. However, there is still a difference between Thai curry products and Indian or Japanese curry products. What are the differences between them? In general, Thai curry has a multi-flavored fragrance, Indian curry is very spicy, and Japanese curry has a sweet taste.

2.8.4 Summary

In summary, in modern society, we have seen that there are some cultural preferences for food existing in different countries, different regions, and different ethnic groups. Technology, industrialization, and diversification run through the entire process of modern food production from food ingredients to food consumption.

Further Exploration and Links:

The food safety traceability system is a key measure and an important means of food safety risk management, and an effective tool to facilitate food safety throughout the production chain. The whole-chain food safety traceability system is not only a modern information technology to help consumers grasp the "past and present" of food, but also an important weapon for governments and food safety supervision departments at all levels to implement precise supervision to prevent and control various food safety risks, and respond to food safety accidents and emergencies.

—Zhang Shouwen. Grasp the past and present of food: on the establishment of a full-chain food safety traceability system to improve the effectiveness of supervision (Part 2). *China Market Regulation News*, 2020-08-13 (005).

2.9   Cultural Interpretation of Public Health

2.9.1 Hygiene, Public Health and Health

(1) Hygiene

Hygiene is a concept from modern medicine, especially in western medicine. Although the word *hygiene* was also used in ancient China, its meaning was different. *Hygiene* in ancient China generally meant "guarding life and protecting its health", which means "health maintenance".

The word first appeared in *Lingshu*. It was also included in *Zhuangzi · Gengsangchu*. As quoted from this book, Nan Rong said: "I only wish to hear the hygienic experience." In Jin Dynasty, Li Yi explained *hygiene* in *Zhuangzi Collection Interpretation*, "One should defend his or her life to make it fit the way". In the Song Dynasty, quoted in *The New Biography of Nan Hua Zhen Jing · Gengsangchu*, "Hygiene means we should guard our life in an all-round way. If we can achieve this goal, we will live forever". This concept of *hygiene* generally refers to the way of obtaining personal health and the public behavior of pursuing health. Some people think that *hygiene* in the context of traditional Chinese culture generally includes the meanings of health maintenance, pharmaceutical and medical care, maintaining life, protecting lives on earth and so on.

Hygiene in the sense of modern medicine generally refers to personal and social hygienic measures taken to improve human health, prevent diseases, improve and create a production environment and living conditions that meet human physiological and psychological needs, including the elimination of diseases and maintaining personal hygiene. Now, the word *hygiene* is generally used to refer to the behavior of maintaining personal hygiene, doing the cleaning and preventing diseases so as to help people keep good health, with much focus given to its significance for human physical and psychological health.

(2) Public health

If "hygieme" is also influenced by traditional cultures, "public health" is completely in the category of modern medicine. In modern medicine, *public health* mainly refers to the implementation of medical measures targeting local community or society, such as vaccination, health education, health supervision, disease prevention and control, and various epidemiological treating methods. It is different from the medical measures taken only for individuals at hospitals. Therefore, "health" and "public health" have different meanings. However, they are both closely related to human health.

(3) Health

Health is relative to disease, but people have different understandings about health to form different health cultures. The World Health Organization Law, which was formulated in New York on July 22, 1946 and formally took force on April 7, 1948, clearly states: "*Health* is the whole state of physical, mental, and social satisfaction, not just immunity from illness or disability. " Therefore, health is actually the organic unity of three human states including their physical, psychological and social adaptation.

In summary, modern public health refers to the perfect state of modern people's physical and psychological health having adapted to modern industrial society. If it is not a perfect state, one should not be said to be in a good health.

2.9.2   Cultural Preferences for Modern Public Health

We mentioned earlier that modern life is compatible with modern industrial society and is characterized by the large-scale production of machines. So, are there any cultural preferences for public health in the industrial society? What are the cultural preferences?

Firstly, we can analyze this problem from the perspective of physiological hygiene and health. In a modern industrial society, personal physiological hygiene habits may affect the prevention and control issues in public health field. For example, in August 2003, there was unfounded claims in Nigeria that the oral poliomyelitis vaccine (OPV) was unsafe and would lead to children's infertility after they have grown up. Therefore, OPV vaccination was suspended in two states in northern Nigeria, and the proportion of population receiving OPV vaccination in other states had also dropped significantly. Cases of polio broke out seriously in northern Nigeria, affecting many other areas of the country where there were no previous cases of polio. The outbreak eventually paralyzed thousands of children in Nigeria and led to the wide spread of the disease to 19 other countries with no occurrence of polio cases before.

Secondly, due to the international spread of diseases, global public health security is unprecedentedly dependent on increasing international cooperation. However, different customs and cultural traditions in different countries will affect the prevention and control actions and effects in global public health field. For example, considering many Westerners' special favor of beef, if the mad cow disease breaks out in a country or region, this food-borne disease will threaten public health with the rapid spread in the food chain.

Thirdly, with the development of transportation in modern society, people have more opportunities to travel around the world, and the chances of rapid transmission of infectious diseases also increase. It is estimated that there are billions of air passengers in the world every year. The outbreak of a disease or epidemic in one area may have a severe impact on another area, and it may take only a few hours for the quick spread.

According to news report released by the World Health Organization on September 3, 2020, the epidemic of Ebola continued to spread to more areas in the Democratic Republic of the Congo. Until September 1, 2020, in 36 health subregions from 11 health regions, 110 cases (104 confirmed cases and 6 suspected cases) had been reported, including 47 deaths (fatality rate of 43%). The SARS virus that appeared in 2003 and the new corona-virus pneumonia virus (COVID-19) that emerged from the end of 2019 to the beginning of 2020 also spread very quickly, and COVID-19 has a greater impact on the health and life safety of human society than SARS. According to the risk assessment report by the World Health Organization, it is believed that "since the beginning of 2020, WHO has not received sufficient Ebola funds and is currently using emergency funds to support epidemiological and public health interventions. With the worsening of the current COVID-19 pandemic, it has been more and more difficult to obtain funding and human resources to deal with this public health crisis, which puts an additional burden on the national health system worldwide. The risk of interference into surveillance and routine public health activities brought by COVID-19 may jeopardize a country's ability to quickly contain the recurrence of Ebola cases. Until August 29, 2020, the Democratic Republic of the Congo has reported 1,044 COVID-19 cases and 258 related deaths"[①].

Finally, the abuse of antibiotics will cause bacterial resistance, extreme climate change, and sudden chemical and radiological incidents, all of which will have a negative impact on public health. Many achievements obtained in controlling infectious diseases in many regions are often severely affected by the problem of antibiotic resistance. Extensive drug-resistant tuberculosis (XDR-TB) has now become a serious public health problem. In addition, different degrees of drug resistance have occurred in diarrhea, nosocomial infections, malaria, meningitis, respiratory infections, sexually transmitted diseases and even AIDS.

According to International Sanitation Regulations (2005), it is believed that human behavior, human impact on the environment, and some sudden chemical and

① 佚名. 埃博拉病毒病：刚果民主共和国［EB/OL］.(2020-09-03)［2020-09-30］. https://www.who.int/zh/emergencies/disease-outbreak-news/item/ebola-virus-disease-democratic-republic-of-the-congo.
Anonymous. Ebola virus case-Democratic Republic of the Congo[EB/OL]. (2020-09-03) [2020-09-30]. https://www.who.int/zh/emergencies/disease-outbreak-news/item/ebola-virus-disease-democratic-republic-of-the-congo.

radiological incidents (including industrial accidents, natural phenomena) may threaten public health safety. The US anthrax mails in 2001 , outbreak of SARS in 2003 , and the large-scale dumping of toxic chemical waste in Côte d'Ivoire in 2006 are all new events that threaten public health in the 21st century.

Experts predict that it is most likely that another major outbreak of influenza would threat the public health. In addition, wars and conflicts will also have a negative impact on public health. For example, the Angolan Civil War in 1975-2000 led to the prevalence of Marburg hemorrhagic fever. After the Rwanda crisis in 1994, a pandemic of cholera occurred in the Democratic Republic of the Congo. In July 1994, about 500,000 to 800,000 refugees crossed the border to seek refuge in the Democratic Republic of the Congo. Within one month after their arrival, nearly 50,000 refugees died of cholera and dysentery. The reasons for the rapid spread of the disease and the infection of so many people included contamination of the only water source with cholera bacteria, poor living conditions, and poor sanitation. On April 7, 1948, the Constitution of the World Health Organization came into effect, declaring the founding of the World Health Organization. Today, the quality of air and water and safety of vaccines and medicines the whole society is concerned about are often supported by relevant technical guidelines developed by WHO. However, the increasing complexity of public health issues worldwide poses even more daunting challenges to WHO.

The prevention and control of the worldwide COVID-19 pandemic that broke out from the end of 2019 to the beginning of 2020 is beyond people's previous knowledge. On September 23, 2020, a joint statement issued by the World Health Organization, the United Nations, and the United Nations Children's Fund pointed out that "in containing COVID-19 pandemic, we widely applied advanced technology and social media to ensure people's safety, to keep them informed, to maintain their productivity and to keep them in touch with each other for the first time in history... We call on member states to develop and implement the action plan to manage the information on COVID-19 pandemic, including timely disseminating accurate information based on science and evidence to all communities, especially to high-risk groups; while respecting freedom of speech, we also should prevent and combat the spread of false and fake information"[1]. Only in this way is it conducive to the prevention and control

---

① 佚名. 管理 COVID-2019 信息疫情: 促进健康行为, 减轻错误和虚假信息的危害 [EB/OL] . (2020-09-23) [2020-09-30]. https://www.who.int/zh/news-room/detail/23-09-2020-managing-the-covid-19-infodemic-promoting- healthy-behaviours-and-mitigating-the-harm-from-misinformation-and-disinformation.
Anonymous. Managing the COVID-2019 information epidemic: promoting healthy behaviors and reducing the harm of error and false information[EB/OL]. (2020-09-23) [2020-09-30]. https://www.who.int/en/news-room/detail/23-09-2020-managing-the-covid-19-infodemic-promoting-healthy-behaviours-and-mitigating-the-harm-from-misinfor mation-and-disinformation.

of the pandemic.

Viruses can spread across borders, so we share the same goal of protecting human lives and health. It should be noted that no country can be spared from the major public health issues under the backdrop of the increasing influence of globalization today. Therefore, people around the world need to remove their cultural prejudices to join hands in public health prevention and control so as to create a civilized, healthy, harmonious and orderly well-off society.

2.9.3 Summary

Hygiene, public health and personal health are closely related, but with different connotations. Modern public health refers to the perfect state of people's physical and mental health in the industrial era adapting to modern industrial society in the modern industrial era. Health of humans knows no borders, so people in all countries and regions of the world need to remove cultural prejudices or preferences to be more engaged in the global public health prevention and control, so as to effectively build a civilized, healthy, harmonious, orderly and prosperous society and a human community of shared destiny that can reserve differences on the basis of common ground.

2.10　Dietary Preference and Causes of Its Formation

2.10.1　What Is a Dietary Preference?

Regarding dietary preferences, different people may have different views. This is not difficult to understand, as people often live in different environments. Different social groups or individuals are shaped in different natural environment, social environment and cultural environment, and even different individuals will be cultivated in the same environment due to differences lying in the culture or habit they acquire in their later life. When manifested in the diet, these differences are what people often say "different strokes for different folks". For example, in 10 counties and one district of Baise City, Guangxi, there are 7 nationalities including Zhuang, Han, Yao, Miao, Hui, Yi and Gelao. Among them, the Zhuang ethnic group accounts for about 80% of the total population, and others account for about 20% of the total population. So the regional culture is composed of many highly interdependent spectacular cultures, with the Zhuang culture as the host. In the long historical process, the unique food culture has been developed in western Guangxi with local people's special favor for wild edible plants.[①]

Therefore, we can understand dietary preferences in this way: this so-called dietary preferences refer to people's inclination to process, make, eat, or drink certain food materials, or foods during a long-term diet. It is under the joint influence of natural, social and cultural environment.

2.10.2   Why Do People Have Dietary Preferences?

As the old saying goes in China, customs vary largely in places which are just 100 or even 1,000 miles away. The eating habits in a region, a country, a nation or a group are formed under the influence of various factors. So, what factors influence people's dietary preferences? To sum up, they include the natural environment and social culture factors.

Firstly, let's take a look at how the natural environment affects human dietary preferences.

We know that in the early days of human society, people lived a primitive life of collecting seeds, fishing and hunting. Since humans entered the civilized society, they began to enjoy much richer food through the cultivation of wild plants and domestication and artificial breeding of animals.

In the past, when science and technology were underdeveloped and the harvest was mainly dependent on the weather condition, people tended to grow different crops in different geographical environments, different seasons and under different climatic conditions. Over time, people gradually developed dietary preferences with regional characteristics.

Generally speaking, in areas where biotechnology was underdeveloped and transportation and storage of food were inconvenient in the past, people's dietary structures are more likely to be affected by the local natural environment and the structure of local food, crops, and livestock types. In other words, for a long time in human history, people's eating habits and preferences were often affected by the local natural environment.

There is another example of how the natural environment affects human dietary preferences. Compared with people living in tropical or subtropical regions with high temperature, people living in cold regions with low temperature prefer pasta, meat, liquor and food with stronger taste, while people living in the south, especially in the

---

① 苏仕林. 桂西壮族文化与植物多样性保护的关系 [J]. 植物资源与环境学报, 2014, 23(2): 107-113.
  Su Shilin. Relationship of Zhuang ethnic culture with plant diversity conservation in Western Guangxi[J]. *Journal of Plant Resources and Environment*, 2014, 23(2): 107-113.

coastal areas, prefer food with bland taste. However, in some hot and humid areas of the south, people also eat some dehumidifying foods, or add seasonings such as pepper, red pepper, sharp pepper, and pepper, or add barley and other foods with dehumidifying effect to the soup.

Secondly, people's eating habits and preferences are also affected by the local natural and social environment.

As we know, in the process of conquering and transforming nature, people have formed different production methods and lifestyles. Generally speaking, crops that are easy to grow or cultivate and have high yields are more likely to be served on the tables as food, while those that are not easy to cultivate and have low yields are only eaten during important festivals such as Chinese New Year. For example, as the main grain in the south, the production of traditional glutinous rice is generally lower than that of hybrid rice. Therefore, in the daily diet, people tend to eat hybrid rice, and glutinous rice is only served in traditional festivals or sacrifice ceremonies. This is the result of the environment affecting the crop harvest, which in turn affects human dietary preferences.

In different social and cultural environments, people's understanding of food is not the same. According to anthropologists, people classify, name and give meaning to the world in which they live.

British anthropologist Douglas in her famous book *Cleanness and Pollution-Analysis of Pollution and Taboo Concepts* starts with people's understanding of "cleanliness" and "dirty" in the Bible and daily life, using symbolic analysis techniques to analyze the characteristics of human thinking and pay attention to the interaction between the symbolic order and social order. She believes that in various social and cultural systems, cleanliness and pollution are parts of a larger classification system. Pollution is considered a violation of social norms and order, which means danger, and fear caused by some inappropriate boundary-crossing. The removal of filth (danger), that is, the occurrence of taboos, the hosting of ceremonies, and the punishment of crimes are the means to re-establish the original social order and maintain social norms. Therefore, eating "clean" food instead of "dirty" food has become a symbol and expression of social order.

However, the definition of "clean" or "dirty" foods varies significantly in different countries and ethnic groups. For many countries or ethnic groups, the internal organs of animals are not "clean", so they are inedible. However, some people think that the animal's internal organs are particularly delicious, and the animal's blood should not be discarded for being tasty. Some people even eat the raw blood of some animals. Some people like to eat sashimi, while others think that sashimi is unhygienic. Their belief is based on the following reason. They think that mustard will stimulate our nasal cavity and can not really kill the bacteria. In addition, if people develop the habit of eating sashimi, they will be prone to be infected with a variety of fish-borne parasites, such as Clonorchiasis, which will cause liver cell necrosis, induce cirrhosis and even liver cancer.

People often say that Guangzhou is the food paradise. This not only shows that Guangzhou has developed a rich food culture, but also implies that the diet of Guangzhouers is so inclusive that it seems anything can be made into delicious food, leading to an increasing risk of being sick due to this dietary habit.

Finally, people's dietary preferences are also impacted by the local food traditions and customs.

For different foods, people cook them in different color, smell and taste with different methods . They even develop the preferences to when and where to eat the specific kind of food. For example, some people like to steam food, some like to fry food, some like to braise food, and some like to deep-fry, stew, or simmer food. People have been contributing varied cooking methods to deal with different foods. Another example is the taste of the Chinese people. People living in the northern region prefer more salty food while people living in Jiangsu, Zhejiang and Shanghai prefer sweet food. People living in Guangdong, Hong Kong and Macao prefer lighter-flavored food and love soups. People living in Hunan and Sichuan are addicted to spicy food, and there are some people living in other areas of China who love sour foods.

According to relative researches, people's dietary preferences may be related to the occurrence of some diseases. Fried and barbecued foods are very popular in area at high latitudes around Beijing and the northeast of China. People in southern Hainan also prefer barbecued foods, as well as people in Guangdong. People who love sweets mainly live in the coastal areas, and people who live in the northern area also has a strong preference for sweets. People who prefer hot and spicy food mainly live in Sichuan. However, people's preferences for deep-fried and grilled food will lead to the higher body mass index, high blood pressure and high incidence of diabetes. These two types of foods are also related to the abnormal rising fasting blood glucose and postprandial blood glucose level, as well the increased incidence of diabetes. Since capsaicin can reduce fasting blood glucose levels while maintaining insulin levels, people's preference for spicy food is inversely related to the incidence of diabetes, fasting blood glucose and postprandial blood glucose levels. However, for people with weak gastrointestinal function, spicy food will irritate the esophageal mucosa and excessive consumption of spicy food will affect the intestinal flora, increase the burden of the gastrointestinal and stomach, and induce excessive internal heat, diarrhea or constipation. In addition, fried or deep-fried foods are not considered healthy, but the boiled or simmered foods.[①] In this view, dietary preferences may also have a certain impact upon people's body functions.

2.10.3　Summary

Dietary preference is developed under the mutual influence of natural environment, social environment and cultural environment. It is a dispositional appetite people have developed to process, make, eat or drink certain foods materials and foods over a long time. Their preferences are also affected by factors such as the natural environment, social culture, and cooking methods to varying degrees.

Further Exploration and Links:

"Spicy" is a distinctive taste sensation. It is found by some researchers that the increase in blood pressure and heart rate caused by spicy food can lead to people's addiction to the spicy food. People who love spicy food usually are often more determined and do things quickly and decisively. They are filled with passion and fiery temper. They are candid with their thoughts and stick to their own ideas.

People who like "unusual" tastes such as sweet and salty or sweet and bitter taste are generally introverted and enjoy being on their own. They are often thoughtful and secretive, who seem a little indifferent and arrogant and difficult to contact.

Most vegetarians are introverted and prefer peace to noisy crowd. They often feel uncomfortable during interpersonal communication .

People who like to eat instantly boiled or barbecued meat are usually more active. They can have a pleasant talk with different people, and always stand out in the crowd.

—Li Su. Dietary preferences and personality traits. *Digest News*, Page 03, January 11, 2014.

---

① 谢开飞, 曹佳奕, 陈旻. 饮食偏好与疾病的发生密切相关 [J] . 中国食品, 2020, (15): 138-139.
　Xie Kaifei, Cao Jiayi, Chen Min. Diet preference is closely related to the occurrence of diseases[J]. *China Food*, 2020, (15): 138-139.

2.11   Interpretation of Human Dietary Preferences

2.11.1   What Are the Dietary Preferences of Humans?

Some people say that Guangzhou is a paradise of food. However, people's standards for delicious food are different. Some people think it is gourmet, while others may not think so.

Due to people's different perceptions of and tastes for food, hotels and restaurants in the city will provide a variety of different cuisines, and fine-tune the flavor and the taste of the food according to the dietary habits of local people. For example, the spiciness of Sichuan and Hunan cuisines in different restaurants of Guangzhou has been subdivided into being slightly spicy, medium spicy and heavy spicy. If the customer does not specify the preference for spiciness when placing an order, the waiter will generally ask and mark it for the convenience of the chef to prepare the food.

Not only Chinese but also foreigners have dietary preferences. Table 2-1 provides information on the dietary preferences of people in some countries of the world. Actually, there are many other countries and ethnic groups that are not included in this table due to limited space of the book. Interested friends can access relevant information by themselves.

Table 2-1   Dietary Preferences of People in Some Countries or Regions

Country or region	Dietary preference
Republic of Korea	Most people do not like lamb, parsley, bitter vegetables or spicy foods; besides bread and cakes, there are few steamed foods that are made of fermented flour; they do not like to put vinegar, sugar or pepper, but they like eating garlic.
Japan	The Japanese do not like spicy food and do not like to eat animal offal; they prefer the light, salty and fresh taste.
Thailand	Thai people do not drink hot tea, nor do they eat beef or sea cucumber; they do not like soy sauce or braised foods; they prefer fresh, sour and pungent taste; dog meat and wild animals are banned in their diet.
Singapore, Malaysia	Muslims do not eat pork and shellfish; they do not drink alcohol; they treat the left hand as unclean and avoid using the left hand to pass items.
Indonesia	Indonesian residents are mostly Muslims. They do not eat pork, drink alcohol, or eat food with bones or thorns. They also avoid passing items with the left hand.
Australia	Australians generally don't like spicy foods but sweet and sour ones. They also don't eat sea cucumber.
Italy	Italians like pizza; various pasta foods (such as spring onion rolls, wontons, macaroni, fried rice, etc.) are served to the dining table as dishes instead of staple food; they like to use a fork to roll macaroni into the mouth and send it to the mouth without cutting it with a knife or using a spoon.

Continued

Country or region	Dietary preference
France	French people like to eat fatty and spicy beef, lamb and various sausages, shrimp, fish, eggs, poultry, oysters, snails and fresh vegetables; they like using garlic, herbs, tomatoes, cloves and other ingredients in their cooking, and love to drink clear soups.
Germany	Germans like pork and pork products; they will have lard when eating bread; they eat soft well-done cabbage together with pork; they prefer medium-done or raw beef; they like deep-fried, roasted, fried, boiled potatoes; they do not like to eat fish or dark red food.
Russia	Russians prefer sweet, salty, sour, and spicy food; they often apply a lot of cooking oil in cooking; they like to drink spirits, hot soup, and cold food.
United Kingdom	The Britons attach great importance to the quality of food, and they like bland and tender food; they are particular about drinking tea and like having tea and snacks before getting out of bed in the morning; they usually prepare two dishes and one soup for lunch or dinner; they love having meat such as beef, mutton, chicken, duck with other snacks, fruit, juice, or coffee; they often have refreshments and tea in the afternoon; they often use less oil in cooking, prefer bland food that is less but refined; they do not like spicy food; they do not like applying monosodium glutamate in cooking; they do not eat dog meat but like fresh and tender, burnt and tasty, sweet and sour food; tipping the salt shaker or making noises are banned in their table manners.
America	Americans use less oil in cooking; they like bland food that is less and refined; they do not like spicy food; they do not like applying monosodium glutamate in cooking; they do not eat dog meat but like fresh and tender, burnt and tasty, sweet and sour food; tipping the salt shaker or making noises are banned in their table manners.
Canada	Canadians love to eat beef, chicken, duck, snails, seafood and other foods; they prefer sweet food, and have fresh and tender food with the wine; they do not drink beer or beverages when dining; they do not like thorny freshwater fish.

Source: Anonymous. Colorful eating habits: table tour of countries in the world. *Guangxi Food Economy*, 2002, (3): 46-47.

2.11.2   Attitude Towards Human Dietary Preferences

Since people's dietary preferences are affected by multiple factors such as different natural environments, social environments, cultural customs, etc. in various countries and regions, we should have an open and tolerant attitude towards different dietary cultures so that we can better understand "others". Only if we can have more reflection and introspection, can we protect the diversity of human dietary culture and achieve what the late well-known sociologist and anthropologist in China Fei Xiaotong ever said: "Every culture has its own beauty and merits and we should respect each other's culture. The harmony in the world can only be achieved when we maintain the diversify of cultures in the world."[1] In 1990, when Mr. Fei Xiaotong looked forward to the prospects of anthropology, he hoped that the research of anthropology should contribute to the above

---

[1] 费孝通. 创建一个和而不同的全球社会: 在国际人类学与民族学联合会中期会议上的主旨发言 [J]. 思想战线, 2001, 27(6): 1-5, 16.
Fei Xiaotong. Creating a harmonious but different world community: a speech at a conference of the IUAES[J]. *The Ideological Front*, 2001, 27(6): 1-5,16.

humanistic glamour. Around 2000, after reflecting on the influence of globalization, he put forward the important viewpoint of "maintaining harmony while reserving differences", and regarded this viewpoint as an important means to realize the coexistence of diversified cultures in the world. From "achieving harmony while maintaining the diversify of cultures" to "maintaining harmony while reserving differences", these viewpoints reflect Mr. Fei's exploration, contemplation and summary of his life from the cultural perspective in his later years. This cultural concept of respecting cultural diversity and tolerance of cultural differences can provide us with effective perspectives for analyzing human dietary preferences.

2.11.3   Summary

From the above discussion in this section, we witness the infinite charm of clothing and food as the main carrier of human culture, which further explains that "we wear culture", "we eat culture", and "our food and clothing are already woven in the cultural world we live".

2.12   Modern Dietary Preferences and Human Health

2.12.1   Main Features of Modern Dietary Preferences

In a modern industrial society, although the eating habits and preferences of different regions, countries, and ethnic groups may be different, they should all carry some basic characteristics of a modern industrial society. In summary, these characteristics are mainly as follows.

(1) The pursuit of health that may lead to overcorrection

From the perspective of modern medicine, the irrational dietary structure is an important inducement of cardiovascular disease and obesity. In order to keep fit and reduce the risk of having cardiovascular disease, some people, especially some females, are often on a diet or become vegetarians in addition to doing aerobic exercises. However, the preference for vegetarian food may also lead to some health problems.

In theory, a vegetarian diet can contain all the nutrients required by the body except vitamin B12, but the premise is that the types and intake of vegetarian diets can meet the requirements. If people only eat carrots, cabbage and other vegetarian food, they may lack a variety of trace elements and high-quality protein, causing anemia and other systemic diseases. Conversely, a diet including mainly animal meat and few or even no vegetables, melons and fruit may increase the physical burden of human heart, lead to excessive saturated fat and increase the risk of hypertension and coronary heart disease. Therefore, for high-risk groups or those who pursue health, nutritionists and doctors give the following suggestions.

1) Have a balanced portion of vegetarian food and meat in his or her diet, eat more highly unsaturated fatty plants (cod, nuts, etc.) and soluble fiber foods (apples, grapes, citrus, oats, brown rice, beans, vegetables, etc.), and even raw onions.

2) Choose whole-wheat, high-fiber, low-sugar, low-fat, low-salt foods and intake at least five different fruits and vegetables every day.

3) Drink six to eight glasses of water a day (or sugar-free coffee, tea, and low-fat milk); take in no more than 150 mL of fruit juice everyday.

4) Eat fish twice a day, and eat less red meat and processed meaty food.

(2) Increasing kinds of processed "junk food" in the food industry

Nowadays, puffed food, carbonated drinks, and milk tea, have even become the favorite food and drinks for a lot of adolescents. However, a long-term consumption of a variety of puffed foods in supermarkets (such as biscuits, yolk pie, potato chips, chocolate and hydrogenated milk cakes, etc.) may be detrimental to human health. In addition, the frequent consumption of instant noodles, ham sausage, bacons, luncheon meats and other ready-to-eat or cooked food products that only require simple processing is also not recommended, for the consideration of one's health.

(3) Modern dietary preferences are developed under the inter-generational influence to a certain degree

As we all know, people's eating habits are not formed in a day or two, but over a long term starting from a young age. In general, parents will exert strong influence on their children in terms of the dietary preferences, and grandparents will also have certain affect as some children may be raised up by their grandparents.

A survey conducted by the China Youth Research Center found that there are three unhealthy eating preferences for the second-generation of "only child" in China: the preferences for sweets, deep-fried foods, and beverages, which is related to the dietary habits of their parents (the first generation of "only child" in China).

2.12.2　Modern Dietary Preferences Affect Good Health

As we know, we need to take in multiple nutrients to keep healthy. Our dietary preferences cannot provide us with the nutrients our body needs, but cause some health problems. For example, researches show that the second-generation of "only child" in China prefer sweets, fried foods and beverages. These foods are said to be the standard kinds of fast food in the industrial society, which are basically processed in the industrialized and standardized mode of production, and provide limited nutrition. A long-time consumption of these foods will lead to malnutrition. According to medical researches, people who like to eat candies or sweet food may increase the risk of having myopia. Therefore, teenagers are suggested to eat less candies or sweets.

In addition, one's dietary preferences may have been formed before the age of 7. A good eating habit developed since an early age will reduce the risk of chronic diseases in adulthood.

At present, obesity has become a widely spread global health problem. According to the World Health Organization, it is estimated that more than 10% of adults in the world suffer from obesity, and 2.8 million people die from diseases related to obesity each year. In 2016, more than 1.9 billion adults aged 18 and over were overweight, of whom over 650 million were obese; more than 340 million children and adolescents aged 5 to 19 were overweight or obese, and the obesity rate rose sharply from 4% in 1975 to more than 18% in 2016.[①] The root cause of obesity and overweight is the diet preference of consuming high-calorie junk foods. Of course, obesity or overweight can be prevented and controlled. The fundamental way is to avoid or eat less high-calorie foods, limit energy intake of total fat and sugar, increase consumption of fruits, vegetables, beans, whole grains and nuts, and keep doing regular exercises (60 minutes of excises per day for children and 150 minutes per week for adults), so as to strengthen the metabolism within human body.

In recent years, more and more people like raw or semi-raw vegetable salads, sashimi, and other similar foods. In fact, eating raw vegetables may not provide comprehensive kinds of nutrition; eating raw meat and seafood not only leads to a low absorption rate, but also a high safety risk for us, such as the parasitic diseases as food-borne diseases; eating raw organic foods can lead to a higher rate of infection with food-borne pathogens such as E. coli and Salmonella.

Many people think that the fresher the food, the better they are. So they drink the milk that has just been expressed. Since milk contains antibiotics and aflatoxins, direct drinking may develop our drug resistance, and even raise the risk of having cancer. Many bean vegetables (such as sword beans, lentils, kidney beans, etc.) contain

① 佚名. 肥胖和超重 [EB/OL] . (2020-04-01) [2020-05-10] . https: //www.who.int/zh/news-room/fact-sheets/detail/obesity-and-overweight.
Anonymous. Obesity and overweight[EB/OL]. (2020-04-01) [2020-05-10]. https://www.who.int/zh/news-room/fact-sheets/detail/obesity-and-overweight.

phytohemagglutinin, which can be poisonous when they are eaten raw, causing nausea, vomiting, abdominal pain, diarrhea and other symptoms, and even threatening our lives in severe cases. During the cultivation of organic food, organic pesticides may also have been applied. If these vegetables are not cleaned or eaten raw, they will also bring hidden dangers. In some other cases, if chemical fertilizers are replaced by animal excrement to be used on some organic vegetables, they will be contaminated with E. coli and Salmonella. Therefore, eating these raw vegetable may cause food-borne diseases.[1]

2.12.3 Summary

In this section, a discussion was conducted on the main characteristics of dietary preferences in modern society and the relationship between dietary preferences and health. In a modern industrial society, although the dietary habits and preferences in different regions, countries, and ethnic groups may be different, dietary preferences cannot provide humans with the nutrients human body needs, increasing the risk of more health problems.

Further Exploration and Links:

Different from the manufacturing process of industrial products, the food production process is not a mechanized manufacturing process, but a cultivation process that has its own law for the growth of the crops and vegetables. Even if modern technology can realize the artificial synthesis of the elements essential for human body that are contained in many agricultural products, this does not mean that humans can recultivate a living body that can grow under the the natural conditions. The tomatoes that are ripened with the application of ethylene look the same as the naturally ripened ones, but they can never match those that ripen in the natural way in quality. From this perspective, the inherent laws of agricultural production are very different from those of industrial production, and mechanized production methods cannot be applied to the production process of food in the same way as we thought.

The most fundamental difference lying between agricultural production and industrial production is that the objects and final products of agricultural production are living things, while those of industrial production are not. The technologies

---

① 罗斌, 吴萍. 生食是健康还是危害？［J］. 保健与生活, 2019, (2): 58.
　Luo Bin, Wu Ping. Is raw food healthy or harmful?[J]. *Health and Life*, 2019, (2): 58.

applied in the agriculture in modern times originated from the industrial production and were then advanced in the agricultural development. When the industrial technologies that contribute to the production of non-living things were transplanted into the production of living things, they will inevitably fail in the agricultural sector and even lead to the food safety problems.

The inherent differences between agricultural and industrial production determine the differences between the two production methods. The industrialized production methods were developed on the basis of the division of labor, specialization, standardization, and marketization. They triggered the industrial revolution and led to the continuous growth of productivity as they inspired the tool innovation and promoted scientific progress to the largest extent. However, the same production method not only plays a limited role in improving productivity in agricultural production, but also leaves behind many "after-effects".

—Li Shaoqing. The after effect of "industrialized food". *21st Century Business Review*, 2011, (7): 97-101.

Chapter 3 Residence and Transportation: Cultural Practices in Human Society

3.1 Cultural Reflections on the Selection of Residential Locations

3.1.1 Cultural Connotation in the Selection of Residential Locations

In modern industrial society, people's choices of residential locations and living environment are no longer made according to people's traditional habits and preferences.

As we know, for a long period of time, people's choices of residence were restricted by the natural environment. For example, in the traditional farming society in China, people generally built houses in places that were convenient for them to be engaged in agricultural production, to have an easy access to water sources, and to have better ventilation and lighting. The ancient Chinese people have formed a culture of residence with a rich connotation in their long-term production and living practices. When this culture is reflected in the selection of residential locations, it is the proposal of popular "*Feng Shui Kanyu*" theory among Chinese people. The core of this theory is to emphasize the importance of "wind and water" in one's residence.

The popular concept and practice of "*Feng Shui*" among Chinese people was actually a simple site investigation technology, in other words, the technology of selecting environment. Later, it became more and more mysterious due to the integration of concepts such as eight diagrams of *Zhouyi* and five elements of *Yinyang*. Now, it has become a "*Feng Shui Kanyu*" culture that still has a certain influence and market in Chinese civil society.

In fact, this so-called "*Feng Shui*" theory is developed due to the influence of China's unique geographical environment and climatic conditions on people's choices of living environment. China is surrounded by mountains on three sides of its territory: the north, west and southwest, and its seas are located in the east. The continental monsoon climate in China leads to the large temperature difference between day and night and little rain in spring and autumn, hot and stuffy summer and cold winter. Considering the geographical environment and continental monsoon climate in China, ancient Chinese people gradually formed a culture of selecting residential sites. They believed that we should always stay out of the wind and be exposed to the sun. Our residence should be close to the water, but should not be built in a low-lying and humid location. The rolling mountains can help us block the cold wind blown from the north in winter. Therefore, the traditional Chinese villages are often seen to be located in a place where there is a mountain behind the house for us to lean against, a mountain in the distance in front of the house, and flat and open areas on the left and right sides of the house that are surrounded by mountains that are lower than the mountain behind the house. If there is a river flowing from left to right in this village, this village will be more likely to be a *"Feng Shui treasure"* for Chinese people. The selection of residential locations in the traditional Chinese farming society actually reflects the harmony between man and nature to a certain extent. The key factors for selecting an ideal residential location include sound ecological accommodation capacity, suitable living density, sufficient sunlight, fresh air, clean water and comfortable sports space.[①]

3.1.2   Diversified Selection of Modern Residential Sites

In the modern industrial society, people's reliance on the natural environment has been reduced. Especially in cities where "every foot of the land costs a fortune", people are often more concerned with the actual economic factors and convenience of work and life when selecting their residential sites. The housing prices, location, public supporting service facilities and the convenience of public transportation in the urban areas have become important factors for citizens' house-purchasing decisions. The saying of "the housing price rises as long as it is close to the subway" has become a sign of selecting residential location in Chinese mega-cities.

As urban houses are subject to the comprehensive development and efficient use of urban land, *"Feng Shui"* is not be taken so seriously by people in the urban areas as in the rural areas when they select their residential locations. Instead, the real estate projects are developed according to the local conditions, urban planning and usage of urban construction land. In addition, because the problems of transportation, water sources, ventilation, lighting, temperature, and humidity have been better solved in modern industrial society, people's dependence on the natural environment and natural conditions has been reduced, which brings more freedom for people to make the

---

① 张磊. 居住环境与健康［J］. 养生大世界, 2020, (6): 57-59.
　Zhang Lei. Living environment and health［J］. *The world of healthy living*, 2020, (6): 57-59.

choices for residential locations. What are the main aspects affecting the diverse choices of modern residential locations?

Firstly, the coexistence of houses for "living" and houses for "comfortable living". For residents living in large cities and mega-cities, owning their own house for "living" instead of renting other people's house for "comfortable living" has become the expectation, dream and need of most young people. Therefore, some inferior properties that either are located in the remote areas far away from the city center or have poor housing orientation, or lie in less favored floor, or have a poor space layout, are still bought by citizens, who are willing to become the so-called "house slaves" of mortgage loans. For those in need of housing improvement, they have higher requirements for residential location. They will comprehensively investigate the natural environment, social environment, cultural environment of their residence, and pursue a life of high quality and good taste. Therefore, it is better to say that they choose a life itself rather than a residential location. High-end residential communities, detached townhouses or duplex villas, have become a choice for urban middle-class or wealthy people.

In a sense, the selection of residential location in a modern industrial society is actually a reflection of social stratification. "Living" and "living comfortably" reflect people's different attitudes towards life and different pursuits of life.

Secondly, the coexistence of urban and rural areas. In the developed countries such as America or some European countries, rich people would rather live in the townhouses or villas in the rural area, drive to work and stay close to nature than live in a tiny apartment in the noisy and crowded urban area. These are all important evidences reflecting human desires of anti-urbanization and returning to their original nature.

The location of residence in modern China is different from that in European countries and America. As the public services and supporting facilities in Chinese cities, especially in large cities or mega-cities in China are more concentrated and advanced, the "siphon" effect is more obvious. Therefore, more and more young people yearn for living in big cities and metropolises. "I would rather have a bed in the city center than a house in the suburbs" has become a vivid portrayal of Chinese youths' aspiration. They have been swarming into cities since the reform and opening up. In Beijing, Shanghai, Guangzhou, Shenzhen and other mega-cities with a population of more than 10 million people, still coexist both the urban and rural areas to meet the needs of different social strata and social groups for selecting their residential locations.

This is true not only in China's first-tier cities, but also in the capitals and mega-cities of other Asian countries. For example, in cities such as Tokyo, Seoul, Kuala Lumpur, and Bangkok, many people prefer to live in a cramped apartment rather than live in a large house in the country, which is different from the situation in America and European countries. Although differences occur between cities and villages in their social, economic, and cultural structures, there are no good or bad choices. The choices are just made out of their different pursuits and experiences. However, in the modern industrial society, when people's residence and transportation, purchase and entertainment are closely related, there are inevitable differences and diversity in selecting the location of urban and rural residences.

Finally the integration of tradition and modernity. In the modern industrial society, tradition has not been completely replaced by modernity, but has found a carrier and an opportunity for its survival.

3.1.3   Summary: Living Environment and Cultural Choices

In this section, we discussed the cultural connotation and diversity of selecting modern residential sites. Through the previous discussions, we can gain the following findings.

Despite the diversity and different cultural expressions of selecting residential locations in different eras, different societies, and different spaces, they are all related to people's choice of the natural environment without exception. However, people nowadays attach more importance to the social environment and cultural environment in the choice of modern living environment. It can be said that people's choices of residence are influenced by multiple factors such as the natural environment, the social and cultural environment. The "reverse urbanization" selection of rural residences in the western countries and the population aggregation in the urban areas in the East or Asia show people's different choices of residence, resulting from people's different cultural choices.

However, no matter what choice people have made, it once again illustrates the fact that "we live in a cultural space". It is hoped that through the discussion and analysis of these issues, we can help you further understand the cultural practices of human society.

Further Exploration and Links:

Many anthropologists believe that the new housing mode is related to the emergence of financial or commercial economy. They believe that this mode may appear when people can sell their labor and products for money, and they can buy their own homes on their own without relying on their relatives. In fact, the new housing model tends to occur in societies where there are financial and commercial exchanges. In societies without finance, couples live more often with relatives or close to each other.

Therefore, the emergence of finance accounts for a portion of the new homes, and money allows couples to live alone. However, this fact does not explain well why they made such a choice. One of the reasons why couples can be independent in a business society may be that related jobs require physical activity or social mobility. Perhaps the reason why couples prefer to live away from relatives is because they want to avoid some interpersonal tensions and escape from the need emerging from their living with close relatives. However, the specific reasons why couples are more willing to live independently after they are financially independent remain unclear.

—Carol R.Ember, Melvin Ember. *Human Culture: Highlights of Cultural Anthropology* (3rd Edition), Translated by Zhou Yunshui, Yang Jinghua, Chen Jingyun. Beijing: Publishing House of Electronics Industry, 2016: 285.

3.2   Modern Interpretation of Residential Culture

3.2.1   Modern People's Living Concept and Its Changes

In the previous section, we discussed the selection of residential locations, which is known to solve the problem of "where to live". Next, we will discuss the "how to live" problem.

For the Chinese, housing is a major event in life. In the traditional Chinese concept of family, the scene of four generations living under the same roof was once regarded as a model of traditional Chinese living pattern, not only symbolizing family harmony, but also metaphorizing family prosperity. A family with a strict father, kind mother, harmony between brothers and also between sister-in-laws, and multiple children and grandchildren, is often the envy of other people.

The traditional Chinese family culture has attached too much utilitarian thoughts to the Chinese way of living. This mode of large family living together is more suitable for traditional farming society with less mobility, but can not adapt to the commercial and industrial society with strong mobility. Especially in urban society, people's ideology of living has changed significantly, which can be said to be a reflection of social changes in the field of living.

So, what changes can be seen in the styles and ideology of living for modern people?

Firstly, people who lead a "nomadic" life frequently change their "nest". Nowadays, young people frequently "change their jobs" or work in different places to become a member of "nomadic family". For the convenience of work, they have to frequently change their "nest" or residence. This is why most young people prefer to live in rented houses instead of buying houses. They think that the house is a daily necessity, like towels, toothpaste and soap. Keeping this in mind, one will discover freedom. They claim that they do not have to buy a house before they are 40 years old but rent a house, as it represents a new way of life.

Secondly, returning to their parents, like a young "kangaroo" returning to its mother's "nest". Today, many financially independent "only-child" youngsters have returned to their parents and lived a new "kangaroo" life. They buy a new house located close to their parents, separated only by a street or a building, or simply on different floors of the same building. Instead of living with parents together, they live next to their parents' homes. In this way, they can care for each other and not interfere with their own lives.

Thirdly, strive to build more "nests" by buying more properties. Today, many people have more than two properties. They believe that "1+1" is an ideal lifestyle in the new century, that is, there is a property in the city center for the convenience of work; there is another property in the suburbs for spending weekends and holidays. Many young people not only like the hustle and bustle in the city, but also the tranquility and fresh air in the suburbs.

Finally, some young people also admire the new concept of hotel-style apartments. Although the apartment with "hotel-style service, apartment-style management" is essentially a hotel, it provides more freedom and convenience at relatively lower price. It is attached with a home layout and sound functions for living, with a full set of furniture and household appliances. In addition, the professional hotel services can be provided in this apartment. This property combining traditional hotel services and modern apartment hardware facilities can offer people a comfortable and cozy living environment with more freedom. It can meet the different needs of people in various industries, especially favored by young people.

3.2.2 Living Pattern in Modern Society

In modern society, cities are often associated with civilization. In the 1990s, the living pattern of Chinese urban residents was basically designed in accordance with the urban hierarchical structure of "residential district–residential community–residential group". After 2003, people began to explore the new living model of "city–residential area–resident", and attached much importance to building the harmony between people and the urban environment in terms of traffic organization, public facilities, greening systems, and parking systems.[①]

The modern model of urban settlement insists that humans should be the master of the city. By sticking to the lifeline of the city, it focuses on environmental protection and ecology and encourages people to share the new life of the city and nature. Therefore, people do not have to stay away from the city or come too close to the country and they also do not have to live in the downtown or on the edge of the city. The prosperity and convenience of modern cities and the purity and freshness of nature, are both indispensable parts of our life. This is the current top-level model of urban settlement.

There have been several popular theories of urban living in the real estate industry, such as the suburbanization of the city, neo-urbanism, neo-naturalism, and so on. Relatively speaking, achieving the balance between urban hustles and rural nature is a new mode of living that is more suitable for human habitation, by people living in the city, getting close to nature, working hard, and enjoying life.

3.2.3   Summary: a Choice Between the City and Nature

In this section, we discussed the modern people's attitudes towards living and the changes of their attitudes, as well as the modern people's living mode and other issues. Urban and rural areas are not incompatible with each other, but can be organically combined. The new model of modern human settlement advocates a living model with people living both close to the city and close to the nature, which is conducive to the combination of work and life, satisfying people's material, spiritual and emotional needs, and reflecting the value, taste and progress of human living.

Further Exploration and Links:

The architecture of Dai ethnic group in Yunnan Province, China shows the regularity and elegance in a theoretical format. Compared with modern architecture built in a scientific and accurate way, it presents the same strict reasoning and shows a greater degree of cultural integrity. People's social life in a traditional society is a

---

① 何禾, 石文华. 新型居住模式初探 [J]. 城市, 2011, (7): 35-38.
   He He, Shi Wenhua. A preliminary study on the new type of residential mode [J]. *City*, 2011, (7): 35-38.

logical and rational organization that fits their cultural values. In modern society, we may not believe in the existence of divinities, but for those societies with a strong belief in divinities, these divinities represent the true social relationships of human society, and other activities in these societies are also based on these relationships. Therefore, we should not judge a person's values in these traditional societies based on our "scientific" point of view.

　　—Gao Yun. *Dai Ethnic Group Houses in Yunnan, China*. Beijing: Peking University Press, 2003: 152.

3.3   Modern Observation of Transportation Means

3.3.1   Development and Evolution of Transportation Means

(1) Ancient transportation means

In ancient society, we travelled in relatively simple means of transportation, which were mainly developed with the help of natural forces such as manpower, animal power, and water power. For example, vehicles that were used for travelling on land included ox carts, horse carts, camels, and so on.

Vehicles driven by manpower mainly includes human-powered tricycles, trolleys, and sedan cars that are familiar to Chinese people. As for waterway transportation, there were common hand-supported boats, wooden paddle boats, rafts, etc. The so-called "boating in water" is a portrayal of this transportation means.

In the era of self-sufficiency and natural economy, this relatively simple transportation means was, not only relatively backward, but also time-consuming and laborious, making it difficult to meet people's increasing social needs.

(2) Modern transportation means

With the invention and application of steam engines and electrical technology, the transportation means in the modern industrial society are more and more advanced, increasingly facilitating people's social life. The streets and alleys in the urban areas are filled with all kinds of cars and steam or electric trains. In the vast rural areas, man-powered or animal-powered vehicles, and some water transportation means such as boats or rafts relying on natural water power still play a key role in rural transportation. In general, changes in the driving power for modern vehicles have changed the scope of travelling space and length of travelling time. The mechanical power of modern transportation has removed our dependence on human, animal power and natural power for transportation, which has significantly increased the speed of travelling and reduced the time of travelling. The time significance of modern transportation has become more and more obvious in the acceleration of travelling speed. On the surface, the realization of this time significance is based on the direct use of modern vehicles, but its internal basis is the result of participation of modern time in its construction. Modern time is a quantified time taken from our life, a homogeneous time away from life, and an abstract time different from anything concrete. Thus, modernity itself is strengthened together by modern transportation and modern time.[①]

(3) Contemporary transportation means

Different from ancient or modern transportation, contemporary transportation mainly features the application of electronic information, artificial intelligence and new energy. It pursues a fast, convenient, comfortable, energy-saving and environmentally-friendly means of transportation, which is not only a daily necessity, but also a symbol of social status.

Nowadays, airplanes, high-speed rail, light rail, coaches and speedboats have become the main means of travel for people; buses, subways, private cars, electric cars, bicycles, etc. constitute the city's three-dimensional transportation system, and people can make flexible choice of transportation according to their own wishes and needs.

During the development and evolution of transportation from ancient times to modern times, it is easy for us to know that technological progress has triggered changes in transportation, and it is not difficult to perceive the impact of transportation on social life.

3.3.2　Types, Characteristics and Values of Modern Transportation

(1) Types, characteristics and values of road transportation

For most landlocked countries or regions, road transportation is still an ideal choice for many people. The means of transportation on the road mainly depends on cars, which can refer to someone driving his or her own car, or hitching a ride in a coach or other people's vehicles. The choice of road traffic varies from person to person.

Generally speaking, it is more appropriate to travel on one's own by car with a one-way trip of less than 200 kilometers; it may be better to ride on a bus for a one-way trip of 200-400 kilometers; for a trip of more than 500 kilometers, it may be better to use other transportation means. Of course, this categorization of travelling

---

① 姚晓霞, 孙大鹏. 现代交通中的现代时间 [J]. 浙江社会科学, 2019, (3): 90-94, 158.
　　Yao Xiaoxia, Sun Dapeng. Modern time in modern transportation [J]. *Zhejiang Social Sciences*, 2019, (3): 90-94, 158.

distance is relative. The main consideration is that traffic accidents might be caused by drivers' fatigue after they hare driven a long distance.

The road traffic network is now well-developed with various types of transportation. The transportation cost may be higher than that of travelling by train but lower than that of air travelling. Moreover, due to its convenience, it is the most popular transportation means for many people. However, there are relatively more traffic accidents linked with this type of transportation. In general, there is still value for the existence of land-based road transportation.

Firstly, the car is currently the mobility tool in the world with the largest number.

Secondly, cars are more flexible, and have advantages that other tools such as railways, airplanes, and electric vehicles cannot compete.

Finally, China's automobile consumption is becoming more and more popularized. The booming automobile traffic makes it difficult to withdraw from the modern transportation market in a short period of time. This is a social and cultural phenomenon that deserves our attention.

(2) Types, characteristics and values of railway transportation

Railway transportation mainly includes the transportation by ordinary railways, high-speed railways, intercity light rail, subways, etc. The construction of this transportation requires more investment and its convenience cannot be compared with that of cars, but it is a much safer means of travelling. However, the travel cost of this transportation is generally lower than that of cars and there is little traffic congestion. Therefore, it is still popular with the public.

(3) Types, characteristics and values of air transportation

There is a single type of air transportation. Due to reasons such as airspace governance and high running costs, there are rare cases of private ownership of aircraft and private routes; aircraft passengers are mostly people on a business trip or tourists. When travelling to a destination over 500 kilometers away, people generally make a choice based on the travel task, time cost, and economic cost. Air travel has its advantages in cross-border and inter-continental travellings, and the probability of air accidents is relatively small, so it is also popular with people. This means of transportation still has its meaning for its existence and target market.

However, in recent years, there have been occasional incidents of aircraft disappearance and aircraft hijacking, which have also affected people's belief in aviation safety and their travel options to a certain extent. Some people even insist that travelling by air should be the last option for safety reasons. Although this view is somewhat one-sided, it reflects people's attitude towards the selection of transportation to a certain extent.

(4) Types, characteristics and values of water transportation

In the riverside and coastal areas with a more developed water system, waterway transportation may become the main mode of transportation for local people. Water transportation mainly includes transportation on the sea or river, and even the ferries along the river have become a way of travel.

Whether it is by sea or river, the transportation cost may be the lowest, but its speed is also relatively slow. Therefore, for those who are more concerned about cost but not in a hurry, water transportation should still be a good choice. Therefore, waterway transportation still has the value for its existence.

3.3.3　Summary: Choose Between Transportation Means and Values

In this section, we discussed various modern means of transportation on different roads, briefly analyzed their types and characteristics, and also discovered the values of their existence. All of these issues are related to culture and people's actions.

People's choice of travel mode and means of transportation seems to be a rational one made following a variety of cost competition. In fact, it is the result of cultural regulation in a country, a region, a nation or an ethnic group. The competition between the "rational choice" of means of transportation and the "rational choice" of what kind of transportation means more "face" presents different outcomes in the travel culture.

Further Exploration and Links:

On June 1, 2020, the Central Committee of the Communist Party of China and the State Council issued the "Overall Plan for the Construction of Hainan Free Trade Port" (referred to as the "Plan"), clearly proposing to implement a highly free, convenient and open transportation policy to achieve free and convenient transportation and to develop Hainan free trade port to be a model and important window leading China's opening up in the new era.

According to the "Plan", by 2035, Hainan will realize free and convenient trade, investment, cross-border capital flow, entry and exit of personnel, transportation, and safe and orderly flow of data. By the middle of this century, a high-level free trade port will be built with strong international influence.

The "Plan" clarifies that the implementation of a highly free, convenient and open transportation policy will promote the construction of a new international shipping hub and aviation hub for land and sea passages in the west, and accelerate the construction of a modern integrated transportation system.

The "Plan" proposes to build the "China Yangpu port" registry port, simplify the inspection process, and gradually liberalize the legal inspection of ships. On the premise of ensuring effective supervision and controllable risks, domestically-built ships registered in the "China Yangpu port" and engaged in international transportation are deemed to be exported and given export tax rebates. For domestic ships that use Yangpu port as a transit port for domestic and foreign trade in the same ship, they are allowed to refill the bonded oil required for this voyage; as to the refilling of ships with locally produced fuel oil required for this voyage, an export tax rebate policy is implemented; for container cargoes that are required to transit and depart via Yangpu port, the port of departure tax refund policy will be implemented on a trial basis.

—Wang Boyu, et al. A clear timetable and road map for the construction of the Hainan free trade port, a highly free, convenient and open transportation policy. *China Communications News Net*, 2020-06-05.

3.4　Contemporary Reflections on Social Interactions

3.4.1　New Ways of Modern Social Interactions

(1) Changes in the way of communication in modern society

Traditional social interaction is a direct face-to-face communication between people, which is the real-world interaction.

In modern industrial society, because people are engaged in different occupations, people's daily life including people's social interaction is dominated by the time spent in "assembly line production". With the invention of modern communication tools such as telephones and telegraphs, people's social interactions have gradually shifted from traditional regular meetings to telephone conversations or telegram messages. With the advent of mobile phones and pagers in the 1980s and 1990s, voice calls became the main method of social interactions.

In the mid and late 1990s, with the development of computer technology and the Internet, online social interactions became a new trend. Through sending e-mails and talking on the later instant messaging tools such as QQ and WeChat, people have built various social interactions between the real world and the virtual world. With the continuously expanded functions of smart phones, the massive information from a smart phone at one's hand provides convenience for people's social exchanges and interactions.

It is safe to claim that people should have had much closer social interactions since the development of modern instant messaging tools provides a strong technical support. But the real situation is that people are more likely to use various network symbols or emoticons to reply to friends or net friends, and the standardized linguistic expressions and communications tend to decline. Even in a real-world gathering of relatives and friends, most people bend their heads to look at their mobile phones and conduct silent "communications" with friends and relatives sitting next or on the opposite through human-machine dialogues. This situation should have been never seen or heard of before. It shows obvious changes occurring in the way of communication in modern society.

(2) Changes in the communication behaviors of modern social interaction

The emergence and development of the Internet have had a huge impact on the daily social life of humans.

Due to the gradual promotion of and popularized access to the Internet, there is a trend for general public to return to everyday social communications from online social communications. So the everyday social communications will still constitute an important part of human social life. No matter how rich and colorful the online life is, and no matter how highly trusted the Internet users are in their exchanges, the reality we must face is that the life online is inseparable from the life we live every day and vast number of netizens cannot always live in the virtual world. Therefore, most of them will still return to real social life.[①]

In fact, it is not high-tech devices including our smartphones that determine what kind of life we are going to live, but our own thinking patterns and attitudes. We should not lose ourselves in the online social interactions, but we should effectively distinguish between the real world and the virtual world, instead of confusing them.

In a long historical period, people often lived in an "acquaintance society", with a rather small communication circle. However, the public life in today's society is more like a "stranger society". People in public life are not limited to acquaintances, but anyone entering public places. The rapid development of science and technology and the increasing refinement of the social division of labor have provided opportunities for people to deal with strangers in unfamiliar public environments.

(3) Changes in the content of social communications in modern society

Today, due to the continuous expansion of WeChat functions, the first thing

---

① 童星, 等. 网络与社会交往 [M]. 贵阳: 贵州人民出版社, 2002.
　　Tong Xing, et al. *Network and Social Communications* [M]. Guiyang: Guizhou People's Publishing House, 2002.

many people do on their smart phones as long as it is activated is to browse related information online. For anyone who has downloaded and installed various APPs, they know that these APPs will push similar related information to them according to the information they have read before. Therefore, visiting Moments on the Wechat or browsing the information pushed by relevant public accounts that you follow constitute the main content of social interactions on the WeChat. As a result, we tend to spend less and less time on real social interactions, while more and more time in chatting online. Nowadays, many people are increasingly addicted to virtual socializing, which may be because of their deep fear towards real socializing. Only after one's gender, appearance, identity, status become invisible in the virtual world does he or she dare to show and expose their emotions in front of others. To a certain extent, this kind of behavior is conducted due to their fear of social reality and want to escape from facing themselves.

3.4.2   Cultural Reflections on Modern Social Interactions

(1) Modern social networking software has brought much more simple forms of interpersonal communication, but this kind of communication does not necessarily lead to spiritual resonance

Since 1998, Tencent has been developing social software, including Chinese people's most familiar QQ and WeChat. It has basically monopolized users and traffic in China's domestic social software market.

In 2011, WeChat was born in Tencent. In just five years, it attracted more than 800 million users. However, some people are beginning to reflect on this phenomenon now. WeChat used to make communications easier than before, but it also leads to the disappearance of the real exchange of information between people. A lot of people's time begins to be consumed on WeChat. When Moments was first invented, WeChat users were fascinated about this new function. They can record every bit of life on Moments and share it with their friends. They can also prove their popularity with countless likes.

Nowadays, WeChat has become the most popular new media for Chinese netizens, with Moments on WeChat becoming a business showcase platform and recorder of customers' whereabouts. Your every move may be exposed to the entire social community. WeChat users mainly use narratives of their lives and WeChat consumption record to reveal their class identity, actively differentiating classes by setting boundaries among friends. They try to discover and confirm their sense of belonging through interactions in the form of expressing likes, posting comments and reposting, as well as by private chats and group chats. Different from real-life class classification, class classification tends to be more diversified on WeChat. Users can simultaneously shuttle between different class groups to discover and confirm their sense of belonging.[①] Moments on WeChat has something in common with the real-world circle of friends, but they also present obvious differences. "Familiar" "strangers" and "unfamiliar" "acquaintances" are the two main types of interpersonal relationships in WeChat Moments. With the help of modern communication media such as the Internet, "friends" have been attached with multiple identities and identity constructions on WeChat. Through the application of various symbols and expressions, the instant interactions across geographic regions on WeChat Moments empower it with the function to mobilize social capital and cultural tensions that cannot be realized in real-world friend circles. Sending and receiving red bags, showing likes, spreading information to the public by individuals, conducting group discussions and even posting advertisements on WeChat, constitute the basic normal scenes on WeChat Moments in the "Internet Plus" era. The emergence and popularity of WeChat Moments are, to some extent, a modern product of the integration of culture and technology. As a medium and carrier of contemporary social communication that integrates culture and technology, there have been some signs of post-modern social life shown on WeChat Moments.[②] Today, some people feel that things tend to be counterproductive, as the social interactions online are just about some superficial communications rather than the soul-touching ones.

(2) Modern social interaction is a kind of cultural exchange in nature

Man is the main agent conducting social interactions, but man is also the carrier of culture. Therefore, in modern social life, people's social interactions have been transformed into cultural exchanges. The cultural exchanges in the social interactions should be an exchange of profound ideas, not a superficial exchange of materials or expression of behavior. It seems that the simple and convenient instant messaging tools have failed in achieving its expected effectiveness in terms of in-depth cultural exchanges.

(3) From social culture to cultural socialization: deep integration of society and culture in the all-media era

The culture of social communication is gradually formed in people's long-term

---

① 杨桃莲. 微信朋友圈中阶层认同的建构 [J]. 当代传播, 2017, (4): 93-96.
　　Yang Taolian. The construction of class identity in WeChat Moments [J]. *Contemporary Communication*, 2017, (4): 93-96.
② 廖杨, 蒙丽, 周志荣. 微信朋友圈: "互联网+"场域中的身份建构与文化表达[J]. 民族学刊, 2017, 8(5): 11-20, 97-101.
　　Liao Yang, Meng Li, Zhou Zhirong. WeChat Moments: identity construction and cultural expression in the "Internet +" field [J]. *Journal of Ethnology*, 2017, 8(5): 11-20, 97-101.

production and living, which regulates people's communications and behaviors. In today's society with highly developed new media and self-media, people's social interactions should be more focused on cultural issues rather than on materials and economic issues. Mr. Fei Xiaotong, a late well-known sociologist, once described cultural exchanges as: "Every culture has its own beauty and merits and we should respect each other's culture. The harmony in the world can only be achieved when we maintain the diversity of cultures in the world. " These insightful remarks provide a good example for cultural consciousness in the all-media era.

3.4.3 Summary: Choose Between the Superficial and Substantive

In this section, we discussed the diversification of modern social communications and cultural reflections on modern social communications, and analyzed the nature of modern social communications and ways to realize them. It should be noted that the innovation of modern communication means and the ever-changing advancement of the instant messaging technology can minimize the space-time distance in people's communication. However, they may not be able to simultaneously reduce the psychological distance or social space among the objects of "communication" space. After all, "tools" and "values" do not belong to the same category, just as the distance in space and time in the physical sense is not the same as the distance in emotion and space in the social sense. This belief can be expressed in the old saying: "Those that seem so far away are actually close at hand."

Further Exploration and Links:

Historical and realistic examples tell us that in the history of human civilization development, the transportation corridor with the watershed transportation system as the main form is an important path for the exchange of civilizations and dissemination of culture, and it also contributes to the emergence of civilization. These watershed transportation systems use watersheds as nodes and hubs, and corridors as connection methods to play an irreplaceable role in realizing cultural exchanges and promoting cultural dissemination.

——Tian Qian. *Introduction to Watershed Anthropology*. Beijing: People's Publishing House, 2018: 102.

Chapter 4　Travel and Purchase: Cultural Logic in the Age of Tourism

4.1　Tourism and Tourism Consumption

4.1.1　Tourism Is Essentially a Cultural Event

(1) Culture is the soul of tourism

Regarding the relationship between tourism and culture, scholars have done many studies and basically agree that culture is the soul of tourism. Why?

We know that there must be reasons for people to temporarily leave their habitual residence and travel to a certain destination. One important reason is that certain scenic spot, tourist attraction, or tourist landscape in this tourist destination attracts tourists to see or enjoy them.

How do tourists perceive whether a scenic spot, a tourist attraction, or a tourist landscape is worth visiting or experiencing? Here tourism-related knowledge is involved.

We know that the construction of tourist attractions, scenic spots, and tourist landscapes needs to be planned, designed and developed, before which it is also necessary to survey tourist resources and evaluate them according to different index systems. Then, based on the abundance and quality of the core tourist resources as well as the local geography and culture, the theme concept and connotation of tourism are refined in order to better plan and design the tourist attractions, scenic spots, and tourist landscapes. Coupled with the redesign and marketing of tourist routes, all these elements are integrated into a larger tourist product to attract more tourists to visit the destination. Therefore, whether it is resource census, planning and design before tourism development, or the route design and construction of tourist attractions, scenic spots and tourist landscapes during the development, or the post-development promotion marketing, management, etc., they are all related to cultural perception and are the result of the perception shared by tourism planners, developers, operators, practitioners and tourists. In this sense, tourism is full of cultural charm.

(2) Tourism is a cultural experience for tourists

From the perspective of tourists, the cultural attributes of tourism are more distinct. Questions like where to travel, how to get to the destination, how long to stay, what to see, etc. are the main factors for tourists to consider when travelling.

Therefore, we consider that tourism is essentially a cultural activity. The temporary leave of their usual residence to travel is actually a different cultural experience and pleasant aesthetic enjoyment paid by tourists.

4.1.2　Cultural Interpretation of Tourism Consumption

With the improvement of living standards, travelling has become a way for most people to improve their quality of life and lifestyle.

On the whole, the tourism consumption for many people remains at a superficial level, mainly focusing on city sightseeing and tourism shopping. There is an overall lack of demand for in-depth cultural tourism, participatory experience tourism, and adventure tourism, and the travel mode for many domestic tourists is relatively simple. Many tourists take overseas travel mainly for the purpose of "being there" and "taking a photo", so much so that some domestic tour guides make fun of those tourists who sleep all the way to the tourist attraction only to take photos and know nothing about the place after returning home. Although these words carry some irony, they reflect to some extent the low-level of tourism consumption.

In addition, some tourists travel internationally not for travelling itself, but for shopping, which also to a certain degree reflects the low level of tourism among some tourists. Although shopping is one of the seven major components of tourism, namely clothing, food, accommodation, transportation, sightseeing, shopping and entertainment, it should be derived from tourism, instead of becoming the main purpose and main activity of tourism. In other words, the kind of travel shopping that does not take tourism as its purpose, strictly speaking, is not in line with the essential features of tourism.

It is worth noting that the consumption behavior of some tourists who travel internationally for shopping sprees has also attracted widespread attention from the international community, showing the strong spending power of Chinese tourists. According to reports, in the past ten years, Chinese tourists overseas travel consumption has covered many kinds of luxury goods such as jewelry, brand name clothing, cosmetics, famous watches, calligraphy and painting, and even daily life utensils are also important options in overseas travel shopping.

According to research, as early as 2011, Chinese tourists' luxury spending has already won the runner-up throne in the global luxury consumption.① It should be noted that Chinese tourists' abnormal consumption in the overseas luxury market is worthy of attention. In recent years, the outbound tourism of Chinese citizens has increased significantly. In 2018, the number of Chinese citizens travelling internationally was 149.72 million, an increase of 14.7% over the same period last year.② In 2019, the number of Chinese citizens travelling internationally was 154.63 million, an increase of 3.3% over the same period last year.③

Obviously Chinese tourists who take overseas tourism need to learn to move from shopping tourism to real and in-depth tourism and maintain a good tourist image during the travel process.

4.1.3　Summary: Betterment Through Travel and Purchase

In this section, we discussed the related issues of tourism and tourism shopping consumption, and analyzed the abnormal consumption and performance of domestic tourists who travel overseas. It is hoped that the cultural reflection on tourism consumption can help you further understand the cultural logic of the tourism era.

Further Exploration and Links:

Tourism anthropology has a theoretical foundation based on the interdisciplinary penetration between tourism and anthropology. There is an internal connection between travel, tourism and anthropology, and the principles of juxtaposition of multiple cultures, "local knowledge" and "cultural mutual subjectivity" compose the methodological principle of the interdisciplinary combination of

---

① 佚名. 中国富裕家庭增速快于他国登上奢侈品消费亚军 [N] . 人民日报海外版, 2010-02-10(12).
Anonymous. China's wealthy households are growing faster than other countries and are ranked second in luxury consumption [N] . *People's Daily Overseas Edition*, 2010-02-10 (12).

② 财务司. 2018 年旅游市场基本情况 [EB/OL] . 中华人民共和国文化和旅游部官网(索引号: 357A04-04-2019-48887), (2019-02-12) [2019-12-25] . http://zwgk.mct.gov.cn/zfxxgkml/ tjxx/202012/t20201204_ 906481.html.
Department of Finance. The basic situation of the tourism market in 2018 [EB/OL] . The Official Website of the Ministry of Culture and Tourism of the People's Republic of China (index number: 357A04-04-2019-48887), (2019-02-12) [2019-12-25]. http://zwgk.mct.gov.cn/zfxxgkml/tjxx/202012/t20201204_906481.html.

③ 财务司. 中华人民共和国文化和旅游部 2019 年文化和旅游发展统计公报 [EB/OL] . 中华人民共和国文化和旅游部官网(索引号: 357A04-04-2020-48897), (2020-06-20) [2020-07-20] . http://zwgk.mct.gov.cn/zfxxgkml/tjxx/ 202012/t20201204_906491.html.
Department of Finance. Statistical bulletin on cultural and tourism development in 2019 by the Ministry of Culture and Tourism of the People's Republic of China [EB/OL] . The Official Website of the Ministry of Culture and Tourism of the People's Republic of China (index number: 357A04-04-2020-48897）, (2020-06-20) [2020-07-20]. http://zwgk.mct.gov.cn/zfxxgkml/tjxx/ 202012/t20201204_906491.html.

tourism and anthropology.

—Liao Yang. Tourism anthropology: interdisciplinary—penetration of tourism and anthropology. *Guizhou Ethnic Studies*, 2004, (4): 74-79.

4.2   Online Shopping, Surrogate Shopping and Overseas Online Shopping

4.2.1   Economic Globalization and the Rise of Cross-Border E-Commerce

(1) Economic globalization and modern life

After we enter the 21st century, economic globalization and free trade are advancing rapidly, bringing global economic prosperity, a surge in wealth, and a general improvement in people's lives.

There is no unified statement about the definition of economic globalization. A report by the International Monetary Fund stated in May 1997: "Globalization refers to the growing economic inter-dependence of countries worldwide through the increasing volume and variety of cross-border transactions in goods and services and of international capital flows, and also through the more rapid and widespread diffusion of technology." According to the Organization for Economic Cooperation and Development, globalization is a process, in which the economy, market, technology, and forms of communication are becoming increasingly global and less dependent on national and local markets. American scholar Robert Gilpin called it "the integration of the world economy".[1]

(2) Economic globalization is an inevitable result of scientific and technological progress and productivity development

In the middle of the 18th century, along with the roar of the steam engine, the first industrial revolution arrived, and an international division of labor took place. Cotton mills in Manchester, England processed cotton from the West Indies and North and South America. British cotton became the first global commodity in human history.

In the middle and late 19th century, generators, internal combustion engines, and production lines were widely used. The second industrial revolution marked the dawn

---

① 钟轩理. 不畏浮云遮望眼：经济全球化趋势不可阻挡［N］. 人民日报, 2018-12-10(2).
Zhong Xuanli. Don't be confused by current situation—economic globalization is an unstoppable trend ［N］. *People's Daily*, 2018-12-10 (2).

of the electric age. Cars, airplanes, telegraphs, and telephones have changed people's traditional way of life, and the world has gotten smaller and more accessible. Industrial and commercial capital is expanding globally, and the production, distribution, and consumption links of different countries are more closely knitted into a large network, giving rise to the first wave of economic globalization. From 1870 to 1913, global trade volume doubled. However, owing to the two world wars and the economic depression between the wars, the process of economic globalization suffered a severe setback.

After the 1970s, the information technology revolution became the core of the third industrial and technological revolution, completely changing the traditional economic operation mode, and giving rise to new economic and social development forms such as the digital economy. People seem to live in a "global village" where they are more interconnected to each other.

From 1970 to 2017, the total global GDP rose from less than 20 trillion to 80 trillion dollars in constant 2010 dollars. Over the same period, GDP per capita rose from 5,185 to 10,634 dollars. The share of global trade in GDP rose from 26.72% to 56.21% in 2017. The net outflow of direct investment rose from 13.04 billion to 1.525 trillion dollars. From 1981 to 2013, the proportion of the world's poor population dropped from 42.3% to 10.9%. And 85% of the global population had a life expectancy of 60 years, twice what it was 100 years ago.[①]

At present, a new round of technological revolutions and industrial transformations such as artificial intelligence, big data, quantum information, and biotechnology is gathering strength, giving rise to a large number of new industries, new formats, and new models, bringing more new changes to global development and people's life. "We need to capitalize the historical opportunities brought by new technologies, industries, and forms of business, to foster an enabling market environment where innovation is respected, protected, and encouraged."[②] It is particularly necessary to establish the multi-chain collaboration which includes the industrial chain, supply chain, value chain, and innovation chain. This new model and mechanism should be suitable for China and also be able to lead the world in development patterns, thus accelerating the establishment of a "dual circulation" development pattern to promote both the domestic economic cycle and the interna-

---

① 钟轩理. 不畏浮云遮望眼: 经济全球化趋势不可阻挡 [N]. 人民日报, 2018-12-10(2).
　　Zhong Xuanli. Don't be confused by current situation—economic globalization is an unstoppable trend [N]. *People's Daily*, 2018-12-10 (2).
② 习近平. 习近平谈治国理政: 第三卷 [M]. 北京: 外文出版社, 2020: 474.
　　Xi Jinping. *The Governance of China III* [M]. Beijing: Foreign Languages Press, 2020: 474.

tional economic cycle.

(3) The rise of cross-border e-commerce

Cross-border e-commerce refers to an international commercial activity in which transaction entities belonging to different customs borders complete transactions through electronic commerce platforms, conduct electronic payment and settlement, and deliver goods through cross-border logistics to complete transactions. It is developed based on the network, and has the characteristics of globalization, anonymity, intangibility, immediacy, paperlessness and rapidity. China's cross-border e-commerce is mainly divided into two trade models: business-to-business (i.e. B2B) and business-to-consumer (i.e. B2C).

According to 2015 China Online Retail Market Data Monitoring Report, the scale of China's cross-border e-commerce transactions in 2015 was 5 trillion yuan, a year-on-year increase of 28.6%, of which the cross-border export transactions reached 4.49 trillion yuan and import transactions reached 907.2 billion yuan. The main cross-border import e-commerce models include the platform model, flash purchase model, direct delivery platform model, self-operated model, and C2C surrogate shopping model. As for the proportion of China's cross-border e-commerce, exports account for 83.2%, and imports account for 16.8%.[1]

At the press conference of the State Council on January 14, 2020, Zou Zhiwu, deputy Customs Commissioner-General of the General Administration of Customs of China, said that in 2019, China's cross-border e-commerce and other new foreign trade forms continued to develop vigorously. Imports and exports through the customs cross-border e-commerce management platform reached 186.21 billion yuan, an increase of 38.3%. Imports and exports through market procurement methods amounted to 562.95 billion yuan, an increase of 19.7%. The total contribution of the two is nearly 14% to the overall foreign trade growth rate.[2]

4.2.2   Online Shopping, Surrogate Shopping and Overseas Online Shopping Have Become a Part of Modern Life

(1) Online shopping

Online shopping is no stranger to everyone. Many people have had online shopping experiences. Let's take a look at the development of online shopping first.

---

① 佚名. 2015 年跨境电商交易 5.4 万亿 [J]. 市场瞭望, 2016, (5): 18.
　　Anonymous. Cross-border e-commerce transactions in 2015 were 5.4 trillion yuan [J] . *Market Outlook*, 2016, (5): 18.
② 高飞. 2019 年跨境电商零售进出口总值 1862.1 亿元增长 38.3% [N]. 电商报, 2020-01-14.
　　Gao Fei. The total value of cross-border e-commerce retail imports and exports in 2019 was 186. 21 billion yuan, an increase of 38.3% [N] . *e-commerce News*, 2020-01-14.

The first online shopping in China took place in November 1996. The shopper was a Canada's ambassador to China, Howard Balloch, who bought a cloisonne, "Dragon and Phoenix Peony" from an online shop owned by Sparkice (Chinese name: Shi Hua Kai). As early as 1999, some Chinese Internet engineers began to build B2C websites, dedicated to promoting the development of online shopping in China. At the end of 1999, the height of the Internet boom, more than 300 Internet companies engaged in B2C were born in China. In 2000, these network companies increased to 700. However, with the decline of the NASDAQ (National Association of Securities Dealers Automated Quotations) index, there were only three or four companies left by 2001. Subsequently, online shopping experienced a relatively long "winter period".

The year of 2007 saw a rapid growth of China's online shopping market. The transactions of C2C e-commerce and B2C e-commerce increased rapidly by 125.2% and 92.3% respectively. In 2007, the market size of China's B2C e-commerce reached 4.3 billion yuan, and that of C2C e-commerce reached 51.8 billion yuan. In 2018, China's e-commerce service industry continued to maintain a steady growth trend, and the market size reached a new level. The annual revenue of the e-commerce service industry reached 3.52 trillion yuan, up 20.3% year on year. As the e-commerce service industry continues to mature, the growth rate of operating income has gradually slowed down, but it is still higher than the 8.9% growth rate of the operating income of service enterprises above the designated size in 2018.[①] Figure 4-1 intuitively reflects the changes in the online shopping penetration rate of home appliances in China in recent years.

At the same time, netizens have also developed online shopping habits. China Internet Network Information Center (CNNIC) released a statistical report on September 29, 2020, showing that as of June 2020, the number of Internet users in China reached 940 million, an increase of 36.25 million from March 2020, and the Internet penetration rate reached 67.0%. The number of mobile Internet users reached 932 million. The number of netizens in China reached 940 million, equivalent to one-fifth of the global netizens. The Internet penetration rate was 67.0%, which is about 5 percentage points higher than the global average. The digital divide between urban and rural areas has narrowed significantly. The difference in Internet penetration rate between urban and rural areas was 24.1%, and

---

① 佚名. 2018 年中国电商代运营市场规模达到 9 623 亿元，预计今后几年 B2C 与 C2C 市场交易规模差距会进一步拉大 [EB/OL] . (2019-07-02) [2020-04-30] . http://www.chyxx.com/industry/201907/754348.html.
Anonymous. In 2018, the market size of China's e-commerce TP reached 962.3 billion yuan, and it is expected that the gap between transaction sizes of B2C and C2C will further widen in the next few years[EB/OL].(2019-07-02)[2020-04-30] . http://www.chyxx.com/industry/201907/754348.html.

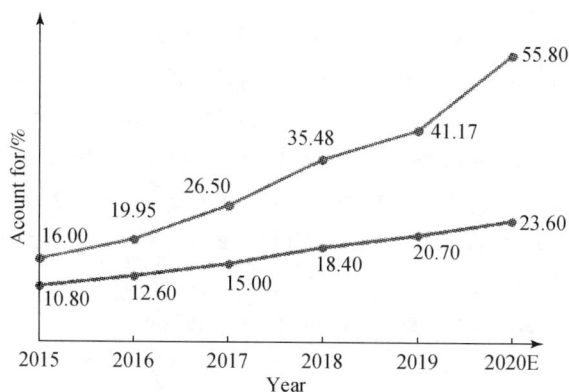

Source: China Center for Information Industry Development. *Report on China's Home Appliances Market in the First Quarter of 2020*, Electronic Information Industry Website, 2020-04, http://www.cena.com.cn/special/2020dyjdjdsc. html. The upper line is the proportion of online retail sales in the total retail sales of the home appliance market, and the lower line is the portion of retail sales of national entity in the total retail sales of consumer goods

Figure 4-1   Comparison of the penetration rate and the average penetration rate of online shopping for household electronic appliance over the same period in China in recent years

it shrunk to within 30% for the first time since 2017. As an important means of poverty alleviation, online poverty alleviation has been increasingly understood and participated by netizens. The number of online education users reached 381 million, accounting for 40.5% of the total netizens; the number of online medical users reached 276 million, accounting for 29.4% of the total netizens; the number of remote office users reached 199 million, accounting for 21.2% of the total netizens. Digital services such as online food delivery, online education, online car-hailing, and online medical services are booming, with the number of users reaching 409 million, 381 million, 340 million, and 276 million, respectively, accounting for 43.5%, 40.5%, 36.2% and 29.4% of the total Internet users, which not only met the needs of netizens, but also contributed to the digital development of the service industry.[1] With the advent of the 5G era, online shopping will become more common.

(2) Surrogate shopping

Surrogate shopping refers to a form of consumption which is done by surrogate agencies or shoppers by purchasing goods in websites, department stores and

---

[1] 中国互联网络信息中心. 第 46 次中国互联网络发展状况统计报告 [R]. CNNIC 中国互联网络信息中心, 2020: 1-52.
China Internet Network Information Center. *The 46th Statistical Report on Internet Development in China* [R]. CNNIC China Internet Network Information Center, 2020: 1-52.

shopping malls outside China and delivering the goods to the buyer through direct mail, transshipment or by people returning to China. Intermediaries or surrogate shoppers will charge a certain commission. Overseas surrogate shopping often involves the issue of credibility and therefore requires caution. The transit cost for surrogate shopping is slightly cheaper with online intermediary agencies. If the foreign website supports direct mail, then there is no need to shop on overseas online surrogate shopping sites.

Although overseas surrogate shopping is relatively cheap, there also exist problems such as credit risk, tax loss and foreign exchange management. Therefore, the "E-commerce Law of the People's Republic of China" was officially implemented on January 1, 2019 to regulate surrogate shopping.

(3) Overseas online shopping

Overseas online shopping is to shop on overseas websites, from where customers search for commodity information and complete online payment. The website then has the goods delivered to it through international express delivery companies or on behalf of transshipment companies and sends them back to China. Generally speaking, the payment method of overseas online shopping is delivery versus payment (online credit card payment, PayPal account payment).

The main difference between overseas shopping and surrogate shopping is the purchase method and whether commission is charged. They are all methods of buying goods abroad. The development of network information and logistics industry has accelerated overseas shopping. In 2020, the overall delivery was sped up by more than 30% in the "6 · 18" shopping spree. Consumers in more than 300 cities across the country have enjoyed hourly, half-day, and same-day delivery services, and even overseas shopping has also offered half-day delivery.[①]

4.2.3 Summary: Choose Between Shopping Online and In-store, at Home and Overseas

In this section, we discussed economic globalization and the rise of cross-border e-commerce. We also introduced modern shopping methods such as online shopping, surrogate shopping and overseas shopping. The development of Internet information technology has accelerated the process of economic globalization, and e-commerce has thus emerged. Whether it is online shopping at home or abroad, or surrogate

---

① 王洋. 配送更快　品类更多　海淘悄然生变 [N]. 消费日报, 2020-06-17(A4).
　Wang Yang. Faster delivery and more choices. Overseas shopping is quietly changing [N]. *Cosumption Daily*, 2020-06-17 (A4).

shopping outside the country (border), they have become part of the lives of netizens in modern industrial society in the age of information. For "homebodies", Internet has become a way of life for them to connect to society. Social informatization, the Internet, and the Internet of Things will reconstruct and shape people's production and life.

4.3   Globalization and Flow of Culture Across Borders

4.3.1   Overseas Tourism: Flow of Culture Across Borders and Cultural Globalization

(1) Overseas tourism: flow of culture across borders

With the development of economy and society and the improvement of living standards, travelling overseas has gradually become a choice for people to spend their leisure time. Recently, a sentence "The world is so big and I want to have a look" went viral online, striking a chord with many netizens, which in fact reflects the actual needs of people for travelling overseas.

China Tourism Research Institute and Trip.com Group jointly released the 2017 China Overseas Tourism Big Data Report entitled "Chinese Tourists' Consumption Upgrade with High Quality Tourism" , which shows that in 2017, Chinese citizens' overseas tourism exceeded 130 million people, and 115.29 billion dollars were spent, an increase by 5% compared with the 109.8 billion dollars in 2016, maintaining the world's largest tourist source country abroad. To some extent, overseas travelling has become a major criterion for measuring the happiness index of urban families and young people in China.

In the process of travelling internationally, scenic spots, tourist attractions, and tourist landscapes in the destination present to tourists the local culture or local people's perception, planning, development and utilization of different tourism resources, such as nature, culture or heritage sites. International tourists can perceive the natural landscape or historical cultural landscape of the destination through sightseeing or participatory experience. This is actually a cross-cultural tourism experience. The transnational flow and global exchange of culture are realized when tourists travel internationally to the tourist destination, where the local culture and the tourists' own culture are brought together. This is actually the result of economic globalization accompanied by cultural globalization.

(2) Overseas tourism and cultural globalization

The cultural globalization brought about by overseas tourism is not a unidirectional export or import of a certain culture, but the conflict, adjustment and negotiation of multiple cultures. For example, many countries or regions, in order to welcome Chinese tourists, have integrated relevant elements of Chinese culture into tourism planning, tourism products (routes), tourism promotion, tourism marketing to varying degrees, especially during the Spring Festival and other traditional Chinese festivals. Various places are racing to create a cultural atmosphere familiar to Chinese people, which brings such a real feeling of being at home that some Chinese tourists wonder if they are outside China. This is the result of overseas tourist destinations taking the initiative to adapt to Chinese culture. As one of the carriers of culture, the transnational flow of tourists promotes the development of cultural globalization. According to the forecast of the World Tourism Organization, international tourists worldwide will maintain an average annual growth rate of 3.3% from 2010 to 2030, and will reach 1.8 billion in 2030.[1] The transnational travel of tourists of this scale will undoubtedly promote the global flow and spread of culture. Cultural globalization is of course inevitable, unless the country is closed and foreign tourists are not allowed to come.

4.3.2 Ethnic Crafts in Ethnic Tourism: Commercialization, Localization and Globalization of Ethnic Culture

(1) Tourist crafts as the commercialization of ethnic culture

In the process of travelling, I believe that everyone has had the experience of purchasing tourist crafts. However, people may not necessarily think about the ethnic cultural attributes of tourist crafts, and the only reason for purchasing the crafts is because they are good, memorable or valuable.

In fact, although a tourist craft is a small object, it carries the understanding of tourist craft designers, developers, manufacturers and sellers to the cultural representativeness of tourist destinations. What kind of tourist craft can represent the iconic local culture? Especially in ethnic regions, what kind of tourist crafts can best represent the local ethnic culture? This should actually be considered as a multi-dimensional cultural negotiation between tourism crafts designers, developers, sellers and tourists, and also a way and result of the commercialization of ethnic culture. The tourist craft is a newly emerged product in the development of tourism. It is an

---

① UNWTO. Tourism towards 2030-Global overview [C] . Madrid: UNWTO 19th General Assembly, 2011: 10.

important carrier of ethnic culture, and its essential connotation is the commer-cialization of ethnic culture. Culture, technology, and ethnic habitat constitute the internal connection between the development of tourist crafts and the commer-cialization of ethnic culture.[①]

(2) Localization and globalization: the development trend of ethnic crafts in ethnic tourism

It is often said that the more national it is, the more international it will be, or it not only belongs to the nation but also the world. This means that although the nation and the world are different, they are related to each other.

The same is true of ethnic tourism crafts, which have both the characteristics of "localization" and globalization. Why?

First, tourist crafts are often made from local material, which is an organic combination of local ethnic aesthetics, arts, thinking, customs, and world advanced technologies. There is no "selling point" for tourist crafts with only ethnic "culture" but backward technology. Only when advanced technology and sophisticated production techniques are matched with unique ethnic culture can an ethnic craft have the value and selling point and be more popular in the tourist souvenir market and more favored by tourists. In this sense, the ethnic culture condensed and reflected in tourist crafts has the obvious "localized" characteristics. Behind the tourist crafts is the cultural identity of the ethnic group.[②]

Second, the globalization of ethnic "culture". This globalization is not only reflected in the global technology and potential global market, but also in the ethnic culture going global through the sale of tourist crafts. Through the form of crafts, a cultural exchange platform between tourists and tourist destinations has been built.

4.3.3   Summary: Culture Flows in Tourism

In this section, we discussed the issues of overseas tourism and cultural flow and cultural globalization and analyzed the relationship between ethnic tourism crafts and the commercialization, localization, and globalization of ethnic culture. It is hoped the discussion and analysis can help you further understand the cultural logic in the tourism era.

---

① 廖杨. 旅游工艺品开发与民族文化商品化 [J]. 贵州民族研究, 2005, (3): 134-141.
Liao Yang. The development of tourist crafts and the commercialization of ethnic culture [J]. *Guizhou Ethnic Studies*, 2005, (3): 134-141.
② 廖杨. 象征符号与旅游工艺品中的民族文化认同 [J]. 民族艺术研究, 2006, (2): 39-44.
Liao Yang. Signs, symbols and ethnic cultural identity in tourist crafts [J]. *Ethnic Art Studies*, 2006, (2): 39-44.

Chapter 5   Entertainment and Enjoyment: Cultural Expressions in Consumption Era

5.1   Entertainment and Social Changes

5.1.1   Entertainment and Enjoyment: Diverse Cultural Expressions in Consumption Era

(1) The meaning of *yu* (pleasure), *le* (happiness) and *yule* (entertainment)

We are no stranger to *yule* (entertainment), but it is never an easy task for us to define the concept of entertainment precisely. *Shuowen Jiezi* says *yu* (pleasure) means *le* (happiness) from "female" and the phonetic "*wu*"[①].

In the ancient literature, *yu* (pleasure) and *le* (happiness) can be used separately, as well as together. For example, in *Lanting Xu*, Wang Xizhi said: "Looking up at the vastness of universe and down at the abundance of life, I enjoy the pleasure of seeing through and hearing about to the extreme. Indeed, it should look as very happy."

An example to show *yu* (pleasure) and *le* (happiness) used together can be found in *Shiji • Biography of Lian Po and Lin Xiangru*. Lin Xiangru offered a plate and jar for the King of Qin to play the music of Qin so that the King of Zhao can "enjoy the music". Here *yu* (pleasure) and *le* (happiness) mainly mean delight and joy. In addition, *yule* (entertainment) also means interesting activities as shown from *The History of the Northern Dynasties* to talk about the cruelty of Emperor Wenxuan, who took pleasure in torturing people by forcing them to sit on a wagon made of thorns and having them dragged back and forth to watch them bleeding. Of course, there are also cases where *le* (happiness) and *yu* (pleasure) are used together. For example, in *Yi Lin • Wuwang Zhigu*, Jiaogan said: "Despite the hardships of life, my families survive, having nothing to worry, which brings me relief and joy." Here *leyu* means rejoicing.

---

① 许慎. 说文解字: 附检字 [M]. 北京: 中华书局, 1963: 262.
　　Xu Shen. *Shuowen Jiezi* (with check characters) [M]. Beijing: Zhonghua Book Company, 1963: 262.

In ancient times, *yu* (pleasure) was used as a phonetic loan character for *wu* meaning "comprehension". *yu* (pleasure) is an emotion after comprehension; *le* (happiness) means ripe wheat in oracle bone script, so entertainment is the feeling after comprehension and the joy after maturity. In modern society, the combination of culture and technology makes entertainment more colorful in terms of content and methods. Especially in today's information society, the convenience, immediacy, customization, networking and globalization of consumption have become the main characteristics of the consumer era and consumer society.

In the consumer era, consumption is made mainly through the Internet and information technology, so network traffic has become the key to a consumer society. In this era of consumption where traffic matters the most, product circulation, transactions, services, etc., all rely on information networks. Therefore, that streaming is king has become a motto for current information consumption. This kind of information consumption makes entertainment content and methods more colorful.

(2) Diverse cultural expressions in consumption era

In the consumer era, consumers not only care about product quality, but also pay more attention to the shopping experience during the consumption of goods. Whether it is shopping in traditional brick and mortar stores, outlets, experience stores or shopping online as well as in overseas online stores, pleasant, novel or meaningful shopping experiences have become an important aspect of consumers' concern.

In terms of consumption content, spiritual consumption, especially information consumption for entertainment, has newly become the darling of consumers, even exceeding people's material consumption. In terms of payment methods, credit, installment and electronic payment have become a new fashion trend for consumers. In terms of consumption patterns, the boundary tends to blur between rational and irrational consumption (reasonable and unreasonable consumption), towards which people's attitudes vary.

5.1.2   Entertainment Changes in Consumption Era

(1) From excessive entertainment to "entertainment to death"

The consumer era is a product of industrial society. It is an era that advocates consumerism, in which the consumption is quite different from that in other eras. As far as entertainment consumption is concerned, it often carries the meaning of "carnival" in this era. Some people believe that in the consumer society, modern entertainment seems to have become more informational, popular and flat. People can consume their favorite information in the online world through smart phones, and use this information to satisfy their material and spiritual needs. This is unimaginable in the agricultural society and the early and middle stages of industrial society. Some consumers indulge themselves with mobile games all day long, without letting go of their phones for a single moment, even spending their youth on mobile games, or immersing themselves in short videos, "entertaining to death". This is worthy of vigilance.

(2) From entertaining the public to "entertaining oneself"

Some have discussed the problem of entertainment turn in contemporary China, holding that China has gone through an era in which entertainment culture was denied and transformed, to one in which entertainment culture is affirmed and publicized. It undergoes a series of changes, from the original sinfulness of entertainment to the sinlessness of entertainment, from the elitism of entertainment to the civilianization of entertainment, from the politicization of entertainment to the commercialization of entertainment, featured by four characteristics, namely the diversified value orientation, the pursuit of self-pleasure, the commercial interest drive, and popularization of expressions. In this era of pan-entertainment, we cannot judge the entertainment culture created by the communication form with the dichotomous paradigm of "right or wrong", but we should recognize that both content and form of entertainment culture have changed in the consumer era. This is the result of the commercialization of information, technology and culture.

The omni-media and self-media in the Internet plus era release the vitality of mass consumption in the consumer era, and also make entertainment more diversified, popularized in terms of content and form and with easy access, which triggers a consumption change from mass entertainment to self-entertainment and "self pleasing".

(3) From complete content to information fragmentation

The third change in entertainment industry in the consumer era is that the integration of entertainment content has been replaced by the fragmentation or miniaturization of information content. It relates to the fast-paced work style of modern people as well as the impact of mobile phone traffic. It has become a common behavior and life style for urban young people to read online works or watch mobile videos for recreation and relaxation when commuting to work and home by taking public transportation or during work breaks. "Phubbing" and human-machine interaction are two characteristics concerning entertainment changes, which reflect the real life of young people in the consumption era.

5.1.3   Summary: Entertainment Changes in Consumption

In this section, we discussed the meaning of pleasure, happiness, and entertainment, and analyzed the diverse cultural expressions and entertainment changes in the consumer era. It is hoped that the discussion in this section will help you to further understand the cultural expression in the consumer era.

Further Exploration and Links:

A consumer society is a society dominated by consumption. It represents a new type of relationship between production and consumption, that is, consumption takes priority in the overall social system arrangement. Its main characteristics are: at the economic level, the tertiary industry based on innovation and service constitutes the main body of the economy; at the social level, the middle class characterized by specialization constitutes the main body of the society; at the institutional level, income growth and distribution, and the social security system constitute the main body of social policy. Historical materialism holds that maintaining a balance between production and consumption is always the basic requirement of economic laws. Since the 19th century, as the degree of industrialization has continued to increase and the world market has become increasingly saturated, the imbalance between production and consumption in western industrial societies has gradually increased, eventually leading to frequent global economic crises. In the first half of the 20th century, the first-mover countries carried out a series of changes in the economic and social fields, regaining a new balance between production and consumption, and gradually transforming from a production-oriented society to a consumer-oriented society. In the second half of the 20th century, consumption has become a leading factor in the development of first-mover countries, and the essential changes in consumption have determined the basic characteristics of a consumer society in different periods. In the 21st century, the first-mover countries have reflected deeply on the limitations of the consumer society and are actively exploring the establishment of a new consumer society that tends to promote sharing and value simplicity. In 2018, the national consumption generates 76.2% of the GDP, and the transition to a consumer-oriented society has begun.

—Fan Ruiping. Accelerating the construction of a consumer society with Chinese characteristics. *Sichuan Learning Platform of Xuexi.cn*, 2019-06-17.

5.2　Consumer Culture and Cultural Consumption

5.2.1　The Concept of Consumer Culture and Cultural Consumption

(1) Consumer culture

Consumer culture, put in a simple way, is the culture of the consumer era or consumer society. Others also argue that consumer culture actually refers to consumerist culture.

Regardless of how consumer culture is understood, it is related to the consumer era, consumer society, and consumerism, and has the following characteristics.

1) Consumer culture is a product of consumer society, so the discussion of consumer culture must be based on consumer society.

2) Consumer culture turns culture into a commodity and works according to market logic.

3) The distinction between commodities and artworks is lost with the emergence of consumer culture, and it has become a major trend to render commodities into artworks and commercialize artworks into commodities in the consumer society.

4) One of the core contents of consumer culture is consumerism which is closely related to hedonism.

5) The important function of consumer culture is to stimulate people's feelings, inspire people's imagination, and then build consumption concepts. Therefore, fashion, sentiment, style, symbolic value, etc. have become the main content of people's consumption.

(2) Cultural consumption

So, how should cultural consumption be understood?

Cultural consumption usually refers to a kind of consumption whose purpose is to meet people's spiritual needs through cultural products or services. It mainly involves culture, education, entertainment, sports, fitness, tourism and other aspects.

Under the condition of knowledge economy, cultural consumption has been given new connotations. Aided by high-tech, it has found its way into the mainstream culture, being popularized and globalized.

From the perspective of sociologists, culture is being constantly created and generated. Cultural consumption is a social behavior, which is perpetually affected by social context and social relations. People are also creating culture in the consumption of text and practice. Therefore, cultural consumption is by no means the end of cultural creation, but just the beginning. In a sense, the process of cultural consumption is also a process of cultural creation.

The history of cultural consumption can be traced back to the late 1950s and early 1960s. At that time, for the first time in Europe and the United States, a relatively affluent working population appeared, capable of meeting not only their "needs" but also "desires": televisions, refrigerators, cars, vacuum cleaners, vacations abroad etc. have gradually become common consumer products. In addition, the working population has begun to form a sense of identity through cultural consumption patterns.

5.2.2   The Relationship Between Consumer Culture and Cultural Consumption

(1) Consumer culture provides a spiritual source for cultural consumption

Consumer culture emerged during the Great Depression of the United States in the 1920s and 1930s, and spread to Western Europe and Japan in the 1950s and 1960s. It advocates conspicuousness, extravagance and novelty of consumption, the pursuit of unrestrained material enjoyment, recreation and hedonism, as a means of personal satisfaction as well as the purpose and ultimate value of life. It is the initial form of consumer culture after the emergence of consumer society in western countries.

The post-modern consumer culture formed after the 1970s is the extension and development of early modern consumerist culture. Although the emergence of consumerist culture is the result of the combined effect of economic, social and cultural factors, modern media has played an important role in spreading and constructing consumer culture.

Encouraged by the idea that symbolic value is higher than the use value and the transformation of material consumption into aesthetic consumption with ideological meanings, cultural consumption based on consumer culture has developed rapidly in western developed countries. This cultural consumption also affects the Chinese society after its reform and opening up. Lots of young people have developed their imagination and yearning for consumerism based on films, TV series or various fashion magazines from capitalist countries, such as the United States, Republic of Korea, and Japan before they come into contact with the modern and advanced consumer society. Many girls from the inland cities quickly repackage themselves based on the image of movies, TV shows and fashion magazines after they arrive in the south. It can be seen that the influence driven by cultural consumption is deep and wide.

(2) Cultural consumption path to happiness for consumer culture

Cultural consumption is a typical activity for non-material pursuit, whose development, maturity, and scale expansion depend on the development of productivity, the size of surplus products, and the increase in residents' income levels.

In consumer culture, advertisements, popular publications, television, film culture, etc. provide a large number of stylized body images. The body is commodified and considered as the carrier of happiness. Therefore, industrialized technology regulates the technical standards of plastic surgery, facial beauty, and body care. On the other hand, the aesthetic consumer culture causes them full of body imagery. People derive pleasure and "happiness" from the body consumption, which in fact, is the result of the manipulation of consumers' desires and interests by the modern media. It also exposes the morality of hedonism in consumer society.

With the emergence of credit consumption, spending future money to have fun and enjoyment has become a fashionable lifestyle for western mass consumers after World War II. Lukács holds that consumer culture is an affirmative culture, which provides a compensatory function for society. It provides people in the alienated reality with an illusion of freedom and happiness to cover up imperfectness in reality. Happiness is equated with consumption, and the "size" of happiness depends on the "size" of goods. [1] This kind of consumerism is actually an ideology, and materialization advocated by consumerism is an abnormal state of alienation in human social life. Marx originally expected that people would eliminate alienation in the future society in order to realize their self-improvement and self-development. In other words, the essential power of human beings can be realized in the objectification of labor products. However, in a consumer society, human creativity has long been transferred from the field of production to the field of consumption, and people's self-realization is mainly reflected in the consumption of various tangible or intangible commodities, rather than in labor products.[2] Can consumption really bring people freedom and happiness? The answer from western Marxists is no. They hold that in contemporary capitalist society, people are under control and manipulation in the process of consumption. On the surface, as long as you have money, you can consume whatever you want. But in reality, people's consumption is steered by manufacturer's intentions and advertisement. People are not free when consuming products in the consumption field, which undoubtedly exposes the beautiful lie of consumption "happiness".

① 卢卡奇. 历史与阶级意识 [M]. 汉译世界学术名著丛书. 北京: 商务印书馆, 1999.
　　Lukács. History and Class Consciousness[M]. Chinese translation of world academic masterpieces. Beijing: The Commercial Press, 1999.
② 李辉. 卢卡奇的物化理论: 兼论其对消费文化的影响 [J]. 山东师范大学学报(人文社会科学版), 2007, (2): 69-73.
　　Li Hui. Lukács's theory of materialization: its influence on consumer culture [J]. Journal of Shandong Normal University(Social Science Edition), 2007, (2): 69-73.

(3) Cultural consumption and consumer culture supplement each other

On the one hand, cultural consumption must meet the spiritual need of the consumer subject, making the subject feel happy and satisfied; on the other hand, it must satisfy the subject's need for spiritual cultural products or spiritual cultural activities. Both needs are influenced and regulated by consumer culture. Therefore, consumer culture is the core of cultural consumption, and cultural consumption is nothing but a means and way of developing consumer culture. The two supplement each other. The rise of webcasting reflects the penetration of media technology into daily life in the "micro-era". Presented by "spectacularization" and "mirrorization", it breeds a "mimetic community" of network subculture, and also heralds the formation of a multifaceted consumer culture. In the process, the proliferation of technology and symbols makes it possible for the carnival of mimesis to further amplify the emotional interaction, and moreover, draws the body of the anchor away from its natural meaning. Therefore, the anchor is given a commodity-like hierarchy value with a regulated aesthetic discourse in a consumption mode of "emotional labor". The formation of this consumer culture not only embodies the exchange and reciprocity between symbolic differences and symbolic capital, but also represents the shift from "survival consumption" to "enjoyment consumption", behind which is the drive and operation of "consumption capitalization"[1].

5.2.3   Summary: Consumption Is a Cultural Expression

In this section, we discussed the meaning of consumer culture and cultural consumption, and analyzed the relationship between consumer culture and cultural consumption. It is hoped that the discussion in this section will help you understand the cultural expression issues in the consumer era.

Further Exploration and Links:

During the Spring Festival of 2020, Zhangyue, a digital publishing company, saw an increase of 20%-30% in user engagement compared with the same period in previous years. Wang Liang, CEO of Zhangyue Literature, said: "Usually during the Chinese New Year, except for online games where user engagement rises, the user click rate and engagement in online literature, music, video and other industries will drop a little bit, because people have to visit relatives and friends

---

[1] 吴震东. 技术、身体与资本: "微时代" 网络直播的消费文化研究 [J]. 西南民族大学学报 (人文社科版), 2020, 41(5): 170-177.
　　Wu Zhendong. Technology, body and capital: a study on consumer culture of webcast in the "micro-era" [J]. *Journal of Southwest Minzu University(Humanities and Social Science)*, 2020, 41(5): 170-177.

and attend gatherings and parties. However, the user engagement of online cultural products increases this year." It is understood that popular science books related to the epidemic are particularly popular. The section of anti-epidemic prevention launched by Zhangyue has received more than 100 million hits via channels like Zhangyue client app and WeChat. E-books like *Handbook of Prevention and Treatment of the Pneumonia Caused by the Novel Coronavirus* are at the top of the hot list.

　　—Zhang He. A wider scope of possibilities for cultural consumption with open content and diversified experience. *People's Daily*, 2020-03-09.

5.3　Advertising, Information and Consumption

5.3.1　The Relationship Between Advertising, Information and Consumption

(1) Advertising and information

In modern life, advertising and information are everywhere and closely related. Generally speaking, advertisement is the carrier of information, and information is the main content of advertisement. In addition, the effective delivery of information relies on the effect of advertisements, but the credibility of an advertisement does not lie in the advertisement itself, but in the authenticity of the advertising message. Different interpretations of fixed information by advertisers and target audiences lead to the discrepancy between the message sent by advertisers and that received by audiences.

(2) Advertisement and consumption

In modern society, people's consumption is more or less affected by commodity advertisements. Advertising information includes commodity information, labor service information, concept information, etc. In addition to conveying commodity information to target audiences, it also conveys conceptual information. Celebrity endorsement advertising is a marketing strategy commonly used by many advertising companies. This is mainly to take advantage of the celebrity's high popularity and the utility psychology.

In the era of self-media and all-media, advertisements are ubiquitous, and even penetrates into every field of people's daily life. Through instant messaging technologies such as WeChat and QQ, advertising information has become a part of real life. It can be said that advertising stimulates consumption, which in turn promotes the development of advertising.

(3) Information and consumption

Information consumption is a prominent feature of the consumer era. In a consumer society, information plays a very important role. What people consume, how to consume, where to consume, etc., are actually closely related to information consumption. Therefore, it is believed that in the consumer era when information is king, consumption naturally flows to whoever controls or owns traffic. Therefore, many businesses and shops provide free Wi-Fi, in order to attract consumers through information consumption.

(4) Advertisement, information and consumption

Various phenomena in the consumer society show that there is a strong logical relationship between advertisement, information and news. Through advertising and information, producers, circulators, distributors and consumers of goods constitute the producers and consumers in the information flow. Advertising information, commodity information, price information, sales information, etc., comprise a fluctuating, non-linear information transmission in the consumer society.

5.3.2　The Essence of Advertisement, Information and Consumption

Over the past 40 years of reform and opening up, China's advertising industry has developed basically along with the development of China's industrialization and modernization. From the ice-breaking and budding period in 1978-1983, the "barbaric growth" in 1984-1991, the upgrading and competition in 1992-2001, to the prosperous development in 2002-2012, and to the transformation and upgrading and the global leadership after 2013[①], China's advertising industry, information and consumption have entered a new era, a new normal of information consumption.

We have just mentioned that in a consumer society, people pay more attention to the symbolic value, cultural and spiritual characteristics and image value of commodities, and pursue unrestrained material enjoyment, pastimes and pleasures. Affected by this, advertising information in the consumer era is inevitably invested in these symbolized and labelled consumer demands. It can be said that advertisement, information, and consumption in the consumer era reflect the value orientation of the consumer society, which is essentially the transition from a modern industrial society to a post-industrial society.

---

① 黄升民, 赵新利, 张驰. 中国品牌四十年: 1979—2019 [M] . 北京: 社会科学文献出版社, 2019.
　Huang Shengmin, Zhao Xinli, Zhang Chi. *Forty Years of Chinese Brands (1979-2019)* [M] . Beijing: Social Sciences Academic Press, 2019.

5.3.3　Summary: Consumption Is a Symbol

In this section, we discussed the relationship between advertisement, information, and consumption, and analyzed the essential issues of advertisement, information, and consumption in a consumer society. In modern society, advertisement is actually a kind of information consumption. In the postmodern society, advertisement is more than a kind of information consumption, and advertisement consumption has become a symbol and value metaphor of the consumer society. It is hoped that the discussion in this section can help you further understand the cultural expression of the consumer era.

Further Exploration and Links:

The China General Chamber of Commerce recently issued a notice requiring the professional committee of media shopping subordinate to the association to take the lead in drafting and formulating two standards including the "Basic Specifications for Live Video Shopping Operations and Services" and the "Evaluation Guidelines for the Credit Service System of Online Shopping". This is the first national standard formulated in the industry and will be issued and implemented in July 2020.

According to statistics from the Ministry of Commerce, in the first quarter of 2020, there were more than 4 million live broadcasts of e-commerce nationwide. The role of online retail in promoting consumption has further improved. "Live commerce" has different forms, such as TV shopping programs, the invitation information of online shopping, and advertising endorsements. The industrial chain is relatively complex, and there is lack of clear management standards and regulatory mechanisms for relevant participants such as network anchors, content release platforms, and product supply companies.

According to reports, the formulation and implementation of the two standards will help lead the development of China's live shopping industry and standardize online shopping, put an end to confusion in the live broadcast industry, reshape the industry ecology, improve the technical management level of the new retail industry, and protect consumers' interest.

—Du Haitao. New rules for live commerce will be released and implemented in July. *People's Daily*, 2020-06-09.

5.4   Entertainment and Consumption in the Era of AI

5.4.1   Entertainment in the Era of AI

In the post-modern society, artificial intelligence(AI) has increasingly demonstrated its usefulness and effectiveness. It can not only realize voice interaction, but also imitate the voice of a star.

AI will touch every aspect of the entertainment industry, even the oldest bedtime storytelling tradition for parents and children. For example, the interactive voice content created by Novel Effect can "summon" vivid visual effects with parents' voice. When parents read *Where the Wild Things Are*, a holographic image depicted in the book would appear simultaneously. Through interactive holographic technology companies like 8i, you can create audio interactive images for reading content. Moms can use these interactive "audio books" to help their children see the characters and scenes in the story directly right on the bed. In short, the application of AI into storytelling in the entertainment field will bring people better interaction and imitation. Whenever you play with, chat with, and observe AI, or make decisions through AI-enhanced devices, they will better understand how to entertain you through their own behavior or content selection.

It has been said that entertainment is the real power of productivity development. Compared with driving and other activities, our entertainment is or has been handed over to AI. For example, someone would like to have a Siri with Hiddleston's voice to chat with themselves, broadcast the weather and provide traffic information, or book tickets and select restaurants for themselves. However, we know that IT can never replace the real Hiddleston.

5.4.2   Consumption in the Era of AI

In the consumer society, online shopping has become the main shopping method for people in the new era. From the perspective of user experience, AI technology has largely changed consumers' habits. Through unmanned and intelligent technologies, such as intelligent search, voice assistants, and unmanned supermarkets, the users' shopping experience is made better. Of course, there also exist the bottlenecks of limited application scenario in shopping and the emotional dissonance to consumers.

Under the guidance of AI, new characteristics have emerged during people's shopping and consumption in this era. First, the scope of shopping is wider, and consumers can place online orders globally. The second is the electronic currency. The third is to accurately customize the production according to different customer needs and deliver at the door. Fourth, there are no difficulties in language communication and currency exchange in the purchase of products from different countries.

In short, consumption in the era of AI will be more personalized, more convenient, and more inclined to the psychological needs and consumption experience of customers. At present, the applications supported by AI have spread to the intelligent application fields of our daily life, such as facial recognition, language translation and voice assistants. With the emergence of these consumer applications, more and more companies are beginning to use AI, which further promotes innovation and productivity. At the same time, it also has a profound impact on people's work and life. Simple, repetitive and highly focused tasks will gradually be completed by intelligent robots. The needs of other occupations will also gradually change with the development of technology. It will soon become a reality for people who have no knowledge, skills, or creativity to have no jobs to do in the future.

5.4.3　Summary: Artificial Intelligence or Intelligence Artificiality?

In this section, we discussed entertainment and consumption issues in the era of AI. It is hoped that the discussion in this section can help you further understand the cultural expression issues in the consumer era.

Further Exploration and Links:

Cloud computing supports technologies such as big data, artificial intelligence, Internet of Things and blockchain. It is based on the three key elements of computing power, data and algorithms and develops in conjunction with 5G and a new generation of automation technologies, which produces fusion and radiation effects. It is a digital infrastructure which promotes the digital transformation of the physical world, traditional companies going cloud, and the digital transformation and upgrading of various industries.

In short, the cloud computing base supports big data processing and artificial intelligence algorithms, reaches the intelligent end in people's hands through 5G, completes a large closed loop of cloud-network-end integration, which together constitutes an intelligent world of all things.

Epitomizing the digital technologies in the new generation, the industrial Internet is the "superposition" and "fusion" of digital technology and traditional industrial technology. In the future, the industrial Internet will be upgraded, iterated, or reconstructed in terms of technology, architecture, model, and ecology.

—Liu Song. New picture of digital production and life. *People's Daily*, 2020-04-28.

Chapter 6 Getting Married: Marriage and Family in Society

6.1 Being Married off, Taking a Spouse, or Neither

6.1.1 Marriage and Family

(1) The meaning of marriage and family

Different academic disciplines have different understandings of marriage and family. The characters *hun* and *yin*, which together form the word "marriage" in modern Chinese, have unique meanings in ancient Chinese.

Shuowen Jiezi interprets *hun* as follows: "When marrying off their daughter, the wife's family, out of courtesy, sends her away at dusk (also pronounced *hun*). Women are also *yin* in nature. Thus, 'to marry off' is pronounced *hun*."[①] It also explains *yin* as follows: "Marriage is the reason (also pronounced *yin*) why she goes to her husband's house, thus marriage is pronounced *yin*."[①] As such, in ancient Chinese society, "the woman, for the purpose (*yin*) of going to her husband, would set off after dusk (*hun*)," became the typical portrayal of marriage. *Cihai*, a dictionary of standard Mandarin, interprets "marriage" as the husband–wife relationship between a man and a woman.[②]

Marxism holds that marriage is a social relationship between men and women, and it states that the nature, characteristics and development of marriage are determined by the economic basis. In socialist society, monogamy is adopted. Both men and women have equal status, rights and obligations. They support each other, care for the elderly and raise children.

Cihai defines the family as "a group of people, related by marriage, blood or adoption, who live together". The narrow sense of "family" refers to individual, monogamous families (nuclear families); the broad sense of "family" generally refers

---

① 许慎. 说文解字: 附检字(卷一二下) [M]. 北京: 中华书局, 1963: 259.
　　Xu Shen. *Shuowen Jiezi* (with check characters) [M]. Volume 1&2 B. Beijing: Zhonghua Book Company, 1963: 259.
② 辞海编辑委员会. 辞海 [Z]. 1999 年版缩印本. 上海: 上海辞书出版社, 2000: 1335.
　　Cihai Editorial Committee. *Cihai* (1999 edition) [Z]. Shanghai: Shanghai Lexicographic Publishing House, 2000: 1335.

to the various familial forms that result from group marriage (such as the consanguine family, the Punaluan family, the dual family and monogamy).[1]

(2) The relationship between marriage and family

In traditional society, marriage and family are closely related. Generally speaking, families are preceded by marriage, as a family is the result of a marital relationship.

As productivity and the relations of production develop, human marriages and families exhibit different characteristics. Under the socialist system, marriage and family are manifestly monogamous. Couples have equal status in the family, respect and love each other, help each other and share the responsibilities and obligations of childcare and old age.

(3) The modern marriage and family

In traditional society, marriage and family are relatively stable. The late, well-known sociologist and anthropologist Fei Xiaotong once regarded the triangular relationship of father–mother–child as an important model for the stability of marriage and the family structure.

In modern industrial society, human marriage and family systems have emerged with the development of society and increasing wealth.

First, the traditional concept of childbearing has grown more diverse, and the infertile "DINK" family has appeared.

Second, pregnancies out of wedlock, illegitimate children and single-parent families are gaining acceptance.

Third, with the diversification of family forms, different family forms such as separated families, non-married cohabiting families, renewed families, DINK families, empty nest families, nuclear families and joint families now exist.

Fourth, the development of modern medical technology has made it possible for artificial insemination, test-tube babies and other forms of procreation, resulting in marriage no longer being a necessary condition or prerequisite for establishing a family.

Fifth, homosexual marriages and families in some European countries and the United States have impacted the traditional forms of marriage and family.

Sixth, the invention and widespread application of intelligent robots in developed countries such as Japan have made "marrying robots" an idea among some avant-garde individuals in Japan. If this becomes a reality, the concept of the human marriage, family and social ethics will be given the characteristics and cultural connotation of a new era.

---

① 辞海编辑委员会. 辞海 [Z]. 1999 年版缩印本. 上海: 上海辞书出版社, 2000: 1236.
　　Cihai Editorial Committee. *Cihai* (1999 edition) [Z]. Shanghai: Shanghai Lexicographic Publishing House, 2000: 1236.

Aside from this, the NHK TV program team found through a survey that against the context of urbanization, aging and declining birthrates, there are now large numbers of so-called "orphaned people" (who have no relatives nor any relationships with others) in Japanese society, and they are lonely. After they pass away, their bodies are left unclaimed.[①]

6.1.2　Modern Marriage: Being Married off or Taking a Spouse

(1) Are you married off or do you take a spouse?

In traditional Chinese society, a man taking a woman as his wife is regarded as the cultural expression of marriage. But this is actually a cultural relic of a patriarchal society, which is prominently expressed in the naming of children born to a married couple regarding whether they take their father's surname or the mother's surname. Undoubtedly, if the father's surname is taken, the woman will live under the same roof with the man's family members as his wife. If the mother's surname is chosen, the man will live under the same roof with the woman's family members as her husband (colloquially known in Chinese as a live-in son-in-law or a *daochamen*).

Surnames are rooted in clans, and the choice of a child's surname thus actually reflects different clan concepts and demands. In this age of family planning, families have few children, and thus the name of a child has a particular effect on the minds of many parents, families and even clans. Why is this?

The reason is simple. Although a child's name is just a symbol, it is related to the lineage of the husband and wife. An only child, as the son or daughter born to a married couple, not only is the hope of two families but is also related to the couple's respective lineages. We naturally want only children to take our own surname. Therefore, the issue of which surnames second- and third-generation only children should take has become a tricky problem for some families. It is gratifying that with China's implementation of its second-child policy for families with only one child, the problem may be solved by one child taking the father's surname and the other taking the mother's surname. In a sense, this question of surnames for only children reflects how to solve the question of whether one is being married off or taking a spouse.

Modern society provides ample mobility, and young people are now particularly independent. Sometimes they live far away from their parents and work hard and get married in a different city. This has led to the modern phenomenon of "neither being

---

① 严蕾. "无缘社会" 困扰日本 [J] . 恋爱婚姻家庭(下半月), 2020, (4): 33.
　　Yan Lei. An "orphaned society" troubles Japan [J] . *Love, Marriage and Family*, 2020, (4): 33.

married off nor taking a spouse".

(2) Neither being married off nor taking a spouse

This type of "non-marriage" is characterized by the residence of both parties to the marriage. In traditional marriages, wives mainly live with their husbands. But "neither being married off nor taking a spouse" means that both husband and wife jointly tend to have a "small family" in a different city far from their parents. Sometimes, the parents of the wife will even buy her a home, though her children still take their father's surname. Superficially, this type of marriage is characterized by the wife's residence and the father's surname, but this is actually a reflection (in Chinese terms) of "neither being married off nor taking a spouse", "half being married off and half taking a spouse" or "being married off and also taking a spouse". This change in the way marriage occurs is a result of China's economic and social transformation, as well as its demographic changes. It is also a sign of the high housing prices in Chinese cities, which young people face during marital and family life.

6.1.3   Summary: Choosing Marriage and Family Amid Tradition and Change

In this section, we discussed topics such as the concepts of marriage and family, the relationship between marriage and family, changes to modern marriages and families, and changes in the ways modern marriages express themselves.

From the discussion of this section's content, we have seen how the concepts, forms and even embodiments of marriages and families have changed. We have also seen how marriage and the preservation of the family are still the main ways for defining legal relationships and kinship in human society. It is throughout this process of social development that some traditions have changed while others have remained the same due to the choices we have made about marriage and family. It is hoped that the discussion in this section will help you understand the sociological issues of marriage and family.

Further Exploration and Links:

In most parts of South Asia, a person will marry someone from the same caste or class. Many parents still insist that their children's marriages should be arranged. But this situation has changed. Let's take a look at how young South Asian people in the UK arrange their own marriages.

Matchmakers have been gradually replaced by personal ads on websites, chat rooms and the internet. Partners who have met online can arrange face-to-face meetings in a practice known as "South Asian Speed Dating". They agree to meet and talk — for just three minutes — at a restaurant or bar, after which they continue to develop their relationship. These participants, all around the age of 20, are typically middle class and consider themselves to be fashionable. They easily integrate Eastern and Western behaviors. Is this also true for South Asians in the United States?

—Carol R. Ember, Melvin Ember. *Human Culture: Highlights of Cultural Anthropology* (3rd Edition), Translated by Zhou Yunshui, Yang Jinghua, Chen Jingyun. Beijing: Publishing House of Electronics Industry, 2016: 262.

6.2   The Modern Evolution of the Dowry

6.2.1   The Betrothal Gift and the Dowry

(1) The meaning of the betrothal gift

China is a state of etiquette, and since ancient times it has paid attention to marriage etiquette. *Nazheng*, one of the six rites of marriage in ancient China (*nacai, wenming, naji, nazheng, qingqi* and *qinying. These six rites refer to proposing a marriage, asking about the bride-to-be's date of birth, divining the bride-to-be's name and date of birth, giving the betrothal, deciding the date of wedding, and escorting the bride to the wedding, respectively*) also known as *nabi*, refers to the groom's family's giving of a betrothal gift to the bride-to-be. This was one of ancient China's main procedures for marital engagement.

(2) The meaning of the dowry

The dowry, also known in Chinese as the *peizhuang* or the *zhuanglian*, generally refers to the wedding supplies and belongings that a woman brings to her husband's house when they are married. Such supplies and belongings can include houses, cars, clothing, furniture and other useful items or daily necessities. Due to the different customs and habits of various regions and ethnic groups, the dowries that they prepare differ.

(3) The relationship between the dowry and the betrothal gift

We know that betrothal gifts are given by the husband's family and that dowries are given by the wife's family. The dowry is closely related to the betrothal gift.

When providing dowries to their married daughters, many families often give dowries worth much more than the betrothal gift. Because some people, like to spoil their daughters or care about "face", the cost of their dowries is sometimes several times that of the betrothal gift. Thus, the traditional Chinese culture of "reciprocity" is clearly reflected in the betrothal gifts and dowries of modern marriages.

Countries or regions outside of China also have similar customs. For example, in India, which has a relatively large population, dowries and betrothal gifts have become a major burden for ordinary families. Indeed, some families are particularly afraid of having daughters. *The Times of India* stated that India's traditional customs hold that the more gold in the bride's dowry, the richer her married life will be. In Kerala, where this custom is especially important, a wedding requires up to 400 grams of gold, and the groom's family will always find ways to ask for more gold. To prepare a dowry for their daughter, some parents have to sell houses, borrow money and make a fortune.[①] Even in the 21st century, this Indian dowry custom has not yet disappeared.[②] This could lead to an imbalance in the sex ratio, which could then lead to serious social problems.

6.2.2   The Evolution of the Modern Betrothal Gift and Dowry

In traditional Chinese society, men farming and women weaving was usually regarded as the ideal agrarian mode of production and life. Therefore, betrothal gifts and dowries generally had "agricultural" or "animal husbandry" characteristics. Both the betrothal gift and the dowry had certain physical properties. For example, in addition to money, seeds, rice and even some production tools in southern China, livestock such as cattle and sheep in northern China often formed a part of the dowry.

In modern society, industrialization and urbanization have altered the original forms of betrothal gifts and dowries. This is not only reflected in an increase to the number of betrothal gifts and dowries but also in the differences in what has constituted a dowry across different periods.

Early after the founding of New China and until the beginning of reform and opening up, the Chinese people's economic conditions were poor. Thus, betrothal gifts and dowries were relatively simple. Even a half ton of rice would suffice. In the 1970s and 1980s, watches, sewing machines and bicycles became the "three big items"

---

① 章鲁生. 嫁女成本高 印度家长"抢新郎"[J]. 东西南北, 2014, (12): 66-67.
   Zhang Lusheng. The Cost of marrying a daughter is high. Indian parents' compete for grooms [J]. *East, West, South, North*, 2014, (12): 66-67.
② 薛克翘. 当前印度的陪嫁之风 [J]. 当代亚太, 2002, (5): 60-64.
   Xue Keqiao. The current dowry customs in India [J]. *Journal of Contemporary Asia Pacific Studies*. 2002, (5): 60-64.

required for Chinese people to marry. In the 1990s, color TVs, refrigerators and motorcycles became the "three big items", in addition to gold, silver and jade bracelets. After entering the 21st century, houses, cars, diamond rings and the like have started to become the main content of people's betrothal gifts and dowries.

In recent years, "national betrothal gift maps" have circulated frequently on the Internet. They are put together by busybodies who have calculated the costs of betrothal gift–giving across the country. Among these maps, the national betrothal gift map of 2018 reflects the changes to current Chinese betrothal gift–giving in certain aspects. Except for Chongqing, the betrothal gifts in other regions range from 10,000 yuan to one million yuan in value.

In the more than 70 years of development and change since the founding of People's Republic of China, betrothal gifts in increasingly many areas of China have been on the rise, and dowries are becoming more and more expensive. Some families even put more than ten kilograms of gold jewelry directly on the bride. As a way to show off wealth, this also demonstrates how industrialization has stimulated the people's material pursuits.

6.2.3 Summary: The Flow of Gifts and the Inheritance of Marriage and Family Culture

In this section, we discussed the meanings of betrothal gifts and dowries, the relationship between dowries and betrothal gifts, and issues related to betrothal gifts and dowries in modern marriage.

From the discussion in this section, we see that betrothal gifts and dowries are actually a matter of circulating gifts, as well as an issue related to the inheritance of marriage and family culture. I hope that the discussion in this course can help everyone further understand the sociological problems of marriage and family.

Further Exploration and Links:

In many societies, especially those based on agriculture, women often bring dowries with them when they get married. The dowry is a share of the woman's parents' property. It is not passed on to her when her parents die but is given to her when she gets married. This does not mean that she retains control of the property after marriage. In the United States, the dowry is sometimes embodied through the custom of the bride's family paying for the wedding.

One of the functions of the dowry is to ensure that women are supported during widowhood (or after marriage). When men engage in lengthy, productive labor, a woman's value lies in her fertility rather than the social work that she does. The dowry is thus an important form of compensation. In such a society, women who cannot have children are particularly vulnerable, but the dowry that they bring with them when they get married helps prevent them from being abandoned. Another function of the dowry is to reflect the economic status of women in a society where wealth differences are important. This also enables women to use their parents and relatives to compete for a desirable (i.e.wealthy) husband through a dowry.

—William A. Haviland, Harald E. L. Prins, Dana Walrath, et al. *Anthropology: The Human Challenge* (14th Edition), Translated by Zhou Yunshui, Chen Xiang, Lei Lei, et al. Beijing: Publishing House of Electronics Industry, 2018: 491.

6.3   Population Migration and Transnational Marriage

6.3.1   Migration

(1) The meaning of human migration

Human migration refers to various short-term, repetitive or periodic movements of human populations between regions.

(2) Types of population migration

According to its duration, population migration can be divided into the following different types.

1) "Long-term population migration" refers to leaving one's place of household registration for more than one year and living elsewhere while the household registration remains unmoved.

2) "Temporary population migration" refers to staying or living elsewhere for more than one day and less than one year after leaving one's registered place of residence, while one's household registration remains unmoved.

3) "Cyclical population migration" refers to regularly leaving and returning to one's place of household registration.

4) "Commuting population migration" generally refers to the migration of people who leave home early and return late, not staying overnight away from home.

5) "Transnational population migration" mainly refers to the cross-border migration of populations between different countries. Its main forms are labor-export

migration, visits to relatives abroad and marriages with foreigners.

6.3.2　Transnational Population Migration and Transnational Marriage

With the progression of China's reform and opening up, the Chinese people's conceptualization of sex has become more tolerant and open, and the number of transnational marriages has increased in recent years. In particular, it is worth mentioning that in large cities in China, the number of transnational ethnic groups and even interracial partners has increased significantly.

According to the data of the Ministry of Civil Affairs of the People's Republic of China, in 2017, there were 100,000 marriage registrations involving a foreign partner or a partner from Hong Kong, Macao or Taiwan. According to CNN, there were 53,000 multinational marriages registered in China in 2012, whereas "Chinese mainland did not register any transnational marriages in 1978"[①].

With the development of the world economy, technology and culture, marriage appears to have been globalized. It is understood that the foreign sons and daughters in law married to individuals from Shanghai come from almost everywhere in world, involving all continents except Antarctica. Among them, the Japanese are the most popular, accounting for 39.6% of the total. Other relatively concentrated countries and regions are the United States (9.1%), Australia (6.1%) and Canada (3.9%).[②]

Due to differences in cultural backgrounds, historical traditions and family values in people from different countries, couples involved in cross-border marriages may have more worries and risks than domestic couples, and some may experience domestic violence. This is mainly due to the shaky recognition of transnational marriages abroad, a lack of familiarity with local laws and disadvantages in terms of language, culture, concepts and customs. Even if marriage is based on emotions, marriage crises can occur due to regional and cultural differences (regarding value orientations and discrimination). Conflicts caused by differing cultural backgrounds can create obstacles in aspects such as communication, customs and values.

Of course, not all transnational marriages are problematic. Many families

---

① 佐伊·墨菲. 中国跨国婚姻，因爱而生 [N/OL] . 甘文凝，译. 环球时报, 2013-10-25.
　　Zoe Murphy. Transnational marriage in China [N/OL] . Translated by Gan Wenning. *Global Times*, 2013-10-25.
② 佚名. 中国当前的跨国婚姻现象 [EB/OL] .(2013-09-18) [2015-04-29] . http://www.bblhls.com/art/view. asp?id=765030234881.
　　Anonymous. The current phenomenon of transnational marriages in China [EB/OL] . (2013-09-18) [2015-04-29] . http://www.bblhls.com/art/ view.asp?id=765030234881.

formed from multinational marriages are also warm and happy. It should be noted that both transnational and domestic marriages require the completion of normal, legal registration procedures, but such procedures for foreign-related marriages are relatively cumbersome.

In both domestic and transnational marriages, blessings from relatives and dowry gifts are generally guaranteed. The dowry and the wedding culture that it carries accompany the population migration resulting from transnational marriages; thus they continue to be passed down through the generations.

6.3.3   Summary: The Flow of Gifts and the Inheritance of Marriage and Family Culture

In this section, we discussed population migration and cross-border marriage issues. Transnational marriages do not simply result in the transnational flow of populations. They also bring the intergenerational inheritance of gifts and transnational marriage and family culture. We hope that the discussion in this section will help everyone to further understand these sociological issues of marriage and family.

Further Exploration and Links:

Large-scale, global immigration, modern technology and many other factors have also affected the cross-cultural mosaic of marriages, families and households. For example, digital communication through optical cables and satellites has changed the way individuals express sexual attraction and possession in romantic relationships.

Nowadays, local, cross-cultural and cross-border romantic relationships are blossoming across the Internet. Many online companies provide dating and blind dating services, allowing Individuals to post personal information and find romantic partners or future spouses in a secure, online environment. Such services have also attracted individuals far and wide based on ethnic or religious terms, helping them find people who match their individual, ethnic or religious backgrounds. For example, today's dating sites in India are also used for the purpose of arranged marriages, allowing parents to upload videos of their children, screen potential suitors and arrange suitable blind dates.

Social media also allow people to privately communicate their forbidden desires or express intimacy through text messages in the pursuit of traditionally forbidden relationships — such as cross-caste interactions between young unmarried men and women in traditional Muslim communities in India.

　　—William A. Haviland, Harald E. L. Prins, Dana Walrath, et al. *Anthropology: The Human Challenge* (14th Edition), Translated by Zhou Yunshui, Chen Xiang, Lei Lei, et al. Beijing: Publishing House of Electronics Industry, 2018: 497-498.

6.4　The Special "Marriages" of Modern Society

6.4.1　Gay "Marriage" and Its Impact on Marriage and the Family

　　(1) What is meant by "homosexuality"?

　　Simply put, "homosexuality" refers to the phenomenon of a sexual orientation that produces love and sexual desire only for people of the same sex, with no interest for the opposite sex. Those who experience same-sex love or same-sex attraction are called homosexuals. According to the objects of homosexual love or attraction, homosexuality can be divided into two types: gay and lesbian, which in Chinese are referred to as *nantong* and *nütong*, respectively.

　　Sexual orientation is related to sexual pleasure, but homosexuality does not equate to homosexual behavior. Under special circumstances, a heterosexual person may exhibit homosexual behavior, and a homosexual person may also exhibit heterosexual behavior. Sexual orientation is a complex issue. Scientists, psychologists and medical experts have done research on human sexual orientation. A document published by the American Psychological Association holds that long-term experimental records prove that homosexuality cannot be "corrected" and that sexual orientation cannot be changed.

　　Rao Yi, a Chinese life scientist, believes that homosexuality has genetic causes, but it is unclear which genes affect human sexual orientation. "Of course, injecting someone with sex hormones will affect sexual orientation, and sex hormones not only change sexual orientation but also other sexual behaviors, as well as some morphological characteristics related to sex. But it has not been proven that genetic changes related to sex hormones are the cause of homosexuality in humans."[1] It should be the basic attitude and moral position of modern civilized society to scientifically examine the issue of "homosexuality" without "turning a blind eye" to it or "concealing it out of fear".

---

① 饶毅. 欲解异性恋，须知同性恋 [J]. 科学文化评论, 2012, 9 (5): 63-74.
　　Rao Yi. To understand heterosexuality, you must know homosexuality [J]. *Science and Culture Review*, 2012, 9 (5): 63-74.

(2) Gay "marriage"

Same-sex marriage refers to the "marital relationship" between two members of the same sex. Supporters of gay marriage call this marriage equality or equal marriage rights. This form of marriage could mean that the diversification of modern marriage will meet the marital needs of homosexuals. From 2001, when the Netherlands became the world's first country to legalize same-sex marriage, until nearly 20 years later in 2019, same-sex marriage and civil unions have become legal in 36 countries or regions around the world. Same-sex marriage is currently not officially recognized in China except Taiwan region as same-sex "marital relationships" cannot be registered at civil affairs departments.

On the morning of December 20, 2019, at the third press conference of the Legislative Affairs Commission of the Standing Committee of the National People's Congress, Yue Zhongming, the spokesperson of the Legislative Affairs Commission of the Standing Committee of the National People's Congress, said that in the process of soliciting opinions on the three drafts of the Marriage and Family Draft of the Civil Code, some opinions held that the legalization of same-sex marriage should be included in the Marriage and Family Civil Code. Prior to this, the NPC Standing Committee meeting held in October 2019 reviewed the draft of the Marriage and Family Civil Code three times. Yue Zhongming said that after this review, from October 31 to November 29, 2019, ideas on the draft of the Marriage and Family Civil Code were publicly solicited from the public through the China National People's Congress website. "A total of 237,057 opinions submitted by 198,891 public individuals were received online. In addition, 5,635 letters from the masses were also received. These opinions mainly focused on improving the scope of what defines 'close relatives', revising the authority for the revocation of marriages, making further improvements regarding the joint debts of husband and wife, and legalizing same-sex marriages."[①]

(3) The impact of homosexual "marriage" on marriage and family

On March 6, 2006, in Los Angeles, Chinese director Li An won an Oscar for best director for a movie reflecting homosexuality: *Brokeback Mountain*. In Beijing at the time, there was also a topic about homosexuality that had attracted much attention: on March 3, 2006, Li Yinhe, a famous sociologist and member of the CPPCC National Committee, while participating in the fourth meeting of the 10th CPPCC National

---

① 王姝. 全国人大常委会法工委发言人: 有意见建议 "同性婚姻合法化" 写入民法典 [N] . 新京报, 2019-12-20.
Wang Shu. Spokesperson of the Legal Work Committee of the Standing Committee of the National People's Congress: some opinions suggest that the "legalization of same-sex marriage" should be written into the Civil Code[N]. *Beijing News*, 2019-12-20.

Committee, formally submitted *A Proposal of Same-Sex Marriage* to the conference. As the most populous country in the world, China lacks official data on the occurrence of homosexuality within its borders, nor are there any comparative figures on people with a typical sexual orientation, but academics estimate that there are about 40 million homosexuals in China. This means that, of every 100 people around us, there may be two to three, or more, who are willing to choose a same-sex partner. Behind this huge number is a group that thus cannot be ignored.[①]

Some scholars have observed and interviewed gay men of different ages in Beijing, Shanghai, Shenyang, Tianjin, Xi'an, Chengdu and other places, and they have found that gay men have developed three special forms of marriage: "marriage" outside of marriage, the "marriage" of two sons, and the marriage of a gay man with a lesbian, all of which are the result of homosexual affection and heterosexual monogamy. There is no legislation that recognizes same-sex marriage in China. The strategic coping mechanisms of gay men and the underlying cultural adaptation thus entailed, as well as a potential heterosexual framework, deserve attention.

Due to their identical sex organs, "married" homosexuals cannot have sex in the way that heterosexual couples do, and thus they cannot produce offspring, as advocated by traditional marriage. Therefore, homosexual "marriages" and the resulting "families" are not readily recognized by traditional, secular society. And although the mechanization and intelligence of the industrial era can help solve the problem of human labor shortages to a certain extent, it is nonetheless difficult for artificial intelligence to completely replace human existence.

6.4.2　Robot "Marriages" and Their Impact on Human Marriages and Families

(1) What is "robot marriage"?

In recent years, with the development of AI technology, some people seem to be particularly interested in sex robots. The question of whether humans can "marry" sex robots has thus become a focus of social attention.

"Robot marriage" refers to the "marriage" of humans and highly intelligent sex robots. The "humanization" of robots still has a long way to go. Some artificial intelligence experts have, however, optimistically predicted that humans will be able to "marry" sex robots in 2045 or 2050. Of course, this "marriage" will not be a

---

① 佚名. 我国首查同性恋人群基数 [EB/OL]. (2004-08-19) [2005-01-15]. http://news.sina.com.cn/c/2004-08-19/16113439105s. shtml.
Anonymous. China's first survey of its base gay population [EB/OL]. (2004-08-19) [2005-01-15]. http://news.sina.com.cn/c/2004-08-19/16113439105s.shtml.

heterosexual marriage in the traditional sense. Robots are intelligent machines, but they are not real people. The result of "human–machine marriage" will not only shake the world; it will also overturn the people's perception of actual marriage and family. If so, "human–machine marriages" will rewrite the history of human marriage and family.

(2) The impact of "robot marriage" on society

Robot ethics is a new field of scientific and technological ethics research. Companion robots that form close relationships with humans will cause a series of conflicts with traditional marriage ethics and sexual ethics, including how to treat love between humans and companion robots, the status and rights of companion robots, and the ethicality of love between two companion robots. Is it possible to abuse such robots? The answers to these questions and their solutions must be examined by philosophers, scientists, manufacturers and users so that robots can better serve humans.

Nowadays, robots are used more and more widely, and the various ethical problems that they can cause are becoming increasingly pressing. Robots, however, are only an important auxiliary tool for mankind and cannot completely replace human beings.

Sex robots can have their artificial intelligence maximized, and they are unlike real-world women whose emotional fluctuations affect the husband–wife relationship due to physiological cycles. They can be adjusted to be more gentle or full of fun according to the needs of the robot's owner, and they will not quarrel. They will not fight, and they might be more easily liked or favored by men. But in the end, robots are just machines; they are not human. It is foreseeable that if "marriage" between people and sex robots in the world is permitted, then humanity itself will eventually be destroyed.

6.4.3   Summary: Recognizing Society in a "Harmonious but Different" Marriage and Family Culture

In this section, we discussed special forms of marriage in modern society: homosexual "marriage" and robot "marriage". This is a controversial topic, and it is also a major challenge to modern marriage and family life brought by the development of modern science and technology. It is hoped that through the discussion in this section, we have helped you further understand the marriage and family problems of human society in the form of "harmonious but different" marriages and families.

Further Exploration and Links:

Among the Lepcha in the Himalayas, if a person eats the meat of uncastrated pigs, they are considered gay. The Lepcha also deny the existence of homosexual behavior among themselves, and they are disgusted with such behavior. Perhaps because many societies deny the existence of homosexuality, in such restrained societies, homosexual behavior is rarely observed. In a free society, the types of homosexuality and attitudes towards its universality are different. In some societies, homosexuality is accepted but restricted to a specific time and a specific person. For example, among the Papagos in the southwestern United States, there is a "Night of the Farming God", where homosexuality can be expressed. Many Papagos men dress up as the opposite sex. They wear women's clothes and do the housework that women often do. If they are unmarried, other men may visit them. Women do not have the same freedom of expression. They can participate in the Farming God Festival Gala, but only with their husbands' permission. Nor are there any female cross-dressers.

—Carol R. Ember, Melvin Ember. *Human Culture: Highlights of Cultural Anthropology* (3rd Edition), Translated by Zhou Yunshui, Yang Jinghua, Chen Jingyun. Beijing: Publishing House of Electronics Industry, 2016: 245.

Chapter 7　Aging and Falling Sick: Old-Age Care in Human Society

7.1　Old-Age Care in the Transformation of Modern Society

7.1.1　Modernity of Social Transformation

(1) What is social transformation?

To put it simply, social transformation refers to the profound transition in social structure, economic patterns, cultural values, etc. from one stage to another. Since 1949, China has undergone an unprecedented social transformation. The social transformation has led to major changes in all aspects of China. With the transition from a poverty-stricken society to a moderately prosperous society, people's livelihood has been greatly improved, and institutional innovation is reflected in the transition from social management to social governance. The change in governance, fairness and justice is embodied in the transition from a pyramid-shaped society to an olive-shaped society, and people's yearning for a better life is reflected in the transition from subsistence-oriented consumption to development- oriented consumption.[①]

(2) Contents of social transformation

Specifically, social transformation is reflected in social structural transformation, transition of social operation mechanism, adjustment of social interests and changes of people's concept.

From the perspective of China's economic system, since the 1980s, a planned economic system has been transformed into a market economic system. In terms of social structure, there are changes in its structure of social stratum, social organization, family, employment or division of labor, income distribution, and consumption. As for the social pattern, social transformation is mainly manifested in the transition from the traditional society to modern society, that is, from the agricultural society to industrial

---

① 孙凤. 70 年来中国社会转型的 "四个向度" ［J］. 人民论坛, 2019, (29): 35-37.
　Sun Feng. The "four dimensions" of China's social transformation in the past 70 years[J]. *People's Forum*, 2019, (29): 35-37.

society, and then the information society. During the period of transition, there will be obvious changes in people's behavior, lifestyle and value system.

(3) Modernity of modern social transformation

In the transformation of modern society, modernity means that the time for line production in the industrial age replaces the time for farming in the traditional agricultural society. What's more, the mass production by machine replaces the manual production with just limited output, and standardized, modeled and stereotyped products or services replace the individualized ones. Organization, coordination, and efficiency replace individuals, decentralization, and inefficiency; the humanistic values of freedom, democracy, equality, and justice replace feudal autocracy, inequality, and injustice.

7.1.2   Old-Age Care in Modern Society

(1) The unsustainable traditional pattern of old-age care at home

Before the industrial society, the main pattern is providing care for the aged by families. This traditional way relies on the transferring wealth from the previous generation to the next, namely vertical intergenerational inheritance. This intergenerational transfer of wealth is almost the only viable pattern before industrialization since no capital market existed then.

In western countries, when the problem of population aging hadn't emerged, and care for the elderly hadn't become a prominent social issue, care by families was mainstreamed. The elderly in Europe, the United States and other developed countries choosing home-based care make up about 80% of the total. Those in China, Japan, Singapore and other Asian countries basically choose the home-based. However, with the demographic transformation and the declining workforce, the traditional way tends to be unsustainable. According to a report, about 5%-15% of the elderly in developed countries choose the institutional model, of which about 5%-12% in Northern Europe, about 10% in the United Kingdom, and about 20% in the United States.[①] In addition, different countries or regions have developed a variety of old-age care methods such as old-age care with assistance from their living communities, through migration, by mortgaging their houses, through mutual help among the elderlies, or with the help of medical care.

Since the implementation of reform and opening-up policy, China's industrialization and urbanization have accelerated rapidly in China, there is a large-scale migration

---

① 杨云帆. 国外养老模式的经验和启示 [N] . 学习时报, 2015-03-09(A15).
　Yang Yunfan. Experience and enlightenment of foreign pension models [N] . *Study Times*, 2015-03-09 (A15).

from rural to urban areas. And the implementation of the family planning policy has aggravated changes in the social demographic structure, for example, smaller family size, more "empty-nest" families, more families with fewer children, and longer time and distance for intergenerational exchange. All these have weakened the support function of the traditional home-based old-age care.

It is predicted that in 2020 and 2050, China's elderly population over 80 will reach 22 million and 83 million respectively. From 2015 to 2035, China's elderly population will increase from 212 million to 418 million, accounting for 29%. In 2012, one senior citizen was financially supported by five people. However, in 2030, two people will provide for one elderly, and in 2050 one person will have to care for one elderly. In addition, the number of disabled elderly people or those losing their only child in China continues to increase. It is estimated that, the total number of only children in China was about 150 million in 2010, and this figure is expected to reach 310 million by 2050. With the increase in the total number of only children, the number of families losing their only child in China due to deaths of only children has also increased sharply, reaching 841,000 in 2010 and exceeding 1 million in 2020.[1] Such a huge number of elderly population and special population and labor structure caused by the one-child policy make traditional home-based old-age care unsustainable.

(2) The population getting old before getting rich poses new challenges for the old-age care scheme

There are two international standards for an aging society: one was set by the United Nations in 1956 that the elderly population aged over 65 in a country or region should account for more than 7% of the total population; the other one was set by the first World Assembly on Ageing held in Vienna in 1982 that the proportion of the elderly population aged over 60 is more than 10% of the total population. The fifth population census in China in 2000 showed that both standards above were met, which means China has become an aging society since the end of 1999 and now it has been such for 20 years.[2]

China is the country with not only the largest aging population but also the fastest growth rate in aging population in the world. At present, the annual growth rate in the elderly population in China is about 3.5%. From an adult society to aging society, it

① 马瑾倩. 立遗嘱的年轻人 [N/OL]. 新京报网, (2019-07-12) [2019-12-10]. http: //www.bjnews.com.cn/news/2019/ 07/12/602682.html.
   Ma Jinqian. The young man who made a will [N/OL] . *The Beijing News Network*, (2019-07-12) [2019-12-10] . http://www.bjnews.com. cn/news/2019/07/12/602682.html.
② 韩维正. 今天, 我们如何养老 [N]. 人民日报海外版, 2018-07-09(10).
   Han Weizheng. Today, How do we care for the elderly [N] . *People's Daily Overseas Edition*, 2018-07-09(10).

took 115 years for France, 60 years for the United States, 30 years for Japan, and only 18 years for China. More importantly, when developed countries entered aging society, their per capita GDP was between $5,000 and $10,000, while China's per capita GDP was only $850 by the end of 1999. Under such severe circumstances, the Ministry of Civil Affairs and the National Development and Reform Commission of China issued the Thirteenth Five-Year Plan for the Development of Civil Affairs in July 2016, which put forward more specific goals for the elderly care system, namely, to establish a multilevel old-age care system based on home, assisted by the community, supplemented by nursing institutions, and combined with medical care.

Against the backdrop of a population getting old before getting rich and unsustainable traditional home-based old-age care, the old-age care in China faces many difficulties in terms of financial support, daily care, spiritual comfort, and care for the disabled elderlies or those losing their only child.

(3) Old-age care provided by individuals, society and country

As it has become unrealistic to depend on "children to provide care for the elderly", what shall we do to prepare for our senile life? Some people say that we should have a partner, a house, savings, good health, old friends, or become prettier or happier as we get old. Of course, all these preparations mentioned above are considered from the perspective of the elderly themselves.

In fact, the issue is not only a matter for individual citizens, but also the responsibility and obligation of the state and society. Only with multi-party cooperation can it be dealt with better. The Chinese-style old-age care requires joint efforts of the government and society.[①] When the living necessities of the individual citizens cannot be fully provided by the state and society, they believe they can live a decent senile life if they enjoy good health. Under the circumstances of inflation and currency depreciation, it seems reasonable that "it is better to keep fit than to save money" for citizens.

7.1.3　Summary: Interpretation of "the Elderly Should Be Looked After Properly" in Social Changes

Caring for the elderly has long been a topic in human society. In this section, we have discussed social transformation and its modernity, as well as old-age care in the transformation of modern society. A full understanding of a population "getting old

---

① 佚名. "中国式养老" 需要政府及社会协同配合 [EB/OL] . (2016-05-05) [2017-03-07] . http://district.ce.cn/newarea/roll/201605/05/t20160505_11241986.shtml.
Anonymous. "Chinese-style elderly care" requires the coordination of the government and society [EB/OL] . (2016-05-05) [2017-03-07] . http://district.ce.cn/newarea/roll/201605 /05/t20160505_11241986.shtml.

before getting rich" and "elderly will be looked after properly" in the context of social changes can help understand the nature and meaning of life. It is hoped that discussions in this section can further help you understand the social issues of old-age care.

Further Exploration and Links:

As the elderly population of a country increases, responsibility of caring for the elderly in the future has increasingly worried analysts. This problem is particularly severe in Western Europe and Japan, which have the largest proportion of elderly people over 65.

——James M. Henslin. *Essentials of Sociology: A Down-to-Earth Approach* (11th Edition), Translated by Lin Juren, Xie Yuxi. Beijing: Publishing House of Electronics Industry, 2016: 302-303.

7.2   Demographic Changes and Old-Age Care Culture

7.2.1   Population Structure and Its Changes

(1) What is the population structure?

The population structure is also called "population composition", which refers to the makeup of population in a country or a region in a certain period of time. It reflects proportional relationships of populations of qualitative differences within a certain region at a certain time. It is relatively stable, and generally changes with the passage of time or development of economy.

(2) Types and characteristics of population structure

According to the characteristics of population composition and the way of population mobility, the population structure can be categorized into three types in terms of the natural, social and geographical composition of population. Among them, the natural population composition can be further classified according to age, gender, etc.; the social population composition can be further classified according to ethnicity, culture, religion, social class, and so on; the regional population composition can be further classified according to the distribution of population in the urban and rural areas, or some specific regions. Although the population is characterized by differences in gender, age, place of residence, ethnicity, class, culture, marriage, occupation, and religious belief, the population structure is still mainly featured in essence by its natural, social, and regional differences.

(3) Changes in population structure

Age and gender are the most basic and essential elements in the population structure, and age composition and gender composition are the most influential in population structure. The ideal age composition features "low birth rate and longevity", while the ideal gender composition is characterized by "the same or close number of men and women at the same age".

The population structure is not only affected by the natural environment, but also by the economy, society, regional culture of a country or region. For example, in some rural areas where people prefer boys to girls, then the proportion of men is higher to that of women; while in cities, the proportions of men and women may be basically the same, and sometimes proportion of women may be higher than men. In addition, people's preference for girl or boy may also be affected by factors such as religion or culture. In the sixth census in 2010, the population of male aged 20 to 29 years old in China was 114.84 million, and females of the same age were 113.58 million. The difference between the two was only 1.26 million, and the overall ratio tended to be balanced. However, by 2013, China's population has shown a new trend, that is, the population structure has become severely imbalanced, and the population's structural contradictions have become increasingly apparent. This has affected the sustainable development of the population and has become the main contradiction in current and future population development and a key factor restricting economic and social development.

At present, the structural contradictions of China's population are manifested in sharply declining birth rate, low total fertility rate, and an aging population. It is necessary to take precautionary measure from the overall and strategic perspective. Timely strategic decisions should be made on population policies, and further improvement should be made in population, economic and social policies, so as to address population problems, promote the sustainable development of future generations and ensure food security and sustainable development of the social economy.

7.2.2 Old-Age Care in the Changing Population Structure

(1) Culture of old-age care with the changing relationship between the "being rich" and "being old" population

In recent years, the relationship between the "being rich" and "being old" population is frequently discussed by the public. China's old-age care culture also varies with the changing relationship between the "getting rich" and "getting old" population.

Since 1999, China has entered an aging society. At that time, China roughly belonged to the "bottom one third" of the countries in the world in terms of its per capita GDP, while it was almost included in the "top one-third" countries in the world in terms of its aging rate. It is increasingly apparent that the elderly "fail to become rich before getting old". Among the elderly in urban and rural areas, only one quarter of them can receive the social old-age pension; only 1/30 of the total population in the country has an access to medical insurance; and only 1/13 of the poor population is covered by the subsistence allowance system.[①]

According to three criteria, namely the 65 year olds and above accounting for 7% of the total population, the World Bank's high-income threshold per capita Constant-Price GDP, and the Population Aging and Economic Development Coordination Index (AECI) ± 50, there may be various degrees of harmony in the relationship between the "getting old" and "getting rich" population. Classified according to the relationship ranging from the least harmonious to the most harmonious, the population can be categorized into five types, being the "old and not rich", "rich but too old", "relatively old but not rich", "rich and old", "not rich and not old", "rich but slightly old" and "rich but not old" types. These seven types actually reflect changes in China's modern population structure. In response to these seven different types of aging society, a cultural trend from "not rich despite working hard" or "old and rich" to "rich but not old" has emerged.

(2) "The future" old-age care culture that "has emerged"

In recent years, the emergence of concepts and models such as "nursing stations", "integration of medical care and nursing", and "smart old-age care" has set new growth goals for old-age care. For 37 years starting from the implementation of family planning at the beginning of 1979 to the universal two-child policy released in 2016, China suffered a steep decline in its population from the era of explosive population growth.

With the ringing of the bell at the New Year in 2019, the post-2010s children are growing up to be teenagers, while post millennials are stepping into their youth. The post-90s have become "uncles" or "aunts", the post-80s have become "seniors", and the post-70s have become "grandpas" or "grandmas". As a result, people commented

---

① 顾严. 暂别 "未富先老", 养老挑战依然严峻 [N]. 中国经济导报, 2018-07-05(6).

　　Gu Yan. Say goodbye to "getting old before getting rich", the challenge of pension is still serious [N] . *China Economic Herald*, 2018-07-05 (6).

with complicated feelings: "How come I become so old, I am really old, and I turn old just in a flash of second." This really fits in the following saying: "Don't lament since the future is coming."

Undoubtedly, the aging society and the problems of old-age care in China are the result of changes in the population structure. However, it is not simply about the dependency ratio, but about the quality of population and labor productivity, which is by no means as simple as just raising the birth rate. The reason is that if there is only the reverse growth of the low-quality population, the population quality of the entire country and nation will decline and the improvement of labor productivity will be difficult to achieve, and the culture of respecting, loving and caring for the elderly will certainly be difficult to form and develop. Therefore, birth rate of high-quality population, dependency ratio and AI is the key to the current and future old-age care.

7.2.3 Summary: Better Understanding of Old-Age Care in Terms of the Changed and the Unchanged Relative Issues

In this section, we discussed the impact of population structure and its changes on old-age care. Through the discussions in this section, you may further understand the issue of old-age care in human society.

Further Exploration and Links:

As one of the largest developing countries in the world, the importance of population aging and its old-age care faced by China is particularly prominent. Considering China's economic structure and its unique economic transformation, the top priority is to solve the problem of old-age care of the aging rural population.

Chinese farmers play diversified roles in their life and their income are unstable and from multiple channels. All these features pose strong constraints and challenges to the rural old-age care...In order to meet the richer and diversified needs of the elderly, various organizations or systems such as old-age care by family, community, individual or through social relief should be encouraged and supported. That means that China's rural old-age insurance or pension system to be established must be a multi-layered, diversified and complex structure...

China's rural old-age insurance system is currently in its infancy and exploratory stage. Related experiences and models have their distinctive regional characteristics, and are targeted at different groups of farmers with various roles or occupations. There is no experience or model that can be simply introduced in all regions or even throughout China.

—Liang Hong, Zhao Deyu, et al. *Population Aging and China's Rural Pension System*. Shanghai: Shanghai People's Publishing House, 2008: 294-298.

7.3   Medical Endowment Insurance for Elderlies Who Have Lost Their Only Child

7.3.1   The Bereaved Elderly and Their Old-Age Care

(1) What kind of people are the bereaved elderly?

As the name implies, the bereaved elderly refer to the old people who have lost their only child. Such families in which the only child in the family unfortunately passed away is called a "bereaved family". Unlike the "empty-nest elderly", the bereaved elderly cannot expect his dead child to return home, and can only hope that the government and society will give them more sense of security and care.

(2) The old-age care of bereaved elderly

Compared with general care to the ordinary senior citizens, the old-age care for the bereaved elderly is different for that such families lack in the filial piety and care, by their children and nor can the elderly obtain any family support and spiritual comfort from their child. Even though their spouse is still living and in good health, what these old people can do may be taking care of each other for a lifetime. In the best situation, there may be grandchild or grandchildren left by their only child, with the grandparents and grandchildren constituting a special family. How the elderly can be cared in their old life in such families is a prevalent public concern.

Some researchers believe that the Ministry of Civil Affairs should make overall research on the issue of elderly care for families who have lost the sole child. They can take the "three-without" elderlies as a reference. "Three-without" elderlies refer to those old people without productive capacity, income and provider. Currently, the "three-without" elderlies and the rural "five-guarantee" elderlies are supported by the government[①] by the decentralized and centralized approaches.

Bereaved elderlies belong to a special group, and the number of such families tend

---

① 周尧, 李欣, 车丽. 我国每年新增失独家庭 7.6 万个 寺院成养老选择 [EB/OL]. (2012-09-29) [2018-10-15]. http://finance.people. com.cn/insurance/BIG5/n/2012/0929/c59941-19155549-2.html.
Zhou Yao, Li Xin, Che Li. There are 76,000 new families which lose their only child every year in China, and monasteries become an option for the elderly [EB/OL]. (2012-09-29) [2018-10-15]. http://finance.people.com.cn/insurance/BIG 5/n/2012/ 0929/c59941- 19155549-2.html.

to increase. According to the *China Report of the Development on Aging Cause (2013)* issued by the Chinese Academy of Social Sciences, in 2013, the number of bereaved elderlies reached 200 million, and is expected to rise by 1 million per year by 2025. Meanwhile, emergence of negative growth in working-age population means the labor supply structure has changed. In 2012, over 1 million families have been bereaved of their child and the number has increased by 76,000 each year.[①] When the elderly lose their only child and tend to get senile, this further exacerbates the complexity of old-age care for them, which is worth our attention.

7.3.2　Health Care for the Bereaved Elderlies

(1) Prone to poverty because of falling sick

According to a survey by the CPPCC, 50% of the bereaved elderly suffered from chronic diseases such as high blood pressure and heart disease; 15% suffered from major diseases such as cancer and paralysis; more than 60% suffered from depression, over half of whom had suicidal tendency. Due to major changes in the family, 50% of the bereaved families have financial difficulties with a monthly income of less than 1,200 yuan; 20% of the bereaved families live on a minimum living standard.[②] After losing their children, these old people have become a "special group" outside the society. They fear to communicate with people and become squeamish and sensitive, thus cannot work normally. China has not yet established a special security system for pensions, old-age care, accidental injuries and medical insurance for the bereaved elderly at the national level.

Following the decease of their only child, parents are prone to self-closure and mental breakdown; families with disabled children are prone to having financial difficulties. According to the survey, more than 50% of the families who seek medical treatment due to their children's injury or disabilities returned to poverty.[③] At the same time, their old-age care is also a problem because most of the existing nursing homes are privately owned and expensive. For a long period of time, it has become a prominent

① 佚名. "失独"家庭亟待精神赡养 [EB/OL]. (2013-05-13) [2018-10-15]. http://www.wenming.cn/wmpl_pd/shzt/201305/t20130514_1223799.shtml.
　　Anonymous. Families which lose their only child urgently need spiritual support [EB/OL]. (2013-05-13) [2018-10-15]. http://www.wenming.cn/wmpl_pd/shzt/201305/t20130514_1223799.shtml.

② 廖君, 周莹珣, 吴晓颖, 等. 老无所依?走近中国失独家庭 [EB/OL]. (2012-07-18) [2018-10-15]. http://www.banyuetan.org/chcontent/sz/szgc/2012718/55652.shtml.
　　Liao Jun, Zhou Yingxun, Wu Xiaoying, et al. Old people have nowhere to depend? Approaching Chinese families which have lost their only child [EB/OL]. (2012-07-18) [2018-10-15]. http://www.banyuetan.org/chcontent/sz/szgc/2012718/55652.shtml.

③ 晓程. 百万家庭破裂了 [J]. 当代工人 (C 版), 2012, (5): 10.
　　Xiao Cheng. Millions of families broke up [J]. *Contemporary Worker: Version C*, 2012, (5): 10.

problem in Chinese basic medical security system that the elderlies generally have trouble seeking medical treatments or cannot afford the treatment.

(2) Solutions to the old-age care and medical insurance for the bereaved elderlies

In view of the fact that some bereaved families in China have a single source of income, it is difficult for them to bear the costs of their own elderly care. What's more, public nursing homes are seriously inadequate, while private nursing homes charge too much. Therefore, it is difficult for the elderly to live there in their old age. For the elderly lacking in family warmth, suffering from psychological emptiness and loneliness, and having difficulty in obtaining spiritual comfort, precise assistance is needed from relative policies, organizations, and economic measures to alleviate the difficulties of the bereaved elderly in their healthcare and old-age care.

Firstly, to strengthen the policy support, formulate or revise relevant laws and regulations, and encourage and help elderly people who have lost their only child to adopt self, home-based or community-based old-age care or other types of elderly care, so as to effectively help these elderly people tackle their old-age care problem.

Secondly, to advocate civilized family values, further adjust the fertility policy, actively support and encourage men and women at the appropriate age to raise two children, support and encourage parents who have lost only child to adopt children, and psychologically help the elderly resolve their loneliness, so as to fundamentally reduce the number of the bereaved elderlies.

Thirdly, to strengthen organizational support, establish special elderly care and security institutions or departments for the bereaved elderly, and provide social services bought by government such as psychological counseling and mental rehabilitation for them, so that the elderly who have lost their only child can be provided for.

Fourthly, to strengthen the economic relief, continuously raise the relief standard for the bereaved elderly, strive to improve the financial situation of such families and help them receive a prompt and affordable medical treatment.

Fifthly, to strengthen the intelligent construction of community hospitals, and promote the transformation of old-age care from traditional home-based one to a pattern combining self-care, home-based care, community-based care with smart health care.

7.3.3   Summary: How Can the Bereaved Elderly Be Happily Cared?

In this section, we discussed the elderlies bereaved of their only child and their old-age care, and the medical security scheme for them. Through discussions in this section, you may further understand the issue of old-age care in human society.

7.4　Empty-Nest Elderlies and Their Medical Care

7.4.1　Empty-Nest Elderlies and Their Main Concerns

(1) What are the empty-nest elderlies?

As the name suggests, the empty-nest elderlies generally refer to the elderlies whose children leave their hometown. They do not have children to care for them, live alone or live with their spouse. They can be generally categorized into three groups: the first group is elder people of no family without children and spouse, the second is the elderly with children living alone, and the last group is those living in the empty nest alone with children far away in other places.

When the children leave home due to work, study, marriage, etc., the middle-aged and elderly couples who live in the "empty nest" will have the symptoms of psychological disorders called family "empty nest" syndrome.

The phenomenon of "empty nest" is a global problem. The proportion of elder people living alone or spouses living in empty nests in developed countries is as high as 70%-80%. With China gradually entering into aging society and its urbanization accelerating, there will be more and more empty nest elderly in the future, and the empty nest period will be significantly extended, and problems faced by the elderly will become more severe. This results from China's changed demographic structure and social transformation.

(2) Main problems faced by the empty-nest elderly

Main problems faced by the empty nesters include:

1) Daily care. As the children do not live at home with the elderly, the daily care and service for the elderlies who are frail and sick in the empty nest has become a major problem. At present, the care services for the elderly in China are not professional enough. There are insufficient professional management companies or elderly care workers. Without much help from outside, the empty-nest elderly can only take care of themselves.

2) Social security. At present, old-age security in rural areas in China needs to be improved. The elderly in empty nests may need to work to meet their living expenses, especially in remote mountain villages. The living conditions of the empty nest elderly in urban areas may be relatively better. Generally speaking, they are financially independent, have their own houses and separate living spaces, and enjoy relatively better quality of life.

3) Spiritual comfort. The children of the old empty nesters are not around, so they have nothing to say and feel lonely. The symptoms of the elder empty nesters include disappointment, depression, loneliness, decreased appetite, sleep disorder, regular sadness, sighs, and even weep. They often have a tendency to blame themselves, thinking that they have not fully fulfilled their parental responsibilities and feel sorry about children. In addition, there is also a tendency to blame the children for neglecting their filial duties. They feel that the children have not fulfilled filial duties, only caring about their own interests and leaving their parents in the "empty nest" alone. According to a survey, the proportion of elder empty nesters with psychological problems reaches 60%. Among them, 10%-20% suffer from mental illness, who need medical attention and psychological intervention.[①] It is showed that there are few television programs targeting at the elderly and insufficient fitness and entertainment facilities, resulting in the poor spiritual life for the elderly. In addition, the social activities of the elderly empty nesters decrease, and the care from their children is not enough, which can easily lead to mental illness.[②] These universal problems is a reflection of transformation and changes of modern society.

7.4.2   Old-Age and Medical Care for Elderly Empty Nesters

(1) The elderly empty nesters need both old-age care and medical care

Old-age care and seeing a doctor is what the elderly must face. As a result, a new model of "elderly care combined with medical care" emerged. The so-called "medical care" refers to a series of services such as rehabilitation, health care, medical treatment, disease diagnosis and treatment, and hospice care. "Elderly care" includes daily life care, spiritual comfort and mental counseling, cultural activities, etc. For this reason, elderly care institutions and medical institutions should seamlessly cooperate with the residential community to "provide treatment if the elderly fall ill, and provide necessary care if they are healthy". In 2009, Shanghai Jiangong Hospital established the Shanghai Jianyang Nursing Home with 180 approved beds, providing a service "combining medical care with nursing care" characterized of "treating minor illnesses in nursing home (Jianyang Nursing Home) and serious illnesses in hospital (Jiangong Hospital)". In 2013, Shanghai Jiangong Hospital and Shanghai Jianfeng College jointly

---

① 徐治. 空巢老人需要重视心理健康［J］. 康颐, 2019, 74(10): 69.
　　Xu Zhi. The elderly in empty nests need to pay attention to their mental health［J］. *Kang Yi*, 2019, 74(10): 69.
② 杨洁, 陈文. 我市户籍老人有近一半空巢　六成有心理问题［EB/OL］.(2012-10-19)［2020-05-10］. http: //www. cnxz.com.cn/newscenter/2012/2012101972056.shtml.
　　Yang Jie, Chen Wen. Nearly half of the old people with household registration in our city are empty nesters, and 60% have psychological problems［EB/OL］. (2012-10-19)［2020-05-10］.
　　http://www.cnxzn.com.cn/newscenter/2012/ 2012101972056.shtml.

established the Shanghai Jianfeng Nursing Home with 230 approved beds, which established a consultation and referral mechanism with Shanghai Jiangong Hospital. Such service is also characterized by "integrated medical and elderly care". The three medical care institutions of Shanghai Jiangong Hospital, Jianyang Nursing Home and Jianfeng Nursing Home have their own advantages, but supplement each other and develop in coordination, providing a practical model solving the elderly care, medical care, and nursing.[1] The government should speed up the development of community care services, encourage market-oriented operations through favorable policies to attract more people to participate in the elderly care services combined with medical care.

(2) Strengthen the training of medical and social workers

The aging population is a worldwide problem, and its impact on human society is lasting and profound. Medical colleges and universities should enhance their efforts to train senior professionals with medical knowledge and to be familiar with the social work of the elderly. For majors related to social work in non-medical colleges, it is necessary to cooperate with medical colleges and community hospitals, hiring medical experts and staff to teach students to achieve deeper integration of social work practices and medical care, include elder care talent training into the development of health talents and accelerate the cultivation of professionals such as elderly service management, medical care, nursing and rehabilitation, nutrition arrangement, and psychological counseling, thus order to better meeting the needs of the elderly group, especially the elderly empty nesters.

(3) The empty-nest elderly need to have their nests warmed by the policy support

Due to the influence of China's traditional culture and the constraints of current conditions, the elderly empty nesters need to "warm their nest" through institution. In the 19th National Congress of the Communist Party of China, it is stated that it is essential to "actively respond to the population aging, establish policy system and social environment favorable to the elderly care, filial piety, and respect for the elderly, promote the integration of medical and elderly care, and accelerate the development of the elderly cause and industry"[2], further promote and develop the Chinese virtues of respecting, providing for and assisting the elderly, improve the home-based care

① 佚名. 上海建工医院: 社区医疗与养老无缝对接 [EB/OL]. (2017-03-01) [2017-12-30]. http://www.rmzxb.com. cn/c/2017-03-01/1370741.shtml.
  Anonymous. Shanghai Jiangong Hospital: seamless connection between community medical care and elderly care [EB/OL]. (2017-03-01) [2017-12-30]. http://www.rmzxb.com.cn/c/2017-03-01/ 1370741.shtml.
② 习近平. 习近平谈治国理政: 第三卷 [M]. 北京: 外文出版社, 2020: 38.
  Xi Jinping. *The Governance of China III* [M]. Beijing: Foreign Languages Press, 2020: 38.

mechanism, and comprehensively build a system of safety and care service for the elderly empty-nesters based on home and supported by the community and institutions, and effectively prevent incidents of elderly empty-nesters' accidental death undiscovered by others, enabling the elderly to enjoy care, happiness, and medical treatment. "China has become an aging society. Let the elderly have a sense of security, support, enjoyment, and peace, which is critical to social harmony and stability. It is necessary for the elderly to live happily in old age."[①] The government and social organizations should vigorously promote the home-based care model. That is, with the community as a platform, to integrate various resources of service in the community, and provide services such as assistance with meal, cleaning, bath, and medical care for the elderly empty-nesters.

(4) Internet + Medical and elderly services

With the development of Internet technology, the smart old-age care service, namely Internet + medical and elderly care, for the empty nest elderly has become a reality.

Nowadays, more and more elder care institutions cooperate with medical institutions to establish medical network information platforms. They make use of the Internet, Internet of Things, cloud computing, artificial intelligence, wearable devices and other new technologies to offer "Internet + health care" and "artificial intelligence + health care" services, so as to improve payment and credit systems and health management and promotion systems, and promote online new model of medical services. They also use smart mirrors to analyze the user's daily health data, detect weight, sleep quality, fat rate, water volume, bone mass, blood pressure, body temperature and other small data of the human body, and then the all-round physical health data will be analyzed for test reports and recommendations. At the same time, through the development of new business formats such as e-commerce, Internet finance, Internet education for the elderly, etc., provide the empty nest elderly with tracking, monitoring, positioning, emergency calls, online shopping, remote emotional care, remote entertainment, and remote literature and arts communication and other services. In this way, through the multi-dimensional linkage between the Internet, medical care and home-based care, smart old-age care will help meet the needs of medical and elderly care of the empty nest elderly.

---

① 习近平. 习近平谈治国理政: 第三卷 [M] . 北京: 外文出版社, 2020: 345.

　　Xi Jinping. *The Governance of China III* [M] . Beijing: Foreign Languages Press, 2020: 345.

7.4.3　Summary: How to Let the Bereaved Elderly Be "Happily Cared" and "Properly Cared"?

In this section, we have discussed the empty nest elderly and the combination of medical and nursing care and smart elderly care. It is hoped that through the discussion in this section we can help you further understand the elderly care problem in human society.

Further Expansion and Links:

Social insurance can best embody the principles of modern social security such as the combination of self-insurance and insurance for others, and the combination of fairness and efficiency. It meets the needs of the market economy and is more accepted by the majority of insured objects. Of course, there are strict requirements to enjoy social insurance, such as pension, medical care, unemployment, childbirth, work injury, disability, death, family allowances, etc. Members who do not meet the corresponding requirements can obtain survival protection only through social assistance. With the transformation of society from traditional to modern and the development of market economy, the number of those who meet the requirements and receive social insurance will continue to rise and become the main body of social members, and fewer and fewer objects will receive social assistance (of course, this group will never disappear completely). As for social welfare implemented by the "welfare state", it is a high-level part of social security system. There still exists a series of problems that have not been resolved in its operation. One of the most fundamental problems is that it hinders the achievement of economic efficiency. Western countries are currently focusing on reform of the huge welfare system. In view of this, the future goal of China's social security system should not be set as becoming a "welfare state", but focus on social insurance.

—Li Yingsheng. *Social Security and the Transformation of Social Structure: A Study of Dual Social Security System.* Beijing: China Renmin University Press, 2001: 193-194.

Chapter 8　Life and Death: The Ultimate Care of Human Society

8.1　Outlook on Life and Its Modern Transformation

8.1.1　Life View

(1) The meaning of the outlook on life

Simply put, the concept of life is people's attitude, principle and standpoint regarding life. Engels gave a scientific definition of life from the perspective of dialectical materialism: life is the existence of protein bodies. This way of existence is, essentially, a complex of protein and nucleic acid. The essence of life is the unity of opposites and contradictory movement of protein bodies in forms of assimilation and alienation. The life process is a process in which the protein body constantly renews itself, replicates itself, and regulates itself. The assimilation and alienation of protein bodies and the constant exchange of matter, energy, and information with the outside world are the basic conditions and fundamental motivation for the existence and development of life. The contradictory movement of assimilation and alienation, inheritance and mutation within the protein body, that is, metabolism and self-reproductions are the fundamental laws of life development.[①] This definition summarizes the basic characteristics of life ranging from the simplest life to human life.

Looking at the overall development of human history, the outlook on life reflects both the degree of civilization of human society and the degree of understanding human beings themselves. People's understanding of life shows a progressive trajectory in line with social development. With the development of modern medical technology and the progress of life science research, human beings have been making fresh progress in exploring the origin of life.

---

① 中共中央马克思恩格斯列宁斯大林著作编译局. 马克思恩格斯文集 [M]. 第九卷. 北京: 人民出版社, 2009: 37-150.

Central Compilation and Translation Bureau. Marx and Engels collected works [M]. Volume 9. Beijing: People's Publishing House, 2009: 37-150.

(2) Marx's view of life

Karl Marx holds that the concept of life is a complete theoretical framework devoted to the realization of the existence of the whole life of man, which is a holistic life concept of the "trinity" integrating natural life, social life and spiritual life. It involves a series of fundamental problems such as life existence and life development, featured by multiple life needs, life alienation caused by capitalist private ownership and life liberation through practical means.[1]

The formation and establishment of Karl Marx's view of life has roughly gone through four stages, covering the four levels of human life: the first stage is the period of "difference between Democritus' natural philosophy and Epicurus' natural philosophy", when the existence of life with "human self-consciousness has the highest degree of divinity" in the coordinates of rationality; the second stage is the period of "Economic and Philosophic Manuscripts of 1844", based on "free and conscious perceptual object activities" as the internal basis of the existence of life; the third stage is the existence of life with the "ensemble of social relations" as the reality in the "Theses on Feuerbach"; the fourth stage is the period of "specific production and lifestyle" as the life existence of dialectical logic.[2] Marx's view of life confirms the meaning and value of human life from the perspective of overall existence, constituting Marx's unique life connotation and life significance.[3][4]

8.1.2   The Change of Modern Outlook on Life

In ancient society, people did not have a deep understanding of life and other natural phenomena, and medical technology was not advanced enough. Therefore, people's views and attitudes towards life were often mysterious to a certain extent, and a self-contained system of life, custom, and culture gradually took shape. For example, in many countries across the world, there has been a tradition of sympathetic witchcraft seeking children.

---

[1] 杨利利. 马克思生命观的理论意蕴及当代启示 [J]. 阴山学刊, 2019, 32(4): 72-77.
Yang Lili. The theoretical implication and contemporary enlightenment of Marx's outlook on life [J]. *Yinshan Academic Journal*, 2019, 32(4): 72-77.
[2] 张懿, 夏文斌. 马克思生命观形成与确立的历史考察 [J]. 东南学术, 2019, (5): 72-79.
Zhang Yi, Xia Wenbin. A historical investigation of the formation and establishment of Marx's outlook on life [J]. *Southeast Academic Research*, 2019, (5): 72-79.
[3] 张懿, 夏文斌. 论马克思的生命观对西方生命哲学的三重超越 [J]. 广东社会科学, 2018, (2): 68-74..
Zhang Yi, Xia Wenbin. On the triple transcendence of Marx's outlook on life to western life philosophy [J]. *Social Sciences in Guangdong,* 2018, (2): 68-74.
[4] 张懿, 夏文斌. 马克思生命观的历史、理论与现实 [J]. 青海社会科学, 2018, (5): 72-80.
Zhang Yi, Xia Wenbin. The history, theory and reality of Marx's outlook on life [J]. *Qinghai Social Sciences*, 2018, (5): 72-80.

In a traditional farming society, children are often the main source of family labor. Therefore, childbearing is a duty for marriage and family life in many countries or regions. The patriarchal notion of "having no descendants is the worst among the three forms of unfilial conduct", which once prevailed in ancient Chinese society, has mainly made many women end up with divorce, for they fail to raise male heirs over many years after their marriage. As a matter of fact, the problems of fertility or reproduction concern both husband and wife, and it is inappropriate or even completely wrong to blame the problem on women only in ancient Chinese society.

In modern society, with the development of science and technology and the improvement of medical and health conditions, people have a deeper understanding of fertility and its culture. It is mainly manifested in:

Firstly, people have realized on a scientific basis that the possibility of having children, or having boys or girls is determined by both spouses rather than by the woman only. This has been proven by modern medical science.

Secondly, eugenics has become a common pursuit. Therefore, pre-marital health check-up has been a new trend in modern society. This is also an important manifestation of modern social civilization in human reproduction itself.

Finally, it is unnatural and unlawful to use modern medical technology to interfere with the natural birth of human life. For example, it is illegal to use B-mode ultrasound technology to identify the gender of a fetus; it is also illegal to use some drugs to change the structure of sperm or egg in order to have twins.

8.1.3   Summary: Transformation of Outlook on Life in Social Changes

In this section, issues such as the outlook on life and the transformation of outlook on life in modern society were discussed, and the impact of modern technology on the outlook on life was analyzed. We hope to help students further understand the ultimate concern of human society.

Further Exploration and Links:

Individual, family, and society are three types of values that parallel with each other and differ from each other. The scope of these three values is arranged from small to large. In traditional society and modern society, the order of importance of these three values is different.

In traditional Chinese society, the family value has top priority, and the individual and society are less valued; in modern Chinese society, the order of importance for the three values is changing in some people's mind.

　　—Li Yinhe, Zheng Hongxia. *The Grandson of a Master: A Case Study of Chinese Family Relations*. Shanghai: Shanghai Culture Publishing House, 2001: 179.

8.2　Modern Health and Traditional Chinese Medicine Culture

8.2.1　Health and Health Culture

(1) What is health cultivation?

Originally, health regimen refers to a kind of medical activity in which Taoists adopt various methods to nourish life, enhance physical fitness, and prevent diseases, thereby achieving longevity. In Chinese pinyin "*yang sheng*", "*yang*" means conditioning, maintenance and replenishment; "*sheng*" refers to life, survival and growth.

In a modern sense, "health cultivation" refers to active maintenance activities undertaken in accordance with the natural laws of human life to keep people healthy, both mentally and physically. Health cultivation is, in other words, to maintain the five internal organs (heart, liver, spleen, lung, and kidneys) to prolong life.

(2) Health cultivation culture

Health cultivation culture refers to the material culture and spiritual culture that people create during the long life practice. Among them, the theoretical classics and practical methods related to health regimen are the main part of health cultivation culture. In all the millennia of history, China's health cultivation culture had formed a basic theoretical thinking and method system before the Qin and Han dynasties (more than 2,000 years ago). With many factors such as natural sciences, humanities and social sciences integrated in the process of its development, Chinese health cultivation culture plays an important role in the world's health cultivation culture.

Among the hundreds of schools in the pre-Qin period of China, *Lao Zi* and *Zhuang Zi* (two books on philosophy in ancient China) ignored appearances but valued temperament. They believed that when the airway was united, the body would not perish, and immortality could be achieved. They also held that "man follows the earth; the earth follows the universe; the universe follows the rules of Tao; Tao follows the laws of nature".

As an important representative of China's medical achievements in the pre-Qin period, *The Medical Classic of the Yellow Emperor* puts forward these health regimen concepts: overall health, conformity to nature, passion and nourishment, refinement of the body and the spirit, and an emphasis on taking precautions to prevent diseases.

During the Han dynasty(206BC-AD220), *Huainanzi* (an encyclopedic work in ancient China) put forward the idea of "Tao" health preservation throughout the year, emphasizing the "trinity" of body, spirit, and *Qi* (vital energy). It can be seen that from the pre-Qin period to the Qin and Han Dynasties, ancient Chinese stressed the cultivation of internal and external wholesomeness, the unity of body and spirit, and the combination of personality and morality through Qi-promotion, food intake, and Daoyin (the exercise therapy of traditional Chinese medicine), which had a great impact on Chinese traditional health cultivation culture.

(3) Modern health cultivation culture

Modern society is an industrial society, whose impact on social life is extensive and profound. In addition to plentiful supply of products and economic development, the industrial society has also brought negative effects such as tension, anxiety, nervousness, and an increasing desire for wealth. Furthermore, the ethical problems on science and technology in the industrial age have become worrying. Therefore, green development, environmental protection, and low carbon have become common pursuits. People have to face many thorny problems: mental state, diet, exercise, sleep, physical therapy, medicine, so eco-awareness marked by a green lifestyle and organic food, simplicity, leisure, closeness to nature, relaxation and stress release have become typical features of modern health cultivation culture.

8.2.2   TCM Health Preservation in Modern Life

(1) Thoughts on cultivating health in traditional Chinese medicine culture

Traditional Chinese medicine is the traditional medical science in China. From the earliest *The Medical Classic of the Yellow Emperor* and *Shennong's Herbal Classics* to *Treatise on Febrile Diseases*, from *Pulse Classic, All Disease Sources* to *Compendium of Materia Medica* written by a famous medical scientist Li Shizhen in the Ming Dynasty in 1578, the major achievements of Chinese medicine in ancient China are highlighted. TCM health preservation is a medical activity that uses various methods to maintain life, strengthen physical fitness, and prevent diseases, so as to achieve longevity. Health preservation in Chinese medicine aims to prevent or cure diseases before their onset, so its holistic and systemic nature is emphasized.

From an ideological point of view, TCM supports these philosophies: preventing diseases before onset, cultivating health before old age days, connecting man and nature, unifying body and spirit, adjusting yin and yang, remedying defects, and correcting errors. Therefore, for different people and in different seasons, traditional Chinese medicine has different health requirements.

For men, Chinese medicine believes that the health of men lies in nourishing the kidneys and protecting the liver. According to traditional Chinese medicine culture, the kidneys govern water; the liver governs wood; water generates wood. Therefore, traditional Chinese medicine advocates that the focus of nourishing the kidneys should be saving energy, which requires abstention from fleshly lusts, avoidance of overexertion, relief from anger, abstinence and a simple and light diet.

For women, traditional Chinese medicine emphasizes these ideas: restoring vital energy and nourishing blood; with proper exercise, *Qi* and blood are stable, meridians in the human body are smoothly connected, and no diseases will occur; with a good mood, melancholy can vanish, so they are healthy both mentally and physically.

For the elderly, due to the degrading physical function, the methods of cultivating health are also particularly important: the elderly should not be gluttonous; processed food like white rice and fine noodle, fatty meat, solid food, excessively hot food, fast food, drinking too much should all be quit to avoid indigestion or low blood sugar.

Traditional Chinese medicine emphasizes that the five viscera (heart, liver, spleen, lungs, kidneys) and six bowels (small intestine, large intestine, gallbladder, stomach, bladder, and triple energizer) cooperate with each other, with the five internal organs playing a leading role and the six bowels playing a supporting role to complete various functions of the human body. The interior-exterior relationship between the internal organs and the bowels can be described as follows: the liver stands in interior-exterior relationship with the gallbladder; the heart stands in interior-exterior relationship with the small intestine; the spleen stands in interior-exterior relationship with the stomach; the lungs stand in interior-exterior relationship with the large intestine; the kidneys stand in interior-exterior relationship with the bladder. In addition, the traditional Chinese medicine culture is also influenced by concepts such as the mutual generation and restraint of the five elements (metal, wood, water, fire and earth) and the Meridian flow.[1]

---

[1] For example, liver and gallbladder belong to wood, heart and small intestine belong to fire, spleen and stomach belong to earth, lung and large intestine belong to metal, kidneys and bladder belong to water, "fire generates earth" (normal heart function can make the spleen and stomach function normally), "mental generates water" (if lung function is good, kidney function is normal) and so on. Zishi (23:00-01:00) has strong gall meridian, Choushi (01:00-03:00) has strong liver meridian, Yinshi (03:00-05:00) has strong lung meridian, at Maoshi (05:00-07:00) large intestine meridian is prosperous, at Chenshi (07:00-09:00) stomach meridian is prosperous, spleen meridian is prosperous at Sishi (09:00-11:00), heart meridian is prosperous at Wushi (11:00-13:00), at Weishi (13:00-15:00) the small intestine meridian is prosperous, the bladder meridian is prosperous at Shenshi (15:00-17:00), the kidney meridian is prosperous at Youshi (17:00-19:00), the pericardium meridian is prosperous at Xushi (19:00-21:00), and the triple-burner meridian is prosperous at Haishi (21:00-23:00).

(2) TCM culture in modern health cultivation

1) Fitness improves health. Gym equipment, as an industrial product, is used by people for physical exercise. Fitness is a common way of keeping healthy for urban residents, especially for the younger generation. People go to the gym either for bodybuilding or for weight loss. Ultimately, they can possess the beauty of body and shape, which is an aesthetic element advocated by TCM health cultivation culture. Therefore, fitness and wellness are favored by urban youth.

2) Food promotes health. The fast pace of modern life and the increasing consumption of fast food and puffed food have brought many adverse effects on people's health. By contrast, dietotherapy of TCM is adjustable based on seasonal changes, which can provide reference for health preservation in the industrial age. As spring sowing, summer growing, autumn harvesting, and winter storing follow an annual cycle, spring is the season of revival and the best time to keep healthy. In traditional Chinese medicine, liver should be nourished in spring, heart in summer, lungs in autumn, and kidneys in winter. Therefore, the focus of taking tonics in spring is on nourishing the liver; it is advisable to choose lighter, milder foods that vital energy can be restored, and the tonic food should also be adjusted according to different constitutions.

The focus of taking tonics in summer is on nourishing the heart, which should follow some basic principles: moistening tonification, strengthening spleen, removing summer heat and resolving dampness in human body, generally by taking light tonic foods. As for early autumn foods, spicy taste should be reduced and acidity should be increased to nourish liver-Qi; Mid-Autumn Festival is still hot, so people should eat more fresh and light foods containing more vitamins and protein.

In the late autumn season, people should eat more foods rich in nutrients such as protein, magnesium, and calcium, which can effectively prevent the occurrence of cardiovascular and cerebrovascular diseases.

According to modern medical science, winter is the coldest season of the year when everything is in a sealed state, and it is the most suitable period of dietary conditioning and supplementation during the year. As the saying goes, "If tonic food is taken during the coldest days in winter, there will be no health problems in the coming year". This makes some sense.

When taking tonic foods in winter, people should pay attention to cultivation of yang mainly for warming. Those with thin body constitution, a quick temper, and nervousness should mainly take moderately tonic food, and they should refuse to eat spicy ingredients; those with a plump figure or poor muscle tone should avoid using cold, wet, greasy and spicy ingredients to prepare their meals; brainworkers should eat more foods rich in protein, vitamins and micro elements.

3) Peace of mind cultivates health. The industrial society is essentially marked by materialism and consumption, which stimulates people's pursuit of wealth and social status, and brings negative influences such as overnight riches, greed, anxiety, restless impetuousness, and quick success. Under the circumstances, people need to make psychological adjustments by restraining their desires, showing no interest in fame and fortune, regulating and invigorating *Qi*, and keeping inner peace.

8.2.3 Summary: in Modern Society, "to Nourish Life", "to Nourish Body" or "to Nourish Soul"?

In this section, we discussed health cultivation and health cultivation culture, as well as TCM health regimen in modern life. The balance and harmony concern "to nourish life, body or soul" in modern industrial society from a holistic perspective of traditional Chinese medicine culture. It is hoped that through the study and discussion in this section, we have helped you further understand the problem of life and death in human society.

Further Exploration and Links:

Traditional culture has always regarded the individual organism as a small universe, therefore, it has also explained the balance and harmony of the small universe with the opposition of yin and yang. The most obvious manifestation of this concept is "cold" and "hot" in food, and the extended concept of "tonic" is popular.

...This concept of yin and yang / cold and warm, has a long origin, so it not only affects the Chinese people's ideas of food and drug, food habits, and cooking methods, but also makes a connection with Chinese medicine and becomes the most important feature in Chinese people's daily life. The opposition of yin and yang / cold and warm is not only prevalent in China, but also influential in the overseas Chinese community because of the abundant material supplies.

—Li Yiyuan. *Human Vision*. Shanghai: Shanghai Literature and Art Publishing House, 1996: 152.

8.3   Death Culture and Its Differences Between Urban and Rural Areas

8.3.1   Death and Funeral Culture

(1) What is death?

Death in clinical medicine usually refers to the deep suppression and loss of function of the medulla oblongata, the disappearance of various reflexes, cardiac arrest, respiratory arrest and brain death. "Death" among ordinary people is more concerned about whether the breathing stops, that is, whether there is still "Qi". This is actually unscientific because human brain function does not necessarily stop in case of apnea. Therefore, life or death is not defined by breathing. Death is the opposite of survival, which means the loss of life, or the end of life, or the cessation of survival.

A study in the United States shows that when the human heart stops beating, the brain still continues to function. In other words, the human brain will be aware of the fact that it has died.

It is understood that China has traditionally adopted cardiac arrest, respiratory arrest and areflexia as the criteria for judging death, which is commonly referred to as "heart death". But in recent years, brain death, which means the irreversible termination of all brain functions, including brain stem function, has gradually begun to be accepted by the public. The respiratory center of the human body is in the brainstem. If structural damage to the brain stem occurs, the respiratory function will consequently stop, and no medical treatment can save the patient's life. At present, brain death has been officially recognized in more than 100 countries and regions across the world, but it is still in controversy for there is no relevant legislation in China.

(2) Funeral culture

Funeral is always associated with death. Different countries, different regions, and different ethnic groups may develop different funeral cultures across time and space.

The funeral customs vary from place to place among all ethnic groups in China. These differences are not only influenced by historical and cultural factors, but also regulated by religious cultures. In traditional Chinese funeral customs, "burial in the earth for rest in peace" has become the basic expression. Before China had fully implemented the funeral reform of cremation of bones in the past, Chinese traditional funeral customs generally include a set of ceremonial procedures: placing the corpse, selecting the date, informing relatives of the funeral, communicating with the soul, sending the soul, cleansing the corpse, putting the corpse in a coffin, expressing condolences, wailing at funeral, and carrying the coffin for burial. In China, burial in the earth adopted by ethnic groups who believe in Islam is influenced by Islamic culture; burial in the earth practiced by those who believed in Catholicism or Christianity is also different from traditional Chinese burial customs. In addition, in the history of some ethnic groups, different funeral methods such as cremation, water burial, tree burial, hanging coffin burial, cliff burial and secondary burial can also be found.

(3) Changes of modern Chinese funeral culture

After the founding of the People's Republic of China, in order to save the land resources and prevent the spread of diseases, it is stipulated that all but a few ethnic groups who believe in Islam should adopt cremation. Therefore, after the death, the body will be transported to the funeral parlour for naked storage. Requested by the bereaved family, the funeral parlour will provide a "mourning hall" for a mourning ceremony and memorial services. Afterwards, the corpse is sent to the crematorium with a "special vehicle", and the corpse is burned to ashes by the fire. The ashes can be kept in an urn by the bereaved family, or they can be sprinkled into the sea or put beneath a tree so that the dead can get back to nature.

8.3.2   Differences in Death and Funeral Culture Between Urban and Rural Areas in China

(1) Changes in mortality rates of major diseases among rural residents in China since the 1990s

According to the data in 2015 China Cardiovascular Report, the mortality rate related to cardiovascular disease in China has continued to rise in recent years, which is much higher than that related to tumors, respiratory diseases, injuries and other diseases. In 2014, the mortality rate related to CVD was 295.63/100,000 in rural areas and 261.99/100,000 in urban areas. CVD-related mortality rate at rural levels has surpassed and continued to be higher than that at urban levels since 2009.

Due to the influence of urban-rural dual economic, social, and cultural structures, the differences in death culture between urban and rural residents in China are also rather obvious.

(2) Differences in death and funeral culture between urban and rural residents in China

1) Rural residents' knowledge of "death" is basically limited by the traditional understanding of "death" (that is, "breathe one's last" or "stop breathing"), while urban residents' cognition of "death" is more in line with "heart death" in clinical medicine, and some residents gradually accept "brain death".

2) Rural residents are still affected by the traditional idea of "burial in the earth for rest in peace". Even if the corpse is cremated, relatives of the deceased still tend to bury the ashes in the earth; urban land and other resources are scarce, so the unit price of the cemetery is even higher than that of a residential building. Therefore, many urban residents sigh and say that they can't afford to die; some residents simply entrust the cemetery columbarium to keep the ashes, and each year they "borrow the ashes" for the sacrificial ceremony on the Qingming Festival and then "return the ashes" to the cemetery for storage. Since the cemetery is a public place, "personal worship activities" carried out there tend to be simplifying traditional funeral and ritual customs.

3) Abnormal or accidental death is a taboo in rural areas. In case of death outside the village or away from home, the deceased's body is not allowed to be carried into the house in the village, instead, the corpse is buried outside the village to avoid bad luck. By contrast, urban residents are not so "choosy". Of course, with the implementation of reforms in funeral customs such as cremation in rural areas, the way of dealing with the ashes may be different from the traditional burial customs featured by "burial in the earth for rest in peace". However, this change in burial customs itself is also a result of modern industrialization. In other words, this reflects the changes of funeral customs caused by industrialization in urban and rural areas in contemporary China.

(3) Choice and dignity: the cultural choice of Chinese urban and rural residents facing death

Influenced by traditional Chinese culture of filial piety, the filial piety of children or juniors to elders is sometimes manifested in the medical treatment given to their parents or elders with serious illnesses.

For those who are seriously ill, their children or juniors have two options: should they do their best to save their patients' life by selling property or even getting into huge debt just for frequent and painful operations, treatments, chemotherapy, and radiotherapy? Otherwise, should they listen to the patients and adopt conservative treatments or even quit treatments? This problem is now arousing more and more attention and rational thinking.

The reality is that the family members of the patient clearly know that even if they spend a large sum of money, it is virtually impossible to cure the severely ill or terminally ill patient. However, they have to complete a mission impossible (neither their parent's life nor their money is saved), because the absence of filial piety is infamous and the worldly blame is dreadful. Patients with severe illnesses or terminal illnesses actually experience great pain both physically and mentally during the course of surgery or treatment, yet their children require the doctor to apply "over-medication" just for the sake of filial piety. Have they ever considered the patient's personal wishes? Should terminally ill patients also have the right to make life or death decisions ? How to treat severely ill or terminally ill patients in a decent way? How to enable these patients to die with dignity? These are difficult problems in modern society.

The right to survive is the most fundamental human right. Is the right to die also a basic right of each human being? Does a patient suffering from severe illness or terminal illness have the right to decide whether he should get a treatment or give up treatment? Which treatment should be used? Although there is a kinship between the patient and the family members, the patient's individual needs and wishes should be respected when it comes to the matter of life rights. If the patient wishes to get conservative treatments, the family members should not consider the virtue of filial piety only, and they should not require "over-medication" for the patient. If the patient hopes to give up treatments, the family members should also obey the patient rather than "make a last attempt to save a hopeless situation". This is a characteristic property that defines a civilized society.

It is worth noting that in 2013, Beijing Lifetime Promotion Association (LWPA) was established on the basis of the "Choice and Dignity" charity website founded in 2006. As the first public welfare website in China to promote "death with dignity", the website keeps promoting the concepts of "death with dignity" and "pre-mortem will", making "my five wishes" in the "pre-mortem will" text implementable and feasible, so that citizens can truly realize "death with dignity through pre-mortem will". It is advocated that at the late stage of the incurable injury and illness, resuscitation should be quit, and life supporting systems should not be used, thus making death occur in a natural way without pre-arrangements or delay. In this process, individual needs and wishes for death with dignity should be respected to the maximum. Needless to say, this is a major step forward in our society.

8.3.3　Summary: Temporal and Spatial Differences and Expressions in Death Culture

In this section, we discussed the culture of death and funeral, as well as the differences in death culture between urban and rural areas in China. Hopefully through the study and discussion in this section, we can help students to further understand the life and death of human society.

8.4　Views of Death in Different Cultures

8.4.1　Views of Death in Traditional Chinese Culture

Traditional culture is different from cultural tradition. The former emphasizes the culture that has come down since ancient times, while the latter stresses the origin of the culture and its ebb and flow or blending in the process of its spread. As far as traditional Chinese culture is concerned, it is the culture formed in Chinese history with Confucianism as the core, which has undergone continuous transformation by Confucians of all ages and whose modification has continued to the present day. From the "Contention of a hundred schools of thought like a hundred flowers in bloom" in the Spring and Autumn and Warring States Period to "Ban of a hundred schools of thought and respect for Confucianism only" proposed by a philosopher named Dong Zhongshu (179-104BC) in the Han Dynasty, to the "Integration of Confucianism, Buddhism, and Taoism" in the Kingdom of Wei(220-265), Jin Dynasty(265-420) and Southern and Northern Dynasties (420-589). The development of Chinese traditional culture can also been seen in Sui, Tang, Song, Yuan, Ming, and Qing dynasties (all together with a time span of more 1,300 years), actually covering the "Hundred Schools of Thought", with Confucianism, Taoism and Buddhism involved. Confucianism is not religion, but some people regard it as "religion" or "quasi-religion". In essence, religion deals with the relationship between man and god, while Confucianism has more to do with people-to-people relations.

(1) Views of death in confucianism

Confucianism holds that death is a natural phenomenon, and people should adopt a detached attitude toward the matter of life and death. There is a saying in *The Analects of Confucius • Yan Yuan*: "Ever since ancient times, there is always death, but people who have no trustworthiness cannot gain a foothold", and there is another remark: "Life and death are determined by destiny; wealth and honor are dominated by Heaven."

Confucius, the founder of Confucianism, once said, "How can we know what death is before knowing what life is?" This was his reply to his disciple Lu's question "How to deal with the matter of death?" Confucius' key point is caring about life without thinking of death, that is, it is necessary to seek knowledge from life rather than from death. Mencius, the "second saint" of Confucianism, also said: "Our attitude toward destiny should be consistent whether our life is long or short. This is the correct way of self-cultivation for good fortune." He emphasized that people should not pay too much attention to the length of life. Mencius also put forward the views of "good fortune" and "ill fate": those who die in a normal way have good fortune; those who die in prison bear ill fate. He advocated that people should die for moral ideas and beliefs, and people should not die for injustice.

On the whole, Confucianism has not deviated from the emotional routine responses: feeling happy in birth and sad in death. *The Analects of Confucius* records that when Yan Yuan died, Confucius sighed with grief: "Heaven will kill me! Heaven will kill me!"

As far as individual life is concerned, human beings only live once, and the dead can never come back to life. Therefore, Confucianism attaches great importance to the mourning and funeral sacrifices for the dead. Confucianism speaks of filial piety: "We should treat the dead and people alive in the same way, and this is the best filial piety." Confucianism holds that deceased ancestors should be treated as if they were still alive. Influenced by this, people often handle funerals as major events. According to a book on governance in ancient China *Mencius and Li Lou*, "Supporting the elderly is not an event big enough, but arranging their funeral ceremony can be a big event". In this way, "a big event" has become a cultural symbol and actual practice of Confucianism.

(2) Views of death in buddhism

As we all know, Buddhism emphasizes reincarnation which originated from the ancient Indian religion prior to Buddhism, and it initially solved the problem of where people would go after death. Later, the founder of Buddhism assimilated the basic idea of reincarnation theory and transformed it into the basic teachings of Buddhism. Earthly Buddhism regards life and death as unimportant, and sees through the fact that the worldly life is always changeable. "Death is a major event in life. Buddhism believes that birth, old age, sickness, and death are all human nature. Death is not the end of life, but the beginning of another cycle of reincarnation. Thus, life and death are the same. Therefore, people should be unconcerned about life and death, and then they can see through impermanence."[1] Those who believe in Buddhism also face the question of life or death. Grand Master Hsing Yun said: "Believing in Buddhism does not mean that people do not need to handle the problem of life and death, instead, people need to see through the relationship between life and death! Life and death are very closely associated with each other. People should be aware that the life-death cycle is endless."[2] In addition, Buddhists "also have smiles and tears, so they have to face the problem of life and death just like other people". Furthermore, "there is no need to fear death. In the face of death, we should take life as it comes and keep ourselves calm"[3]. According to Grand Master Hsing Yun, "When a person is born, death is destined to be an inevitable result. Therefore, everybody dies. Is there any joy? The death of a person is just as winter goes before spring comes. Is there any sadness? Life and death coexist side by side. Life, death, and rebirth, they form an endless cycle together"[4]. All these views of life and death reflect the Buddhist philosophy of reincarnation and immortality.

(3) Views of death in Taoism

Taoism is a native religion in China, which originated in the late Eastern Han Dynasty (25-220) and is characterized by the pursuit of immortality. It is believed that as long as people are good at health cultivation, they can become immortals, thus living forever.

Taoism advocates the homogeneity of life and death. Lao Zi said: "Man follows the earth; the earth follows the universe; the universe follows the rules of Tao; Tao follows the laws of nature."[5] In Lao Zi's view, the changes in life and death of man and everything in nature come from the combination of yin and yang: "Tao begets one, one life makes two, two begets three, three begets all things. All things bear yin and hold yang, as a result, harmony and balance between yin and yang can be achieved."[6] In addition, Taoism also advocates the necessity of life and death, the

① 星云大师. 人间佛教语录: 中册 [M]. 台北: 香海文化事业有限公司, 2008: 236.
  Grand Master Hsing Yun. *Buddhist Quotations on Earth* (Volume 2)[M]. Taipei: Xianghai Cultural Enterprise Co., Ltd., 2008: 236.
② 星云大师. 人间佛教语录: 中册 [M]. 台北: 香海文化事业有限公司, 2008: 244.
  Grand Master Hsing Yun. *Buddhist Quotations on Earth* (Volume 2)[M]. Taipei: Xianghai Cultural Enterprise Co., Ltd., 2008: 244.
③ 星云大师. 人间佛教语录: 中册 [M]. 台北: 香海文化事业有限公司, 2008: 251.
  Grand Master Hsing Yun. *Buddhist Quotations on Earth* (Volume 2)[M]. Taipei: Xianghai Cultural Enterprise Co., Ltd., 2008: 251.
④ 星云大师. 人间佛教语录: 中册 [M]. 台北: 香海文化事业有限公司, 2008: 253.
  Grand Master Hsing Yun. *Buddhist Quotations on Earth* (Volume 2)[M]. Taipei: Xianghai Cultural Enterprise Co., Ltd., 2008: 253.
⑤ 陈鼓应. 老子注译及评价 [M]. 北京: 中华书局, 2016: 159.
  Chen Guying. *Annotation, Translation and Evaluation of Laozi* [M]. Beijing: Zhonghua Book Company, 2016: 159.
⑥ 陈鼓应. 老子注译及评价 [M]. 北京: 中华书局, 2016: 225.
  Chen Guying. *Annotation, Translation and Evaluation of Laozi* [M]. Beijing: Zhonghua Book Company, 2016: 225.

unity of life and death, and the integration with "Tao" to achieve the ideal state of "to die is not to perish".

In short, when facing the problem of death, Taoism does not use natural laws to seek self-comfort immortality on the spiritual level to alleviate the anxiety caused by death; instead, Taoism believes that people can use their wisdom to understand the truth of universal creation and operation, that is, by ingesting the power of circulation in the world, the result of life can be reversed.

Although the concept of life and death advocated by Taoism that "to live a long life and become immortal" is an illusion, it has the connotation of loving life, enriching life, sublimating life and transcending life.[①] Taoism's "pursuit of worldly success and merits" is in stark contrast to Buddhism's "purity of mind with few desires". Taoism's idea of "life and death do not share the same way" is also different from the "three reincarnations" of Buddhism. In terms of life and death, the difference between Taoism and Buddhism, Christianity and other religions is that the fairy world of Taoism is unified with the mundane world we live in. The shift from this mundane world to that fairy world can be a continuation of a natural life, so the process of death is not necessary. Taoism's view of life and death is rooted in the desire for life and the love of the world, hoping to live forever, reflecting the ethical attitude of the Chinese nation in pursuit of a happy life. As the fusion of Confucianism, Buddhism, and Taoism appeared in the period of Kingdom of Wei, Jin Dynasty, and Northern and Southern Dynasties, the traditional Chinese concept of life and death was also influenced.

8.4.2   Views of Death in Western Religious Culture

Christianity believes that death is an inevitable process of human life. Christians believe that death is a journey of life, not the disillusionment of life, let alone the end of life.

Christianity regards death as a "rebirth". In this sense, "life" is not a "rebirth in reincarnation", but a "life" of transition from the present life to heaven, from impermanence to eternity, and from a foreign land to homeland.

The Bible states that the death of a person is "dust to dust", which means that human body will return to the soil, and the spirit will return to the God who gave human beings the spirit. The human body, in essence, is soil. People are from the soil, so they must return to the soil. This is the return of the physical body. The soul comes

---

① 赵博超. 道教的生死观 [N]. 中国社会科学报, 2018-03-20(4).
　　Zhao Bochao. Taoist view of life and death [N]. *Chinese Social Sciences Today*, 2018-03-20(4).

from God, but it must return to the God who gave the spirit. This is the return of the soul. However, the meaning of "return" in Christianity is different from that of "reincarnation" in Buddhism.

Christianity regards death as a "new life" rather than as a "rebirth" in Buddhism; this is an "eternal life" featured by transition from the present life to heaven, from impermanence to eternity, and from foreign land to homeland.

In fact, every religion tries to answer the ultimate question of human existence, that is, the question of death. According to research, Christianity's answer to the death question is based on Greek philosophy and Hebrew faith. Christian theology believes that whether physical death, spiritual death, or eternal death is actually an inevitable result of sins, but Jesus Christ used his own death to break the power of death over man, and he interpreted the Christian views of life and death in a Christian theological way.[①]

8.4.3   Summary: the Cultural Expression of the Relationship Between Man and God in Life Course

In this section, we discussed the cultures of death and funeral ceremony; we also made a simple analysis of the death culture and its temporal and spatial differences. It is hoped that the discussion in this section will help students further understand the issues of life and death in human society.

Further Exploration and Links:

Old age and sickness are not to be feared: what is dreadful is laziness in youth. When people are old and sick, their empty life will perish with grass and trees; death is not something sad; what is sad is that people do not know how to contribute to the society, regretting a future full of uncertainty at the end of their life.

—Grand Master Tsing Yun. *Collected Essays on Earthly Buddhism* (Volume 1). Taipei: Xianghai Cultural Enterprise Co., Ltd., 2008: 698.

---

① 宗晓兰. 死亡是生命的终结吗?——简论基督宗教的死亡观 [J]. 西南民族大学学报(人文社科版), 2015, 36(9): 81-87.
Zong Xiaolan. Is death the end of life? A brief discussion on the Christian view of death [J]. *Journal of Southwest Minzu University* (*Humanities and Social Science*), 2015, 36(9): 81-87.

Chapter 9　Filial Piety and Sacrifice: Temporal and Spatial Differences in Human Culture

9.1　Changes in Traditional and Modern Culture of "Filial Piety"

9.1.1　The Culture of Filial Piety in Traditional Chinese Society

China is a country that values filial piety, the philosophy and practice of which constitute the basics of the country's traditional "filial piety" culture. In China, "filial piety comes first," and "filial piety is the foundation of goodness". According to scholarly studies, the culture of filial piety was born during the age of Yao and Shun. *Historical Records: A Book of Five Emperors* says, "Shun was famous for filial piety at the age of twenty". In the first story "His Filial Piety Moves Heaven and Earth" in China's *Twenty-Four Paragons of Filial Piety*, Shun is filial to his parents and loves his brothers. Emperor Yao knows that Shun is filial, so he offers his two daughters to Shun in marriage. During the Han dynasty, filial piety was a means to govern society, thus becoming a code of conduct for life.

During the Qin and Han dynasties, the *Classic of Filial Piety* preserved and developed Confucian ideas on filial piety such as those of Confucius, Zengzi and Mencius, thus becoming an authority on Confucian filial piety culture and having a significant influence on traditional Chinese filial piety culture.

The first chapter "The Scope and Meaning of the Treatise" of the *Classic of Filial Piety* states, "It commences with the service of parents; it proceeds to the service of the ruler; it is completed by the establishment of character". This clearly combines filial piety with "the service of the ruler," thus equating "the service of parents" with filial piety for the state. As such, "the service of the ruler" became an indispensable part of filial piety, representing the politicization of this practice.

In addition, the *Classic of Filial Piety* divides filial piety into "five classes". It spends five chapters discussing "the filial piety of the emperor", "the filial piety of princes", "the filial piety of doctors", "the filial piety of scholars" and "the filial piety of ordinary people", thus reflecting the different levels of filial piety.

In general, the theme or biggest feature of the ideology espoused by *the Classic of Filial Piety* is the philosophy's popularity, politicization and even wonder. The *Classic of Filial Piety* portrays a world with filial piety as an attractive picture. "The ancient kings had a perfect virtue and all-embracing rule of conduct, through which they were in accord with all under heaven. By the practice of it the people were brought to live in peace and harmony, and there was no ill-will between superiors and inferiors." Its first chapter goes on to state that were one to govern in this way, one would win the "hearts and minds of the people", achieving "a world of peace" without disasters and chaos. This text of less than two thousand characters repeatedly discusses "governance" and "filial piety". The practice of filial piety is a means of "governing all of society" and "earning obedience". There is a profound historical background to all of this, but what is it?

We know that the Spring and Autumn period and the Warring States period were an "axial age" in the history of Chinese philosophy, as there was a diversity of popular ideologies and cultures due to the chaos and turbulence of the times. After Qin Shihuang forcefully reunited the six kingdoms, he opposed the "ritual and music culture" under the Western Zhou dynasty's institution of slavery. Instead, he promoted the doctrine of legalism throughout his rule and attempted to establish a new social order in the spirit of law. But this led to an unprecedented intensification of social conflict, paving the way to ruin. The rulers of the Western Han dynasty drew lessons from the Qin's demise, and after a period of trial and error, they finally selected Confucianism as their main philosophy and simultaneously adopted the applicable parts of various schools of thought to form their own theory of governance, in which "filial governance" was an important component. This way, filial piety was incorporated into this feudal system of ethics and began to become the ideological basis for feudal, patriarchal, autocratic rule. At the time, filial piety had thus extended beyond the scope of family ethics and became the all-encompassing moral consciousness of traditional Chinese society throughout economic, political and cultural life.

In ancient Chinese society, where "family and country were one," the culture of filial piety became an important part of a patriarchal system. After the Western Han dynasty, Chinese feudal filial piety changed little. From the historical evolution of the concept of filial piety, it can be seen that filial piety culture in China underwent a transformation from religious ethics to family ethics and then to political ethics. In this process, the concept of filial piety constantly evolved, with increasingly many unreasonable and negative factors being included. This is worth people's attention and reflection.

9.1.2　Modern Changes to the Culture of "Filial Piety"

Some people say that the traditional Chinese culture of filial piety is mainly related to agricultural society and that the "filial piety" culture of modern industrial society has changed due to transformations in production and lifestyles. These changes have mainly manifested as follows.

(1) Changes in the ways relatives are taken care of and respected

The traditional concept of filial piety not only requires children to be dedicated to their parents but also emphasizes that children should have respect for their parents. For example, chapter two "On Government" of *The Analects* states, "The filial piety nowadays means the support of one's parents. But dogs and horses likewise are able to do something in the way of support. Without reverence, what is there to distinguish the support given from the other?"

In modern society, although children still love their parents, those who neither work nor live with their parents tend to feel that they are insufficiently filial. Sometimes they do not go home and visit their parents during the holidays. They just call them or send video greetings, and thus they feel heavily indebted to their parents.

Of course, there are some only children who have been over-indulged by their parents from a young age. Despite growing up, they are not willing to find work and cannot bear hardships. Instead, they stay in their parents' homes without supporting them. Just the opposite, they rely on their elderly parents. How is this support and respect?

(2) Showing genuine filial respect to parents is determined by the parent-child relationship

Traditional filial piety requires obeying one's parents and following their will. Everything must be based on their standards. Otherwise, one is rebellious and unfilial.

In modern society, due to the high degree of social openness, people's values have grown more diverse. In some families where children have not been sufficiently educated and have instead been spoiled, quarrelling and confrontation with parents happens from time to time. Some young people are particularly selfish and only consider their own personal feelings. Sometimes they abuse or beat their parents or elders. This is especially unfilial and is even illegal and criminal.

(3) The continuation of lineages has been replaced by personal emotions

The concept of continuing one's lineage was a way of repaying and comforting parents in ancient China, as well as a complex form of filial piety. Chapter nine "The Government of the Sage" of *The Classic of Filial Piety* states, "The son derives his life from his parents, and no greater gift could possibly be transmitted". Likewise, the birth of a boy was regarded as the main purpose of marriages in ancient times. "Of the three conducts of being unfilial, the worst is not having children." Such ideas have caused numerous marital and family tragedies in ancient Chinese society.

The modern concepts of marriage and family have changed. Though the main purpose of marriage varies from person to person, most people pursue love and "happiness". Marriage nowadays is more about meeting the emotional and psychological needs of both parties rather than the traditional physiological need to have children. Thus, "DINK" families, late marriages and even remaining single, among other phenomena, have developed a certain "market" among some young people with open minds.

From the perspective of social development and population reproduction, however, late marriages, remaining single and "DINK" families cause population decline for countries, regions or ethnic groups. This shows a lack of responsibility for both country and society, and it is a real problem worth considering. How "loyalty and filial piety" between individuals, families, society and the country should be balanced requires more society-wide attention.

(4) The bereavement and honoring of lost relatives has been simplified, but honoring parents through personal success is still prevalent in modern society

In traditional Chinese filial piety culture, funerals and sacrifices to lost relatives are highly valued. *Doctrine of the Mean* says, "Honoring the dead is like honoring the living. That is the essence of filial piety". "The Meaning of Sacrifices" in the *Book of Rites* also says, "One may be able to support one's parents; the difficulty is in doing so with the proper reverence. One may attain to that reverence; the difficulty is to do so without self-constraint. That freedom from constraint may be realized; the difficulty is to maintain it to the end". It can be seen that the traditional Chinese concept of filial piety attaches great importance to matters related to death. Zengzi summarizes the filial act of bereaving and honoring lost relatives as mourning them upon death and regularly making sacrifices to them after death. Thus, holding funerals and making sacrifices to lost relatives is how children show filial piety to lost parents; that is, once parents or relatives pass away, funerals should be held and sacrificial offerings should be made.

Aside from such rituals, Chinese tradition requires children to establish their character, on the basis of which the establishment of virtue, successful service and speech is also required. The first chapter of the *Classic of Filial Piety* states that children must "make a name of themselves as a way of honoring their parents, which is the end of filial piety". Children must study diligently, embark on their careers and make a name of themselves to uphold the wills of their fathers, manage family businesses and fulfill their parents' hopes. *Doctrine of the Mean* states, "Filial piety is about upholding one's parents' will and skillfully carrying forward their undertakings". It can thus be seen that the highest form in which children traditionally express filial piety is about bringing glory to their family and ancestors.

In modern society, "horizontal" spatial mobility and "vertical" social mobility have increased. Thus, children sometimes live in different cities from their parents, or they live in the same cities but in different neighborhoods. They are busy with work and have little time to spend taking care of their parents, and when their parents pass away, they hold simple funerals and sacrificial ceremonies. But as far as modern parents are concerned, most just hope that their children will go to good universities and find a good job and a suitable marriage partner. Thus, a parent's love is a treasure indeed, and this is the most unchanging aspect of China's transforming culture of "filial piety".

9.1.3　Summary: a Modern Expression of Traditional Filial Piety Culture

In this section, we discussed China's traditional filial piety culture and its modern changes. We also offered a brief review of the changing and unchanging aspects of filial piety culture. We hope that through studying and discussing this section, you will better understand spatial and temporal differences in human culture.

Further Exploration and Links:

China's endlessly many descendants will always enjoy and protect their ancestral temples while also making sacrifices. The Chinese regard such behaviors as timeless, along with the establishment of virtue, successful service and speech. Our only expectations for the following generations are that they uphold the various moral, political and cultural requirements of human relations and society. These requirements have become the greatest values. For thousands of years, the cultural practices of the Chinese people have not exceeded these eternal limits.

　　—Li Xiangping. *Death and Transcendence*. Shanghai: Shanghai Culture Publishing House, 1997: 132.

Further Exploration and Links:

Banners sway on the field in front of the farm. More than a dozen wreaths are placed in the corner of the farm, and a tall pergola is erected in the yard. It is obvious that someone has died and a funeral is proceeding, but one would not know that from the electro band performing on the stage set up on the farm. Throughout the scene, except for the dull expressions on some people's faces, others laugh and look expectant; no one appears sad.

　　We returned to our place with a sense of incredulity. How can funerals be turned into happy events? Why didn't I see any sadness? In the Chinese tradition, it is indeed a good thing for someone to die in old age. The saying *baixishi* in Chinese suggests that it is a happy occurrence, but the death of a person is always a cause for sadness. It is a major turning point for a heartbroken family or even a group of relatives and friends. How, then, could such upbeat music be used? Was it an electro band? Upon asking the secretary of the town committee, we learned that he was not from Shuyang. He said that funerals had been held in Shuyang this way for more than ten years. Of course the young girls in their makeup didn't come to cry but to sing. What did they sing? They sang, "Sister, go forward boldly". The secretary also thought that it was absurd and incomprehensible to sing such a song at a funeral. But such absurdities are a tradition, and the locals are quite used to them. Thus, the villagers went to see the performance of the electro band invited to the funeral as if they were watching a play.

　　—He Xuefeng. *New Rural China*. Guilin: Guangxi Normal University Press, 2003: 17-18.

9.2　Differences Between Chinese and Western Sacrificial Cultures

9.2.1　Traditional Chinese Sacrificial Culture

　　China is a unified, multi-ethnic country, and its various ethnic groups have formed varied and colorful cultures through long periods of development.

　　Sacrificial offerings are an important part of any culture, and they are conducted differently among the various ethnic groups of China. Nonetheless, traditional Chinese sacrificial culture has basic characteristics. Let's first try to understand what traditional Chinese sacrificial culture is.

　　Simply put, traditional Chinese sacrificial culture is the country's sacrificial culture formed throughout its history. It is centered on Confucian filial piety and has elements of other schools of thought. In addition, it has experienced the continuous transformation of generations of Confucians. Let's now discuss and analyze its objects, places, offerings, methods and etiquette.

(1) Traditional Chinese sacrificial objects

According to the rituals in the literature, we know that traditional Chinese sacrificial objects were quite complex and included objects of religious belief and the various "mysterious forces" of nature, dead human souls and deceased ancestors. Notably, such objects included the various gods in the heavens and even the strange, chaotic gods from the nether world. The reason is that the traditional Chinese system of beliefs was complex.

We know that in the traditional Chinese belief system, there were not only sages, wise men or outstanding historical celebrities who were adept at martial arts and were worshiped by the people as gods, as there were also the spiritual systems of Buddhism, Taoism and Confucianism — "three religions in one". During the Wei, Jin and Northern and Southern dynasties, such practices appeared and were strengthened throughout later historical development, thus leading to the diversity and complexity of traditional Chinese sacrificial objects.

Next, let's discuss the places of traditional Chinese sacrifices.

(2) The places of traditional Chinese sacrifices

In traditional Chinese culture, sacrifices are an important part of etiquette. In a culture where families and the state are structured in the same way, the state is the infinite enlargement of the family and the clan, and the king is the largest and highest "patriarch".

In traditional Chinese society, sacrificial offerings are a ritual that the country, clan, household and family all value. "The greatest events a country can experience are sacrifice and war." Sacrificial offerings were prioritized over the protection of one's family and country, which shows how important they were in ancient Chinese society. Under the influence of traditional Chinese patriarchal culture, the ancient sacrificial venues in China differed due to the different social statuses of the individuals performing the rites.

In ancient China, the graded classification of rituals was strict. It was said that: "The gods couldn't use sacrificial offerings made to other gods, and people shouldn't make sacrifices to the ancestors of others." Sacrifices to the heavenly gods could only be made by the emperor. Princes could make sacrifices to the mountains and rivers, and scholars were only permitted to make sacrifices to their ancestors and the god of the stove. This division of sacrificial objects — from heaven, the earth, mountains and rivers to the ancestral stove god — also reflects the differences in the sacrificial levels separating ancient Chinese emperors, princes, doctors and scholars as determined by the civilization's patriarchal culture and their different places of worship. Temples of heaven, temples of earth, flat ground, ordinary temples, ancestral halls and tombs, among other venues, have become the main venues for traditional Chinese sacrificial offerings.

(3) Traditional Chinese offerings

"Sacrificial offerings" refer to supplies or articles offered in sacrifice. Traditional Chinese offerings vary depending on the object of the offering. In traditional Chinese sacrificial religious activities, the "ripeness" of a sacrifice is often used to symbolize the significance of the role of the god receiving the sacrifice.

In ancient Chinese society, people usually made sacrifices to heaven with animal blood. They made sacrifices to ancestors with raw meat, using half-cooked meat for mountains and rivers in addition to cooked meat for small sacrifices. The ancient Chinese preferred eating tender, "young" meat and used this preference as an analogy for the gods' appetites. They considered using young calves as sacrificial offerings to heaven to signify that integrity is most valuable. The size of a sacrifice was also used as an analogy for the status of the object of the offering. Thus, the cow horns produced during sacrifices to heaven and earth during the Zhou dynasty were as small as silkworm cocoons, whereas the cow horns produced during sacrifices at ancestral temples were so large that they could be held by hand.

Anthropologist Mr. Li Yiyuan believes that Taiwan's folk religious sacrifices are usually expressed as "raw" or "cooked" sacrifices, reflecting the closeness or lack thereof of the relationship between the person making the sacrifice and the person receiving the sacrifice. The more "raw" the sacrifice, the more distant the relationship. Conversely, the more familiar the relationship, the more "cooked" the sacrifice would be. Specifically, whole pigs and whole sheep during the worship of the "Duke of Heaven" or Confucius are not cooked; they are all raw offerings, representing the distant relationship with the objects of worship. When making sacrifices to ordinary gods such as Mazu, Guandi, Wangye and Chitose, sacrificial animals are cooked lightly before making the offerings, though they are not fully cooked. This is done to show respect to gods that are not quite of "heavenly" caliber, though the light cooking also demonstrates the closer relationship with such gods, unlike that with the heavenly emperor who does not meddle in human affairs. Sacrifices dedicated to ancestors not only have to be cooked but sometimes must also be seasoned. This clearly indicates that such ancestors are unlike other gods and belong to one's family. Such ceremonies are treated entirely as family affairs, and intimate respect is offered. In addition, the offering of a "complete animal" or just a "portion" is used to distinguish degrees of respect. Generally speaking, a complete offering offers the highest respect and grandeur, whereas smaller "portioned" offerings represent lesser degrees of respect or grandeur.[①] Different points of emphasis, such as meditation and incense, are used during offerings to different sacrificial objects, such as gods and ancestors, see table 9-1.

Table 9-1　Chinese People Offer Different Sacrifices to Different Gods

God Type		God		Spirit	
		God of the Sky	gods	ancestor	little ghosts
Burned Paper and Paper Money for Deceased Ancestors		golden paper money		silver paper money	
		big golden basin, pot of gold	*shou* paper money, "cut" paper money	big piece of silver	small piece of silver
Sacrifice	Shape	complete	big piece	small piece	small piece
	Cooked or Uncooked	uncooked	half-cooked	cooked, seasoned	ordinary cooked food
Incense	Form	whole joss-sticks	three joss-sticks	two joss-sticks	one joss-stick
	Dividing Incense or Not	no	dividing incense, cutting incense	dividing incense	no

Source: Li Yiyuan, *Human Vision*, Shanghai: Shanghai Literature and Art Publishing House, 1996: 292.

(4) Traditional Chinese sacrificial methods and etiquette

According to the rituals in the literature, the ancient Chinese used different methods for different objects. For example, when we worship gods such as the heavenly emperor or the sun and the moon, among others, fire was generally adopted. In "Offices of Spring" in the *Rites of Zhou*, there is a record of "building a fire with real wood to make sacrifices to the sun, the moon and the stars".

Sacrifices to the earth god generally used the method of liquid infusion. In "Minister of Rites" in the *Rites of Zhou*, it is stated that "blood should be used for sacrifices to the state." Likewise, the text's section on "The Great Border Sacrifice" in the *Book of Rites* states, "The libations were poured from cups with long handles of jade, (as if) to employ (also) the smell of the mineral. After the liquor was poured, they met (and brought in) the victim, having first diffused the smell into the unseen realm". In addition, the ancient Chinese people dropped offerings into water to make sacrifices to the water god, and they hung offerings to make sacrifices to the mountain god. These different sacrificial methods reflect how people related to other people and things in ancient China.

---

① 李亦园. 人类的视野 [M]. 上海: 上海文艺出版社, 1996: 291-292.
　　Li Yiyuan. *Human Vision* [M]. Shanghai: Shanghai Literature and Art Publishing House, 1996: 291-292.

9.2.2   Western Sacrificial Culture

The sacrificial culture in the west is different from the traditional sacrificial culture of China. This difference is not only manifested in sacrifices but also in the underlying religious beliefs and practices of the two regions.

The biggest difference between Chinese and Western offerings may be that the Chinese people like to worship using food. Westerners, however, tend to use flowers when they visit and commemorate cemeteries. An interesting story in the field of anthropology says that in 1935, the famous British anthropologist Radcliffe-Brown visited Yanjing University in Beijing. He was once accompanied by a young assistant to investigate village society. He found that the halls of one family were filled with food to worship their ancestors. Curious, he asked his young assistant, "Do the Chinese people really believe that the souls of your ancestors will come to eat these sacrifices?" The young assistant asked the British professor rhetorically, "Do the British people really believe that your ancestors will smell the fragrance of flowers dedicated to their tombs?" This interesting dialogue reflects the symbolic meaning of Chinese and Western sacrifices. "In the Western world, people are imperfect. They need the help of a perfect God to restrain their lifestyles and behaviors. This is the western concept of the supernatural concept. In the Chinese world, people can be perfect, so such people who behave nearly perfectly are worshipped as gods, thus serving as models for everyone else. This is the Chinese concept of the supernatural. In the Chinese supernatural world, gods and ghosts must coexist. If there are no ghosts, the perfection of the gods could not be brought out. But Chinese ghosts are not like Satan in the West who coexists with the universe. Our ghosts are what a person becomes after death."[1] These different conceptions of man, gods and ghosts actually reflect the differences between Chinese and Western cosmology.

Regarding the factors that have influenced its root sacrificial culture, Chinese traditional sacrificial culture has been more influenced by its traditional Chinese ritual system. The closer one gets to the bottom levels of Chinese society, the more one is influenced by non-institutionalized rituals (such as folk religious customs). In the societies of western countries, however, the culture of institutionalized religion has had a significant effect on the regulation of their sacrificial culture.

---

[1] 李亦园. 人类的视野 [M]. 上海: 上海文艺出版社, 1996: 293-294.
　Li Yiyuan. *Human Vision* [M]. Shanghai: Shanghai Literature and Art Publishing House, 1996: 293-294.

9.2.3   Summary: Different Chinese and Western Sacrificial Cultures

In this section, we discussed the concepts, objects, places, offerings, methods and etiquette of traditional Chinese sacrificial culture, and we briefly analyzed how and why western sacrificial culture differs from that of traditional Chinese sacrificial culture. We hope that through studying and discussing this section, you have come to further understand these spatial and temporal differences in human culture.

Further Exploration and Links:

What is the religious situation in contemporary western society? It resembles in curious fashion the picture which the anthropologist gets in studying the religion of the North American Indians. They have been converted to the Christian religion but their old pre-Christian religions have by no means been up-rooted. Christianity is a veneer laid over this old religion and blended with it in many ways. In our own culture monotheistic religion and also atheistic and agnostic philosophies are a thin veneer built upon religions which are in many ways far more "primitive" than the Indian religions and, being sheer idolatry, are also more incompatible with the essential teachings of monotheism. As a collective and potent form of modern idolatry we find the worship of power, of success and of the authority of the market; but aside from these collective forms we find something else. If we scratch the surface of modern man we discover any number of individualized primitive forms of religion. Many of these are called neuroses, but one might just as well call them by the irrespective religious names: ancestor worship, totemism, fetishism, ritualism, the cult of cleanliness, and soon.

Do we actually find ancestor worship? Indeed, ancestor worship is one of the most widespread primitive cults in our society and it does not alter its picture if we call it, as the psychiatrist does, neurotic fixation to father or mother. Let us consider such a case of ancestor worship. A beautiful, highly talented woman, a painter, was attached to her father in such a way that she would refuse to have any close contact with men; she spent all her free time with her father, a pleasant but rather dull gentleman who had been widowed early. Aside from her painting, nothing but her father was of any interest to her. The picture she gave of him to others was grotesquely different from reality. After he died she committed suicide and left a will stipulating only that she was to be buried by his side.

—Erich Fromm. *Psychoanalysis and Religion*, Translated by Jia Huijun. Beijing: China Translation and Publishing Corporation, 1995: 21.

9.3   "Internet Plus" Internet Sacrifice Culture Analysis

9.3.1   "The Internet Sacrifice": a New Form of Sacrificial Culture in the "Internet Plus" Era

As the name implies, an "internet sacrifice" is short for an online sacrifice. It is different from the traditional sacrificial methods. It does not require one to go to a site of worship, as it opens up a space for worship on the Internet and simulates a real worship site for performing a virtual sacrifice. This form of Internet worship is currently dominated by public worship activities. For example, Internet sacrifices are performed on the birthdays or dates of passing of revolutionary heroes and other important public figures who have passed away. This kind of online worship is generally initiated by nonprofit organizations or enthusiastic netizens, and its participants are mostly young people.

It is worth noting that in recent years there has been another variant of online sacrifices in which intermediaries can be hired to make ceremonial visits to ancestral tombs. The development of Internet technology and instant messaging tools has spawned many new such formats and business models. Among them, it is worth paying attention to this particular form.

For those who have moved abroad or work diligently all year round and lack the time to go home on ceremonial visits to their ancestors' graves, paying people online to make the trip on their behalf saves them the trouble of returning to their hometowns to make such visits in person. This is yet another way for people to express their grief. Therefore, around 2012, these outsourced visits to family gravestones, as well as the phenomena of online sacrifices, emerged in some parts of China. Other similar sacrificial methods also appeared at this time.

1) Musical sacrifice: playing the favorite song of the deceased and expressing nostalgia for it.

2) Flower sacrifice: paying respect to the deceased using their favorite flowers or participating in the cemetery-organized "tossing of flowers instead of the burning of paper money".

3) Tree planting sacrifice: celebrating the deceased through tree planting.

4) Tomb-washing rituals: washing tombstones to express one's thoughts.

5) Family remembrance meeting: making photos and video materials of the deceased's life into a CD and organizing family members to watch and recall

memories.

6) Community ceremonies: after full-time teachers of sacrificial etiquette are stationed in a community, community residents organize the display of portraits of the deceased and also provide fruits, nuts, balloons and the like; family members of the deceased read sacrificial words aloud, and the public offers sacrificial flowers.

7) Online sacrifices: expressing condolences to deceased relatives through the internet.

8) Flying remembrances: communities organize residents to launch white balloons into the sky, sending off their memories.

In addition, the civil affairs departments of some cities have also advocated and encouraged residents to adopt modern forms of sacrifice, such as Internet sacrifices, community ceremonies and musical remembrances, as well as to use flowers instead of firecrackers and incense to mourn. This has had a positive effect on the innovation and development of the sacrificial culture of Internet sacrifices and the "Internet plus" era.

9.3.2   How Should We Approach the "Internet Sacrifice" Culture?

The Internet sacrifice culture has only just emerged in recent years, and people have different opinions about it. How we should approach the Internet sacrifice culture is perhaps a matter of benevolence and wisdom.

People who have lived abroad for many years or who are unable to visit their ancestors' gravesite or cemetery in person due to old age might need to pay for this service through the Internet. People can understand and support this. Some people, however, think that the actions of others cannot replace their own filial piety. In particular, asking someone to "cry on behalf of someone else" seems hypocritical and unable to convey true familial affection. Some vendors that provide such intermediary services have also made it clear that they will not "cry on behalf of others".

People who have reservations about the "Internet sacrifice" culture, such as through hiring someone to visit a gravesite or hiring someone to cry on your behalf — phenomena that have appeared in recent years — tend to have more traditional ideas. They believe that filial piety is the moral foundation by which the Chinese people should abide. If a person does not even have the most basic sense of filial piety, what moral code could you expect him or her to abide by? Although filial piety is largely a personal matter, it also largely reflects a person's "ethics".

In fact, whether or not you go to a gravesite or a cemetery in person — or even if you make your sacrifices online or entrust others or a professional institution to go on your behalf — you are simply engaging in a unique form of worship. What is most important is the actual sacrifice and expression of filial piety. Are you truly revering and remembering deceased relatives, or are you just showing off? Only you can answer this.

In fact, the best time to express filial piety is when your loved ones are alive. Thus, you should spend time with the elderly at home as much as possible, and you should strive to be healthy, happy and joyful every day, instead of waiting until one's loved ones have passed away. The logic of being unfilial before death and filial after death is absurd. It is not worth advocating, and it also deviates from the traditional Chinese spirit of filial piety.

In a modern industrial society, this logic is definitely absurd and unworthy of advocating, and it also deviates from the traditional Chinese spirit of filial piety. Modern society is an industrial society. And an essential feature of industrial society is that goods can be exchanged and consumed for a price. Internet sacrifices and their various forms such as sending an intermediary to a grave on one's behalf or hiring someone to cry on one's behalf reflect the commercialization of sacrificial culture. In this regard, we should dialectically view and analyze these phenomena and simply affirm or deny them, as we have no way of accurately interpreting them.

9.3.3   Summary: the Temporal Expression of Sacrificial Culture

In this section, we discussed Internet sacrifices in the "Internet plus" era and their extended "modern" cultures, such as hiring intermediaries to visit gravesites on one's behalf and hiring others to cry on one's behalf. In addition, we offered a simple analysis of how to treat the "Internet sacrifice" culture. We hope that through the study and discussion of this section, we have helped you further understand the spatial and temporal differences in human culture.

Further Exploration and Links:

The special circumstances this year promoted the development and popularization of Internet sacrifices. Sacrificial processes such as offering flowers, offering incense and writing eulogies have all been completed online, breaking temporal and geographical restrictions. As such, the memorialization of deceased relatives can now be carried out anytime and anywhere, making online sacrificial offerings entirely popular.

Statistics show that during the Qingming Festival, offline sacrifices dropped sharply. There were more than 1.25 million online sacrifices in Danzhou, but the number of people who actually went to cemeteries to make sacrifices on site decreased by 80% compared with the same period last year. More than 100,000 people in Guangzhou participated in online remembrance, and in Shenyang, Internet sacrifices for 9,413 people were conducted.

Corresponding to this has been an increase in the number of companies offering these services. It is understood that there are currently 60 companies offering services related to Internet sacrifices in China. In 2019 alone, 19 such companies were added to this list, accounting for 31.7% of the total. The number of registered companies in Guangdong province ranks first among China's companies offering Internet sacrifices, with 16 companies in total, and Hubei province and Fujian province rank second and third, respectively, with 9 and 5 such companies.

Among these businesses, the launch of a new network sacrifice platform, *Siniantang*, made waves. According to the big data officially released by *Siniantang*, the number of user visits on the platform exceeded 300,000 on the day of the Qingming Festival.

Such data proves that the people's acceptance of online rituals is increasing, and participation is also rising. Compared with traditional sacrificial methods, Internet sacrifices are more convenient and efficient. Take *Siniantang* as an example. Register an account and fill in the basic information of the sacrifice. It only takes two or three minutes to create a memorial hall. Images of the deceased can be permanently retained here, and their biographical profiles can also be created. On this platform, you can offer flowers and electric candles. You can also leave messages and pray for the dead. People can also forward these profiles to relatives and friends or share them on social media so that people living in different places can pay homage anytime and anywhere, thus expressing their longing for their deceased relatives and friends.

In addition, on the *Siniantang* platform, users can set up family ancestral halls and share them with relatives and friends to pay homage. They can also pay homage to famous deceased individuals, scholars, scientists and the like in the Memorial Hall of Fame. *Siniantang* provides users with a variety of options.

At a moment when China is advocating "green sacrifices" and "civilized sacrifices", the emergence of Internet sacrifice platforms couldn't be more appropriate, and the people's acceptance of such services is growing higher and higher, with much expected future development.

——Drive China. Online sacrificial offerings are entirely popular, and future development is worth looking forward to. *NetEase News*, 2020-05-03.

Chapter 10 The "Global Village": Human "Civilizational Conflict" and Cultural Integration

10.1 Industrial Civilization and Culture

10.1.1 Industrial Civilization and Industrial Society

Simply put, industrial civilization is a form of modern social civilization dominated by industrialization, mechanization, standardization and mass production.

Compared with traditional agricultural civilization, industrial civilization is much more colorful, a character mainly manifested through its urbanization, legalization and democratization, as well as its increased social class mobility, popularization of education, accelerated messaging, significant uptick in the proportional size of the non-agricultural population and sustained economic growth.

In industrial society, due to the improvement of machine productivity and the mass production of standardized products, homogenization or homogeneity has become an important symbol of industrial civilization distinguishing it from agricultural civilization. Unified markets, unified languages, universal social mobility and equality, as well as ubiquitous standardization, are all manifestations of homogeneity. In this sense, industrial society is a homogeneous society, whereas agricultural society is a heterogeneous society with many heterogeneous subcultures.

The development of science and technology has played an important role in promoting the transformation from agricultural society to industrial society. Science and technology, however, are a "double-edged sword". While creating a better life for mankind, they can also have negative effects on human society. The key is in determining how human beings can use science and technology to improve livelihoods and serve society on the basis of ensuring ecological civilization.

We know that early industrial civilization created problems such as environmental pollution, resource wastage and a widening gap between the rich and the poor. These problems still exist in some developing countries today. Questions about industrial revolution, science and technology, as well as modernity, have caused widespread concern and discussion.

At present, developed western countries have entered the post-industrial era, and they have been reflecting on the consequences of industrialization since the 1970s. China is still in the process of industrialization, which means that we must learn from the experiences and lessons of the developed countries in the West. This will allow China to take as few detours as possible on the road to industrialization, thus entering the information era of civilization sooner. In other words, science and technology in an industrial society should be applied in a "civilized" manner to benefit society rather than "harm" people.

Although an industrial society follows its own logic of development, technological progress in this society should not set back human civilization. Instead, technology and civilization should push each other forward.

10.1.2   Civilizational "Conflict" in Industrial Society

Is there a civilizational "conflict" within an industrial society? This question deserves in-depth consideration.

(1) The "conflict" between material civilization and spiritual civilization

No country or society can do without the development of material civilization and spiritual civilization. This question deserves in-depth consideration.

The industrial era is essentially an era of material pursuits. Factory machines consume raw materials to produce more and better products, and people continue to consume freshly produced industrial products.

In an era of swelling "material desires", people's spiritual pursuits may have lessened. This has inevitably led to a "conflict" between material civilization and spiritual civilization. In addition, some people may have also experienced a moral decline on the spiritual level.

(2) The "conflict" between industrial civilization and ecological civilization

Compared with traditional agriculture, industries create more wealth and value than traditional agricultural production. Thus, the industrial civilization of industrial powers, industrial provinces, wealthy industrial cities and wealthy industrial counties drives people to pursue the value and wealth created by industry.

When prioritizing the development of industry, some local governments have implemented preferential policies or measures, intensified efforts to attract investment, developed industry and sometimes even introduced energy-intensive and highly polluting foreign capital or foreign enterprises. As a result of lax regulation, the environmental protection efforts of companies are substandard, or they secretly discharge untreated exhaust gas, waste water and other waste to reduce their environmental protection costs, seriously polluting or destroying the ecological environment. This path of industrial development at the expense of environment directly challenges the sustainable development of human society.

(3) The "conflict" between globalization and a community with a shared future for mankind

Globalization first started at the economic level. It relies on the global allocation of economic factors such as funds, resources, products and markets. The result is a "conflict" between the "many-in-one" world economy and "one-among-many" human cultures. Human beings live together on the same planet — the earth — but we cannot live like estranged neighbors, only talking about "ethnic diversity" while denying "globalization". Nor can we only talk about "global economic integration" while neglecting the "community with a shared future for mankind".

The common sense of anthropology tells us that the integration of economics and politics with culture is the basic proposition of human society. Facing the challenges of growing multinational corporations, as well as geo-economical and geopolitical issues, building a community with a shared future for mankind throughout the process of participating in coordinated global governance has become an urgent task facing all nations and ethnic groups in the world. "At present, with the world's multi-faceted polarization, economic globalization and cultural diversification, as well as the significant digitalization of society, human society is full of hope. But simultaneously, instability and uncertainty of the international scene have grown more serious, and the global challenges facing mankind have become more severe. All the world's countries must work together and respond to these challenges together."[①] This kind of response requires not only economic and technological power but also cultural and civilizational power. Only by deepening the exchanges and mutual learning between human civilizations can we truly build a community with a shared future for mankind.

10.1.3 Summary: Culture and Civilization in the Industrial Age

In this section, we discussed industrial civilization and industrial society, as well as the civilizational "conflicts" of an industrial society. We also conducted a simple analysis of culture and civilization in the industrial era. We hope that by studying and discussing this section, we have helped you further understand the civilizational

---

① 习近平. 习近平谈治国理政: 第三卷 [M] . 北京: 外文出版社, 2020: 465.

　Xi Jinping. *The Governance of China III* [M] . Beijing: Foreign Languages Press, 2020: 465.

"conflicts" and cultural integration of human society.

Further Exploration and Links

The pragmatic and analytical world view of the West has gained new power from its combination with modern science and its application through technology. An equation seems to be forming: if a society wants to achieve material and economic development, it must accept and appropriately use modern technology. And if it wants to master modern technology, it must accept the Western rationalist culture of pragmatism. This equation seems convincing; it affects the thinking of most leaders in the world. But whether this equation is completely correct is another matter.

Notably, this equation requires the assumption of a special combination of technology and culture. The latest technologies are considered to be the most needed technologies: these technologies ensure the highest productivity and determine the ability of each country to compete in the world economy. As a source of wealth creation in the civilian economy, these technologies are assumed to be the overall foundation for socio-economic development. Because these technologies are mainly products of Western culture, people believe that mastering their use requires Western-style thinking and behavior.

The new technologies produced by the rational thinking of Western science are not the only tools of the culture that produced them, and their use is not limited to the development goals of the Western world. But because all methods of development are thought to rely on the use of new technologies, and since the use of new technologies requires Western-style thinking and goal-oriented preparation, Western rationality and empiricism have been adopted worldwide. As a result, this emergence of a technological civilization and its strong, consistent impact threaten the world's cultural diversity. Local cultures face an inevitable responsibility: either accept Western culture and use new technologies, or maintain their own traditions and disappear into history.

But this equation consisting of the Western culture of rationalism and empiricism, as well as the use of new technologies, is not universal. As far as the Western world is concerned, the culture of carefully crafting new technologies is the culture of using these technologies. This may be true or at least logical. But for other cultures, this is not true: in these cultures, new technologies help propose goals that are completely different from standard socioeconomic development goals. No technology is inevitably confined to a certain way of thinking and behavior nor confined to achieving certain goals.

　　—Ervin Laszlo. *The Multicultural Planet: The Report of a UNESCO International Expert Group* (2nd Edition), Translated by Dai Kan, Xin Wei. Beijing: Social Sciences Academic Press, 2004: 226-227.

10.2　An Information Civilization and Culture

10.2.1　Information and the Information Culture

(1) The concept of information

It is generally believed that information refers to that which is transmitted and processed by audio, messages and communication systems, generally referring to all content transmitted by human society.

As a scientific term, "information" first appeared in the article "Information Transmission" written by R. V. Hartley in 1928. In the 1940s, C. E. Shannon, the "founder of information", gave the concept a clear definition. In 1948, Shannon pointed out in a paper entitled "Mathematical Theory of Communication" that "information is something used to eliminate random uncertainty". This definition is regarded as the classic definition of information and is frequently quoted.

(2) The information culture

The information culture was born and formed throughout the information age. It is a new form of culture created and characterized by the wide use of information technology in social life. Compositionally speaking, there are roughly four different forms of information culture.

The information culture in its material form and as a social norm is the materialized foundation of a broader information culture, though it can also be broadly and rationally analyzed as a behavioral mode and as a spiritual concept. Thus, some people tend to regard its expression as a behavioral mode and as a spiritual concept as a narrow definition of information culture. In addition to the general characteristics of culture, the information culture also has the following four characteristics.

Firstly, digitization and globalization reflect the material and cultural characteristics of the information age.

Secondly, a virtual nature and interactivity reflect the characteristics of behavioral culture in the information age.

Thirdly, openness, autonomy and self-discipline have become the characteristics of institutional culture in the information age.

Finally, the concepts of freedom, equality and sharing regarding the exchange of information are gradually evolving into the spirit of the information age.

Given the increasingly developed information science of today, the importance of information is self-evident, as it has a major impact on society and the entire human race. It can thus be said that the information culture constitutes the third major technological breakthrough in human history and will play an increasingly powerful role.

10.2.2   Information-Based Society and Information-Based Civilization

(1) Information-based society and information-based civilization

"Information-based society" is a new type of society based on electronic information technology. Information resources are its basic resources for development. Information service industries are its basic social industries, and digitalization and networking are its basic methods of social interaction.

In this information-based society, information has become a resource more important than materials and energy resources. Economic information-related activities that seek to develop and use information resources have expanded rapidly, and they have gradually replaced industrial production activities as the main component of national economic activities. Thus, the information technology revolution, which is dominated by computers, microelectronics and communication technologies, constitutes the main source of power for the deepening integration of information in society.

(2) Information-based civilization

Due to the wide application of information technology in the production of data, scientific research, education, medical care, enterprise applications, government management and household use, it has had a huge and profound impact on human society and economic development, fundamentally changing economic formats and business models, as well as lifestyles, behaviors and values. Thus, information-based civilization can be regarded as a new type of civilization with additional layers of factors: it is both a characteristic of material civilization and a characteristic of spiritual civilization.

Information-based civilization has given human society new characteristics.

Firstly, information and knowledge have become important productive factors. Together with matter and energy, they constitute the three major resources on which society depends.

Secondly, in an information-based society, technology and culture are more closely integrated through the use of informational know-how, with such knowledge having become a basic necessity.

Finally, the economy of an information-based society is dominated by the information economy and the knowledge economy — unlike industrial society, which is dominated by the industrial economy.

Of course, information-based civilization also has its own problems that must be solved. These issues mainly go as follows.

1) information pollution, such as fake information, spam, information interference, disordered information, defective information, outdated information, redundant information, misleading information, information overflow and unhealthy information.

2) information infringement, such as intellectual property rights infringement, the violation of personal privacy and cyber manhunt or doxing.

3) information crime, such as hacking, pornography, online gambling, online drug trafficking, internet fraud and the stealing of information.

4) information aggression, such as information-intensive countries using their information monopolies and hype to promote their own values, influence other countries with their own cultures and lifestyles, and carry out "color revolutions" and other evolutionary activities.

In short, information-based society is actually a "double-edged sword". Whether such civilization is good or bad depends not on the "sword" itself but on the person who wields it. With the development of information technology, informatization and globalization have become irreversible trends in the contemporary world economy. Thus, we should take the initiative to respond to them, seek benefit and avoid harm, thus promoting the healthy development of information-based civilization.

10.2.3   Summary: Information in the "Global Village"

In this section, we discussed the concepts and characteristics of information and the information culture. We analyzed issues regarding information-based society and the development of information-based civilization, and we conducted a simple analysis of the characteristics and negative effects of such civilization. We hope that by studying and discussing this section, we have helped students further understand the civilizational "conflicts" and cultural integration of human society.

Further Exploration and Links:

Billions of people are now connected to each other through electronics, optical fibers and digital communications technology. There are about 1,000 satellites orbiting the earth at an altitude of 400 to 35,000 kilometers. Around 560 of them are dedicated communications satellites. The others operate as military, scientific and meteorological observation satellites. This figure also includes 24 global positioning satellites (GPS) 16,000 kilometers from the ground. Countless pieces of communications equipment are accessible through mass-produced, light-weight mobile communications equipment: information on telephones, TVs and computers can be accessed by these small devices, continuously and instantly connecting billions of people worldwide.

The political situation in which humans are growing closer to each other consists of the circulation of people, products and ideas around the world. Modern mass transportation and media have made these things possible. This has also led to many external similarities between cultures, forming a spectacular scene in which the future of mankind will become a single, homogeneous global culture. Around the world, people increasingly share the same forms of entertainment, watching and listening to many of the same world news programs, eating the same fast foods, wearing the same clothes, playing the same sports and dancing to the same music. They also now communicate in a few common languages.

The far-reaching influence of modern, electronic digital technology has created a global media environment that plays an important role in how individuals and society perceive their positions in the world. Together with radio and television, the Internet has become the main channel for communication for people around the world. The global information flow transmitted through optical fibers, signal towers and terrestrial communications satellites has been almost completely digitized, and it takes place in a new, infinitely large cultural space called the "global media".

In recent years, the power of companies has become stronger through the expansion of media. Over the past 20 years, the development of global commercial media has been controlled by a small number of large American companies (such as General Electric, Time Warner and Disney). They have controlled television, the Internet and other media, as well as the advertising industry. These multinational companies have profoundly affected the daily ideas and behaviors of hundreds of millions of ordinary people around the world.

— William A. Haviland, Harald E. L. Prins, Dana Walrath, et al. *Anthropology: The Human Challenge* (14th Edition), Translated by Zhou Yunshui, Chen Xiang, Lei Lei, et al. Beijing: Publishing House of Electronics Industry, 2018: 645-657.

10.3   Religious Civilization and Culture

10.3.1   Religious Culture and Religious Civilization

Religion is a special cultural phenomenon in human society and an important part of traditional cultures. It affects people's philosophical outlooks and customs. Religion itself is based on faith, and it is an integral part of overall social culture.

(1) Religious culture

As a cultural phenomenon, religion has its own cultural system and patterns of development.

In a broad sense, all cultures that are involved with religion are religious cultures. A religious culture, in a narrow sense, consists only of the cultural system of religion itself, which includes religious ideas, concepts, classics, teachings, emotions, priests, believers, venues, buildings, ceremonies, morals and customs. In short, religious culture is a broad concept. But the meaning of religious civilization itself is relatively narrow.

(2) Religious civilization

For a long time, people have had different understandings of the differences and connections between culture and civilization.

It is generally believed that civilization is relatively static but that culture is full of flowing dynamism. Civilization is the result of the long-term accumulation of culture, but not all cultures can accumulate into civilizations.

From this perspective, religious culture can be regarded as a type of human civilization. It is what precipitates out from a religion that has continuously adapted to social needs and grown throughout its long development. Conducive to social peace, stability and harmony, it is the crystallization of religious culture. Whether or not it "crystallizes" or "can crystallize" is the largest and most primary difference between religious civilization and religious culture.

A "crystalized" religious civilization is not as easy to change as a flowing religious culture. Thus, such civilizations have become a type of human civilization with strong religious colouring.

10.3.2   Religious "Civilizational Conflict" Versus Mutual Growth

(1) Religious civilizational "conflict" or integration?

According to Samuel Huntington, a famous American political scientist, the world's major civilizations are at odds with each other. This "conflict of civilizations" theory proposed by Huntington is actually the "conflict" theory of religious civilization.

In truth, Huntington only saw "conflict" between the world's religious civilizations, thus ignoring inter-civilizational blending and symbiosis.

Regarding the development of major religions in China, Confucianism, Buddhism and Taoism appeared during the Wei, Jin, and Northern and Southern dynasties, respectively. Despite repeated developments since then, this "confluence" of Confucianism, Buddhism and Taoism has become a trend of historical development. Since then, even though Islam was introduced into China during the Tang and Song dynasties, it has also experienced "Sinification" forming the *menhuan* system of Islam in the country's northwest region. During the Ming and Qing dynasties, some Hui scholars who believed in Islam also used the Confucian classics to interpret the Quran, and thus the practice of the "Sinification of Islam" through the "Confucian interpretation of the classics" appeared.

During the Ming and Qing dynasties, when Christianity was introduced into China, a "conflict of rituals" occurred. Catholicism and Christianity are incompatible with traditional Chinese practices such as the worship of heaven, ancestor worship and idol worship. Thus, it was difficult for Christian missionaries to achieve success in China. The frequent occurrence of religious events in modern Chinese history seems to serve as a footnote for the "conflict" between Christian civilization and Chinese civilization. The Chinese civilization, however, with Confucian civilization as its core, is actually quite open and inclusive.

During the 1920s, the "localization" movement of Chinese Christianity reflected how Chinese civilization and Christianity could be merged instead of existing in a state of "conflict". The history of the development of Chinese religions shows that the major religious civilizations in the world are not necessarily "contradictory" but can indeed integrate. Whether they "conflict" with each other or integrate depends on dialogue and exchange between religious civilizations.

The history of the development of Chinese religions shows that the major religious civilizations in the world are not necessarily "contradictory" but can be integrated and exist symbiotically. The basic path for this lies in religious dialogue and communication. "Globalization has given new vitality to the religious world, and it has narrowed the distance between beliefs. Traditional belief models are facing deconstruction, and new forms of belief models have emerged. Driven by different beliefs through modern technological civilization, the East and the West, tradition and modernity, sacred and secular, are all placed in the same space and time to collide, making dialogue and exchange between different religions and beliefs both possible and necessary."[1] This shows how religious and academic circles have reached a basic consensus on the importance of religious dialogue and exchange.

(2) Religious integration and symbiosis

The key to religious integration and harmony is to actively carry out religious dialogue and exchange between different religions and sects, seeking common ground while reservings differencess and allowing for mutual accommodation.

All normal religions persuade people to do good and teach believers to be useful to their countries, societies and families. In this regard, the various schools are consistent, but their paths for realizing these objectives, as well as their methods and understandings of doctrines, may differ. This requires religious dialogue and exchange, and on this basis, the achievement of religious harmony and symbiosis. In addition, it is also necessary to actively guide religion to adapt to socialist society and "to actively practice the core socialist values, promote Chinese culture and strive to integrate religious teachings with Chinese culture"[2]. "Think deeply and perceive both thoroughly and accurately when providing 'guidance' so that 'guidance' is well-directed, powerful and effective."[2] Only in this way can we better realize the harmonious coexistence of religion and human society.

10.3.3　Summary: Religious Civilization Is in a "Conflicting" State of Symbiosis

In this section, we discussed the concepts of religious culture and religious civilization, and we analyzed how religious civilization can coexist in symbiosis, as well as other issues. We hope that by studying and discussing this section, we have helped students further understand the civilizational "conflicts" of human society and the issues of cultural integration.

10.4　A Civilized World Featured by Harmony in Diversity

10.4.1　The Diversity of Human Culture

Diversity is an important symbol of human culture. Like the natural ecological

---

① 释了意. 觉醒的力量: 全球宗教对话与交流 [M]. 北京: 宗教文化出版社, 2010: 2.
　　Shi Liaoyi. Seeking the similarities and containing the differences: global religious dialogue and communication [M]. Beijing: China Religious Culture Publisher, 2010: 2.
② 习近平. 习近平谈治国理政: 第二卷 [M]. 北京: 外文出版社, 2017: 301-302.
　　Xi Jinping. *The Governance of China II* [M]. Beijing: Foreign Languages Press, 2017: 301-302.

environment, the human cultural ecology should also be diverse, but why?

The reason is actually quite simple. From a circular structure perspective of culture, human culture from the outside to the inside runs from material culture, behavioral culture and institutional culture to spiritual culture.[①]

Material culture at the outermost periphery is inseparable from the natural ecological environment. Therefore, human material culture is naturally characterized by the diversity of the natural ecological environment.

The second level of culture, which represents a move from material culture toward the cultural core, is behavioral culture. The behavioral cultures of human beings are constrained by their social systems. Behavioral cultures under the regulation of different social systems naturally exhibit different cultural characteristics, and their cultural diversity is thus naturally self-evident.

It goes without saying that institutional cultures and spiritual cultures are diverse. Institutional cultures are a morphological or outward projection of spiritual cultures. Whatever kind of spiritual culture there may be, there is a corresponding institutional culture, and vice versa. As the sayings go, "the water and soil of a particular place nurtures the people there" and "one type of rice can feed different kinds of people". Such sayings clearly illustrate the diversity of human cultures.

In addition, due to the influence of multiple factors, such as the historical, regional and national characteristics of a culture, the cultures of different countries and regions are quite different. Such differences exist even among the various ethnic groups within a given country or region, as well as among a given ethnic group across different countries, regions or eras. Likewise, large cultural differences will exist among different ethnic groups during one particular era.

10.4.2　A Harmonious and Diverse Cultural Future

Harmony and diversity are the most dazzling cultural images in this era of globalization. Although the industrialization and standardization of modern society will bring a certain degree of superficial "convergence," this does not imply the homogenization or integration of human culture. On the contrary, the superficial convergence brought about by globalization has actually stimulated people's cultural perceptions and their identification of the "self" and "other". As a result, people have emphasized and revived their individual cultures so that they and their subordinate groups can stand among all nations in the world.

---

① Yang L, Li M, Cultural understanding of global governance: a perspective of religious culture [J] . *Advances in Applied Sociology*, 2018, 8 (5): 359-365.

Around 2000, when Fei Xiaotong, a well-known Chinese sociologist and anthropologist, was thinking about the cultural world and cultural development throughout the 21st century, he proposed to himself in his early years the thesis that "each ethnic culture has its own beauty and should be respected, and all ethnic cultures should coexist, maintaining and promoting cultural diversity," which he then revised to "each ethnic culture has its own beauty and should be respected, and all ethnic cultures should coexist, both harmoniously and diversely". Of course, Mr. Fei Xiaotong regards "harmonious and diverse" as an important means and path of realizing "universal harmony". Indeed, this is insightful. It should be said that these sixteen revised characters (in Chinese) provide a relatively objective and comprehensive outlook on the cultural future and trend for human society's development.

The direct result of economic globalization is an increased frequency of exchange among the countries, regions and ethnic groups of the world. But the real integration of culture still has a long way to go, and their differences are still the direction of human development in the future. This suggests a development proposition worth cherishing: is the culture of harmony amid diversity a driving force or friction to globalization?

10.4.3   Summary: the Multi-Cultural "Planet" and the Harmonious and Diverse Cultural World

In this section, we discussed the diversity of human cultures, as well as the futures of harmonious and diverse cultures. We hope that by studying and discussing this section, we have helped students further understand the "conflicts" of human civilization and the issues of cultural integration.

Further Exploration and Links:

From a cultural perspective, balancing the diversity of today's society with a new level of unity is the greatest challenge. Culture is not just one of society's factors but is also its decisive feature. In the final analysis, what distinguishes one society from another is not only its wealth in terms of money or natural resources but also the values, enthusiasm and creativity of its people. One nation can establish modern industry, develop high technology and gradually form a consumer society, but another nation can quickly catch up with it. A third, however, can adopt an attitude of resistance and seek other paths of development. This situation is not primarily due to climate or geographical location, and it cannot be fully explained by economic factors. Its cause is cultural and is related to the distinct characteristics of each culture, their different ways of thinking and the ways of life of each organization and each individual in society. The Mexico City World Conference pointed out that, compared with the economic growth process measured by gross national product, the development process is much more complex, deep and more extensive. Indeed, "only when it is based on the independent will of each society, and only when it truly shows its basic characteristics" can development prove to be effective.

In seeking peace, understanding, solidarity, unity and, ultimately, a diversity of harmonious cooperation, because diversity and unity are all determined by culture, people's pursuits can only be realized through cultural dialogue and cooperation.

Through dialogue and cooperation, various cultures and culturally diverse societies consciously and purposefully lay a solid foundation for promoting integration. Their success will depend on the mutual respect of all parties and their willingness to cooperate on an equal footing. It does not matter whether various cultures are good or bad; they are diverse, and their diversity is crucial.

—Ervin Laszlo. *The Multicultural Planet: The Report of a UNESCO International Expert Group* (2nd Edition), Translated by Dai Kan, Xin Wei. Beijing: Social Sciences Academic Press, 2004: 7-9.

Chapter 11 Conclusion: Life Is Culture, and Culture Is Life

11.1 Industrial Culture and Modern Life

Modern society is a society whose development is based on industrial technology. Industrial technology and its cultural system have deeply penetrated every aspect of modern life. Regardless of whether people like this or support this, the modern cultural system, which is adapted to industrial technology, deeply controls the lives of people all over the world.

From the topics and content discussed in the previous chapters of this book, it should be easy for us to understand the basic meaning of "life is culture, and culture is life".

It must be emphasized that mechanization, modeling and standardization, as well as the shift toward set procedures, batching, marketization and even globalization — all necessitated by industrial technology and its cultural system — now completely dominate clothing, food, housing, transportation, travel, shopping, entertainment, marriage, funeral, birth, old age, sickness, death, burial, sacrifice and other aspects of life. It is practically impossible for people living in modern societies to rid themselves of technology's grasp of these areas.

In modern life, though people seem to have many choices, they actually have few. They can only choose products produced by existing technologies or emerging technologies. Even modern agriculture, especially "facility agriculture", has strong industrial characteristics.

From crop breeding to cultivation, and from pest control, as well as increasing production and income, to harvesting, processing, transportation and storage, which of these is not an application and supporting example of modern agricultural technology? The modern, industrialized poultry and livestock industry, for example, is the result of the popularization and application of modern agricultural technology. It can be said that the "three good" technologies of good seeds, good methods and good skills constitute an important cornerstone of the modern agricultural industry system. This is still the case for the agricultural industry, which is the most important undertaking for providing people with food, as well as for other industries such as clothing, medical treatment and transportation.

Therefore, we believe that modern life is created by industrial technology, and the ways and methods in which we live our lives are thus inevitably regulated by industrial culture. This is especially true during the later stages of industrial society, in which people are more affected by industrial technology and culture.

In an information-based society, the work lives and personal lives of the vast majority of people are increasingly dependent on the Internet and instant messaging technology. But it is essential that we ask, "In modern life, does technology serve us, or do we serve technology and become 'slaves' to it?" Technology is a double-edged sword. We should have faith in technology, but we should neither obsess over it nor be superstitious about it. Technology should serve people instead of serving as a tool for slavery. Keeping these ideas and thoughts in mind, we will have more confidence in technology, culture and life in modern society, thus perhaps living better lives.

11.2　The Non-linear Expression of Culture and Its Temporal and Spatial Differences

Throughout the process of its development and evolution, culture expresses temporal and spatial differences in non-linear ways.

Culture is historical in nature. Culture reflects history more than society itself. In other words, culture is less reflective of society than it is of history: culture has more historical genes. Therefore, cultures have differed temporally throughout the ages. These temporal differences have been represented by cultural changes, whereas the spatial changes to culture have been represented by cultural variation.

In modern society, cultures have existed at different times and spaces in different parts of the world. These differences have mainly been related to the industrialization process.

In general, the earlier industrialization started in a country or a region, the more mature it became. Likewise, the industrial cultures in such places have had a deeper influence on their modern ways of life. In some countries or regions that were industrialized late, however, the influence of industrial culture on the lives of locals sometimes grew in leaps and bounds, thus presenting a non-linear effect.

From the topics and content discussed in the previous chapters of this book, the impact that industrial technology and its culture have on the lives of locals reflects these non-linear characteristics to varying degrees. Relatively speaking, modern industrial technology and its culture have a greater impact on clothing, food, housing, transportation, travel, shopping, entertainment and other areas of life, though they also affects marriage, funeral, birth, old age, sickness, death, burial and sacrifices in varying ways, reflecting the non-linear influence of industrial culture on modern life.

11.3   Summary: Culture Is Life, the Basic Proposition of Modern Life

We discussed industrial culture and modern life on the dimensions of industry, technology and society, and we conducted a cultural interpretation of anthropology.

Culture itself is complicated, but modern life is all-encompassing. In an industrial society and an information-based society, however, the basic proposition of modern life is that "culture is life, and life is culture".

Further Exploration and Links:

Through the numerous cross-cultural connections that have been discovered between a particular cultural variation and its assumed reasons, we are able to work hard to understand cultural changes. All cultures change over time, and variation is the product of differential change. Therefore, the variation we see is the product of the process of change, and the predictors of those variations that have been discovered can explain the reason and method of the change.

——Carol R.Ember, Melvin Ember. *Human Culture: Highlights of Cultural Anthropology* (3rd Edition), Translated by Zhou Yunshui, Yang Jinghua, Chen Jingyun. Beijing: Publishing House of Electronics Industry, 2016: 65.

Postscript

After earning my Ph.D. in June 2002, I started teaching at Guangxi Normal University, offering general elective courses such as Anthropology and Modern Life, China-ASEAN Ethnic Religions and An Overview of Tourism, as well as undergraduate elective courses such as The Anthropology of Tourism and Historical Anthropology. I also taught postgraduate courses such as Economic Anthropology, Religious Anthropology, Topics in the Anthropology of Tourism, Theories and Methods of Ethnological Anthropology and The Folklore Classics of Ethnological Anthropology, constantly working on related courses in anthropology.

After leaving my post-doctoral "mobile station" for Ethnology at Lanzhou University in October 2008, I worked at South China Agricultural University, where I continued to offer general education courses such as Anthropology and Modern Life. To meet my requirements for professional development, I lectured in courses such as Social Survey Theory and Methods, Field Research and Societal Practice, Cultural Anthropology, Ethnic Sociology and Cultural Sociology, among other undergraduate courses. I also taught Qualitative Public Management Research Methods, MPA Social Research Methods and other graduate-level management courses open to the public, thus continuously enriching the understanding and knowledge of cultural phenomena, such as social systems and social behaviors, through interdisciplinary cross-pollination.

At the beginning of 2012, the public elective course Anthropology and Modern Life, which I taught, was selected as one of the school's A-series courses, thus becoming one of optional general education courses that students ought to take before graduation. In July of the same year, the textbook Anthropology and Modern Life, which I edited, was published. In December, I was nominated for my outstanding social science popularization work in Guangdong province. I was also recognized as a "national outstanding master for the popularization of the social sciences". Since then, I have been inspired to interpret modern life from the cultural dimensions of anthropology.

The year 2013 is regarded as the first year that MOOCs started being taught at Chinese universities, during which famous Chinese teachers began designing and launching their own MOOCs. Likewise, I began planning and building a brand-new course on the analysis of modern life culture. This course was based on courses and teaching materials relating to anthropology and modern life. In July 2015, I participated in the MOOC training meeting organized by Wisdom Tree Online Education Company in Qingyuan, Guangdong province. At the end of the same year, I applied for the school's first MOOC project —Cultural Interpretation of Modern Life — and received funding.

Since these original anthropology and modern life courses were major-specific video courses open to the public and produced at both the school and provincial level, they were put together according to the "quality curriculum model" and did not meet the characteristics and requirements of MOOCs. Therefore, I decided to expand and reorganize these teaching resources and start a new MOOC (established as the 2018 Guangdong Province Online Open Course Project), but the difficulty of this undertaking was beyond my imagination. After many setbacks, the Wisdom Tree online education platform was finally launched after the Chinese National Day in 2019. At that time, I also signed a textbook-publishing contract with Science Press, but once again, converting video content into textbooks was another hurdle, as the two forms of media differ too greatly.

The division of work for the preparation of this textbook was as follows: The preface and the first, second, sixth, seventh, ninth and tenth chapters, as well as the conclusion, were written by Liao Yang. The third, fourth, fifth and eighth chapters were written by Meng Li and drafted by Liao Yang.

Currently, this textbook is officially completed. I would like to express thanks to all the leaders and staff of the Academic Affairs Office of South China Agricultural University for their help and support in compiling this course and in the publication of this textbook. I would also like to thank the leaders and editors of Science Press. In addition, I would also like to thank the translation team (including translators from home and abroad: Zhang Huan, Li Zhiying, Long Yuqiong, and Eliot Wycoff from the United States) led by Associate Professor Chen Xihua from the College of Foreign Studies of South China Agricultural University for their professional translation and proofreading for the English manuscript of this book! Due to limited time and ability, some errors may still exist in this book. Readers and friends are welcome to provide your precious opinions and help us correct them.

Liao Yang
June, 2021
Guangzhou